ISLAM IN A POST-SECULAR SOCIETY

Studies in Critical Social Sciences Book Series

Haymarket Books is proud to be working with Brill Academic Publishers (www.brill.nl) to republish the *Studies in Critical Social Sciences* book series in paperback editions. This peer-reviewed book series offers insights into our current reality by exploring the content and consequences of power relationships under capitalism, and by considering the spaces of opposition and resistance to these changes that have been defining our new age. Our full catalog of *SCSS* volumes can be viewed at https://www.haymarketbooks .org/series_collections/4-studies-in-critical-social-sciences.

ISLAM
IN A POST-SECULAR SOCIETY

Religion, Secularity and
the Antagonism of Recalcitrant Faith

DUSTIN J. BYRD

Haymarket
Books
Chicago, IL

First published in 2016 by Brill Academic Publishers, The Netherlands.
© 2017 Koninklijke Brill NV, Leiden, The Netherlands

Published in paperback in 2018 by
Haymarket Books
P.O. Box 180165
Chicago, IL 60618
773-583-7884
www.haymarketbooks.org

ISBN: 978-1-60846-841-6

Trade distribution:
In the U.S. through Consortium Book Sales, www.cbsd.com
In the UK, Turnaround Publisher Services, www.turnaround-uk.com
In Canada, Publishers Group Canada, www.pgcbooks.ca
All other countries, Ingram Publisher Services International, ips_intlsales@ingramcontent.com

Cover design by Jamie Kerry of Belle Étoile Studios and Ragina Johnson.

This book was published with the generous support of Lannan Foundation and the Wallace Action Fund.

Printed in Canada by union labor.

10 9 8 7 6 5 4 3 2 1

Library of Congress Cataloging-in-Publication Data is available.

This book is dedicated to the memory of
David Ward Thomas.
Eternal student, devoted friend and blues man of deep faith

∴

The best of people are those that bring most benefit to the rest of mankind.

– PROPHET MUHAMMAD

• • •

Preach the Gospel at all times, and when necessary, use words.

– ST. FRANCIS OF ASSISI

• • •

When Philosophy paints its grey in grey, a shape of life has grown old, and it cannot be rejuvenated, but only recognized, by the grey in grey of philosophy; the owl of Minerva begins its flight only with the onset of dusk.

– GEORG WILHELM FRIEDRICH HEGEL

• • •

Indeed, ask every man separately whether he thinks it laudable and worthy of a man of this age to hold a position from which he receives a salary disproportionate to his work; to take from the people – often in poverty – taxes to be spent on constructing cannon, torpedoes, and other instruments of butchery, so as to make war on people with whom we wish to be at peace, and who feel the same wish in regard to us; or to receive a salary for devoting one's whole life to constructing these instruments of butchery, or to preparing oneself and others for the work of murder.

– LEO TOLSTOY

• •
•

Contents

Preface

The idea for this book came about when I attended the 38th annual *Future of Religion* conference in Dubrovnik, Croatia, in April of 2014. The director, Dr. Rudolf J. Siebert, of Western Michigan University's Comparative Religion Department, has been my academic mentor, friend, and guide for over 20 years. Always faithful to the advancement of dialectical philosophy and theology, Dr. Siebert has never missed a year of the Dubrovnik conference since it was founded in 1976 at the request of Ivan Supek, a Croatian anti-fascist physicist, philosopher, and humanist author. The theme of the 2014 conference was *Witnessing and Confessing* – a perfect theme for my interests in Muslim communities in Europe, relations between the West and the Muslim world, as well as my main theoretical foundation, the Critical Theory of Religion, as developed out of the Frankfurt School's critical theory of society. After presenting my paper in the Inter-University Centre in Dubrovnik, and listening to the other scholar's valuable critiques, I chose to continue my research and expand it into a book. The result is this modest volume.

To the reader, I hope my use of technical and foreign language, born out of philosophy, religion, theology and sociology, doesn't prove to be too impenetrable. For some this verbiage may seem like mesmerizing jargon; I assure you it is not. Certain categories, concepts, and notions (and some in languages other than English) are necessary in order to clarify, analyze, and debate the subject at hand. As philosophers dealing with complex issues that pertain to a multiplicity of cultures, wherein we both have to speak about the universal and the particular, the use of various languages to penetrate into the heart of the vexing problem is sometimes necessary. Each language provides another avenue by which the thinker can journey into the darkest recess of the dilemma. Through our conceptual language and categories we come to understand, interpret, differentiate and engage the world. If we are lacking in the conceptual tools to do so, we experience the world as an untranslatable phenomenon that lacks determinacy, lacks clarity, and consequently lacks subjective importance. In this blunted form of living, existential issues are reduced to a series of experiences and sensations that do not find sufficient articulation in meaningful language, which essentially leaves us with an amorphous biography of random impressions and passions. However, the world becomes unlocked to many students and scholars once they've acquired the language and conceptions to think systematically, abstractly, dialectically, concretely, as well as through what Walter Benjamin called "constellations." Without such philosophical, theological, sociological and religious language, the status quo remains *reified* – it is experienced as simply "the given" and not the socially constructed and therefore mutable phenomenon that it is. Although much of mankind's history is the product of mere nature, most of it is the product of the way man choses to be through his labor, his passions, and his will. History and society are not fixed, nor are they on an unalterable trajectory, nor are they simply the product of the natural world. Society, and therefore history, can be changed when we can first understand their internal dynamics and characteristics. If we are able to articulate our worldview, identify our disagreements, and find the courage to transcend the status quo, than we can construct better and more penetrating arguments through which social change can be imagined and actualized.

In Marx's article, *The Ruthless Critique of Everything Existing,* he calls upon his reader to (1) have courage to accept the consequences of one's critique, and (2) to not be afraid to challenge the status quo, i.e. to be martyr material if history calls one to be such. In light of the increasing barbarity of the modern world, it may be an absolute necessity to adopt this attitude if we are to remedy the seemingly intractable ills that plague our present world. As every student of political philosophy knows, Karl Marx's famous 11th Thesis on Feuerbach states, 'Philosophers have hitherto only *interpreted* the world in various ways; the point is to *change* it.' In this quote, Marx presupposes that philosophers already have the linguistic and conceptual capabilities to interpret the world adequately – some more than others for sure – but does not slip into a state of *ataraxia* (ἀταραξία – tranquility) in doing so, but rather becomes maladjusted to the pathological sickness of their society. Philosophers, and consequently those who learn from philosophers, must go beyond the mere conceptualization of the world – although it is the necessary precondition – they must also contribute to a radical praxis *adversus mundi* (against the world) with its unnecessary injustices, and must never *fuga mundi* (flee the world) like cloistered mystics.

This same desire to transubstantiate the world for the better was echoed in a religious form by Pope Francis in his 2013 exhortation *Evangelii Gaudium* (The Joy of the Gospel) when he wrote,

> An authentic faith – which is never comfortable or completely personal – always involves a deep desire to change the world, to transmit values, to leave this earth somehow better than we found it.[1]

---

1   Pope Francis, *Evangelii Gaudium: The Joy of the Gospel.* (Washington D.C.: USCCB Communications, 2013), 93.

For the critical theorist of religion and society, it is the role, some may even say the duty, of those who find themselves with the intellectual tools to see beyond the necessary appearances of the given, who have escaped Plato's Cave, who can pierce through the façade of the mesmerizing consumer society, and see clearly through the impenetrable darkness of the night-side of neo-liberalism, to engage not only the world via thought, but through deed as well. The Slovenian philosopher Slavoj Žižek encourages intellectuals to return to thinking, especially after the collapse of the Soviet Union and the Marxist international. For him, we need to think through the catastrophic that was communism, and to also take stock of the ingenuity of capitalism to survive its own inner-contradictions, catastrophes and frequent collapses. However, as right as Žižek is, and he *is* most assuredly correct about the need to *re*-think, we must also not lose sight of revolutionary and Socratic praxis. The victims of the world's pathological exploitation and oppression – created by the distorted logic and rapacious greed of globalized neo-liberalism – are still being manufactured, still being abused, and still being oppressed, and have not the time for self-satisfying intellectual theorizing. Yet this is not a call for action for action's sake. It is clear that the immediacy of unnecessary human, animal and environmental suffering needs not to be rethought. As such, we should avoid a perpetual state of *praxis paralysis* – satisfied within ourselves to only *think* about the victims but *do* nothing concretely to stop the creation of new victims. If religious believers and secular revolutionaries cannot change the world entire, or bring about the utopian Kingdom of God on earth, and must content themselves with waiting for the long-awaited and long-delayed messianic figure, we must not in our activist-slumber forget the suffering that is in the world at this very moment. Those whose suffering will never be recorded in the footnotes of history must not be forgotten, but rather their suffering must be expressed, as all perennial suffering, Adorno reminds us, has the right to be expressed, and academics are in a privileged position to articulate the suffering that today's societies fights to mute. It may be the appropriate moment in which philosophy retires its feeling of intellectual superiority and once again learns from the prophetic religions, especially as it has been articulated today by Pope Francis, who encourages the faithful to live *in* solidarity *with* the poor, which means to 'eliminate the structural causes of poverty and to promote the integral development of the poor.'[2] Pope Francis reminds us to remember that,

> as long as the problems of the poor are not radically resolved by rejecting the absolute autonomy of markets and financial speculation and by

---

2   Ibid., 95.

attacking structural causes of inequality, no solution will be found for the
world's problems, or, for that matter, to any problem. Inequality is the
root of social ills.[3]

In light of the overwhelming social degradation that is occurring around the
world with the spread of values that are diametrically opposed to the prophetic values of mercy, solidarity, and brotherly love, Pope Francis bravely calls
the world to cultivate its inner sense of fairness and justice as a countervailing force to the tyranny of the markets and to engage in loving praxis in the
hopes of redirecting our ailing world towards a greater sense of brotherhood
and equality. Critical theorists of religion share this sentiment, albeit through
humanist philosophy.

In the process of writing this book, I attended not only the 2014 Dubrovnik
conference in Croatia, but also the Loyola University conference on Critical
Theory in Rome, Italy, a week later. However, during the Dubrovnik conference, I listened intently to an individual with nationalist leanings voice some
of the crudest stereotypes about Muslims and their faith. Astonishingly, he
boldly articulated his belief that Muslims were inherently incapable of enlightened thought, inherently undemocratic and unwilling to accept the superiority of European religious culture. No matter how much I argued against his ill-
informed thesis, he remained steadfast in his narrow and shallow beliefs about
a community comprised of 1.6 billion individuals. The cacophony of Muslim
opinions, philosophies, cultural practices, etc., were all artificially harmonized
and reduced to a single concept: *the Muslim,* just as the Jews had once been
conceptualized as *der Jude* (the Jew). Once singularized, he could dismiss all
the Muslims with crude generalizations and stereotypes. An echo of fascism
hung thick in the cool Adriatic air.

In Rome, under the shadow of the Pantheon – once dedicated to "all the
gods" and now to Saint Mary and the early Christian martyrs – I was appalled
to witness a tourist couple from Northern Europe berate an African immigrant
trying to sell them a knock-off luxury purse. In front of their child, they yelled
at him, hurled insults, and brushed him away like a vexatious fly. The pain of
being belittled and disrespected in front of a child could be seen in the weary
face of the already broken man who was only there trying to scratch out a mea-
ger existence, most likely to send most of what he earned back home to his
family in Africa. What was most poignant to witness was the tourists' young
boy, who was no more than ten years old. Without any thought, he mimicked
his father's dismissive gestures – waving away the immigrant man without

---

3   Ibid., 102.

ever recognizing the humanity that dwelled within him. The father clearly approved of the boy's mimetic actions as he looked down at his son with pride. Unfortunately, this abusive and dehumanizing behavior ensures a cycle of antagonistic relationships with the "other," one that further entrenches already deeply held racist beliefs as well as their after-effect, a feeling of disrespect among the immigrants – especially those of Islamic faith. However, from the solidarist perspective of Pope Francis, it was in the suffering of that despised immigrant that one can find the presence of Jesus of Nazareth; he too, for Francis, was dismissed by the tourists – when history offered an opportunity to express Christian *agape* with the suffering, dejected and despised, they instead showed cruel and cold callousness, more typical of the bourgeoisie. These two footnotes of history shows us that this kind of hatred and disgust for others is not natural, it is not inborn, and it is not genetic; it is a learned phenomenon and an acquired attitude. It results in a cycle that is blindly repeated through the generations unless people who can think critically voice their firm opposition and begin to work against a world that devours itself based on small differences. Auschwitz – the inevitable outcome of pathological hatred and misguided metaphysics – begins with such inherited attitudes and gestures.

In his reflection on metaphysics after the horror and terror of the Shoah, Theodor Adorno wrote,

> a new categorical imperative has been impose by Hitler upon unfree mankind: to arrange their thoughts and actions so that Auschwitz will not repeat itself, so that nothing similar will happen.[4]

In order to make forbidden to history that which is already forbidden in Abrahamic morality – pathological hatred of the other – all instances of injustice must be opposed by an equal commitment to justice, mercy, and solidarity. The mass annihilation of others, rooted in a mass disgust, contempt, and hatred for their existence, must be forever eradicated as a potential for human relations.

Auschwitz, which forever doomed mankind's optimism about itself, cannot and must not be repeated. Yet, only decades after this great catastrophe, the conditions for another conflation of worldviews and peoples are already being produced in Europe, North America and the Middle East. In Europe, the ranks of anti-Immigrant political parties continue to swell while ISIS continues to call for lone wolf attacks on targets in the capitals of western nations.

---

4   Theodor Adorno, *Negative Dialectics.* (New York: Continuum, 1999), 365. '*Hitler hat den Menschen im Stande ihrer Unfreiheit einen neuen kategorischen Imperativ aufgezwungen: ihr Denken und Hendeln so einzurichen, dass Auschwitz nicht sich wiederhole, nicht Ähnliches geschehe.*'

The potential for fascism and fascistic-like tendencies survived the Third Reich and are now once again being exploited within the debate about Islam in the West. The mirror image is happening among the Muslims, as the growth of extremist and terrorists groups in the Middle East continues unabated, but thankfully do not represent the vast majority of believers. Fascism has many forms and, like a cameleon, can camouflage itself in many different cultures; from the far right in Europe to ISIS in Syria and Iraq, the human capacity for absolute destruction of the other is swiftly becoming a renewed reality. The "new imperative" of "never again," that resulted from fascism's cruelty and destruction, has gone unheard between the clamor of militaristic slogans and the battle cries of war between nations and religions.

Despite the rise of the often Islamophobic and neo-Randian Tea Party in American political life, the situation has become worse in Europe. In the Netherlands, Germany, France, Italy, Switzerland, Greece, etc., political parties whose platform includes anti-immigrant rhetoric have made significant headways into the political system. For the first fifty years after World War II, or the Great Patriotic War as it is called in Russia, xenophobic far-right political parties were unthinkable, fascistic policies and thoughts were unspeakable in the public sphere, but now they have been reborn with a sense of credibility. Then the target was the communists and Jews, now there is a new target: the Muslims. The language that Europe thought it had left behind after WWII has reappeared and has forcefully made its way back into political discourse. The critical theorists Horkheimer and Adorno already foresaw the folly of believing Europe could resign its fascistic tendencies after the catastrophe of World War II. With the proper catalyst, all of Europe was capable of the same authoritarian and violent tendencies that were cultivated in Nazi Germany. They wrote,

> fascism triumphed under a crassly xenophobic, anti-cultural, collectivist ideology. Now that it has devastated the earth, nations must fight against it; there is no other way. But when all is over, a spirit of freedom need not spread across Europe; its nations may become as xenophobic, as hostile to culture, and as pseudocollectivist as the fascism against which they had to defend themselves. Even its defeat will not necessarily break the motion of the avalanche.[5]

---

5   Max Horkheimer and Theodor Adorno, *The Dialectic of Enlightenment: Philosophical Fragments,* edited by Gunzelin Schmid Noerr. Trans. Edmund Jephcott. (Stanford: Stanford University Press, 2002), 183.

Conversely, the Muslim community hasn't always given their fellow European and American counterparts a sense of security, as many within the community have often contributed to the suspicion of violence that surrounds them. From rallies that fanatically condemn European culture, to terrorist acts upon European and American cities, radical Muslims – having rejected the values of European society as well as traditional Islam – have often pushed their American, Dutch, British, German, Italian, French, etc., neighbors into the anti-Islamic political parties for fear that they are losing their culture, their nation, and their way of life.

This new and rabid Islamophobia draws upon a different legitimation than the neo-pagan fascism of Hitler and Mussolini; it is often clothed in the language of "defending the Enlightenment" itself. These far-right and often neo-fascist politicians and activists are drawing their legitimacy by appearing to defend what was once thought to be the *universal* values of the European Enlightenment, and they often have help in this endeavor from liberals and anti-religion leftists. Having traveled around Europe often in the last ten years, I've witnessed this growing trend firsthand and have noticed that it has only worsened as Europe has become increasingly entangled in Middle Eastern and North African affairs and as emigration from Muslim countries to Europe has increased beyond its capacity (or national will) to accommodate them. Unfortunately, I see that a new dark and ominous specter is forming over Europe: *neo-fascist Islamophobism*, or what I have defined as *miso-Islamism*, or "pathological hatred for Islam." The hatred of Islam will spread like a virulent cancer unless people of good will, revolutionary faith and Socratic faithlessness, who are committed to the peaceful cooperation between the religious traditions and secular citizens – a being-with-each-other that is rooted in mutual recognition, respect and shared commitments – work together for a common goal: a more reconciled future society. Absent a discourse movement such as this, both the neo-fascist nativists of Europe and the extremist Muslims who find no real attachment to their western societies, and who dream of an "Islamic Europe," will continue to pull western society to the political and cultural margins – an unsustainable situation under any analysis. Without discourse there will be no true knowledge of the other; without knowledge there will be no potential for reconciliation; and without reconciliation there will only be a state of war.

When examining Dr. Siebert's time in Dubrovnik during Yugoslavia's civil war, it's important to note the great courage that was demonstrated as he continued to travel to the Balkans during the fighting; he never missed a year despite the heavy bombardment that surrounded him; he refused to take sides between the Croats, the Serbs, and the Bosnian Muslims, but rather stood steadfast for what he believed was morally right; he suffered with whomever was suffering unjustly. Dr. Siebert not only brought a penetrating philosophical analysis and critical religiology to the Balkans but also cared for the physical and material needs of the victims. Medicine was given to whoever was in need, regardless of their national identity and/or ethnicity, and he welcomed any discourse partner who was willing to offer their constructive and critical thoughts. Amidst the artillery shells falling on the worker owned Hotel Argentina, in which the conference was being held, he had the prophetic and Socratic commitment to continue his lectures on Immanuel Kant's most hopeful proposition for *Perpetual Peace* (1795). In the face of war, he embraced a revolutionary yet illusive peace. It is in this light – the undiminished search for a better world – that I offer this book as a small attempt to help find a way towards that more reconciled future society that Dr. Rudolf J. Siebert taught about and longed for since he was a soldier in World War II, through the Yugoslav civil war, and until today. *Dum vivimus, vivamus.*[6]

> *Dustin J. Byrd*
> Dubrovnik, Croatia
> Rome, Italy

---

6   'While there is life there is hope.'

Acknowledgments

Like all academic works that take a long time to produce, this book was the result of many long conversations with good friends, colleagues, students, and even my children: Benjamin, Layla and Maxwell. They have all challenged the way I see the world, the way I interpret international political, economic and cultural events, as well as my ethical and moral reasoning. I owe them all a great debt of gratitude for their unrelenting commitment to my work.

I would especially like to thank Jamie Groendyk for all her hard work formatting and editing my often long, complex, and philosophically tortured language. Without her dedication and perseverance this book would not have been possible. I cannot thank her enough for all she has done for me over the past decade. She is the light in my life and foundation of my being.

I am most grateful to Dr. Rudolf J. Siebert, my mentor and friend. As I have benefited from his knowledge and wisdom for over twenty years, he has instilled in me the ability to look critically at the ugliness of nature and history, and most specifically the unnecessary suffering men have forced upon each other. At the same time he has solidified my personal resolve, so I do not lose myself within the despair of the suffering – for what good is genuine empathy with those who suffer if one becomes paralyzed by that suffering. If the world is blind (O Cieco Mondo) to the misery of others, the Critical Theory of Religion and Society, which Dr. Siebert has developed over the course of his career, is not. In proleptic solidarity with those destroyed by the slaughterbench of history, global Golgatha, and the innocent victims of war, torture and exploitation, who often don't appear even in the footnotes of history, the Critical Theory remembers their agony, their misery and their longing for the totally other.

I would like to thank my most devoted companions: Mikel Cloman, Spencer Michaud, Steven Chamberlin, Mladjo Ivanovic, Walter Jensen, Michael R. Ott, Mary Louise Ott and Kirk Hendershott-Kraetzer. They have all influenced my work in their own ways. All that is good within this book can be attributed to their brilliance; all that is flawed is my own.

I must acknowledge Olivet College for its support of my work in and out of the classroom, especially President Steven Corey and Provost Maria Davis. Olivet College began in protest against slavery, misogyny and class oppression. In 1844, it opened its doors to those who were told that they were not worthy of education on account of their race, gender and class. To this day, its tradition of radical egalitarianism guides its path towards a more reconciled future society. Being dedicated to the 'divine art of doing good to others,' and their commitment to 'those who are not rich in this world's means,' makes Olivet College one of the most prophetic and Socratic institutions in the state of Michigan. In a world that desperately needs critical voices, it instills a sense of 'social and individual responsibility' that is unmatched. As its motto states, it is *Pro Christo et Humanitiate.*

Lastly, I cannot forget one of my dearest friends, David Ward Thomas, who lost his battle with his failing heart on February 7, 2015, in Ann Arbor, Michigan. A long time resident of Kalamazoo, Michigan, and a proud graduate of Western Michigan University, David was one of the most giving human beings one could ever be blessed to have in one's life. The University of Michigan hospital kept him alive long beyond what his own heart was capable of, and I am eternally indebted to them for giving us the time we had with him. He was a man of quiet heroicism, a modern saint who embodied the best of his Catholic faith. I speak for all his friends when I say we all miss him dearly. He left us too soon, but he will not be forgotten. 'Keep your stick on the ice' David! *Requiem Aeternam dona eis, Domine, et lux perpetua luceat eis.*

Professing Islam in a Post-Secular Society

Introduction

The post-September 11th world has brought a new concentration upon the nature of Islam and the Muslim world, especially in light of the millions of Muslims that live in the West. The turmoil in Syria and Iraq, as well as in parts of North and East Africa, has brought hundreds of thousands of Muslim immigrants and refugees to the shores of Europe. Once there, they join the millions of other Muslims who have already made their homes in the West. Although the secular democracies of Europe are seen by many as places of opportunity and freedom, many Muslims find their presence to be unwanted, unwelcomed and hated; their religious sensibilities disrespected; their culture maligned, and their faith positions mocked and degraded. Indeed, the post-secular society, in which both religious communities remain an important and powerful presence despite the continual secularization of the lifeworld, is a contentious mix of worldviews, cultural norms, epistemologies and moral systems. Following the philosophical work of Jürgen Habermas and the Frankfurt School, such a society can either chose to embrace the diversity and live in a dynamic democracy, or retreat into stagnant provincialism, in which the various secular and religious communities fail to engage in a productive discourse. As such, the challenge of the post-secular society can either result in a vibrant multicultural and cosmopolitan democracy, where constitutional values are the basis for shared citizenship, or the various factions can continue their discourse avoidance and fragment into waring faction, which will inevitably lead to increased social conflict.

The purpose of this study is to probe the various points in western society, especially Europe, where the issue of professing Islam can either be a force for solidarity among religious communities and secular citizens, or a force of division. Informed by the Frankfurt School for Social Research, especially Theodor Adorno, Max Horkheimer, Erich Fromm, Herbert Marcuse, and the 2nd generation philosopher and sociologist Jürgen Habermas, this study will be attempt to shed light on the future possibilities of a more reconciled future society wherein Islam finds a welcoming place within the post-secular society. As both a critical scholar of religion as well as a citizen of a secular state, I and many others wish to avoid the situation in which western societies degenerate into rigid communities of exclusivity; we wish to arrest and reverse the entrenched economic marginalization that so many experience, as well as to abolish the religious bigotry that plagues both the Muslim community as well as the post-secular – and post-Christian – West. Rather we choose to seek out ways to peacefully co-exist and thrive together as one community regardless of the other's faith or faithlessness. In order to explore the possibilities of such a future reconciled society, we, like the Frankfurt School's critical religiology, will turn to philosophy, sociology, history, psychology, cultural studies and even theology. Although some remain skeptical, I find a turn towards theology to be extremely insightful, as its transcendent nature can inform us of the inner-dynamics of any given situation and help point us towards the *ought*, as opposed to simply abandoning the future to the *is*. Furthermore, "reconciliation," which is an underlying theme throughout this work, is not simply a matter of eschatology, but one that we recognize as being within the realm of possibility in the here-and-now. Just as Karl Marx's vision of a classless society reconciles the antagonism of class by the removal of that which antagonizes – oppression and exploitation of one class over all others; just as 'Ali Shariati's visions of a society beyond the colonial/colonized paradigm pointed to the reconciliatory potential of revolutionary Islam; just as Malcolm X, in his last days, saw a vision of the world that no longer used the yardstick of *race* to judge others, but rather judged based on the *deeds* of individuals; and just as Che Guevara had a radical vision of a society unified under the principle of equality and social justice, so too do we want to search for the potential for reconciliation within the context of our contemporary times. In order to do this, we will examine, interrogate, and critique both religion and secularity in a dialectical fashion, hoping to determinately negate that which leads mankind into continuous cycles of hatred and violence, while simultaneously preserving, augmenting, and fulfilling the prophetic and Socratic spirit that dissolves such irrational and destructive antagonisms. That being said, our aim, predicated on the permanence of the modern secular society in the West, wishes to see the construction of a more humane post-secular society; a society that values both the achievements of secularity as well as enlightened religion.[1] In working for such a better society, we must turn our attention to one of the most vexing issues within western society today: the trouble with recalcitrant faith, especially Islamic faith, in the context of the post-secular West and its post-Christian society.

---

1 One should not confuse the 'post-secular society' as being a society that has returned to religion. Many religious believers, seeing the destruction that secularity has had upon their faith, the moral values, and the pious way of life, engage in wishful thinking when they hear the phrase 'post-secular,' thinking that secularity is finally over. This is not the notion of 'post-secular' that we are discussing or attempting to advance in this study.

On the Contemporary Possibility of Witnessing and Professing

Professing a religious position can be a perilous proposition in a world that has been thoroughly secularized. It is an even greater problem when the faith that one professes is thought to be suspicious or threatening by the dominant group within one's society, which is the case for Islam in much of Europe.[2] When a community's deeply held beliefs, the basis of their identity, spiritual life, and cultural norms, is thought to be backwards, oppressive, undemocratic and unenlightened, it becomes easy for that community to internalize those accusations and close themselves up within their particular religious lifeworld (*religiöse lebenswelt*) and refuse to engage the broader society in a non-antagonistic and/or open way. When the marginalized religious identity is the source of social scorn, many within the faith community often cannot bolster the courage to engage other voices as equal members within that society, despite the fact that the believers may be the carrier of all the same civil rights afforded to them via their status as equal citizens of such a society. The notion of "equality" through mutual recognition, as often articulated by the Critical Theorist Jürgen Habermas, is the precondition for democratic and pluralistic deliberation. When society fails to adequately internalize and/or practice such notions of equality, democracy becomes distorted and degenerates into a hollow state-ideology in service to a single class, race, creed, etc. Therefore, when an undemocratic and therefore unfree situation presents itself within a context of social hostility on the basis of religious faith, especially Islam, the Muslim believers are often confronted with three choices; (1) abandon the faith, (2) engage in "religious dissimulation" (*taqīyah*), or (3) retreat into fundamentalism – the cutting off of an individual from the symphony of voices within the national discourse and adopting a staunch and unyielding attitude towards their own beliefs. Religious fundamentalism, by its nature, deprives the national discourse of the authentic voices of religious communities, as the believers often refrain from the social and theological risk created

---

2   I would like to note most forcefully that Islam and Muslims are not monolithic. The Muslim community, whether it be in the West or in the traditional Muslim world, are divided by the same antagonisms as westerners. Despite the unifying factor of the Islamic tradition, Muslims are separated by race, gender, class, sect, political philosophy, geography, schools of law, sexual orientation, language, nationalities, etc. While Muslims tend to agree on the basics of their religion, the interpretations and orientations within the religion is as numerous as the stitching in the *Kiswat al-Kab'ah* (shroud on the Ka'bah in Mecca). Managing such diversity itself has become a problem for the global ummah as many fundamentalist find such diversity threatening. With this in mind, the diversity of faith positions, etc. should be tacitly understood whenever the general terms of "Islam" and "Muslim" are used in this book.

by subjecting their beliefs to democratic deliberation. Many can no longer believe that the discourse partner in any way respects their sincere beliefs, as that partner seems not to find any value in what is offered. A poignant example of this retreat into one's own particular community can be found in the 2005 Muhammad cartoon affair, where Muslims experienced the Danish newspaper Jyllands Posten's portrayal of Muhammad as a terrorist to be extremely offensive and disrespectful of their most sacred figure. The perceived disrespect left many western Muslims feeling deeply alienated from the broader society whom they previously thought had some respect for their Islamic identity even if they couldn't be reverential towards their Islamic faith. Consequently, the post-protest withdrawal from Danish society diminished the possibility of a future reconciliation between people of different faiths and those of no faith.[3] If there is no discourse partner then there is no discourse; if there is no discourse then there is no real possibility for reconciliation and peace.

On the other hand, irreverent and critical thought, which is often perceived as insulting, is essential in the modern world, as it helps diminish the temptation of dogmas, authoritarian ideologies and political economic idolatry. Yet, on the other side, the tyranny of relativism, which plagues modern society, leaving it without any philosophical and/or ethical anchors, cannot simply go unchecked and unquestioned. Joseph Ratzinger, later to be named Pope Benedict XVI, pointed out in a conversation with the philosopher Jürgen Habermas that there is a danger in the over extension of relativism, multiculturalism, and tolerance within a society that is rooted in the Enlightenment and the secular state. The danger is especially acute when that state fails to adequately integrate minorities into the overall national culture.[4] The national anxiety concerning the non-integration and assimilation of Muslims within European society cannot be ignored as it is rife with future possibilities, both negative and positive; this anxiety can either be a source for discourse amongst European and Muslims or a source of continual antagonism and future violence.

---

3   Jyllands Posten wasn't the only publication to experience the ire of radical Islam. The left-wing French newspaper *Charlie Hebdo*, which routinely satirizes religion, especially Islam, Muhammad, and Muslims, was firebombed on November 2, 2011, and was later attacked by gunmen on January 7, 2015. In the last attack, twelve people were murdered including the senior editor Stéphane "Charb" Charbonnier. The killing was believed to be motivated out of revenge for the disrespect of the Prophet Muhammad. This subject will be taken up later in this work.

4   Jürgen Habermas and Joseph Ratzinger, *The Dialectics of Secularization: On Reason and Religion*. San Francisco: Ignatius Press, 2005.

The modern identity crisis of Europe – the question of *what does it mean to be European* in a post-secular society – is compounded by the mass immigration of Muslims who often are more oriented towards their national-cultural-religious place of origins as opposed to the culture and politics of their newly settled nation. As many of the center-right continuously proclaim, this problem is further compounded by the fact that many Muslim immigrants (both legal and illegal) enjoy the social benefits that Europe provides its citizens while seemingly contributing little-to-nothing of social value to their host countries. These "concerned" or sometimes "nativist"/"nationalist" voices view Muslims simply as parasites – enjoying the social benefits that Europe has created while at the same time delivering crime, poverty, and social chaos to their once peaceful and orderly cities and villages.[5] There is a sense that the near-utopia of Europe has been sullied and destroyed by people of an inferior and alien culture. *If they would only leave,* it is thought, *Europe could once again return to its happy retirement.*

However, the non-integration of Muslims risks the production of the "perpetual other" within the secular European society, which threatens the very stability of Europe. In terms of assimilation, the retreat into the comfort of Islam, the culture of national origin, and the Muslim community's often refusal to integrate within the national life of the host nation – the self-ghettoization of Muslims – creates a parallel society within Europe. They are not fully integrated but not fully segregated either, but rather a state of limbo exists. Coupled with the historical suspicion of Islam being anti-democratic, authoritarian, patriarchal, and violent, Muslims are seen not only as the suspicious "other" but also the lurking enemy within. In light of this, immigration by Muslims appears to many Europeans to look more like a stealth invasion, especially during the refugee/immigrant crisis of 2015 and 2016.[6] The fact that this society within a

---

5 Since September 11th, 2001, there has been a remarkable incline in anti-Muslim rhetoric, politics, and political parties in both America and Europe. These can be seen in the Netherlands, Germany, Switzerland, France, Greece, Italy, Ukraine, etc. Many of these parties have gained seats in the national legislatures but have failed to gain any substantial amount of control of any government body. Nevertheless, the frightening amount of silence – or lack of opposition – by others in the society could represent a tacit – not publicly endorsed – agreement with the center-right on the issue of immigrants and specifically Muslims. The silence of the majority is, to my thinking, the greatest threat to peace for Muslim immigrants in Europe.

6 Due to the Syrian civil war between the government of Bashar al-Assad, the Western (NATO) coalition and their Syrian allies, Russian forces and ISIS, hundreds of thousands of Syrian refugees flooded into Europe. Amidst those refugees were also many immigrants from Afghanistan, Pakistan, and Iraqis who were simply looking to Europe for a better and more prosperous life. Such a mass migration sparked a fierce debate with the EU countries as to

society is rooted in a *religious* identity only causes more suspicion and distrust within the national secular cultural, which trusts neither their religiosity nor the content of their religion. The refusal of both sides, the native European and the Muslim immigrant, to engage in a robust dialogue, discourse, and debate; to subject their deeply held claims – both religious and secular – to democratic scrutiny; and the refusal to think in terms of humanistic commonalities as opposed to *ethnos* and culture, all contribute to a situation where either violence will continue to be inevitable because discourse – the precondition for acceptance and respect – has been made impossible.

The Post-Secular Society

The Critical Theorist Jürgen Habermas is keenly aware of the antagonism between the religious and the secular, the immigrant and the native, the democratic and the authoritarian, and the religiously devout Muslims and their European neighbors who are just as committed to their secular values. In order to look for democratic means to address the antagonism between these antagonisms, Habermas, in his chapter, *What is Meant by a "Post-Secular Society"? A Discussion on Islam in Europe* revisits the sociological debate about secularism and religious communities within Europe, especially the particular challenges presented by Islam. Reviewing former thought about the inevitability of global secularity, he points out the three basic premises of traditional secularization theory; (1) that science, technology, positivism, natural causation, i.e. the anthropocentric vision of the world, can no longer be reconciled with a worldview that is rooted in a theological and/or God-centric understanding of ultimate reality; (2) that religion has resigned itself to the private sphere after the loss of its social power within the state, economy, and national institutions; and (3) that the material abundance that was created with the capitalization and industrialization of the West, the availability of consumer goods, the advance of medicine resulting in the increase in the lifespan and healthy living, the reduction of existential and material anxiety, and the alleviation of ubiquitous violence, all made religion superfluous to the average individual – where once God provided for the people, now the markets provide; where once Christians prayed for their "daily bread," now the bread factories see to it that it's available. The scarcity of necessities and the uncertainty of life, which was

---

what responsibility the EU has for such refugees and migrants. Not surprisingly, this influx of non-European Muslims became a flash point for the far-right and other liberals concerned about the influence of more Muslims in Europe.

the precondition for such religious faith, no longer exist for most people living in advanced industrial societies. Man provides where once God did, and thus religion in unnecessary.[7] Religion, according to many of these theories, would become superfluous as the roles and functions it once exclusively held were taken over by secular civil society and the secular state. For many of them, including Marx, Nietzsche, Freud, Weber and many 20th century sociologists, religion's long life was soon to come to an end, as it could no longer sustain its theological claims and traditional roles within the conditions of secular modernity.

Yet Habermas is aware that those who have dogmatically held onto such theories of secularization have become frustrated by the failure of religion to fully disappear in the late 20th and early 21st centuries. Their claims, that religion belongs to the adolescence, or even infancy of human history, that it's a *gestalt des geistes* as Freud believed – and thus has no place in the adulthood of the modern humanity – are frustrated by religion's stubbornness to find history's exit door. In this sense, religion is *fluctuat nec mergitur*.[8] Most stubbornly, and despite the ever-increasing secularization of the cultural, economic, and political realms, religion continued to infuse itself into the lifeworld of billions of people. The rise of religious fundamentalism, especially amongst Muslims both in Europe and the Middle East, the growth of conservative orthodoxy amongst the older denomination of Christianity, the move towards religiously infused governments in Iran, Turkey, Egypt, Iraq, etc., and the international and ecumenical popularity of the Pope Francis, all point to a resurgence of religion on a global scale.[9] For the secularization theorists, religion's shelf-life has long expired but it is still held onto by the masses, despite that it is understood by the expert cultures to be a roadblock to man's progress and an entrenched impediment to his survival. Religion, for the militantly secular, scientific, and atheistic, is man's poison – one he is too foolishly eager to consume. Confusingly, they wonder why so many continue to swallow the religion pill on a daily basis when they should know the pill is a placebo.

Like the religious believer who retreats into a purist way of thinking about the world, many secular fundamentalists also take refuge in Logical Positivism's *metaphysics of what-is-the-case* – deeming all non-materialist, non-scientific, and non-causational explanations of ultimate reality to be

---

7   Jürgen Habermas, *Europe: The Faltering Project* (Malden, MA: Polity Press, 2009), 60.

8   'Tossed by the waves but does not sink.'

9   Habermas, *Europe*, 61–62.

misguided, mentally deficient, and ultimately dangerous.[10] They see the continual existence of sacred stories, rituals, sacred space, and sacred persons to be nothing more than the mad ramblings of the mentally-disturbed, obscurantists, and hucksters, who may mean well, but are inevitably misguided by their reluctance to abandon their superstitious beliefs about God, angels, revelation, miracles, etc. For the logical positivist, that which cannot be measured through quantitative measures cannot be real and only that which is real can be measured. Therefore reality is limited to physicality and/or appearances. Additionally, they view the religious believers' commitments to divine revelation, which they find to be devoid of reason and epistemologically unsound, to be a sign of man's inability to mature and think rationally, abstractly, and systematically. From the perspective of positivists, religion, and all forms of *mysticism* as Ayn Rand would describe it, circumvent reason, make a mockery of the human intellect, and will ultimately lead human history into the ditch.[11] The worldview of the positivist has consequences. According to the German sociologist Max Weber, the increased rationalization of society leads to the inevitable *disenchantment* of the world. Man's emancipation from traditional religious metaphysics – that once connected him to the totality of his own being through sacred space, sacred texts, sacred figures, rituals, and religious institutions – leaves him disconnected and existentially adrift. Where religion once provided a comprehensive interpretation of reality and orientation of action, the bureaucratization and rationalization of the world disconnected him from that holistic wholeness and left him isolated, without unconditional meaning, afraid of others as well as the anonymous bureaucratic system he created by his own hands. This modern disenchanted man experienced himself locked within an "iron cage" without religious or metaphysical consolation. The modern world, which promised both material abundance and freedom from old and misguided dogmas, failed to replace the *connectedness* and sense of ontological and eschatological certainty that man once had living in a religious world. This sense of non-belonging, non-connectedness and the non-sense nature of a disenchanted world left him in a state of longing for the innocence of prior times. This being the case, a door for religion was left open by the failure of modernity to adequately address man's psychological and spiritual needs outside of his material necessities.

---

10   Clearly a retreat into positivism wasn't the case for dialectical thinkers such as Marx and
      the Frankfurt School.
11   Dustin Byrd, *A Critique of Ayn Rand's Philosophy of Religion: The Gospel According to John
      Galt.* Lanham, MD: Lexington Books, 2015.

From the perspective of the Critical Theorists of the Frankfurt School, who recognized man's spiritual bankruptcy post-Enlightenment, the inadequacies of religion, including its criminal and pathological history, cannot be the final word on religion as a human phenomenon, as religions contain within themselves the accumulation of human wisdom, experiences, protests, and thoughts which cannot be easily discarded without vacating much of human knowledge and abandoning the cause of those who, in their suffering, took refuge in the comforting arms of its absolutes.[12] As Max Horkheimer wrote, 'religion is the record of the wishes, desires, and accusation of countless generations.'[13] For Horkheimer, the longing for "perfect justice" remains an integral part of religion even within the modern period, and for that reason alone the critical theory of the Frankfurt School has to take seriously the human-centered claims of religion.[14] For the Critical Theorist of religion, proleptic solidarity (solidarity with past victims) is a sufficient reason to preserve some forms of prophetic religion in the secular world, even if it is only in its distorted form (manifest religion) or through its transformation and migration into secular philosophy.

The continuation of religion's existence amidst the thoroughly secularized world points to the fact that there is either (1) some persistent *longing* for something *other* than what-is-the-case (the world as it is) and (2) that religion still provides something to mankind that the secular world has yet to discover.[15] Most dialectically, it appears that the very coordinates of secularity have produced the necessary conditions for religions' continual presence – and/or rejuvenation – in society. In other words, secularity has produced a new form of religiosity: one that has become immune to secularity's attacks, or at least has found the capacity within itself to deter secularity's aggressively corrosive nature – a *post-secular* form of religion. This is not a world in which religion has triumphed over secularity, as could be misunderstood by reading "post" as being simply "after" in terms of time, but one where religion remains a continual and persistent presence *within* the increasingly secular world. Indeed, like a elastic band that is stretched at both ends, the more secular the contemporary world becomes, the more it creates the conditions for this new post-secular form of religion. The dialectic within secularity is such: as secularity expands

---

12   Karl Marx and Friedrich Engels, *The Marx-Engels Reader,* ed. Robert C. Tucker (New York: W. W. Norton & Co. Inc., 1978), 54.

13   Max Horkheimer, *Critical Theory: Selected Essays* (New York: Continuum, 2002), 129.

14   Horkheimer, *Critical Theory,* 129.

15   See Habermas' discussion of Max Frisch's funeral in St. Peter's Church in Zürich. Jürgen Habermas, *An Awareness of What's Missing: Faith and Reason in a Post-Secular Age* (Malden, MA: Polity Press, 2011), 15–16.

further into the lifeworld, it unintentionally produces the conditions which are filled by religion; as it alienates and disenchants more people, the more they turn to religion to fulfill their longing for transcendence; the more atheistic and meaningless the modern world becomes, the more it simultaneously calls for the messianic, i.e. the return to religion as a complete and total way-of-being.

As scholars of history, society, religion and secular philosophy, we are challenged by this paradoxical phenomenon. Surely we in the West cannot go behind history and return to religion as a comprehensive worldview that determines the trajectory of the state and civil society, nor can we anachronistically return behind the Enlightenment without collapsing civilization into a false utopian dream of what society should look like now that we've experienced the horrors of secular modernity. Indeed, as Adorno has remarked in his essay *Reason and Revelation*, any attempt to return to religion post-Enlightenment is rooted in what we perceive as our *needs* and *desires*, not our being *convinced* of the metaphysical truth of religion's claims.[16] No, we are forced to muscle our way through secular modernity with one eye turned back towards history in proleptic solidarity with past victims and the other sternly directed towards the future with the object of creating a more-reconciled future society, which must include space for religious voices. This situation imposes an important question upon us: what can we as Critical Theorists do on the practical level to address the growing antagonism between the secular and the sacred; between the atheistic citizen and their religious counterpart; between the secular West and the *dar-al-Islam* (abode of Islam)?

In the realm of society, Habermas' late writings on religion are increasingly sensitive to the antagonism between the sacred and the profane and how it manifests itself in the life of the nation-state and body politic. In light of his time diagnosis and prognosis, he proposes an answer to the vexing conditions of *post-secularity* – one that lays a challenging burden on both the religious and the secular if we are to see that the fundamental antagonism between the sacred and the profane within our current transition period – that is exacerbated by the ever-increasing power of capitalist markets and their global expansion – does not bring the world to total violence, i.e. alternative future No. 2, the totally militarized world capable of ABC (atomic, biological and chemical) wars.

According to various critical religiologists of the Frankfurt School tradition, including Rudolf J. Siebert – a second generation Critical Theorist and the pioneer of the Frankfurt School's systematic study of religion – the secularization process continues undisturbed by the "return to religion" movements that can

---

16   Theodor Adorno, *Critical Models: Interventions and Catchwords* (New York: Columbia University Press, 2005), 137.

be witnessed throughout the world.[17] In the West, these movements are primarily in response to the near complete secularization of the public sphere, the lifeworld, the economy, and the family. They are born from the continuing infiltration of secular values, consumerism, commercialism, the neo-imperialism in the Muslim world, and the globalization of the secular ethos in other parts of the world that are desperately attempting to hold onto their traditional religious values and cultures. These religious people, like the fundamentalists, are deeply wounded by secular modernity and have become painfully aware of the corrosive effects it has had upon their lives. However, Habermas also points out that these victims of secularity rarely acknowledge the beneficial side of the secular Enlightenment that they themselves benefit from. Too often the positive side of the Enlightenment, i.e. the attempt to make every individual the master of their own fate; to liberate them from the bounds of kin, class, region, and familial expectations and traditional roles; to free them from magic, superstition, and nature; the advance of technology; and to place temporal power in the hands of the people, is often not adequately articulated by the proponents of secularization. Yet, much of these so-called positive aspects of Enlightenment are not universally experienced as being beneficial. Definitions of what can be considered "positive," for example, are very different in the West than among the devoutly religious. Emancipation, which in the West is often associated with an autonomous and democratic lifestyle, is rarely reconciled with the religious idea of true freedom that can only be found through the complete submission to the will of the divine. Yet, for the secular West, as Horkheimer and Adorno articulated in the first lines of their *Dialectic of Enlightenment*, the Enlightenment is to be understood in the broadest sense as the

> advance of thought,... aimed at liberating human beings from fear and installing them as masters... Enlightenment's program was the disenchantment of the world. It wanted to dispel myths, to overthrow fantasy with knowledge.[18]

However, even when individuals have been emancipated from their fears, myths and fantasies, many intrinsically feel the price has been too high for

---

17 Rudolf J. Siebert, *Manifesto of the Critical Theory of Society and Religion: The Wholly Other, Liberation, Happiness and the Rescue of the Hopeless, Vol 1–III*. Boston: Brill, 2010.

18 Max Horkheimer and Theodor Adorno, *Dialectic of Enlightenment: Philosophical Fragments*, ed. Gunzelin Schmid Noerr. trans. Edmund Jephcott (Stanford: Stanford University Press, 2002), 1.

such liberation. They would be much happier to retreat into a traditional worldview and way of life. Freedom from the strictures of traditional societies is too heavy of a burden, too disorienting, too confusing, and is devoid of the necessary metaphysical moorings that anchor the individual in a worldview that orders their existence and renders it meaningful. Although much of the anxiety felt by secularized individuals stems from the fear of being isolated, standing on their own two moral and intellectual feet, and appropriating the responsibility for their own lives, there is nevertheless a legitimate *awareness that something is missing* in the secularized lifeworld that is independent of individual angst and anxiety.[19]

Beyond the purely subjective answer, secularity has failed to answer the most basic questions about life, its end point, its meaning, and how to console the grieving person in their moment of inner-most despair and torment. Consequently, there is a pervasive feeling of nihilistic *emptiness* in today's secularized world. It continues to create mentally, physically and spiritually broken and crippled individuals, who are isolated and on the margins of society. Despite the problems, the pain of spiritual vacuousness is being globalized through the secularization process via aggressive forms of capitalism; the pain that was once limited to secular Western nations is swiftly becoming *weltschmerz* (world pain) and many are looking once again towards religion for anesthetic answers.

It is important to note that for Habermas, the object of the post-secular society can only be the society that has already been thoroughly secularized and not one presently struggling to become secular.[20] In other words, to be *post-secular* presupposes a prior state of *secularity*. Therefore, post-secularity is limited to only those nation-states which have a secular constitution, secular polity, and a secular state; those states that have constructed a secular way-of-being-in-the-world through some kind of rational deliberation or non-theistic philosophy as opposed to a traditional theocracy or any other form of governance that relies on revelation or divine command for its legitimation. Furthermore, the cultural climate of the nation-state must also be one that is not only *open* to secularity, but accepts it as a basic norm, i.e. that the desireability of secularity is not a subject of disagreement and contestation (even if the degree of secularization and what that ultimately means can be a matter of debate). States in which the secular constitution and secular government is imposed from above upon a people who identify themselves as predominately

---

19   Erich Fromm, *Escape from Freedom* (New York: Henry Holt & Co., Inc.: 1994), 1–21; Habermas, *An Awareness of What is Missing,* 15–23.

20   Habermas, *Europe.* 59.

religious and in favor of some form of religiosity within the government, cannot be describes as a secular nation per se, as they fail to reflect the general consensus of the people. A current example can be found in post-Mubarak Egypt. When given the opportunity to democratically elect their leaders, the majority of Egyptians elected a religious political party – the *Ikhwan al-Muslimun* (Muslim Brotherhood) and Muhammad Morsi, who, despite being democratically elected, was overthrown in a coup d'etat in 2013 by the secular military under the direction of General Abdal-Fattah el-Sisi, who later banned the *Ikhwan al-Muslimun* under the pretext of being a "terrorist" group. Egypt, despite its "secular" constitution, secular military and secular-oriented ruling class, can hardly be considered a secular nation as the will of the people is thoroughly divided between those who want religion to have some influence on the government and those who advocate for a purely secular state. Because secularity itself is still bitterly contested among the people, resulting in a lack of consensus about the desirability of secularity, we should not regard it as a secular nation even if religion has been forcibly removed from governmental institutions. It is a *formal* secularity at best, and not one that has been adopted as a way-of-being for the vast majority of citizens.

For Habermas, if the secular West has moved into a post-secular condition, we then have to have a change in consciousness concerning three important factors.[21] First, Habermas points out that citizens of secular states find themselves anxious at the sight of resurgent religion which 'shakes the secularistic confidence that religion is destined to disappear.'[22] He believes that they must begin to resign themselves to the inevitability that religion will persist despite the growth of secularism. Second, secular citizens are becoming more aware that religious voices are increasingly contributing to various discourses within the public sphere; that they are 'assuming the role of communities of interpretation' and that they can contribute as a 'sounding board' for society when engaged in difficult moral and ethics decisions and dilemmas. Additionally, the existence of other religions within the multicultural societies of the West confronts Christianity's exclusivism and privileged status by presenting alternative interpretations of reality and moral problems, and in doing so can offer previously unimagined solutions.[23] Habermas points out that religions have increasingly become sources for meaningful thought-material in a world that has become increasingly malcontent to accept the finality of the status quo or the simply given. Lastly, the influxes of religious minorities into secular

---

21   Habermas, *Europe*, 63–65.

22   Ibid., 63.

23   Ibid., 64.

Europe are a constant test of the Enlightenment values that Europeans have claimed to be universal.[24] The physical presence of the foreign "other," their alternative lifestyles, and their persistent questioning of what Europe takes to be *self-evident* pushes Europeans into a self-reflexive mode – a rethinking of the way-of-being that was previously understood to be normative and inherently good and ethical. The limits of multiculturalism, the respect for diversity, and the belief in the universality of *Liberté, Egalité, Fraternité* regardless of national origin, are fundamentally tested by the cultural and religious "other" within European society. Yet, Europe must ask: can such "enlightened" values persist when other cultures read those same values through religious lenses? Does such an alternative reading of "core" values bring to light the tacit "Europeanness" of how they've been traditionally articulated since the Enlightenment? For example, can an Islamic reading of liberty, equality, and fraternity deepen and expand the vitality of such values in Europe or are the different readings – the secular European Enlightenment and the Islamic tradition – too radically different to be complimentary or reconcilable?

To view these questions from the standpoint of the 'neutral observer' is to take the wrong perspective. According to Habermas, we must rather ask a series of pertinent questions, 'How *should we understand ourselves* as members of a post-secular society, and what *must we* expect from one another if *we* want to ensure that social relations in secular nation-states remain civil despite the growth of cultural and religious pluralism?'[25] Indeed, how does both the religious foreigner practice their religion in a secular society and how does the secular citizen embody their convictions within a society in which religion remains an active component in the public sphere? How do these groups of believers, non-believers, and agnostics learn to engage in conversations that do not descend into crude stereotypes, crass innuendos, disrespect, and hatred? Can they witness for their different religious and philosophical positions together as citizens, or is shared citizenship too deficient in providing them a platform by which they could discover an "overlapping consensus" on a variety of issues? Additionally, can secular society regain a healthy admiration for religion, and can religious communities understand and appreciate the role and achievements of secularity within the modern world despite their absence of divine legitimation? How should these two work together so that their living together does not descend into hating and killing? Can Habermas' notion of post-secular society prepare a space in which professing a religious worldview – especially one that is associated primarily with foreigners – can

---

24   Ibid., 64.
25   Ibid., 65.

be done safely and as equal citizens? Can the political, economic, and culture spheres of the nation-state be widened enough to allow for full integration and democratic participation of the "other"? Complete and meaningful *integration* through honest and universal discourse, not *toleration* through faux-respect, seems to be the current challenge in our current secular societies, but do the conditions of the post-secular society allow for such integration and acceptance? In order to answer that, we must delve into what it means to be Muslim in the post-secular society.

What Does It Mean to Profess Islam?

Through their adherence to five pillars and the moral code of Islam, Muslims profess every day to the most basic of theological claims: *tawḥīd*. 'There is no god but Allah, and Muhammad is the Messenger of Allah' (*La ilaha il Allah, wa Muhammad Rasul Allah*). It is both a statement about ultimate reality, that the world and all it contains is a creation of a divine being that interjects its will into human history – a belief that is also shared by Jews and Christians – and a statement about how and why the divine has entered into history, not as an divine incarnation like Jesus of Nazareth in Christianity, but through a human messenger, a Prophet. For Muslims, the religion that was *perfected* by the divine is a *complete* and *total way of life* – a way of being that is meant to be understood as a total 'submission' (*islam*) to the will of the creator: a radicalization of what Jesus said in the Gospel of Luke: 'not my will Lord, but yours be done.'[26] For Muslims, this Christian statement has to carry through to all aspects of life, not just during *ṣalāt al-jumʿah* (congregational Friday prayers), the *'eids* (holy days), or in moments of crisis. Similar to the Calvinists, who find religious devotion in the everydayness of work, Muslims see the potential for *ibādah* (worship) in all things at all times (as long as they're permitted activities). As such, all aspects of daily life take on a religious significance.

 Profession is bearing witness through words – through the speech act – through language that expresses the ultimate commitments, ultimate concerns, ultimate values, and core beliefs of the individual.[27] It articulates the

---

26 The Gospel According to Luke: 22:42.

27 This conception of profession is obviously different from the *act of confession* which is seen as a sacrament within Catholicism. For Catholics, the sacrament of confession is the confession of sins and transgressions to a Priest in exchange for penance and hopefully absolution. Outside of this particularistic ritual, Catholics share the same phenomenon with other religion, the confession of beliefs as a public act of religious affirmation.

utmost concerns, the essence of being, the spiritual aspects of human existence, and it affirms the duty of the believer to embody the values expressed and revealed by the divine. Additionally, Islamic professing is the merging of both words and intentions (*niyyah*) so that the speech-act itself stands as a testament to the identical nature of the believer's sincere intentions. Through their public profession, the believer offers their belief and praxis to the judgment of history, their peers, their community, and their God. For the devout Muslim, both the public and private sphere are arenas in which they either succeeds or fail to incorporate the ideals, potentials, principles, and the Islamic social values that are expressed in both the Qur'an and the Sunnah. As such, the devout believe that they will be questioned on the Day of Judgment (*Yawm al-Qiyāmah*) about how they fulfilled their time on the earth, which includes time in both the public and private realm. Did they dedicate the time Allah provided by engaging in *shirk* (polytheism) via the devotion of the earthly idols of wealth, fame, status, power – living in the *having* mode of being – or did they commit themselves to the furthering of justice, compassion, and mercy – living in the *being* mode – the embodiment of *tawḥīd* (oneness of God) and *taqwá* (God consciousness)?[28]

Because of the integrated wholeness of the Islamic tradition, the bifurcation of the lifeworld into a religious private and secular public sphere is a problem for the devout Muslim; faith does not stop at the threshold of the home and it cannot be artificially locked within the home. The five pillars of Islam are to be equally confessed in the realm of the family, civil society, and the state, regardless of whether they reside in a secular or religious society.[29] Therefore for most Muslims, Islam cannot be relegated and/or isolated to the home without doing considerable damage to the integrated wholeness of the believer's lifeworld. If the individual Muslim in praxis remains steadfast in separating the two spheres of life they often senses that they violate the very creed they professes which recognizes no such distinction, causing great difficulty, anxiety, and fear of divine punishment. If Islam is the *perfected* religion established by the God of the Qur'an, and that the Prophet instituted it in such a way that it is a religion that regulates – and therefore liberates – all spheres of life, and if the individual is a modern European who only confesses his religious beliefs behind closed doors while living the secular life in the public sphere, then they effectively forsake the sunnah (the way of the Prophet) and the divine

---

28   See Erich Fromm, *To Have or To Be?* New York: Harper & Row, Publishers, 1976.

29   See G.W.F. Hegel, *Elements of the Philosophy of Right* (New York: Cambridge University Press, 2010) §§142 – 329. Also see Rudolf J. Siebert, *Hegel's Concept of Marriage and Family: The Origin of Subjective Freedom.* Lewiston, NY: The Edwin Mellen Press, 1979.

command to submit to the will of Allah (at all times).[30] Muslims fail to engage in a meaningful *imitatio Muhammadi* if the bifurcation of the lifeworld separates their religious life into private and public praxis. In light of this inner-conflict, western Muslim are often trapped between two imperatives, (1) to faithfully integrate their religion in all spheres of being and be alienated – or even marginalized – from the society in which they live – which is often hostile towards outward displays of religion, or (2) to isolate the religious life to the private and abandon the constitutional example of the Prophet. Steadfastness to the first may insure salvation; steadfastness to the second may insure social survival but engender salvational anxiety. Sincere profession of faith in a bifurcated society often instills great pains of conscience within many Muslim. For many believers, the question is: *where is the balance,* and *is it even possible to be a good secular citizen as well as a devout Muslim?* Surely one can be a law-abiding citizen, engage in civil affairs, and advance the interests of one's nation-state and community, but can one do this while openly professing Islam as the motivation for such actions?

Witnessing in Islam: On the Tradition of Radical Praxis

The practice of "witnessing" for the faith of Islam takes on two fundamental dimensions. First, when in times of peace, the propagation of the Islam via *da'wa* (invitation to Islam), or activities associated with calling others to Islam. Muslims are encouraged to present Islam to non-believers in the most peaceful, merciful, and loving way, as to interest them in an alternative and *truthful* way-of-being, learning more about the will of the divine, and ultimately welcoming them into the *ummat al-Islamiyah* (Islamic community). Despite the stereotype of the Muslim that conquers by the sword, forcefully compelling anyone into Islam via violence or the threat of violence has been strongly condemned by an unequivocal verse in the Qur'an (*Sūrat al-Baqarah,* 2:256): *there shall be no compulsion in religion.* According to Islamic *fiqh* (jurisprudence), if a non-Muslim is ever wrongly forced to accept Islam, they are within their rights to revert back to their original tradition (or non-tradition). Da'wa is meant to be an open invitation to Islam, not an attempt to incarcerate within Islam. In peacetime, Muslims are to stand as witnesses for the Islamic tradition both in word and in deed through their submission to the moral and ethics principles laid out in the Qur'an, the *Sunnah* (way of the Prophet), *ahl*

---

30   Al-Qur'an 5:3, 'This day, I have perfected your religion, completed my favor upon you and have chosen Islam as your religion.' My translation. We will return to this issue briefly.

al-bayt (The House of the Prophet), and the *ḥadīṯ* (reports of Muhammad's words and deeds).[31] Muslims are to stand as examples of righteousness in a world that is post-righteous (or even sometimes pre-righteous). Although this command goes beyond the clothing that one wears (which is a form of witnessing), it is often the *Muslima* (the Muslim woman) that stand at the frontline of this struggle in secular societies, as she is the most readily identifiable because of her hijab or other head-coverings. Muslim women are the ones that are approached most often with questions about Islam; they are the ones that will most often be harassed because of the faith; they are the ones most often pitied (in the West) because they're seen as oppressed under their headscarf and behind their *niqāb* (face veil); and they're the ones most often singled out for discrimination because of the suspicion of terrorism that surrounds the Muslim community. Like the women who openly wept for the executed Jesus on Golgotha, Muslim women are on the frontlines for the struggle for recognition while often the men hide behind their western clothing and practice *taqīyah* (religious dissimulation) to the best of their ability. Amidst those with anti-Islamic sentiments, it is the *Muslima* that are most often the bravest *mujahideen* (those who struggle for the sake of Allah).

Whereas professing is inherently concerned with the individual and the divine – a relationship that can easily retreat exclusively into the private sphere – the practice of *witnessing* is a public praxis that is geared primarily towards the individual believer and the society around them. The social aspect of witnessing is one that cannot be overlooked in understanding how the dynamic of Islamic witnessing works. It is within society that the subjectivity of the Muslim can transcend itself, go out to the other, and return back to them and complete their faith. The "other" in society is that which makes possible the realization of the believer's moral commitments, social obligations, and divine commandments. It is with the "other" in society that the Muslim is commanded by his religion to practice the humanistic values of compassion, mercy, solidarity, and unconditional love. Although the mystics of Islam, the Sufis, often stoically shy away from the world outside of themselves and seek refuge in a deeply personalized relationship with the divine, and therefore sometimes forget the social demands of the *ummah* (community), the non-mystic Muslim, adhering to the prophetic model of religious life, is compelled to realize their religiosity in concert with others – whether that be in a community of believers or in a community of adversaries – either one of which serves as the

---

31   The *ahl al-bayt* is especially important for Shi'i Muslims, as it is the house of the Prophet via 'Ali that they take as another source moral authority.

basis for the social dimension of the Islamic creed.[32] For example, the poor make it possible for those who have resources to purify and therefore make ḥalāl (permissible) their accumulated wealth (if it wasn't gained through illicit means, in which case purification does not follow charity). Without the fulfillment of their obligations to the poor, the subjective religiosity of the individual Muslim is suspect; their commitment to the divine command is insufficient, diminished, and stands unfulfilled. It is through the other, especially in this case the poor and marginalized, which allows the individual to abide by the divine laws and dictates of the Qur'an. Therefore, witnessing in Islam inherently means *being-with-others* and *being-for-others*. In the end, it is a freely chosen *altruistic* commitment that stresses the absolute need for social justice, social equity, and social harmony – where the subjective desires of the individual are superseded by the objective needs of the community. Without the witnessing of Islamic values in society, Islam retreats into a private hyper-personalized faith that depletes it of its social potentials, its social force, and its commitment to the furthering of a future reconciled society. This same phenomenon can be seen in the historical privatization of Christian social values in the West. Only in times of great need, such as the Civil Rights struggle in the U.S., do these humanistic values reappear in individuals of great moral courage, such as Dr. Martin Luther King Jr., who not only called for civil rights but also for the "redistribution of wealth," which was not popular among capitalists and the white majority of the United States. For King, it was a moral disgrace that the U.S. massively produces poor people like commodities, even though it is the richest nation on earth.[33]

New Religion as Return of the Old

Islam, like Christianity, is not *only* a matter of a personal relationship with the divine, but is also a matter of active and dynamic social solidarity with the poor, the suffering, and the victims of nature and history, the tyrannized and the oppressed, and all those forced to live under unjust conditions. It was for these innocent victims, created by *al-Qur'aysh* (Muhammad's tribe in Mecca),

---

32   It is certainly not the case that all Sufis shy away from social life but it is a general orientation among mystics to find a deeply personal relationship with the divine that often overshadows the commitment to the greater world.

33   According to Dr. Martin Luther King Jr.'s son, MLK III, the demand for the "redistribution of wealth" was the reason his father was murdered. See Martin Luther King III's interview by Rev. Al Sharpton, *PoliticsNation*, MSNBC, 20 January 2014.

the Roman Empire, and racist America that Muhammad, Jesus, Dr. Martin Luther King Jr., Malcolm X and many others fought on the side of. Their religious faith led them to bind themselves to the plight and predicament of those who were despised, neglected, and abused: the social outcasts and those who found themselves the victims of systematic discrimination, oppression, and violence. Furthermore, the advancement of hyper-individualization, egoism, narcissism, and bourgeois coldness, that is characteristic of modern civil society as advanced by global capitalism, is a great fear of the *ummah* and other religious communities, as it undermines the communicative rationality that is the adhesive of their community. Many Muslim scholars identify how western Christianity has been privatized and depleted of its social force and relevance, leaving civil society to be steered by corporate greed, individual competitiveness, and the politics of unaccountable power. They fear precisely what Nietzsche accused the West of doing: turning God's cathedrals – and possibly his mosques – into God's tombs, and thus handing the keys to the earthly kingdom over to tyranny of the markets. *Requiem aeternam deo*.[34] The idea that this *market-zeitgeist* could migrate – and has migrated – into the *dar al-Islam* (abode of Islam) is alarming to Muslims who see Islam as the antithesis to the values that drive global capitalism. Summing up their stance against this radical social change, a devout Muslim once told me: *you can keep your Gucci, Prada, and Mercedes-Benz, and we'll keep our faith, traditions, and families*. The threat of the displacement of Islam for secular capitalism, which according to the Critical Theorist Walter Benjamin is a new religion itself, is real and should be taken seriously by both Muslims and the West, as it is one of the greatest contributing factors in the resentment that the Muslim world has against western nations.

In order to witness the encroachment of corporate capitalism within the most holy of spaces within the Muslim world, one need only visit Mecca – the most sacred space for Muslims – where the commercialization of the surrounding area continues unabated. Every western fast food chain, designer clothes, technological gadgets, or luxury items most associated with western bourgeois culture and the consumer society can be purchased within the city. It is a very modern city dedicated to a pre-modern religion *and* the modern cult of consumption. This phenomenon is the result of the collaboration with Saudi Salafism and corporate capitalism; the most poignant symbol of this alliance being the new *Makkah Royal Hotel Clock Tower* or *Abraj al-Bait Tower* that looms ominously over the great mosque of Mecca – a grotesque display of

---

34   'Eternal rest of God.' Friedrich Nietzsche, *The Gay Science* (New York: Barnes & Noble, 2008), 104.

cheap grandeur in the city of the most humble prophet; it is symbolic of cor-
porate style capitalism awkwardly superimposed on prophetic religious faith.
Additionally, it continues on the tradition of the Wahhabi-Salafi destruction of
Islamic architecture that begun with the conquest of Mecca by the Wahhabi-
Salafis in 1803. Just as was done to Islamic monuments and dwellings to build
the new petro funded *Clock-Tower* and the grandiose expansion of the Grand
Mosque, Abdul Aziz, a leader of the puritan reform movement, destroyed any
edifice that didn't conform to his narrow and puritan interpretation of Islam,
including tombs, shrines, and homes associated with the *Sīrat Rasūl Allāh*
(biography of the Prophet). However, as the 19th century Wahhabi-Salafis destroyed historically significant edifices in the name of religious reform, today's
Wahhabi-Salafis destroy in the name of other goals: profits.[35]

Critics have dubbed this commercialization of sacred space the "Las Vegas-
ization" of Mecca, as the "other-worldliness" of the sacred geography appears
increasingly diminished in contrast to the secular and capitalist oriented culture. In the end, the "otherness" of Mecca is giving way to the "sameness" of
every other major city in the world, as it sheds the aura of sacredness for ubiquitous advertisements and the same consumer goods that are found throughout the world. Apart from the Grand Mosque and other features of the city
associated with Muhammad and the early Muslims, Mecca becomes indistin-
guishable from other Middle Eastern cities where the influence of corporate
capitalism is abundant. For many Muslims, it appears that Mecca has returned
to the market ethics of al-Qar'aysh, the primary enemies of the early Muslims,
who also maximized profits from the pilgrims on their way to visit the holy
Ka'ba, just as the first century money-changers did around the Jewish Temple,
which sparked Jesus' earthly *dies irae* (day of rage) against their profit making.
For these Muslim critics, it appears that the globalizing secular force of capitalism has created a *new jāhilīyah* (age of ignorance) and its *destruktiven geist* (destructive spirit) has pierced the very heart of Islam's most sacred space. Mecca,
in many ways, stands today as a city divided between two religions. First, the
religion of Islam that has always resisted its integration within the antagonistic
spirit of capitalism, and secondly, the new "religion" of globalized capitalism –
which has a way of quietly undermining the communicative nature of revealed
religion, leaving behind a pitiful shadow of what religion once was. Additionally, from the perspective of Walter Benjamin's dialectical materialist historian,
the catastrophe of elegance and luxury comes at the cost of the more than

---

35   Alastair Crooke, "You Can't Understand ISIS if You Don't Know the History of Wah-
      habism in Saudi Arabia," August 27, 2014. www.huffingtonpost.com/alastair-crooke/isis
      -wahhabism-saudi-arabia_b_5717157.html (Accessed 11/3/2014).

half a million foreign workers in Saudi Arabia that live in squalid conditions, are abused at the hands of their employers, and are denied their basic human rights by the Kingdom. According to a report by Human Rights Watch, these workers often times live in conditions reminiscent of slavery.[36] Echoing Benjamin's *Angelus Novus*, who sees all of history as a singular event of barbaric tragedy, the dialectical materialist historian sees the new skyscrapers, shopping malls, and luxury office buildings as testaments to the sickness within today's Saudi (and broader Muslim) society. When the Islamic command to clothe, house, and feed the poor, the sick, and the broken gives way to gaudy and vainglorious displays of unmerited wealth and undeserved luxury, then the prophetic values of Islam have been overtaken by the corrosive nature of a very secular globalized capitalism. They have, in this sense, exchanged the religious morality of the Prophet Muhammad for the secular philosophies of Ayn Rand, Friedrich Hayek and Milton Friedman. It is capitalism with an Islamic façade.

Witnessing in the Time of War

Witnessing in the time of war is of utmost concern in the latest period of Islamic history, as it has come to the forefront under European colonialism, post-colonialism, the "War on Terror," the Arab Spring, and the various civil wars that have recently plagued the Muslim world. Although the western World's fascination, condemnation, and distortion of the Islamic concept of *jihād* has gone on since the rise of the first Islamic empire that displaced the crumbling and oppressive Byzantines and Sasanians in the Middle East, and later threatened the lands of the Roman Catholic Church, it has yet to fully understand what *jihād* means from *within* a normative Islamic perspective. Whether this is intentional or through neglect is a continual topic of debate. On the other hand, a pervasive symptom of the nouveau-*jahili*-status (state of modern ignorance) of today's *dar al-Islam* is that many Muslims aren't able to adequately define or intellectually defend the notion of *jihād* either. When it comes under scrutiny, many Muslims adopt a reactionary attitude that levels the complex concept down to a simple slogan of "holy war," the very same misconception of *jihād* that many uninformed westerners have. Religious illiteracy is not only a symptom of secularization, but of deficient religious education in supposed religious societies, and the Muslim majority countries are no exception. In a

---

36   See Human Rights Watch, "Bad Dreams: Exploitation and Abuse of Migrant Workers in Saudi Arabia." July 14, 2004. www.refworld.org/cgibin/texis/vtx/rwmainpage=search&do cid=412ef32a4&skip=0&query=saudiarabiamigrantworkers (Accessed 10/12/2014).

classical understanding of *jihād*, especially in times of *peace*, it is a struggle within oneself to perfect that which is confessed and witnessed; it's a struggle to be just, fair, honest, and life-affirming; it is an concerted effort to 'enjoin what is right and forbid what is wrong' (Qur'an, 3:110); it is a struggle to direct one's energies, resources, and time towards realizing a society that does not brutalize, oppress, and make into idols the gods of the market: success, fame, status and wealth. In times of war, *jihād bil-saif* (struggle of the sword) is an active struggle to defend the Muslim *ummah* from those who wish to inflict harm upon it. Although the laws governing Muslims engaged in warfare are precise and extensive, and are therefore beyond the scope of this discussion, it is clear both from the Qur'an and the ḥadīth that Muslims are (1) not to initiate hostilities with others, (2) not to attack innocent civilians, whether they be men, women, children, clerics, etc., (3) must cease hostilities if the enemy surrenders or sues for peace, (4) cannot abuse captives, (5) cannot force Islam upon captives, and (6) cannot poison wells (engage in biological and chemical warfare).[37] Lastly, similar to the Augustinian Just War Theory (*jus bellum iustum*), the war against the enemy must be proportional and must avoid civilian casualties at all costs.[38] Of course, history demonstrates to us that the Muslim world is not a society of saints and often violates its own prescribed norms, as Muslim so often justify violence against innocent civilians by creatively interpreting away certain prohibitions, by declaring them non-applicable, or by anachronistically making normative certain actions of past Muslims that have been since rejected or abandoned via *ijma'* (consensus) by Islamic scholars over the centuries.[39] Furthermore, the practice of *takfīr,* or declaring a Muslim to be a non-Muslim (a form of excommunication), and therefore mistakenly believing it is permissible to kill these "*murtaddīn*" (apostates), is also become a commonly held belief among some orientations, and is likewise a symptom of the modern condition in the Muslim world. This is most certainly not limited to the Muslim community, as all religions have a criminal history when we see the core of the faiths transformed into an ideology that crudely legitimates and/or masks limited self-interest. From the perspective of the critical religiologist, the Christian religion of 'becoming and liberation' is distorted into the Crusades, witch burning, and the Inquisition; the Jewish religion of

---

37 Al-Qur'an, 2:190–193; 4:84; 2:216; 2:244; 2:217; 2:246–251; 4:74–76; 8:39; 8:65; 9:5–6; 12:13–16; 9:29; 9:123; 22:39–41; 47:4; 47:20; 48:17.

38 The Augustinian Just War Theory was a compromise between Christians and the Roman state that betrayed the radical pacifism of the earliest Christian communities.

39 This neglect of Qur'anic norms concerning warfare can be witnessed most poignantly in ISIS (Islamic State in Iraq and Syria) repeated human rights abuses.

'sublimity' is turned into an ideology of state sponsored repression and murder of Palestinians as well as the denial of their most basic human rights; the religion of 'imagination' turns into Hindu nationalism and fanaticism against Muslim minorities; and likewise the Islamic religion of 'law' turns into 9/11, hijackings, beheadings, and suicide bombers.[40] We also see this same phenomenon among secular states that also espouse prohibitions against exacting violence among innocent people but fail to uphold such standards precisely when they are most necessary. 'The land of the free' – predicated on the American Constitution – degenerates into the slaughter of Native Americas, the enslavement of Africans, the internment of Japanese citizens, and the so-called "war on terror" which itself terrorizes innocent victims of Iraq, Afghanistan, Yemen, Pakistan, etc.[41] The nation that fights against terror has refused to close its own terrorist training camp in Fort Benning, Georgia, i.e. the *School of the Americas*, now known as *Western Hemisphere Institute for Security Cooperation,* which is responsible for some of the most brutal and repulsive human rights abuses in Latin America. A nation that obsessives over abortion but finds no flaw in napalming pregnant Vietnamese women and their toddlers is hardly a nation that can claim to be rooted in the Gospel tradition of loving one's enemy. What kind of enemy can the unborn and newly-born be? The already historically dubious claim that the United States is a "Christian" country is made even more unbelievable by the militaristic praxis of the "hawks" in Washington d.c. – both Republican and Democrat – whose instrumental rationality – which allows them to think strategically about the destruction of nations – outweighs any remnants of communicative reason which would inform them of the intrinsic worth of the life they will inevitably destroy. From the perspective of the Frankfurt School's Critical Theory, nations are invaded, undermined, and overthrown for profit, not for the Orwellian notions of freedom, justice, and liberty, which may provide ideological justification but are rarely the true motivation for aggressive militarism. Millions of martyrs, both American soldiers and the citizens of nations that they were ordered to invade, can attest to the "aims" and "benefits" of neo-imperialism, which have profited the few – especially western corporations – while the many, *including* American citizens, suffer.

---

40   See G.W.F. Hegel's *Lectures on the Philosophy of Religion: Determinate Religion Vol. 2,* ed. Peter C. Hodgson. New York: Clarendon Press, 2007.

41   This same country is the only western country that still exacts the death penalty upon its own civilians. See Gladstone, Rick. "Amnesty International Find Executions Rose in 2013." March 26, 2014. http://www.nytimes.com/2014/03/27/world/amnesty-international-2013 -death-penalty-report.html?_r=0 (Accessed 3/29/2014).

For traditional Islamic *fiqh*, in order for a military struggle to be a legitimate *jihād*, i.e. to be justified by the Islamic tradition itself, its war aims must be just, honest, and in accordance with the spirit of compassion and mercy. Both the theory that guides the aims and the praxis that carries it out must be in congruence otherwise it risks its Islamic legitimacy. In Islam, the Orwellian functionalization of principles, whether they are purely Islamic or "universal," such as freedom, justice, and liberty, etc., is condemnable, as it delegitimates the concepts, undermines rightful authority, and breeds cynicism concerning publicly stated intentions. It also has a more perverse and pervasive affect: the continual impoverishment of language – its impoverishment of substantive meaning via its functionalization as cover for ulterior motives – is a major problem both within the Islamic and western world. Words just do not carry the same credibility that they once embodied because they have been so woefully distorted by various powers looking to camouflage their plans behind universally accepted values. This is true both for states as well as groups, especially terrorist groups such as al-Qae'da and ISIS.

Ultimately, all attempts to engage in a *jihād bil-saif* must be justified via rational discourse and legitimately rooted within the Prophetic tradition. It must therefore also maintain the standards, regulations, and prohibitions that were articulated both by Muhammad and the Qur'an, as these are the constitutional sources of the normative values that govern all forms of *jihād*.

Just as the once-revolutionary nature of Bourgeois philosophy is twisted into its opposite, the revolutionary and compassionate nature of *jihād* has also been transformed into the very opposite of its original emancipatory intention. Suicide bombers have not only become the fear of non-Muslims flying on Russian Aeroflot (Аэрофлóт) airlines, United States and NATO soldiers in Iraq and Afghanistan, bus riders in Britain and Israel, and trains in Spain, they are also feared by Muslims in historically Muslim lands who reject extremism, who visit Shi'a shrines, or who work for peace and reconciliation between warring factions. Indeed, if one was to adopt a quantitative methodology, one should clearly see that Muslims have been the victims at the hands of such terroristic activities more so than westerners.[42] The Islamic *ummah* is targeted both by

---

42   While I do not like to engage in the fashionable counting of victims in order to make a quantitative statement about who has suffered more, I do believe that the reality of human suffering at the hands of injustice both in the Islamic and western world can be a point of mutual recognition, discussion, and eventually reconciliation. This is what I call *intersubjective-passiology*. Through an honest discourse centered on the common human experience of suffering, different peoples can come together and hopefully overcome their animosity towards each other. The grieving faces of western mothers and fathers are

the great powers of the West and those who claim to fight for the preservation of Islam through its "purification." The Muslims who find themselves within one of the many conflict zones in the world are doubly victimized.

Although what is deemed "radical" in today's discussion of religion – those that bend religion to their extremist and often violent ideology – the real "radical" nature of Islam is in the opposite approach; the prophetic trajectory that Muhammad directed the early Muslim community towards was the truly radical approach, if we understand the term "radical" as being to "grasp the roots" of a given subject or action. In this case, the roots are in the prophetic tradition of the Biblical and Qur'anic prophets. When we examine what in Islam is described as the "age of ignorance" (*jāhilīyah*), there we see the prototype of those contemporary Muslims who brutalize, oppress, and murder, embodying not the example set forth by Muhammad, but by his enemies: *al-Qur'aysh*. Likewise, in the example of the Roman Empire, its sociopathic Caesars, its Legions, and its Praetorian guard, we see the prototype for those "Christians" who brutalize, oppress, and murder today; and in the example of the ancient Egyptians and Babylonians we see the archetype for the Israeli Defense Force (IDF) that deprives Palestinians of their native land, their families, and their lives. In the victims of *al-Qur'aysh*, the Roman Empire, and the ancient Egyptians and Babylonians, we see the model of the unjust martyr-manufacturer, whose spirit can be found today in the authoritarian and violent expressions of the religions that were once their victims.

From the perspective of the critical religiologist, the prophetic tradition, initiated by Abraham, as he accepted the call of his unseen God, laid down the geography for the prophetic and therefore radical tradition of love and mercy, justice and peace, that permeated the history of religious revolutions through Muhammad ibn 'Abdallah of the 7th century Arabia.[43] Furthermore, it is the radical commitment to equality, equity, justice, compassion, which manifests itself in the care of the poor, the orphan, and the widow that was translated into secular language – forsaking the theological legitimation – by socialists and even many communists. Impatient for a heavenly manifestation of a reconciled and therefore peaceful and un-alienated society, they attempted to construct a world in which the messiah could endorse upon his arrival (even if many, like Marx himself, could no longer believe in such religious figures). Regrettably, such lofty values in secular form are also subject to distortion, denigration, and functionalization for the means of oppression and brutality, as

---

the same grieving face of the Islamic mothers and fathers. That shared grief is fertile soil for solidarity and reconciliation.

43   In the Islamic Tradition, Abraham ('Ibrāhīm) is call *al-Khalil Allah,* the "friend of God."

had happened under the brutal regime of Stalin and other communist despots, who shrouded themselves in altruistic values while systematically denying and destroying the humanity of millions. Nevertheless, both secular and religious martyrs have been created throughout the millennia while in search of more just and equitable social conditions. With the ongoing struggles in the Ukraine against the 2014 neo-fascist coup d'etat of the Right Sector and Svaboda Party in Kiev, the struggle between secularization and religious politics in Turkey, the struggle for democracy against military dictatorship in Egypt, the struggle for Shi'a and Sunni reconciliation in Iraq, and the struggle against both the 'Alawite state and ISIS terror in Syria, it is clear that history will continue to produce more of what it has always produced: martyrs.

"Perfected Religion": A Problematic Conception

The historic rise of Europe out of the Dark Ages has come at the expense the traditional Muslim territories, especially in the Middle East and North African, which was the principle bearer of advanced civilization in the Mediterranean area after the fall of the Roman Empire in the 4th century. Despite the fact that the early Muslims severed the southern part of the Mediterranean from its northern half – which was culturally integrated via the shared Greco-Roman culture and later Christianity – the southern Mediterranean was quickly integrated into a more progressive society than the European one: the various Islamic Caliphates and dynasties. Chief among the reasons for the Muslim's rapid advancement, in terms of intellectual achievements and not territorial gain, was its insistence on education, the emergence of scholarship, and the unconquerable drive to absorb the knowledge of the previous civilizations into the growing Islamic empire.[44] By the 8th century CE, the Islamic empire was vast, stretching from India to Western Europe, from the southernmost point of Arabia to deep within central Asia. In order to organize such an empire, in order to codify the Islamic tradition, in order to provide for the needs of the new Islamic territories, the Muslims had to be practical, less dogmatic, and learn from those who came before. They were rich in religious zeal, piety, and morality, but lacked the worldly experience of being rulers of empires. This reality would require gaining and expanding upon knowledge received from the previous civilizations. From India the Muslims learned complex mathematics; from the Romans they learned about logistics of city building, from the

---

44   George Makdisi, *The Rise of Colleges: Institutions of Learning in Islam and the West.* Edinburgh: Edinburgh University Press, 1981.

Chinese they learned about paper (and later gunpowder), and from the Greeks they learned philosophy; the latter being the most important for the advancement of Islamic thought, Qur'anic exegesis, systematic theology, and the art of logic. Platonism and Aristotelian logic, which fertilized the earliest of Muslim philosophers such as al-Kindi (801–873 CE), resulted in an unprecedented depth in understanding the sources of Islam. Al-Qur'an, the ḥadīth, and the Sunnah, were also supplemented by the great works of Greek philosophy, such as Plato's *Republic, The Dialogues,* and his other works on epistemology and metaphysics.[45] Aristotle played an important role among the intellectual elites in the Muslim world, to the point where some scholars claimed that his works were close to having near-revelation status. These texts and may others delivered to the Muslims the categories and concepts they needed in order to become a world power and to systematize their own religious tradition. These ancient sources of knowledge were continually developed further in the *Bayt al-Hikma* in Baghdad as well as in the great libraries and universities of *al-'Andalus* (Islamic Iberia). The great works of Abū Naṣr al-Fārābī (Alpharabius), Ibn Rušd (Averroes), Ibn Sīnā (Avicenna), Ibn 'Arabī, Nasir al-din al- Tūsī, etc., were all steeped within the thought of both Islamic theology and Greek philosophy – religious revelation and autonomous reason; by way of Islamic Spain, this mixture would later fertilize the intellectually sterile grounds of Europe itself, thus laying the foundations for the European Renaissance. Philosophy, no matter where it derived from, whether it be a work of ethics, metaphysics, ontology, epistemology, or politic-economic, was not rejected by the Muslim intellectuals simply because it was of foreign origin or was originally developed by those men of different faiths or no faiths at all, but was governed by a different criteria: can "truth" be found in these pagan philosophies? And in light of the Qur'an, could these truths be reconciled with divine revelation? As the Islamic empire grew, so too did its rapacious desire to learn the knowledge of other peoples. Muslim scholars remembered two important proverbs: 'seek knowledge from the cradle to the grave' and 'the ink of the scholar is more sacred then the blood of the martyr.'[46]

For the early Muslim intellectuals and scholars, the truth of philosophy could be reconciled with the faith of Islam via reason and sound logic. No

---

45   Roy Jackson, *What is Islamic Philosophy?* (New York: Routledge, 2014), 8–40.

46   There is some debate as to whether the former phrase is something the Prophet really said or if it is just a pious truism that is common within the Muslim community. The second phrase seems to be authentic according to the scholars of ḥadīth but has a weak *isnad* (chain of transmission). Either way, both represent the *zeitgeist* of the Muslims in the early empires.

one exemplified this more than al-Kindī, better known as the *philosopher of the Arabs* in the 9th century, who attempted to demonstrate that the believer could read the Qur'an and other sacred texts through reason. He did not believe that reason was the enemy of revelation, but rather it was a divine gift to humanity for the understanding of all that exists. Arguments made by Socrates, Plato and Aristotle were no strangers to arguments concerning *īman* (faith), *ʿaqīda* (creed), *kalam* (theology), *fiqh* (jurisprudence), etc., but were deeply engrained in the logic of the arguments themselves. Early Islamic philosophers, seeing the tremendous accomplishment gifted to the world by Greek thinkers, absorbed their works into Islamic thought. This syncretism rescued Islam from the intellectual stagnation that was already potentially there; it gave Islamic thought a more complex and sophistication vocabulary by which one could interpret the Qur'an and other sources of Islam more effectively.[47] Additionally, this also gave the Muslim intellectuals the philosophical and scientific categories by which they could fulfill the divine command to investigate the world and all it contains, without which they would have to either (1) reinvent such intellectual tools or (2) remain intellectual underdeveloped. By engaging the Greek texts and translating their wisdom into Islamic thought, philosophy was not only infusing the new religious tradition with the ability to comprehend itself in a much more precise and in-depth way, but philosophy was also pressed into service of the broader Muslim community.

Yet for some, the Islamic practice of interrogating non-Islamic thought and inviting the wisdom of others into the Islamic domain was not a virtue that brought about a more progressive and beneficial society, but a dangerous mixture of Allah's religion and man's fallible thought. For these believers, whatever comes from Allah should never be conflated or "diluted" with the thoughts of man, let alone those who were outside of Islam: *kāfirūn* (disbelievers). The preservation of the "purity" or *authenticity* (*ṣaḥīḥ*) of Islam was of utmost importance, and so *damnant quod non intellegunt.*[48] This aversion to outside thought remains within much of the *ummah* of Muslims today, especially among those of a more fundamentalist trajectory.

This reactionary response to those who are unable to experience Islam as a dynamic religion as opposed to a stagnant one have made their objections to Islamic philosophy known from the beginning of the Islamic empire until today, and still hold a considerable and undeserved tyranny over many Islamic intellectuals who, as a consequence, isolate themselves within academia

47   Marshall G.S. Hodgson, *The Venture of Islam: Conscience and History in a World Civilization. The Classical Age of Islam* (Chicago: The University of Chicago Press, 1977), 410–443.

48   'They condemn what they do not understand.'

where such thought can occur without any influence on the masses. Those who could help the Muslim world the most are often the ones least likely to enter into civil discourse within the Muslim public sphere for fear of reprisals. It is not because these Muslim intellectuals are not engaged in robust and powerful critiques of the Muslim societies that they have little to no influence in the Muslim world, but it's because of the lack of legitimacy that they have with the common believer. They are often seen as outsiders, those influenced by western ways of thinking, and insufficiently Islamic, as if being Islamic means to be anti-intellectual. In the end, the contribution of the Islamic philosophers, who learned from their teachers the Greeks, cannot be forgotten. From the perspective of Habermas and other critical philosophers, the Muslim world cannot engage in a *damnatio memoriae* (damnation of memory) to expunge the Muslim philosophers from Islamic history, but rather must return to them in the modern period, as such philosophy may hold the key to an Islamic form of modernity that is both sufficiently Islamic and also valid within the conditions of an increasingly secular global society.

However, this distrust of "outsider" knowledge is not unique to the Muslim world, as this bifurcated intellectual tradition, or the *double truth thesis* – which is intrinsic to the divisions of class and education – was also the case in the Roman empire: *let the plebeians have their religion and we'll keep our patrician philosophy*; the western Enlightenment period: *let the peasants keep their superstitious religion and we'll keep our reason and rational civil/natural religions*.[49] Rational truth had to be protected from the mythologically enamoured and exclusivist masses, who, from the perspective of the intellectual elites, had not the mental capacity to understand reality for what it really was, but rather needed "pictorial" and/or simple representations of reality. Two forms of faith were thus produced: unenlightened religion for the "riff raff" (*Ḥashwiyya*), faith justified by reason for the elites.

As stated before, *Sūrah al-Maʾida* (5:3) of the Qur'an states, 'This day, I have perfected your religion, completed my favor upon you and have chosen Islam as your religion.'[50] From the position of those who attempt to preserve the intellectual chastity of the Islamic tradition, this verse is taken to mean that Islam is a "closed" religious system, as if through "perfecting" Islam it has been made impenetrable to any other knowledge, wisdom and/or thought. Perfected is taken to mean "without lack," "fully developed," "already identical with itself," and "complete." Additionally, it is assumed that by 'perfected' any other

---

49   Terry Eagleton, *Culture and the Death of God* (New Haven: Yale University Press, 2014), 20–26.

50   My translation.

form of thought that may migrate into Islam is inherently invalid due to its origins outside of Islam. If the knowledge is not *sui generis* to Islam, then it is not Islam at all. Yet this is a completely unphilosophical and non-dialectical way to approach the meaning of the phrase 'perfected your religion.'

In order to understand the Qur'anic language that is used to describe the ontological state of Islam during the time of Muhammad, we have to think in terms of Islam *in-and-of-itself* and the believer who approaches the Islamic tradition from the outside (even if they are a Muslims). Islam is the object of study and the Muslim is the subject that studies. These are two very different phenomenon and therefore have two very different ontological statuses: the Qur'an is – for lack of a better word – the incarnation (*incarnationem*) of the divine for Muslims; it is the word of Allah (*Kalam Allah*) made present in the finite and fallible world; it is *Deum in libro.*[51] For most devout Muslims, it is the uncreated but historically bound presence of the divine that is accessible – on the surface level – to all believers. The Qur'an as such is the door to the divine presence. The believer accesses this presence through recitation, contemplation, and study. Furthermore, it is a record of Allah's thought concerning historical (particular) and ahistorical (universal) issues, problems, etc., revealed to Muhammad ibn 'Abdallah in the 7th century Arabia. Being that the believer is a finite creature, the product of history, and bound to their own mortality, moral fallibility, and incomplete knowledge, they are in need of guidance. Therefore it is the duty of the believer to not only come to *know* the Islamic tradition from within itself but also to incorporate and embody the values, principles, and ideals of the Islamic tradition so that the object (Islam) and the subject (the believer) become identical with each other to the best of the believers ability. This attempt to be a believer who has incorporated the Qur'anic way-of-being-in-the-world requires a certain amount of intellectual and philosophical tools, as the Islamic tradition is not one that asks its devout to be "childlike" in faith, to be without education, or to mortify intelligence, but rather demands of its followers to be people of intellect as opposed to simply being people of *taqlīd* (imitation).

When the proponents of the "closed" theory put forth their argument concerning the inability of Islam to appropriate the wisdom of others into itself without diluting its purity and authenticity, they cancel its *entelechy,* its process of "becoming" – the internal development of all there is beyond that which has already been and that which is to be. Since Aristotle, philosophers have insisted that nothing is what it was, and nothing is yet what it will be, all is "becoming" – the present is but a moment within the dialectical relationship between the

---

51   'The divine in the book.'

past and the future. With the cancelation of "becoming" the religious purists forces a stationary state upon the Islamic tradition; they imprison it within its own history, which inevitably impedes its ability to deliver the necessary and adequate moral and intellectual tools, concepts, and categories needed within the 21st century for Muslims to address their very modern problems. This stationary state, this petrification of what is an inherently *dynamic* (as in it embraces its own inner-development) religious tradition – as all religious traditions that remain beneficial to mankind must be or they will become historically irrelevant – has unfortunately handicapped the Muslim *ummah* as they have become ill prepared for the challenges and predominate coordinates of life in the modern age.[52] The main source of the community's identity, their interpretation of reality and orientation of action, is somehow stuck within the 10th century (or slightly beyond) because it is not allowed to recognize its own development as it passes through (and creates) history. This development – often accompanied by social, intellectual, and politic-economic forces from outside of it – is condemned as *bid'a* (innovation) by those who fail to recognize the internal dynamics and perpetual recreation of Islam from within itself. For these intellectual idol makers, Islam is a *fetish* – having magic-like powers that can deliver the Muslim world from its enemies all on its own, as long as it is "pure." Contrary to the approach of the philosophers, who emphasized the dynamics of Islam, fundamentalism forces the religion into a state of *stasis* (στάσις – "standing still"). This "islam" is formal, without prophetic and revolutionary content, without internal development, and as such cannot adequately address the problems of the modern period; it remains locked in an "iron cage" of history; a perpetual looking backwards without genuine self-propelled movement forward. This diminished form of "islam," with its crippled philosophical immune system, stands completely alien in the contemporary world that surrounds it. This is the dead-idol that fundamentalism and extremism has made of Islam, and one of the primary reasons why the Muslim community remains bewildered within the post-secular conditions, stuck without the philosophical capacity to navigate the religion in a rapidly changing global situation.

---

52 Some scholars attribute this artificial arrest of the Islamic tradition to the thinking of Ibn Taymiyyah, a 13th/14th century Islamic scholar, theologian and logician, who was skeptical of what he thought was *bid'a* (innovation) in the daily religious lives of Muslims. His thought is seen as an early attempt to exorcise the Islamic tradition from the innovations that Muslims had brought into it. Many of the Muslim world's most reactionary and purist movements lay claim to Ibn Taymiyyah as their intellectual precursor.

To the point about purity and authenticity, a historical example that may shed light on the present situation is available. Post-Revolutionary Iran experienced a conflict between two "forms" of Islamic intellectualism. Those who wished to keep Islam pure from all outside influenced argued for a *Islam-i maktabi* or "authentic Islam," while those who saw no contradiction with Islam being supplemented, or even fertilized by other philosophies – especially third world liberation thought inspired by Karl Marx, Che Guevara, Albert Camus, Franz Fanon, Jean Paul Sartre and even Nietzsche – argued for *Islam-i iltiqati* or "syncretic Islam." The later was predominately influenced by the works of the left-wing Shi'a intellectual 'Ali Sharī'ati, whose legacy was claimed by the non-clerical *raushanfikran-i mazhabi* (religious intellectuals).[53] These religious intellectuals confronted what they saw as the intellectual stagnation of the *'Ulamā'* (religious scholars), which wished to place tradition above intellectual creativity and "independent reasoning" (*ijtihād*). They believed the petrified religious thought that the ulema faithfully guarded was unsuitable for the modern problems of Iran and the broader Shi'a community, as it had lost the revolutionary and socially progressive *geist* that early Islam embodied. Additionally, they argued for a place among the leadership of the revolutionary republic partially due to the fact that their "ideology" – in the Sharī'ati sense of a *comprehensive system of ideas* – played an important role in revolutionizing the Iranian public.[54] Although he never expressly admitted it, it was the deep well of *Islamized* political-leftist language and arguments of Sharī'ati that Khomeini drew from in his opposition to the Shah.[55] The religious intellectuals understood that traditional Shi'a Islam, as embodied by the political quietism of most of the clerics, would not sufficiently motivate the masses in their rebellion against the Shah's "White Revolution," and therefore a spirit of revolution had to be provoked in Islam from outside.[56] "Safavid Islam," to their minds, had become stagnant, conservative, and reserved, but leftist theory and political praxis would force the Shi'a in Iran to recover the revolutionary potentials that were latent within their tradition, especially in what Sharī'ati called *Alavi*

---

53   Hamid Algar, *Roots of The Islamic Revolution in Iran* (Oneonta, NY: Islamic Publications International, 2001), 99.

54   Hamid Algar, *Roots*, 93.

55   Dustin Byrd, *Ayatollah Khomeini and the Anatomy of the Islamic Revolution in Iran: Toward a Theory of Prophetic Charisma* (Lanham, MD: University Press of America, 2011), 98–102; Ervand Abrahamian, *Khomeinism: Essays on the Islamic Republic* (Berkeley: University of California Press, 1993), 60–87; 'Ali Shari'ati, *On the Sociology of Islam*, trans. Hamid Algar (Berkeley: Mizan Press, 1979), 31.

56   See Mohammad Reza Pahlavi, *The White Revolution of Iran*. Tehran: Kayhan Press, 1967.

Shi'ism or Shi'ism before it was co-opted by the Safavids.[57] Just as the working class, dark skinned people, and other Third World peoples were persecuted by the imperialist, whites, and the "First World," so too were 'Ali and Hussein persecuted by the rich and powerful, and now the people of 'Ali and Hussein were being persecuted and oppressed by the new Yazid, the Shah of Iran.[58] Did 'Ali not fight his oppressors, the religious intellectuals asked. Did Hussein not fight his oppressors? Should not revolutionary Shi'a Islam, or what is sometimes called "Red Shi'ism," fight its western and monarchical oppressors? Lest the Shi'a forget Karbala, and make the same history-changing mistake again, the Shi'a – with the conceptual aid of Islamized leftist language – overthrew the Shah in 1979 and regained their independence from foreign domination. Unfortunately, after the revolution, the Islamic Republic of Iran chose to suppress the thought of 'Ali Shari'ati as it attempted to build a nation more aligned with the traditionalism of the Shi'a clerics that had little space for western philosophy – especially of the Marxist variant – despite its important contribution to the success of the revolution. It is possible that the philosophical basis for Shari'ati's work was too alienating for many of the more conservative *'Ulamā'*, which looked with suspicion at all his secular western (and leftist) influences. Nevertheless, according to Hamid Algar, 'many people were ready to participate in the Revolution under the leadership of Imam Khomeini to a certain degree because of the influence upon them of Dr. Shari'ati.'[59] It is to a major degree that the Iranian people owe their successful revolution to the recovery of the philosophical heritage of Islam as it was ignited by 'Ali Shari'ati's reintroduction of philosophical conceptions into Islamic thought and praxis. It was the revolutionary spirit of *Islam-i iltiqati* that broke the back of the Shah, not the religious conservatism of the quietist clerics.

In his June 2014 article on aljazeera.com, the author Hasan Azad asked the perplexing but pertinent question, *Why are there no Muslim philosophers?*[60] As we've already demonstrated, this is a highly complex question that had garnished a tremendous amount of attention from academics and scholars, both western and Muslim. From the perspective of the Critical Theory of

---

57   Hamid Algar, *Roots*, 96–97.

58   In Islamic history, Yazid was responsible for the murder of Hussein, the Prophet Muhammad's grandson. His murder and the penitence movement that it sparked was the true beginning of Shi'a Islam.

59   Hamid Algar, *Roots,* 111.

60   Hasan Azad, "Why are there no Muslim Philosophers?" June 12, 2014. http://www .aljazeera.com/indepth/opinion/2014/06/muslim-philosophers-2014610135114713259 .html (Accessed 6/29/2014).

Religion, the absence of "Islamic Philosophers" – in the strictest sense of a "philosopher" as being the inheritor of a philosophical tradition which began with the Greeks – has to do with the legitimation crisis that philosophy went through in Islamic history. As was stated before, from the most gregarious of intellectuals within the Muslim world's golden age, philosophy, regardless of its origin, was investigated for its truth content and much of it was translated into Arabic, debated, and infused into Islamic theology, political thought, and jurisprudence.[61] However, as the Muslim world began to collapse upon itself due to outside pressures as well as internal divisions and weaknesses, a reactionary and defensive attitude towards Islam became increasingly common among the believers. Unfortunately, if the religion can no longer be intellectually defended due to the absence of qualified "apologists" (ἀπολογία – to speak in defense), it is inevitably defended through violence. The idea that a "return to Islam," i.e. the de-intellectualized fundamentalist orientation, was the only way to rescue Islam from a world in which the balance of power began to shift away from the *dar al-Islam,* took hold among many intellectuals and layman alike. It is important to remember that it was Islamic philosophy, its own articulation and augmentation of Greek philosophy, which laid down the intellectual and scientific roots of the European Renaissance. Because of this, Muslims inadvertently rescued Europe from perpetuating its own catastrophic collapse into barbarity. Yet simultaneously, it abandoned one of the more important sources of its own vitality. Europe's philosophical gain was the Muslim world's loss; Europe recovered the wisdom of the Greeks, the mathematics of the Hindus, the architectural genius of the Romans, etc., while the Muslim world fell into decay. The suppression of philosophy and human rationality in favor of blind faith in revelation – that was incomprehensible to most without theo-philosophical categories by which to read it – led to the Muslim world's intellectual decline. In the process, blame was shifted towards philosophy and the philosophers as being the *bid'a* that caused the collapse; philosophers were accused of being heretics, apostates, and introducers of "foreign" ideas; their books and the books of their Greeks predecessors were suppressed, and the Muslims world slid into its own "dark ages." In the place of an *Islam that thinks* and *believes* came an *Islam that only believes*; thus abandoning the Qur'anic demand to think, ponder, reflect, and investigate the world and all it contains through reason and imagination. With the abandonment of philosophy under the accusation that it imported foreign ideas into the Muslim community and thus made Islam corrupt and weak, came the complete de-legitimization

---

61   Marshall G.S. Hodgson, *The Venture of Islam: Conscience and History in the World Civiliza-tion,* 410–443.

of philosophy in the Muslim world. Philosophers of the Islamic faith are still today tepid in their thought, unwilling to antagonize those who still remain in Plato's now *Islamized* cave.

Looking critically back into history, we see that a very serious problem occurred in the 10th century. The closing of *ijtihād* (independent reasoning) among the Sunnis, in favor of what the 19th and 20th Turkish scholar Bediüzzaman Said Nursi described as *taqlīdi-Islam* (Islam by imitation), had created the conditions for intellectual stagnation, at least in the case of Islamic jurisprudence.[62] Scholars believed that the major questions concerning the true and proper Islamic way-of-being were decided among the first few centuries after the death of the prophet and therefore the development of Islam beyond the already established customs and norms of the first generations endangered Islam: as the boundaries of the empire grew, more and more "foreign" influences crept into the *ummah* and threatened the orthodoxy of the "perfected" religion. In light of this, Sunni scholars moved to replace *ijtihād* with *taqlīd*, or *reasoning* with *imitation/precedence* – as a way of preserving their notion of the "perfected" religion.[63] However, what such a move actually did was cancel the natural development of the tradition and its ability to adequately address the problems and challenges of the times precisely because it robbed the Muslims of the dialectical tension that would have driven its development when confronted with thought and praxis that opposes Islam or Islamic tenets. From the philosophical perspective, as thought continues to become more differentiated, more complex, and more dialectical, as the old answers no longer hold sway, new answers determinately negate the thought that proceeded them, and the development of thinking continues unabated. As ways-of-being and ways-of-thinking approach the boundaries of Islam, Muslim philosophers and theologians had to engage in critical evaluation of these alien philosophies and were therefore motivated to engage in a higher degree of critical analysis. When the reactionaries forced Islam to retreat behind its own dogmatic and un-reflexive precedents, it consequently cut itself off from its own capacity for creativity and dialectical imagination concerning religion, philosophy, culture, and polity, and thus it became stale, inflexible, and enslaved to its own past. Being systems of thought that are naturally self-reflective and self-critical, religious traditions must be able to continue to engage in a constant rethinking

---

62   Colin Turner and Hasan Horkuc, *Said Nursi* (New York: I.B. Tauris, 2009), 47. Also see G.W.F. Hegel, *Lectures on the Philosophy of Religion: The Lectures of 1827*, ed. Peter C. Hodgson (New York: Oxford University Press, 2006), Pt. 2.

63   One should note that the Shi'a tradition, for the most part, continued with the practice of ijtihad and did not follow the Sunnis into their stagnation.

and reexamination of their own creeds, dogmas, and principles as not to become stationary and intellectually obsolete. If a religion fails to articulate itself within language adequate to the difficulty of the contemporary task at hand, then it inevitably dies. History, as Hegel has reminded us, is full of dead religions that could no longer speak to the needs and intellectual challenges presented to them.[64] As of yet, none on the major world religion have died, but even the smaller ones that have died did so amidst massive amounts of human suffering and violence. How much greater would it be if one of the world religion were to descend rapidly into extinction? If the future historian does an autopsy of the Islamic world, he will see that it was the rejection of philosophical thought that partially led to the Muslims' inability to remain relevant, vital, and dynamic in modernity. It was also the primary cause of much of the descent into violent barbarity that unfortunately can be witnessed in much of the Islamic world today.

Yet the contemporary situation in which the Muslim world finds itself is forcing many scholars and jurists to rethink the wisdom of closing *ijtihād*; they see that this self-inflicted wound is partially responsible for the abysmal state of the Islamic community. Not only has the Muslim world lost its place as a world leader, but the most dynamic developments within the Muslim community tend to be some of the most violent and reactionary, this being the result of the forced *de-hellenization* of Islam. The life of the mind, and not just the study of the West's instrumental rationality – numerate thought: engineering, computers, chemistry, etc. – but also the communicative rationality imbedded in the arts, in literature, and especially in philosophy, must also be once again revived if the Muslim world is to have its own humanistic *renaissance*.

From the perspective of the critical religiologist, for Islam to survive the onslaught of secular modernity, it must come into contact, recover, and integrate into itself its own philosophical and intellectual heritage and history. Although the heritage is deep, it is currently neglected in the *dar al-Islam*. The language and conceptual material that was determinately negated from earlier philosophical thought by the early Muslim empire, which allowed the Muslim world to advance far beyond those cultures that preceded it, must be rediscovered and re-imagined *within* the Islamic context: an Islamization of philosophy and its critical-analytical-dialectical potentials. This process not only means returning to al-Kindī, al-Fārābī, Ibn Rušd, Ibn-Sīnā, and other Islamic intellectuals, etc., to uncover that which was buried by the heap of intellectual ashes that

---

64   See G.W.F. Hegel, *Lectures on the Philosophy of Religion, Vol 1: The Lectures of 1827*, ed. Peter
      C. Hodgson trans. R.F. Brown, P.C. Hodgson and J.M. Stewart. New York: Oxford University
      Press, 2006.

smothered its potentials, but also to critically examine the heirs to their Greco-Islamic philosophy: "occidental" philosophy. Regardless if Muslims scholars, intellectuals, and common believers think that philosophy's importance is limited because it lacks theological legitimation, unlike theology, western philosophical thought predominates throughout the global economy as well as international institutions, international law, and global culture. At the moment, some Muslim intellectuals can speak the language of liberalism, socialism, and cosmopolitanism, but the intellectual concepts that steer the majority of Muslims – which are bound to a religious way of life – remain irrelevant to world affairs, as the world has already moved into a secular epoch that remains entirely hostile – or at least alien – to prophetic religion. Not only would the works of the classical liberal philosophers, Locke, Hume, Smith, Rousseau, Voltaire, etc., reignite certain revolutionary qualities within the Islamic tradition, but the much more radical philosophies of Kant, Hegel, Marx-Engels, Sartre, Nietzsche, and the Frankfurt School could aid in the articulation of a vision of society that remains buried deep within the hidden recesses of the Islamic tradition; a vision of more reconciled society of freedom, justice, mercy, and compassion, free from irrational compulsion and oppression. To uncover and incorporate, transplant and translate such philosophical material could once again give life to the Muslim world and help release it from its self-imposed isolation, self-ghettoization, and metaphysical nihilism; for it is in the secular language of philosophy that the revolutionary potentials reside in the modern epoch. It is no longer the theological that motivates mankind in his praxis in an increasingly secular and capitalist world, but rather the philosophical sentiments that have already migrated from the religious into the secular; values like freedom, liberty, justice, democracy, equality, and fraternity, whether those values are articulated in their bourgeois, Freudian or Marxian formulations. Philosophy, pressed into the service of Islam, coupled with the spirit of inquisitiveness about the world, life, truth, and thought, could help liberate Islam from those who've disfigured it into a deformed lifeless "whitened sepulcher," and resurrect that which once made it the envy of the "known world."

From the perspective of Islam, the religion itself is "perfected," which means that it understand and accepts its own internal development, its own increasing differentiation within the context of the times, and the unending strive to be *identical with itself* (to embody its own constitutional values, principles, and beliefs). Nevertheless, the active agent that can allow Islam to do such things is the Muslim *ummah* itself, as it is the only entity through which Islam can be made manifest. Yes, it is true that Muslims can say (or repeat) that Islam is perfected, but no they cannot allow the concept of perfection to become a barrier to the attempted "perfection" of society (if that is even possible). The Qur'an does not state that the Muslims are perfected, and therefore every articulation of Islam's tenets from the mind of an imperfect interpreter must be assumed to be fallible, and therefore subject to robust scrutiny and criticism. Yet the perfectability of the believer is not a given, and therefore it must continually be realized through the realization of the perfect nature of the Qur'an – which can only be comprehended via categories worked out by generations of philosophers, theologians, and scholars. Therefore, it is an absolute necessity that Muslims rejuvenate and resurrect their own philosophical heritage as well as engaging in an honest and robust discourse with modern philosophy.

Fear of Philosophical Blasphemy

In light of the antagonistic conditions fostered by secular globalization as well as the post-secular society, one can imagine the uproar that would happen if a Muslim philosopher were to reenact Nietzsche's insightful tale of the madman exclaiming the death of God in a devout Muslim country. The self-proclaimed anti-Christ wrote about the murder of God as such,

> *We have killed him* – you and I! We are all his murderers! But how have we done it? How were we able to drink up the sea? Who gave us the sponge to wipe away the whole horizon? What did we do when we loosened this earth from its sun?... Do we not hear the noise of the gravediggers who are burying God? Do we not smell the divine putrefaction? For even Gods putrefy! *God is Dead! God remains dead! And we have killed him!*[65]

What would happen to such a "madman" had he articulated this thesis in the presence of those de-Hellenized fundamentalist believers who fail to see the deeper point and more philosophical point of Nietzsche's rhetorical claim? On the surface level, this appears to mock those who continue to believe in a living divine being. However, beyond the surface is a deeply philosophical statement that expressed absolutely nothing about the ontology of God but rather the conditions of the possibility for believing in the divine in our secular-scientific and industrial age.[66] Would this madman spark outrage? Would there be an international riot, burning of the philosopher in effigy, attacks on western

---

65   Friederich Nietzsche, *The Gay Science* (New York: The Barnes & Noble Library of Essential Reading, 2008), 103. We will return to Nietzsche's *Death of God* latter in this volume.

66   Walter Kaufmann, *Nietzsche: Philosopher, Psychologist, Antichrist* (Princeton, NJ: Princeton University Press, 1974), 96–118.

embassies, would it be ignored by the masses as the insane rambling of a man whose lost touch with his sanity, or would it be considered an invitation to discourse about state of the world and its alternative futures? The recent history may shed light on what may occur in this hypothetical situation.

Delivering an addresses in 2006 entitled *Glaube, Vernunft und Universität – Erinnerungen und Reflexionen* (Faith, Reason and the University – Memories and Reflections), then Pope Benedict XVI warned about the dangers of "de-Hellenizing" religion, i.e. the separation of the faith and reason. In his speech in Regensburg, Germany, he quoted the Byzantine emperor Manuell II Palaiologos, who said 'Show me just what Muhammad brought that was new and there you will find things only evil and inhuman, such as his command to spread by the sword the faith he preached.' This speech emphasized the theological claim that God limits himself within his own dictates, his own rationality, his own self-imposed limitations, and does not transcend or violate himself through an absolute will; he limits his will as not to become unrestrained, or, as it can be conceptualized, God is not pure will over logos. The discussion about the use of reason within religious faith was an attempt to ignite a discourse between religions concerning the importance of maintaining rationality as an integral and necessary component of religion. However, the language that the Pope was using was steeped in philosophical concepts and not theological protocol-sentences that religious fundamentalism is typically expressed through. As a result, many outraged believers, both within the intellectual elites as well as the laymen, took to the streets to condemn the Pope for offending Islam and disrespecting the Prophet. On the other hand, many fundamentalist Christians, instead of expressing solidarity with their co-religionists, condemned the Muslims for being wantonly violent in the face of the Pope's statements, despite the fact that secularist and atheists would accuse those same Christians of the same religious obscurantism as they do the Islamic community. Additionally, while post-religious Europe found itself in a strange position of defending the very Pope that many had often deemed "our Taliban," they emphasizing that if the Pope's speech had been considered in its entirety, one could easily see that it was an invitation to discourse about the nature of faith and reason – which is not a foreign subject in history of Islam, even if it is foreign to modern fundamentalism. However, many within the Muslim community reacted violently, while being misinformed of the particulars of the Pope's speech and the subject it was addressing. One need not question the sincerity of the protests – for many thought the *Pope* and not an *emperor* of a bygone age said such disparaging words against Islam. However, some Muslims critically studied the entire document, such as Tariq Ramadan, while others abandoned any attempt for dialogue in favor of an emotional outrage, despite the fact that the subject is an important theological issue for both Christianity and Islam. This was not a failure to communicate, but a failure to think.

Discourse on difficult matters such as this simply can't happen when one side no longer possess the philosophical language that is the precondition for such a discourse, while the other can no longer put themselves into the perspective of the religious believer, and therefore garnished little sympathy for their wounded sensibilities. While the use of the emperor's speech may have been unfortunate, the Pope's intentions were neither to antagonize nor to cast aspersions on Islam and Muslims per se, but rather to warn his listeners of the dangers when reason is excommunicated from religion. Had there been a discourse partner within the Muslim community who could speak the philosophical *and* theological language required for such an intricate discussion, such as Ibn Rušd and/or his Catholic student Saint Thomas Aquinas, then the tensions would have a greater potential for reconciliation. Until the Muslim community can once again recover its own philosophical heritage and once again bring it to the foreground of thought, it will continue to be needlessly antagonized by critical-philosophical thought emanating from the secular West, even when it isn't motivated out of ill will or hatred. From the perspective of the critical theory of religion, invitations to discourse about uncomfortable matters should not be taken as signs of disrespect, but as an opportunity for mutual-understanding and potentially future reconciliation. A "perfected" religion remains open to discourse as it has confidence in its own claims while at the same time is prepared to re-examine itself based on better and more differentiated categories and arguments. It does not shy away from debate but rather invites it and invests itself in it. This episode demonstrates the depth to which much of the Muslim world has suppressed its own philosophical resources that were once the envy of Europe. Therefore philosophy is desperately needed in order to avoid the predictions of the neo-Conservatives' *clash of civilizations*: the democratic secular rational West vs. the authoritarian religious irrational East.[67]

Clearly, from a theological perspective, the perfection of Islam fears no critique of itself. The question is rather, can modern believers enter into a meaningful discourse with those who can no longer believe, or speak a philosophical language to express a more differentiated way of engaging the world?

---

67   I do not ascribe to the *clash of civilization* thesis. It is ultimately too simplistic to think of the Muslim world as being monolithic, just as it is a mistake to think of the West as being equally monolithic. The reader should not mistake my use of the words "Muslim," "Islam," and the "West" as somehow endorsing such a thesis, but rather these words are being used in a general way to avoid the necessity of excessive qualifiers.

Can the Muslim community, not just individual intellectuals, find within its own resources the necessary tools to engage in such a conversation without truly mining its own philosophical heritage – the language that both the West and the Muslim world once shared? Can the *ummah* adopt the attitude of the Muslim philosophers who cared little if wisdom of older philosophers came from non-Muslims, but were rather solely concerned with the truth claims of their statements? If it cannot, and the tyranny of the fundamentalist position – which cares little about the nuances of theology or philosophy – continues to suppress dialectical, analytical, and critical thought, all in the name of purity of creed, we may not see any new Muslim philosophers and the Islamic philosophical tradition may remain with one foot in the crypt of history. However, the appearance of the crypt is but a warning signpost for all religions that fail to adequately development within themselves through history, for if they don't, they will become the next victim of history: another dead religion within an already crowded cemetery of religions.

Adversity in Post-Secular Europe

The Dialectics of Martyrdom: Death as Witnessing and Professing

Like Judaism and Christianity before, Islam has a long history of *martyrs* (μάρτυς – "blood witnesses" or "witnesses by death"). Yet unlike in Christianity, where Jesus of Nazareth himself was martyred at the hands of the Roman Empire, Pontius Pilate (the Prefect of Judea), and those Jewish authorities who collaborated with Rome, Muhammad escaped all assassination attempts and eventually died peacefully with his family in the city of *al-Madīnah al-Munawwarah*.[1] Although his adversaries attempted to kill him on more than one occasion, the *zeitgeist* of barbarism they wished to perpetuate was broken by the establishment of Islam in Arabia, which brought relative peace to the Arabian Peninsula. For the believer, Muhammad's long life attests to Allah's mercy and protection, especially in considering that Muhammad was fully prepared to be a martyr for his cause. For twenty-three years he lived under and accepted the very real threat of violence. There is no doubt in the Islamic tradition that he was entirely prepared to be sacrificed for his message, but his martyrdom was not the purpose of his life and message. When the Qur'aysh tribe asked his Uncle Abū Ṭālib ibn 'Abd al-Muṭṭalib to intercede on their behalf hoping to persuade him to abandon his call, Muhammad said 'even if they put the sun in my right hand and the moon in my left, I will not give up this mission until either Allah is victorious or I die in the attempt.'[2] Even non-Muslim biographers praise his resolve to see his message through to the end.[3] Not even the promise of great wealth and pleasure could dislodge his determination to construct a society of *tawḥīd* (oneness of God) and *taqwá* (God-consciousness) based on the Qur'an. Muhammad's message was essentially what the psychologist Erich Fromm describes as *biophilic* (love of life), as opposed to *necrophilic*

---

1   It should be noted that the Muslims do not blame "the Jews" for the execution of Jesus of Nazareth. Indeed, since the Qur'an states, 'they slew him not,' 'the Jews' cannot be made responsible for what did not happen. (Qur'an 4:157).

2   My translation.

3   See Karen Armstrong, *Muhammad: A Biography of the Prophet*. New York: HarperSanFrancisco, 1992.

(love of death or inanimate objects), as it promoted a society predicated on equality, justice and mercy.[4]

Nevertheless, the earliest Muslim community, those who risk their lives pledging their allegiance to the prophet and witnessing their faith in his message, felt the wrath of the Qur'aysh tribe, the wealthiest and most brutal opponents of Islam. Before Muhammad ultimately triumphed over his pagan adversaries in 630 CE, the pagans had sent hundreds of Muslims to *Jannah* (paradise) as *šuhadā'* (martyrs).

Yet the historical record demonstrates that Muhammad refused to make martyrs out of his adversaries when a just peace could be established. For example, when conquering Mecca from the pagans, Muhammad forbade any of his followers from engaging in any form of revenge, despite the fact that there were legitimate reasons to do so.[5] *Qiṣāṣ*, or the right of retaliation, was suspended by the command of Muhammad, as he believed it would only perpetuate violence and vendettas, and would therefore close the door to reconciliation between the Muslims and the pagan inhabitants of Mecca. If the Meccans, who spent the last two decades oppressing and murdering Muslims, would lay down their arms and live in peace, Muhammad could not allow his followers to retaliate, despite the fact that they had an abundance of legitimate reasons to seek revenge. The Qur'an states, 'fight for the cause of Allah those who fight you, *but do not violate the limits; Allah does not love those who transgress*.'[6] By this *ayat* (verse) alone, Muhammad was obliged to offer peace to the Meccans as long as they were willing to live peacefully with their Muslim neighbors. This situation has been pointed out by many scholars as being an example of the capability of Muslims to live peacefully with those who do not share their faith, as the *ṣaḥābah* (companions) of the Prophet could even live with their former enemies who did not convert to Islam and had previously oppressed them, confiscated their properties, and murdered their kinsman.[7]

---

4   See Erich Fromm, *To Have or To Be?* New York: Continuum, 2000.

5   Yahiya Emerick, *Muhammad* (Indianapolis: Alpha Books, 2002.), 227–248.

6   Qur'an. 2:190. My Translation and my emphasis.

7   Another paradigmatic example of an inter-faith community of early Muslims is when many Muslims escaped persecution at the hands of the pagan Arabs by traveling to Abyssinia, in East Africa. There, King Negus, a Christian, overrode the objections of the pagan Meccans and offered these Muslims sanctuary. The King was impressed by their reverence of Jesus and Mary and in kind protected them from their enemies. According to Ṣaḥīḥ al-Bukhārī, Vol. 5, Number 218, Jabir bin 'Abdallah Al-Ansari related that the Prophet even held a funeral service for King Negus when he later died, despite the fact that Negus did not convert to Islam. Regardless, the Prophet was impressed by Negus' ecumenical spirit and willingness to embody the Christian value of charity and mercy.

According to Asma Afsaruddin, the earliest conceptions of Islamic martyrdom were not limited to military activities, but were just as applicable to scholars who died in their pursuit of knowledge and other pious believers. She notes that in contradiction to our current conceptions, early exegetical works on the Qur'an did not privilege military or fighting-martyrs above the pious, the scholars, and the suffering believer; they were all given the same reward for the devotion to the divine and his religion.[8] However, as Islam expanded into increasingly hostile territories outside of the Arabian Peninsula, and as Islam split between the Sunni and the Shi'i, the concept of martyrdom took on an increasingly martial meaning. Today, at least in the public sphere in both the West and the Muslim world, martyrdom has almost become synonymous with those who either fight or die *fisibillah* (for the sake of Allah), whilst those who *live* for Allah and his religion are no longer understood to be martyrs at death. This martial definition of martyrdom is more akin to the Christian conception martyrdom that was conceived under the conditions of the Roman Empire where Christianity was brutally persecuted until Emperor Constantine's *Edict of Milan* in 313 CE, which legalized the faith. To the consternation of the Roman authorities, the more the early Christians were suppressed, the more the religion grew. The same phenomenon can be witnessed among Muhammad's ṣaḥābah, many of which were persecuted for not only being slaves, women, orphans, or for just simply being weak, but also for following Muhammad's "new" religion. Being a Muslim denied the "inferiority" claim that the society imposed on slaves, women, orphans, and the weak, and thus provoked a backlash from the socially "superior." However, the more the unjust power structure manufactured martyrs, the more their suffering created new converts.

From a historical and theological perspective, the production of martyrs is only called upon when the bonds of brotherhood, as expressed in the Abrahamic traditions, are broken and violent conflict ensues. For many non-fundamentalist schools of thought, it is one of the primary goals of Islam to retire the concept of martyrdom by bringing into existence a society that no longer produces the conditions for which martial martyrs are needed – a reconciled society rooted in justice, peace, and friendly living together.[9] It light

---

8   Asma Afsaruddin, 'Martyrdom in Islamic Thought and Praxis' in *Martyrdom and Terrorism: Pre-Modern to Contemporary Perspectives,* ed. Dominic Janes and Alex Houen (New York: Oxford University Press, 2014), 40–58.

9   A "reconciled society" is a society that has resolved its antagonisms, i.e. its class antagonisms, its gender antagonisms, it racial antagonisms, etc. Although prototypically belonging to theology, this term, via the Frankfurt School and others has been brought down from metaphysics and into sociology and philosophy.

of this, it is the height of irony that martial martyrs are praised in the modern day struggles in the Muslim world when Islam itself is an attempt to emancipate mankind from the conditions that produce these sorts of martyrs. In other words, the fact that Muslim martyrs are still being created is evidence that Islam itself has not been fully realized; its "perfection" is not perfectly imminent. Unfortunately, a society free from the need of warrior martyrs has yet to be achieved as humanity has not yet resolved the conditions that stirs the hatred for the other; it has yet to live within a sane balance of autonomy and solidarity; it has yet to value each individual as an ends and not as a means; and it has not learned how to identify and embrace the humanistic points of commonality which transcend cultural differences. Neither the secular western nor the Islamic worlds have been able to adequately overcome the antagonistic tendencies dwelling deeply within mankind's nature and psyche (*Thanatos*), despite the lofty ideals of peace, love, and reconciliation, which are found both in religious and secular thought. Although various world religions and philosophies, and various political and economic theories, have made such a reconciled society an aim to be achieved, history testifies that such goals remain elusive. The utopian vision – the messianic realm of peaceful existence – is an intangible dream of the prophets, philosophers, mystics, and activists. As to the present, these ideals belong to the metaphysics of hope, but not to the metaphysics of the really existing world.

Yet despite the despair that history creates, humanity has not yet abandoned this longing for messianic reconciliation. For many it cannot be forgotten; to do so would be to deliver the world entirely to the "given," to forfeit any possibility that the world could be other than what it is. In this sense, the utopian ideal remains preserved in both prophetic religion and critical philosophy, as the "longing for the totally other," and in some occasions such a longing has called for martyrs: Dr. Martin Luther King Jr., Mahatma Gandhi, Malcolm x (al-hajj Malik al-Shabazz), Che Guevara, ʿAli Sharīʿati, Thomas Müntzer, Fra Dolcino, John Brown, Archbishop Óscar Romero, Sophie and Hans Scholl, Dietrich Bonhoeffer, Kwame Nkrumah, Steve Biko, Hussein ibn ʿAli, and Jesus of Nazareth.

In the Islamic tradition, the martyrs, who have either been killed fighting or have been unjustly murdered for their faith (*fisibillah*), stand as testaments to what they believed to be ultimate reality concerning this world and the next. From the *hadīth* (reports of the Prophet Muhammad) literature, it is said that the martyr's blood-soaked clothes, in which they are buried, stand as silent but powerful witnesses to their dedication to Allah and his religion. Like Michelangelo's *Pietà*, which stands as a silent witness to the suffering of the innocent in St. Peter's Basilica, the blood of the martyr need no words to convey the injustice of this world; its presence both before the divine and mankind invoke an endless well of desire to erase the suffering within the human condition: to overcome man's hatred and violence towards himself and others. In other words, the blood of the martyrs is meant to send a message not only to the masses but also to the divine; the blood itself testifies on behalf of the martyr – it reveals their willingness to accept the ultimate price for their beliefs and testifies to their devotion on judgment day (*yawm al-Qiyāmah*). Conversely, the blood of the martyrs also bears witness against the unjust, heartless, and soulless conditions of this world; it is a protest against the cruel and barbarous life that mankind continuously creates for itself. However, mankind may not be the only one responsible for such barbarity.

From the perspective of the critical religiologist – steeped in the reality of the *theodicy* problem – martyrdom is understood as a dialectical phenomenon; the blood of the martyrs is not only a sign of the believers' commitment to his *dīn* (religion), but also can be understood as an active protest *against* the divine, as it is the divine's world in which the barbaric conditions call for the blood of martyrs.[10] According to the critical religiologist Rudolf J. Siebert, it is the social, political, and economic conditions that the divine is *ultimately* responsible for that lead to the necessity of martyrdom, which viewed dialectically, is an indictment leveled by the believer against their creator.[11] Every televised suicide confession of an Islamic terrorist can be read not only as a profession of faith – evidence of their willingness to be sacrificed – but also a tacit denunciation of God's world that creates the need for brutal self-sacrifice. Indeed, behind the bravado, the courage, and the strength (or cowardice) of the suicidal confession, lies the odious resentment that the life of the individual has to be scarified in order to fix that which the divine has allowed to be broken. It is quietly recognized, but painfully felt, that it is the family of the martyred who have to suffer the loss of their beloved while the one responsible for the situation remains *absconditus* (absent), or worse yet, reveals itself as the author of man's misery (as in the book of Job). The world-as-it-is, so often absent of the values that the divine claims as its essential characteristics – mercy, compassion, empathy, and love – compels the believer to protest this godless and soulless situation with an act of supreme sacrifice. Out of love of family, companions, and/or nation, whom the divine seems to show no mercy, the martyr shows mercy, compassion, empathy, and love. Although the Islamic tradition does not openly encourage dissension within the discourse between the believer and Allah – there is no substantive tradition of "protest

---

10   See Rudolf J. Siebert, *From Critical Theory to Critical Political Theology: Personal Autonomy and Universal Solidarity* (New York: Peter Lang, 1994), 153–269.

11   Siebert, *From Critical Theory,* 153–269.

theology" – as in the case of Judaism. For many Jewish believers, the martyr's death is a historical signpost that marks his frustration with God's creation and ultimately with the composer of such disharmony. Therefore, whether openly admitted or not, every martyr is not only obedient to the divine but also protests against him through the act of self-sacrifice. In this view, redemption for the suffering of this world is brought about through the martyrizing act of the humanity – its sacrifice for the living – not though an act of the divine. In a perverse dialectic: the more self-seeking and self-sacrificing martyrs, especially the "suicide-martyrs" – whose aim is to kill others – the more rebellion there is against the divine.

To continue this dialectical approach to martyrdom, we must examine the martyr's protest against the divine further: what is its function and who is its prototypical protest-actor in the Abrahamic traditions?

In Judaism, the adversary of God is *Ha-Satan* (Satan) who stands in opposition to the will of the divine as an "adversary." Etymologically, "satan" is the noun deriving from the verb "to oppose."[12] Satan's opposition to the will of the divine becomes acute in the book of Job, where he not only remains steadfast against God's commands, but also *accuses* him of wrongdoing. He wants to demonstrate that the divine is deliberately provided a false consciousness – he veils Job's potential faithlessness by giving him everything he needs. Of course Job is "blameless and upright" and "fear[s] God" because no calamity has every struck him.[13] If God's divine protection and blessings were withdrawn from him, and he had to experience the world in all its misery, pain, and suffering, this same saintly Job would curse his creator for his unfortunate fate. Although Job remains faithful to the divine, even after experiencing the loss of everything he holds dear, including his family, the act of accusing God of lying about the reality of his creation – that if it was not for his active intervention human life would be absolutely cruel and barbaric – is the essential role of Satan in his text. Satan, having knowledge of human frailty because he is 'going to and fro on the earth, and from walking up and down on it,' believes God to be duplicitous, an author of chaos, and the creator of the conditions by which man will suffer, murder each other in war, and curse the absence of God's mercy.[14] Whereas Satan walks were men walk, God remains seemingly *absconditus*, separate from his creation by nature and design. From a Christian reading, where the Holy Spirit should be, the unholy pervades. Does not Satan, in his accusative moment, speak in the name of his fellow – seemingly

---

12   Numbers 22:22, Samuel 29:4 and Psalms 109:6.

13   Job 1:1.

14   Job 1:7.

abandoned – creations? In the context of theodicy, is not the *devil as advocate* the advocate for a suffering humanity in God's cruel world? Continuing with this biblical story, is it not the case that the modern suicide-martyr (*jihādist*) also takes upon themselves an element of *Ha-Satan* through the act of self-sacrifice, especially when that martyrdom itself is a sign of protest against the divine? If we can legitimately claim that the martyr both witnesses and professes *for* their faith while simultaneously protests *against* the author who creates the history that creates martyrs, is not the "satanic" element a significant component within the ontological being of martyrs? Can the martyr act exclusively through obedient faith without the satanic act of accusing God of neglect and sadism, or are we forced to say that the martyr died not only for the *sake of God,* but also died *accusing* God in the same way that Satan accuses God? The dialectic tension within martial martyrdom – the antagonism between obedient faith and accusation – pierces through the ideology of death that has become prevalent in the modern period. Martyrdom is not a pure act of faith when it is wedded to the violent act of self-sacrifice – especially when it intends to kill the innocent other; it appropriates within itself the diabolical and blasphemous nature of the satanic, the bloody accusation against God and his seemingly "Godless" creation.

If we carefully read the history of martyrs within the Abrahamic faiths, we can see that the *theodicy* problem, the question of the divine's justice, is at the core of the concept of martyrdom for all of them. The history of warrior-martyrs, whether they be in Judaism, Christianity, and Islam, reveals that the good, the just, and the faithful have to sacrifice themselves on the altar of history while the bad, the unjust, and the *infidelious* (unfaithful) prosper in this world, live rich lives, and reside in safety and comfort. No other martyr is more expressive of this point than Jesus of Nazareth when he was brutally executed on the Roman's most humiliating execution device: the cross. While dying in excruciating agony, he voiced the words of Psalm 22:1, '*Eli, Eli, Lama Sabachtani?*' (My God, my God, why have you forsaken me?).[15] Had the Gospel writer recorded all of Rabbi Jesus' lamentation, if he was capable of continuing his recitation, he may have heard the rest of King David's Psalm.

> My God, my God, why hast thou forsaken me?
> Why art thou so far from helping me, from the words of my groaning?
> O my God, I cry by day, but thou dost not answer;
> and by night, but find no rest.[16]

---

15 Matthew 27:46.

16 Psalm 22:1–2. *Holy Bible: Revised Standard Version* (New York: Thomas Nelson Inc., 1972), 484.

This honest moment of human frailty, these words of despair written by the very earthly King David, briefly allow us to witness the humanity of Rabbi Jesus in all his human anguish, far from the sanitized Jesus of the later Church which had a tendency to over-emphasize his divine nature ($\mu o\nu o\varphi\upsilon\sigma\iota\tau\iota\sigma\mu\acute{o}\varsigma$ – monophysitism) at the expense of frailty of his human reality, a heresy that today's church still suffers from often in *praxis* if not in doctrine.[17] On the tendency to de-emphasize the humanity of great religious figures, the biographer of St. Francis of Assisi, Donald Spoto, claims that,

> The lives of saints are often composed by those who offer them and us a grave distortion when they fashion literary halos over their lives, effectively diminishing or even erasing the humanity God assumed and has given us, and which He uses to bring us to Himself. Sanitized stories of holy men and women too often describe them as essentially perfect, always pious, suffering without complaint, ever clear about their commitment and their destiny. In no way would such a description suit the life and character of Jesus of Nazareth, who fully shared our frail humanity.[18]

Like so many other historical martyrs, in which the plan of the creator is questioned, Rabbi Jesus briefly defies his willingness to become a martyr; the price may have been too high, and the pain too deep, for him in that moment of hopeless despair. Sharing in his agony, his mother Mary – the *stabat mater dolorosa* (the standing suffering mother) – and his disciple Mary Magdalene prepared themselves for his unjust death. Surely, one can imagine so many other soon-to-be martyrs having such agonizing moments of doubt, where they question the mercy of the divine as well as their own convictions in the face of impending execution. Thus, the religiously obedient "event" of martyrdom produces its antithesis – doubt, despair, and often *misotheism* (hatred of god), for how could a loving and just God allow such evil.[19]

The Critical Theorist remembers the trial of God that the Rabbis engaged in while awaiting their deaths in Auschwitz; so deep was their agony that God

---

17   It is interesting to note that from the Christian perspective, God, via Jesus, quotes the lamentation of a human King. In this case, human words express the pain that is being suffered by a divine figure. The fact that "God" quotes man to express his suffering on the cross cannot be overlooked in an attempt to understand the theodicy problem.

18   Donald Spoto, *Reluctant Saint: The Life of Francis of Assisi* (New York: Viking Press, 2002), 183.

19   Bernard Schweizer, *Hating God: The Untold Story of Misotheism*. New York: Oxford University Press, 2011.

himself was emphatically indicted for what he allowed to happen (or had authored).[20] God's perceived indifference to the suffering of his "chosen people" led many Rabbis to believe he had broken the covenant with Israel, that he may have even made a new covenant with another people – maybe even the Germans, or that the Germans were the "hand of God" – smiting the Jews for their disloyalty and abandonment of their faith.[21] Many Jews, although they could not abandon their belief in God, chose to rather hate him for his purposeful indifference to their suffering, his cruelty, and his evilness. Nevertheless, as Jesus witnessed the barbarity of the Roman soldiers, the scorn of their commanding officers, the rancor of the wealthy among the Jewish authorities who collaborated with Rome, the irrepressible spirit of protest in the name of the victims of history – those viciously executed on Golgotha and throughout what Hegel describes as the *slaughterbench of history* – is coupled with the protest against the world that the divine has designed and engineered. Their suffering indicts the divine and its *absconditus* (absence) or *otiosus* (idleness) in the history of mankind's existence.

In light of the modern barbarity of war, cannibalistic civil society, and the international exploitation of humanity, the pessimistic philosopher, like Nietzsche and Schopenhauer, can easily come to the conclusion that the world is forsaken, for it is under God's dominion that all the suffering, catastrophe, and destruction occur. Indeed, Deism, the 17th and 18th century Enlightenment answer to the theodicy problem, could only postulate that the divine bars itself from entering into history as the only logical reason for his apparent absence. As such, God leaves the problem of suffering for man to resolve. Martyrs may call out to God, according to the Deists, but they should expect no answer; he has taken leave and refuses to reenter into human history. The suffering masses can transcend their misery through prayer, fasting, and other vain rituals, but they should expect no countermovement from the divine. Deism fails to provide a consoling God.

In a Nietzschian world post-death-of-god, what came from the prayers of the suffering Jews in Auschwitz were only the *Schutzstaffel* (ss) and their sadomasochistic brutality. Yet, where God failed to deliver, the Bourgeois Enlightenment in the form of the United States Army, and the Marxist Enlightenment in the form of the Soviet Red Army, liberated what in the *vernichtungslager*

---

20 Schweizer, *Hating God,* 161–165; Jenni Frazer, "Wiesel: Yes, We Really did put God on Trial," September 19, 2008. http://www.thejc.com/news/uk-news/wiesel-yes-we-really-did-put -god-trial (Accessed 8/14/2014).

21 See Elie Wiesel, *The Trial of God* (*as it was held on February 25, 1649 in Shamgorod*), trans. Marion Wiesel New York: Random House, 1979.

(extermination camp) was called the *muselmänner* – the *dead-not-yet-dead*, or the walking corpses of the Holocaust. The longing for the intercession of the divine was rooted in a time where believing in the divine was still a true possibility, but in Auschwitz no god seemed to exist. The liberal and Marxian Enlightenment liberated the Jews while the God of Judaism remained silent and seemingly absent.

However, the preponderance of death at the hands of the unjust is not the last word on religious faith. Regardless of God's seeming absence and like the ardent faith that the author of the Psalms expressed, the martyr remains *semper fidelis* (always faithful) to his creator, and to his mission, despite his moments of doubt and fear. From the view of the critical religiologist, the dialectics of martyrdom demonstrate the internal antagonism between faith and doubt, suffering and joy, transcendence and destruction, which is manifested through the martyrdom of the finite believer for the cause of the infinite. Because the dialectic persists regardless of history, such suffering and misery cannot be the final nail in god's coffin nor can it be the final word on religion. Because religion points in the direction of another possibility, an abandonment of metaphysics or theology in the face of earthly despair can only deliver the world over to the already given, the status quo, the despairing world-as-it-is, and thus forsake a world that could be – that which the martyr died for.[22] However, metaphysical thought that brings a positive meaning to the suffering of the martyr may also be dangerous and unacceptable.

In Hegel's optimistic philosophy of history, the dialectical movement through time is predicated on the negation of that which came before; the determinate negation of the negative gives birth most painfully to the positive. However, as Adorno discovered in his *Negative Dialectics*, Hegel's optimism did not always prove to be true, as no positive was born from the near complete destruction of the Jews in Europe.[23] For Adorno and the Frankfurt School, not even the birth of Israel can justify such inhumanity as displayed in the "final

---

22   John Abromeit. *Max Horkheimer and the Foundations of the Frankfurt School* (New York: Cambridge University Press, 2013), 362–366.

23   Many Israeli Rabbis have articulated the idea that the Jews of Europe were the sacrificial lambs for the rebirth of Israel as a modern nation-state: a returning of the chosen people to the land that God delivered to them in the Jewish Bible. From the perspective of the Critical Theorist, this argument lends a positive metaphysics to history, positing that it has a telos that is discernible and therefore meaningful; history, by way of providence, made those Jews into victims and therefore their suffering should be accepted as a necessary but painful good. Consequently, Hitler himself becomes the agent of providence in service to the creation of the Jewish state. For these reasons, and in agreement with Adorno, such arguments must be rejected for they revictimize the already victimized.

solution of the Jewish question" (*die Endlösung der Judenfrage*). Such positive metaphysics which give objective meaning to the purely negative within the dialect of history, i.e. Auschwitz, was to engage in ideology – false but consoling consciousness – that results in the double victimization of the victims, as it not only recognizes their suffering and murder as tragedy, but violently impinges upon it a farcical metaphysics.[24] In the face of such absurdity, Adorno says that our feeling 'balk at squeezing any kind of sense, however bleached, out of the victim's fate.'[25] Without collapsing into a positivistic maxim, Auschwitz simply remains what it is: objective meaninglessness, history without purpose, and a pure event that signifies nothing beyond the barbaric given. It can only be falsely imbued with distorted meaning; such meaning arises from a subjective dissatisfaction with its inherent meaninglessness. Such a disturbed subjectivity reveals itself as the source of the *Holocaust as distorted ideology*.

The senselessness invoked in Adorno's *Negative dialectics* plays an important role in the history of Islamic and Christian martyrdom. Many individuals who had sacrificed their lives for their faiths, their values, and their core principles, have found, like Rabbi Jesus, not the "rose within the cross," the rational within the real, but only the inadequate consolation of newly formed institutions – the Church in the case of Christianity and the state of Israel in the case of Judaism – that can neither fully reconcile the individual to their agonizing fates nor can they negate the conditions that led the individual to sacrifice themselves. Despite the piling up of martyred corpses, the world remains the same: an ever-destroying mechanism manifested in the cruelty of nature and history. No matter how many martyrs are honored with Islamic *panegyrics* (πανηγυρικός – "speeches praising martyrs") in the West Bank and Gaza, no matter the number of rousing *jihadi khuṭbah* (sermons), the conditions which call for the production of martyrs continues; no matter how many Shi'a, Christian, and Yazidi martyrs accumulate at the hands of ISIS (Islamic State in Iraq and Syria), the conditions that perpetuate martyrdom continues; no matter how many poor, weak, and suffering homeless and stateless immigrants die in the streets of Europe, Africa, Asia, and the Americas, the coordinates that create such human catastrophes continues unabated. The negation of their suffering brought about no objective alleviation of suffering within the world, even if it was thought to have done so subjectively. Martyrdom has often failed to overcome that which creates martyrs, and so, despite Hegel's

---

24   We will return once again to Adorno's discussion of metaphysics post-Auschwitz in a later chapter.

25   Theodor Adorno, *Negative Dialectics* (New York: The Continuum Publishing Company, 1999), 361.

optimistic diagnosis and prognosis about history and its so-called "progress" towards absolute freedom i.e. the concrete transcendence of the world-as-it-is, such freedom fails to arrive.[26] Due to the lack of concrete negation, humanity stubbornly continues to abide by the self-perpetuating dictum: *si vis pacem para bellum,* which in itself cancels out the possibility of a true peace; it rather expresses a vortex of violence that man seems incapable of escaping.[27] In this case, the negative only gives way to a new form of negativity: the *negativity-of-the-now-time (negativität der jetztzeit)*, which resembles that of the past and already determines the future. Ironically, and at the risk of sounding like a devotee of Schopenhauer's metaphysical pessimism, martyrdom may well be the only way out of sorrow-inducing cycle of perpetual return solely through anamnestic solidarity; remembrance that the victim's sacrifice may have made but a small crack in the edifice of history as barbarity.[28]

Witnessing against Islam: The Case of Theo van Gogh

Although western protests against Islam have a long history, since September 11, 2001, an awareness of the "other" within the western midst has led to a whole new wave of protests against Islam that have been aided by the ubiquity of modern media and the 24 hour news cycle. This constant awareness of the other has been a net negative for Muslims. In the Middle Ages, and even during the Enlightenment period, Islam was consistently represented as a form of Christian heresy, Muhammad was a fraud, and the Qur'an was the work of the Devil. Thousands of books, tracts, and treatises were written to prove the fraudulent nature of Islam and to convince Christendom of the evil intention of the Muslims.[29] For example, Dante Alighieri places Mohammad in the realm of hell with the schismatics. Another example can be found in France, where, although criticizing the Catholic Church was his main objective, the

---

26 As has been noted by many critical scholars, the notion of "progress" has often been made into the ideology of bourgeois societies. All technological, social, economic, and political changes in favor of the ruling class have been designated progress, while all that resists and/or challenges bourgeois interests are dubbed retrogressive, obscurantist, or degenerate.

27 'If you want peace prepare for war.' "True peace" is predicated not on the threat of war, but in a state of being that requires both war and *the threat of war* to be absent.

28 Rudolf J. Siebert, *Manifesto of the Critical Theory of Society and Religion: The Wholly Other, Liberation, Happiness and the Rescue of the Hopeless. Vol 11.* (Leiden: Brill, 2010), 465–466.

29 Minou Reeves, *Muhammad in Europe: A Thousand Years of Western Myth-Making.* New York: New York University Press, 2000.

Enlightenment philosopher Voltaire's 1736 play *Le fanatisme, ou Mahomet le Prophete* (dubbed *Mohomet the Imposter* in English), tacitly disguised such criticism of the church behind the manifest images of Islam, which was perceived to be the universal enemy, as it was perceived to be both pre-Enlightenment and "other." For the unenlightened audience, the message was clear; Muhammad was considered diabolical and was both a spiritual imposter and a purveyor of religious violence.[30] For the Protestant or secular audience member, it was understood that "Mahomet" not only represented the evil of Islam, but was simultaneously symbolically representing "religion" all together, including the Catholic Church. Voltaire had systematically merged the two in his popular play, manipulating his audience's distrust for both the turban and the miter. Nevertheless, the illiterate population of Europe was hardly interested in inter-faith polemics, and was more preoccupied with base issues such as the challenges of poverty, disease, feeding and caring for their families, as well as the state of their immortal soul. Therefore the literary crusade against Islam had limited consequences on the vast majority of Europeans who may have only been exposed to anti-Islamic sentiments through the occasional sermon and other religious exhortations. Unless one resided on the border regions of Christendom, Islam remained abstract and foreign. However, the modern era proved that this would not always be the case.

Two important advances in human history have determined the modern form of "Islamophobia." First, the material abundance and acquisition of wealth within the western world have given opportunities to its people in education, liberation from agricultural toil, urbanization, and industrialization. All these developments have made it possible for people to gain the minimum education necessary to both read and engage in religious discussions within the public sphere. However, the same modernity that expanded basic literacy, failed to deliver to the masses the ability to think critically, systematically or dialectically, thus leaving them, in the thought of many, with an incomplete education. This "half-education" remains detrimental to the future of the West. First, it makes the masses increasingly susceptible to sophistic propaganda. Second, and in additional to the incomplete education, technology has brought the expanses of geography and culture into the home. Either via television or internet, the outside world, that which was never to be witnessed by the majority of westerners in the pre-modern periods, can now be witnessed by the touch of a bottom. In terms of its relationship with the West, this accessibility of information has been both of equal benefit to Islam as well as a

---

30   Denise Spellberg, *Thomas Jefferson's Qur'an: Islam and the Founders* (New York: Alfred A. Knopf, 2013), 27–33.

hindrance. Because modern communication technologies in-and-of-itself are neutral as to its content, it allows Muslims to speak directly to non-Muslims, but it also allows their adversaries to speak directly to the masses as well.[31] Post-9/11, the western world was flooded with images of civil airliners crashing into the World Trade Center; Muslims beheading Americans who "only came to help" in Iraq and Syria; the video-confessions of suicide bombers in Palestine; mobs of Pakistanis burning American flags; Afghani "mujahideen" killing Marines via IEDs; and various "irrational" outbursts of Muslims due to Qur'an burnings; irreverent and derisive cartoons; and a YouTube video depicting Muhammad as a pedophile and fanatic.[32] Consequently, according to the FBI, the growth in anti-Muslim hate crimes in the United States jumped 1600% from pre-9/11 levels.[33] In addition, there were other incidents of violence that greatly contributed to the idea that Islam is an inherently violent religion and that Muslims are all willing to kill for their faith. All of these incidents led to both a growing trend in Islamophobia, which is strictly a "fear of Islam," as well as *miso-islamism*, which is the "hatred of Islam." Although the United States has often been seen to be in the center of the conflagration between the West and the Muslim world, most of the day-to-day conflicts have happened in Europe.

In August of 2004, Dutch public television aired an eleven-minute film entitled *Submission* (translated from the Arabic word "Islam") that was made by the Dutch filmmaker Theo van Gogh and the Somali apostate Ayaan Hirsi Ali.[34] The film was critical of what they saw as the violent nature of Islam, its

---

31   Here I make the claim that although the content that technology advances, i.e. TV shows, music, blogs, etc., are bound to given subjective tastes, opinions, etc., technology itself remains neutral. However, this is only a surface observation, as technology itself advances a certain form of thinking, a certain way-of-being-in-the-world that determines human interaction and relations. Technology is predicated on instrumental reason, the reason of work and tool, manipulation of the physical world, and the reduction of all that cannot be subject to scientific scrutiny down to the physical. In this sense, even where communicative reason is still a powerful force in society, instrumental reason undermines its ability to serve as the basis for a healthy and cooperative society.

32   Richard Esposito et al., "Anti-Islam Film Producer Wrote Script in Prison: Authorities," September 13, 2012. http://abcnews.go.com/Blotter/anti-islam-film-producer-wrote-script -prisonauthorities/story?id=17230609#.UFLmFK4dWVk (Accessed 3/30/2014).

33   Muslim Public Affairs Council, "What you Need to Know," http://www.mpac.org/programs/ hate-crime-prevention/statistics.php#.UzixcChDx94 (Accessed 3/30/2014).

34   Ayaan Hirsi Ali, *Infidel* (New York: Free Press, 2007), 311–335. Ali refers to Van Gogh as a "Lord of Misrule," invoking the Renaissance tradition of appointing an individual to direct the "Feast of Fools" for Christmas. She says 'his house was a shambles, but he focused intensely on his work. He was a mess of contradictions, an impossible man, a genius in some ways.' Ali, *Infidel*, 312.

misogyny, and its supposed theological legitimation of patriarchy. Telling the story of four young Muslim women who were abused in various ways by their fathers and husbands – who together symbolically represent Islam – the short film's main critique was that Muslims (especially women) are not free to follow their own individualistic paths towards happiness, but are bound by archaic laws that limit their subjective autonomy and enslaves them to religiously inspired violence and oppression. According to Ali, the film was meant to show that "submission to Islam causes many other kinds of sufferings" and that "we should be free to interpret it [the Qur'an]; we should be permitted to apply it to the modern era in a different way, instead of performing painful contortions to try to recreate the circumstances of a horrible distant past."[35] In their attempt to provoke a reaction from the Muslim community – and thus demonstrate that Islam is irreconcilable with western values – the makers filmed a naked woman's battered and bruised body with Qur'anic verses written on her. The symbolic merger of the *Qur'an* and the *abuse of the weak,* in this case of young women, was very offensive for Muslims living in the Netherlands who (1) rejected the claim that Islam condones violence upon women, and (2) who previously thought that their adopted home was a bastion of European multiculturalism and tolerance. In making the film, knowing that it would provoke a vocal and potentially violent protest, Van Gogh and Ali wanted to get across to the Dutch population that Europe has a foreign faction within its midst who do not, and cannot, share their same political (secular democratic) and cultural (enlightened and multicultural) values precisely because of their religious beliefs. In the minds of the filmmakers, this foreign group is a latent threat to the existence of liberal freedom within the Netherlands and by extension all of Europe. The message of the film was very clear and well received by some, as Ian Buruma states in his book *Murder in Amsterdam*, 'this was a disturbing message in a society used to public figures preaching multicultural tolerance, but it was something many people wished to hear.'[36] From the perspective of the critical theorist of religion, we must ask why so many people wished to hear that Islam is violent, that the Qur'an encourages and legitimates violence against women, and that the Muslim community is a threat to European freedom? What were people thinking that they felt they could not express in public, although they had the desire and right to? What did they want to say about their Muslim neighbors and what forces stopped them from doing so?

---

35 Ibid., *Infidel,* 314.

36 Ian Buruma, *Murder in Amsterdam: Liberal Europe, Islam, and the Limits of Tolerance* (New York: Penguin Books, 2006), 5.

For the far-right nationalists, the Somali apostate Ayaan Hirsi Ali was a god-send, for it allowed them to openly proclaim the end of what they hated the most in modern Europe: multiculturalism and the idea of tolerance. It was only a "bonus" that the warning came from a former Muslim woman who had publicly renounced and denounced her former faith as being barbaric and backward, as it lent credibility to their attacks, thus shielding them from the accusation of xenophobia and/or racism. For many liberals as well as those on the political-right, Ayaan's voice of dissent was overdue and was subsequent-ly championed by other prominent individuals. For too long, they believed, the native Dutch population begrudgingly lived with the peculiarities of their Muslim neighbors. Their rituals, their languages, their religious sensibilities, and their cultural baggage hardly seemed to fit with liberal Dutch society. They believed these Muslims, mainly from North Africa, ruined their schools, took away thier jobs, brought violent crime and took advantage of the Dutch wel-fare state. Finally, with Ayaan Hirsi Ali, they had a voice from within the Is-lamic world that would trumpet the threat these immigrants posed to Europe.

One such personality that captured the attention of the Dutch population was Geert Wilders, a parliamentarian whose rise to fame was predicated on his anti-Islam and anti-immigration stance. Like Pim Fortuyn, a Dutch populist politician who also had anti-Muslim and anti-immigrant views, but was later assassinated in 2002, Geert Wilders saw Islam as a cultural and political threat to Dutch society. For him, immigration had allowed too many Muslim in; mul-ticulturalism had welcomed in the most "backward" elements of Islamic, and tolerance of such backwardness has proven to be the Achilles heel of Europe. Europe was slowly being *Islamicized.* Speaking in 2007 for the anti-immigrant movement in the Netherlands, Wilders forcefully stated,

> ... the Islamic incursion must be stopped. Islam is the *Trojan Horse* in Europe. If we do not stop *Islamification* now, *Eurabia* and *Netherabia* will just be a matter of time. One century ago, there were approximately 50 Muslims in the Netherlands. Today, there are about 1 million Muslims in this country. Where will it end? We are heading for the end of European and Dutch civilization as we know it. Where is our Prime Minister in all this? In reply to my questions in the House he said, without batting an eyelid, that there is no question of our country being *Islamified.*
>
> Now, this reply constituted a historical error as soon as it was uttered. Very many Dutch citizens... experience the presence of Islam around them. And I can report that they have had enough of burkas, heads-carves, the ritual slaughter of animals, so called honor revenge, blaring minarets, female circumcision, hymen restoration operations, abuse of

homosexuals, Turkish and Arabic on the buses and trains as well as on town hall leaflets, halal meat at grocery shops and department stores, Sharia exams, the Finance Minister's Sharia mortgages, and the enormous overrepresentation of Muslims in the area of crime, including Moroccan street terrorists.[37]

Witnessed from his statement that 'I don't hate Muslims, I hate Islam,' Wilders believes that all things Islamic are foreign to Europe and are therefore not reconcilable with liberal Dutch values.[38] For all intents and purposes, this statement, often repeated by many who disdain all things Islamic but do not want to appear to be xenophobic, is a distinction without a difference; to hate Islam is to hate Muslims, for without Muslims there is no Islam, and without Islam there are no Muslims.

Wilders took to the habit of likening the Qur'an to Adolf Hitler's *Mein Kampf,* but pointed out that he wasn't the first to do so; Winston Churchill also made this erroneous connection.[39] To the dismay of the Netherland's Muslim faithful, Wilders aggressively advocated the banning of the Qur'an as a "threat to our society" just as *Mein Kampf* was banned in the Netherlands.[40] The filmmaker Theo van Gogh couldn't have agreed more, as he shared many of the same Islamophobic sentiments.[41] Nevertheless, Van Gogh never had the opportunity to work closely with Wilders. On November 2, 2004, a Dutch-Moroccan named Mohammed Bouyeri murdered Van Gogh. Van Gogh and Ayaan Hirsi Ali's disrespect of Islam, Muhammad, and the Muslim community outraged Bouyeri, and he was determined to send a message to Ayaan Hirsi Ali for her insolence and Van Gogh's mockery.

---

37   Geert Wilders, "Mr Wilders' Contribution to the Debate on Islamic Activism," September 29, 2007. http://web.archive.org/web/20080614074737/http://www.groepwilders.com/website/details.aspx?ID=44 (Accessed 3/30/2014).

38   Ian Traynor, "'I Don't Hate Muslims, I Hate Islam' says Holland's Rising Political Star," February 16, 2008. http://www.theguardian.com/world/2008/feb/17/netherlands.islam (Accessed 3/30/2014).

39   Geert Wilders, *Marked For Death: Islam's War Against the West and Me* (Washington D.C.: Regnery Publishing, Inc., 2012), 121.

40   Wilders, *Marked For Death,* 122.

41   Although they agreed on the threat of Islam, Geert Wilders and Theo van Gogh never worked together. Wilders thought Van Gogh to be too outlandish and anti-religious. Whereas Wilders was solely critical of Islam, Van Gogh was equally hostile to Christianity and Judaism. Whereas Van Gogh was an equal opportunity hater of religion, Wilders emphasized the Judeo-Christian legacy of Europe as a source for its rejuvenation. See Wilders, *Marked For Death,* 8–9.

In light of the tensions between the Muslim community and their secular counterparts in the post-secular society, seeing that both sides claim to defend the higher principle, we must ask the question, can we consider Theo van Gogh a martyr for secular society? Within a context of acute social antagonisms, especially between the religious and the secular, can someone be martyred whiled witnessing *against* something, or was Van Gogh's death a death *for* something? If his death and his film were acts of witnessing *for* something, what would it have been precisely? Ultimately, can we regard him as the first post-9/11 martyr for *miso-Islamism*?

From the perspective of the critical theory of religion, it is certainly possible for the secular-humanist individual to be a martyr for their cause. Max Horkheimer, in his *Critique of Instrumental Rationality,* reminds us that 'both of them [religion and atheism] have been responsible for good and evil throughout history... and both of them have had their tyrants and their martyrs.'[42] Che Guevara, an atheist Marxist and physician who dedicated himself to the revolutionary advancement of the working and poor classes in Latin America was brutally executed by the Bolivian military with the aid of the CIA in 1967. Che was religiously unmusical, but he remained sensitive to the important role religion played in the lives of the many poor people he fought for. For Che, when religious praxis was identical with its core social values, then it naturally took the side of revolutionary love, justice, and solidarity, and as such he had no qualms with those members of his revolutionary movement who remained religious. However, when it sanctified the existing status quo of oppression, he vehemently attacked religion as a tool of the ruling class. With Fidel Castro, Che supported the removal of the Catholic Church from Cuba after the revolution precisely because it had supported the ruthless dictator Fulgencio Batista against the interests of the Cuban population.[43] Che, like many other revolutionary Marxists, would attempt to make an alliance with religion if it was possible; where it was not, it had to be fought as a reactionary and counter-revolutionary ideology. For his work on behalf of the poor, for his fight against dictatorship, and for his ultimate martyrdom for a Latin American revolution, Che was thought by many to have been a secular *alter Christus* (other Christ).[44] According to Fidel Castro, 'if Che had been a Catholic, if Che had belonged

---

42   Max Horkheimer, *Critique of Instrumental Reason* (New York: The Seabury Press, 1974), 49.

43   Fidel Castro and Frei Betto, *Fidel and Religion: Conversations with Frei Bretto on Marxism & Liberation Theology.* New York: Ocean Press, 2014.

44   Candida R. Moss, *The Other Christs: Imitating Jesus in Ancient Christian Ideologies of Martyrdom.* New York: Oxford University Press, 2010; Michael Casey, *Che's Afterlife: The Legacy of an Image.* New York: Vintage Books, 2009.

to the church, he would probably have been made a saint, for he had all the virtues.'[45]

Patrice Lamumba, the secular revolutionary leader of the *Mouvement National Congolaise,* who fought and defeated colonial Belgium to gain independence in 1960, was assassinated by Belgium forces and their Congolese collaborators.[46] Both the CIA and the MI6 bear responsibility for his murder. Lamumba is remembered as a martyr for African independence for colonial powers. The atheist Leon Trotsky, murdered on the orders of Josef Stalin, is seen by many followers as a martyr for the cause of working class liberation and worldwide revolution. Fred Hampton, the deputy-chairman of the Illinois branch of the Black Panther Party, was executed while sleeping in his apartment by the Chicago Police Department in 1969 and today is still seen as a martyr for the cause of Black emancipation in America. These and many other non-religious, militantly secular or atheistic activists have be brutalized, oppressed, and murdered along side of their explicitly religious comrades. As such, martyrdom has no exclusive sectarian or religious/secular preference. It is not bound to one religion or to any religion at all, but manifests itself in times of crisis. Consequently, a martyr is one that is murdered *unjustly* while standing up for what they believe to be the truth and refusing to bend their knees in *proskynesis* (προσκύνησις – "prostration") to those who unjustly set themselves above others. The 27 million Soviets communists that were murdered in the "Great Patriotic War" (World War II) must be remembered as martyrs *against* fascism and for the communist ideal of equality.[47] However, by that broad definition, can we classify fascists like Benito Mussolini and Hitler as martyrs? Do we want to lend the term "martyr" to individuals who are nearly universally despised for their destructive activities and philosophies? Were they *unjustly* murdered or was their demise indeed just? Mussolini certainly died for his

---

45   Castro and Betto, *Fidel and Religion,* 289.

46   Although Lumumba was born into a Catholic family and was educated in a Protestant school, he nevertheless believed in the separation of church and state that would end the legitimization of government policies by clerical authorities.

47   I make a point to remember the 27 million Soviet communists who were killed fighting the Third Reich for the expressed point that they are so easily forgotten in the West. With all our emphasis on the D-Day invasion, the Holocaust, and the Western Front, we hardly remember that the Communists were the first and primary enemy of the Fascists. For that the Soviet Union lost 27 millions citizens – the highest loss of one country in the entire war. This observation in no way diminishes the commitment and loss of Americans, British, French, Canadians, and the partisan forces in occupied Europe. Additionally, it may be the case that anti-fascism was a stronger motivational force in the war against the Germans that was their dedication to Communism.

unwavering belief in fascist ideals, what he often called "corporatism."[48] Can those who are responsible for the death and destruction of hundreds, thousands, or even millions in the case of the Nazis, be considered martyrs for their causes, or should the *aims* and *goals* of the movements be taken into account when determining whether or not they are martyrs? In other words, is the definition of martyrdom constitutionally bound to goals and aims associated with a certain political, economic and cultural trajectory, i.e. the expansion of substantive freedom, the cancelation of the alienated life and towards a society beyond the realm of necessity? Can an unpopular "martyr" be legitimately stripped of that designation because they represent the authoritarian, the xenophobic, the misogynistic, the racist, and the romantic – who sees the ideal future only in the idealistic past?

From the perspective of the critical religiologists who are concerned with the translation of the revolutionary potential of religious semantic and semiotic material into secular philosophy, the *aims* of the murdered matter in whether or not they can be legitimately classified as a martyr. The modern notion of martyrdom, rooted in the Abrahamic faiths that gave birth to the West, as well as in the "post-metaphysical" thought of Greek philosophy, cultural, and political life of Athens, Sparta, and other Greek city-states, takes seriously the claims that martyrs not only die witnessing for a faith, but also die witnessing for *specific* and *substantive* political-economic and cultural values such as freedom, justice, equality, and liberty even when they're emancipated from their religious legitimation and motivation. Revolutionary values, which are rooted in communicative rationality, and therefore resist the colonization of instrumental rationality and the functionalization of language via empty and manipulative slogans, attempt to broaden the scope of human emancipation, human actualization, and human reconciliation, not further the trend towards barbarism or the totally administered society. When human energy, resources, and life are directed towards creating a society that does not exploit one side of the human family by the other, that works in cooperation for social flourishing instead of petty competitiveness and aggression, that resists

---

48   See Robert O. Paxton, *The Anatomy of Fascism*. New York: Alfred A. Knopf, 2004. Corporatism is a structural-functionalist theory of social organization that is rooted in St. Paul's letter to the Corinthians (12:12–31), where the community is understood to be structured like a body, with certain parts playing various but necessary functionalist roles. All parts work together to create a single organic whole. For Italian fascists, including Mussolini, all segments of society work as a whole for the benefit of the nation-race. For Marxists, this social theory fundamentally sanitizes the class divisions within a given nation and serves the ideological function to suppress class-consciousness and therefore revolution of the working class against their masters.

the society of the fascist *übermensch* in preference for a society that is based in mutual-recognition and respect, compassion for the poor, elderly, sick, and abused (the *untermensch*), and sees a social imperative to create a society of *biophilia* as opposed to one permeated with *necrophilia*, then that movement has legitimate claim to the "revolutionary" title.[49] From the perspective of the critical religiologist, it is the *revolutionary* or *prophetic* nature of the unjustly murdered that makes them a martyr, not the simple fact that they were killed for a cause. If by "revolutionary" we mean the furthering of human emancipation in this world, revolutions serve as movements that increase the realization of human freedom within the context of space and time. In this sense, *counter-revolutionaries*, those authorities, groups or movements that attempt to limit the freedom, rights, and liberties of individuals; those who attempt to re-enslave those formerly emancipated from the drudges of oppression, exploitation, irrational authority and alienated existence; those who attempt to establish the conditions by which the surplus value of the those who toil endlessly is wrongfully appropriated by one group of people for their own benefit, can never fall on the battlefield of history as revolutionary martyrs. They are, in the view of the critical historian who sees history through the eyes of the victim, fallen tyrants.[50] Spartacus, who led the slaves in their rebellion against the slave masters in Rome, was a martyr, as he attempted to liberate his fellow slaves from their tyrannical masters. John Brown was a Christian martyr, as he attempted to liberate the slaves of America from their sadistic and cruel masters. Malcolm X was a Muslim martyr, as he attempted to liberate Afro-Americans from the tyranny of American racism and white supremacy. 'Ali Sharī'ati was a Shi'i Muslim martyr, as he attempted to liberate the minds of the Iranian masses from their enslavement to the quietist orthodoxy of the clerics as well as the counter-revolutionary policies of the u.s. imposed Shah. These and many other freedom fighters attempted to expand the geography of freedom, respect, self-reliance, and inter-subjectivity based on the principles of justice and equality. For their efforts they were murdered by the forces of oppression, tyranny, and the necrophilic disdain for those whom the powerful felt were beneath them. It is with this in mind that the critical theorist believes

---

49   Erich Fromm, *The Anatomy of Human Destructiveness* (New York: Holt, Rinehart and Winston, 1973), 325–368. See Dustin Byrd, *Ayatollah Khomeini and the Anatomy of the Islamic Revolution in Iran: Toward a Theory of Prophetic Charisma*. Lanham, MD: University Press of America, 2011. I use these terms, *übermensch* and *untermensch*, more in the spirit of the Third Reich and not Nietzsche's philosophy, which the Nazis distorted.

50   See my later chapter on Walter Benjamin's philosophy concerning the historical materialist historian.

the "martyr" should be reserved for the fallen revolutionary, not the unjust counter-revolutionaries, whose death was in service to those who diminish human emancipation, functionalized humanity for the benefit of the few, and exploit, neglect, and oppress the weak.

In light of this analysis, we must again ask ourselves what exactly it was that Theo van Gogh died for? What did he stand for? What were his philosophical, political, and cultural commitments? In whose tradition did he stand for? Did the conditions of post-secularity, in which he lived and worked, produce a new kind of martyr – one that is based on a contested definition of freedom? Was Van Gogh the first to be martyred in the struggle against the conditions of post-secularity?

It is clear that the murder of Theo van Gogh was unjust, unwarranted, and criminal (both legally and morally). Although some outspoken clerics among the Salafis were in support of an interpretation of religious law (*sharīʿah*) that exacts the death penalty against those who blaspheme or disrespect the Prophet, the Qur'an, or Islam in general, the concept of freedom of speech, a value that Theo van Gogh embraced, is an important concept within Islam itself, as it was this freedom that was denied the Prophet Muhammad in Mecca at the beginning of his prophethood. Additionally, Muhammad himself never executed someone simply for freely denying his prophethood – not even when they did so directly in front of him. He often opposed those of his followers that wanted to exact punishment on those who denied his prophethood.[51] Freedom of speech, even if it was speech against the Muslims, was an Islamic ideal that needed to be protected both for Muslims and non-Muslims. For Muhammad, the Islamic value of free speech, which has been too often eclipsed in many Muslim countries by leaders who they didn't elect, was extended even to those who used it to attack Muslims.

Since 9/11, the conflict between the West and the Muslim world has been constructed in a symbolic binary form: the narrative is one between the freedom of speech and the respect for religious figures. In other words, the core antagonism is between the secular "free" values of the West and the religious "authoritarian" values of Islam.[52] Upon a critical analysis, it becomes clear that

---

51   During the signing of the Treaty of Hudaibiyyah, the Meccans refused to recognize Muhammad's title "Messenger of God," but would instead sign it if he wrote the "son of 'Abdallah" by his name. Muhammad agreed to this despite the fact that it was explicitly denying his prophethood. Nevertheless, he did not retaliate against them for it, nor did he seek revenge for their disrespect.

52   Asad et al, *Is Critique Secular: Blasphemy, Injury and Free Speech* (New York: Fordham University Press, 2013), 14–57. This conflict wasn't necessarily new. One should remember the

not all Muslims deny the right of citizens to speak their minds freely, nor does it mean that all Europeans lack respect for religion and religious figures. What is the case is that shared values inherent within the western Enlightenment and Islam are weighted differently. Within the Islamic tradition itself, respect for sacred figures, especially Prophets, is of the highest value, whereas in the West, the freedom of the individual to critique religion or sacred figures – being a form of freedom of speech – is equally of the highest value. A critical stance, or sometimes even crass irreverence towards religion, whether it is healthy or not, has been at the core of the modern Enlightenment since its early struggles with the church. In other words, freedom of speech in the West brought with it the *right to blaspheme* without the fear of a violent reprisal by institutional power, be it the church or the state, which was a tremendous step towards freeing the population from the tyranny of the authoritarian church and the corrupt state. Henceforth, this ideal has become normative in the West and a constitutional part of democracy.

Beyond politics, many Enlighteners were motivated out of their distrust and disagreement with the church's pronouncements on morality, epistemology, ontology, and metaphysics, especially concerning the natural world and the priority of revelation and tradition over reason, as well as the church's abuse of power. Out of this conflict with the church and the ultimate triumph of the Enlightenment, the modern West was born. Blasphemy won its right to exist in the public sphere.[53] As the secular Enlightenment progressed, it would in time emancipate itself from the religious elements of mundane life as well as its dominating religious institutions.[54]

Since Luther broke open the doors to *individualism* through his "priesthood of all believers," or what Alister E. McGrath dubbed the "dangerous idea" of Christianity, Rome struggled to dictate the morality of the West. Under the influence of Protestantism, each individual would be guided by their own reason and conscience – and that reason and conscious has increasingly become

---

1988–1989 Salman Rushdie controversy when his novel *Satanic Verses* was released. The debate between freedom of speech and respect for sacred figures erupted then as well.

53   See Talal Assad's chapter in *Is Critique Secular: Blasphemy, Injury, and Free Speech,* 14–57.

54   Historically, the process of secularization pertained to the state's appropriation of church property, i.e. monasteries, convents, monastic lands, priories, and other church edifices, which occurred under King Henry VIII's dissolution of monasteries, having occurred after the Act of Supremacy was passed by Parliament in 1534, thus making the British King the *supreme head* (royal supremacy) of the Church of England. This seizure of properties – which transformed religious property into secular property – continued during the French Revolution and well into the 18th and 19th century by various European countries.

more secular.[55] In many ways this turn away from dogmatic obscurantism and unquestioned metaphysics towards the conscious of the individual was liberational in the West, while at the same time we can see that some of the religious values, principles, and beliefs that were beneficial in pre-Reformation Christendom – especially the sense of community and shared fates – have been lost in our now secular and thoroughly atomized society. Despite the obvious gains from western modernity, especially on the level of the individual, Habermas and Pope Benedict XVI believe the West has paid a high price for such a radical dissolution.[56] Nevertheless, the constitutional protection of speech is one of the uncompromisable benefits of the Bourgeois Enlightenment and the West is not willing to relinquish such a hard earned right for the protection against being offended.

From the perspective of the critical religiologist, the modern Muslim world could benefit much from a greater understanding of those same values associated with the western Enlightenment – secularity of the state, democracy, individual rights, etc. Just as equally true, the West could benefit from an increased understanding of those Muslim voices that harbor legitimate fear of secularization, democratization, and capitalization. For Habermas, the West should cultivate a greater understanding of such fears and apprehensions, while the Muslim world should come to appreciate the benefits of secular western values while simultaneously maintaining their Islamic identity?[57] Discussions like these have undoubtedly lead many Muslims and non-Muslims scholars to ask *can there be an Islamic movement that determinately negates western modernity and creates an Islamic modernity; one that could fully integrate itself into the modern world without abandoning the Islamic identity?* This type of move would include a categorical rejection of a simplistic and blind emulation of the West, which the Iranian Marxist scholar Jalal Al-i Ahmad aptly diagnosed as "Occidentosis" (*gharbzadegi*), as well as a simplistic retreat into a reactionary Islamic fundamentalism.[58] As Hans Küng as noted, the *failure* to engage in a meaningful discourse, to gather together the unlimited discourse community – which can enter into a robust discussion on what it means to be

55   Alister E. McGrath, *Christianity's Dangerous Idea: The Protestant Revolution – A History from the Sixteenth Century to the Twenty First* (New York: Harper One, 2007), 2–3, 57–58.

56   See Jürgen Habermas et al., *An Awareness of What is Missing: Faith and Reason in a Post-Secular Age,* trans. Ciaran Cronin (Malden, MA: Polity Press, 2011), 15–23; Jürgen Habermas and Joseph Ratzinger, *The Dialectics of Secularization: On Reason and Religion.* San Francisco: Ignatius Press, 2006.

57   Habermas, *Europe, 59–77.*

58   See Jalal Al-i Ahmad, *Occidentosis: A Plague from the West,* ed. Hamid Algar and trans. R. Campbell. Berkeley: Mizan Press Berkeley, 1984.

Muslim, what it means to be European, what it means to be modern, cosmopolitan, accepting, and enlightened – too often leads to senseless violence.[59] Mohammed Bouyeri and Theo van Gogh most likely would not have come to some kind of agreement on "ultimate truth," but discourse is a practice of the philosophically and religiously brave; such brave discourse has the potential to lead to the diminishment of tensions and future reconciliation. It demonstrates one's willingness to risk one's own beliefs, entertain a change in thinking, critically reflect on one's own deeply held convictions, and defend them via publicly accessible reasoning.[60] Theo van Gogh's defense of the Netherlands' notoriously liberal culture, with its legalized drug use, legal prostitution, pornography, unlimited sex partners, gay-rights, consumerism, i.e. its post-religious ethos, etc., which is rooted in the secular idea of individual happiness, freedom of choice, and the autonomy of the individual to direct their life in the way one sees fit, can hardly be reconciled with a religion that places a premium on the collective over the individual, the obedience to divine command, and/ or a religion that condemns the objectification of the body, and sexual licentiousness. Islamic morality cannot be reconciled with the individualistic *geist* of the ethical-egoism that animates modern secular society, a society in which each individual devises their own ethical and moral norms autonomously as opposed to following that which was divinely revealed in scripture and tradition. Nevertheless, in a democratic society, all members of the discourse community – no matter if they are religious or secular – not only have the right but the duty (some believe) to engage in a discussion about the values that will be considered normative within the society. As Habermas insists, all those affected by the decisions made by the discourse community must be included in such a process in order for it to bear any democratic legitimacy.[61] A consensus among the governed has to be found and that can only be done via discourse.

However, this line of thinking presupposes that there is already a universal consensus concerning the validity of governance via the "will of the people" as opposed to the "will of the divine." For some like Usama bin Laden, it is the "will of the people" that is precisely the problem with modern democracies, because the people's will stands in direct contradiction to the will of the

59 Hans Küng, *Islam: Past, Present & Future* (New York: Oxford University Press, 2007), xxiii-xxx, 3–24.

60 Jürgen Habermas, *The Inclusion of the Other: Studies in Political Theory* (Cambridge, MA: The MIT Press, 1998), 49–74.

61 One should also bear in mind the symbolic language of silence. Silence is often a way of registering one's refusal to engage in a discourse, and thus through the silence one engages in the discourse.

divine as expressed in sacred scripture and tradition. In other words, the independence of the human will is a problem when that independence fails to reconcile itself with the rule of God, and therefore stands in rebellion against the divine. Seeing this dynamic as one of the most fundamental disagreements between Islam and democracy, in October of 2002, Usama bin Laden stated,

> You [the United States and Europe] are a nation who, rather than ruling by the *sharia* (way) of God in its Constitution and Laws, choose to invent your own laws as you will and desire. You separate religion from your politics, contradicting the pure nature which affirms Absolute Authority to the Lord and your Creator. You flee from the embarrassing question posed to you: How is it possible for God the Almighty to fashion His creation, grant men power over all creatures and land, grant them all the amenities of life, and then deny them that which they are most in need of: knowledge of the laws which govern their lives?[62]

A society in which divine guidance is separated from the masses, where the masses are allowed to follow their *nafs* (instincts and desires) over and above divine revelation was anathema to his conception of a just and righteous society, as it would inevitably lead man into error and barbarism. In essence, man's animalic nature could never lead mankind into a society that is truly free, but would only enslave him to his animality, i.e. his "first nature." A second nature, one rooted in and governed by divine revelation, was the only way to create such a desirable nation, and that second nature, according to bin Laden, could only be crafted through divine guidance. Secular democracy not only ignored such divine guidance, but let loose man's destructiveness and gave that animalistic destructiveness the power of the state. If Plato thought democracy to be a failed form of government because it gave power to those who do not have the mental capacity to wield such power – the demos – then bin Laden believed it was because of their moral deficiency and their incapacity to justly guide themselves that democracy was faulty. He believed that by democratic consensus, a nation legitimizes the blindness of the first nature – thus alleviating the populace of it hatred of the superego in the form of the religious civilization. Democracy, in the name of civilization, unleashes civilization's nemesis: animality.

Usama bin Laden was not the only person who determined democracy to be a retreat from man's higher self and an affront to divine sovereignty. In his book

---

62   Osama Bin Laden, *Message to the World: The Statements of Osama Bin Laden,* ed. Bruce Lawrence (New York: Verso, 2005), 167.

The Bitter Harvest: The Muslim Brotherhood in Sixty Years, Ayman al-Zawahiri's critique takes on a theological tone; he condemns democracy for its 'deification of man,' stating,

> Know that democracy, that is, 'rule of the people,' is a new religion that deifies the masses by giving them the right to legislate without being shackled down to any other authority. For sovereignty, as has been shown earlier, is absolute authority; nothing supersedes it. Regarding this, Abu al-Ali al-Mawdudi said: 'Democracy is the deification of man... and rule of the masses.' In other words, democracy is a man-made infidel religion, devised to give the right to legislate to the masses – as opposed to Islam, where all legislative rights belong to Allah Most High... In democracies, however, those legislators from the masses become partners worshipped in place of Allah. Whoever obeys their laws worships them.[63]

Both bin Laden and Zawahiri are partially correct in their critique; a Muslim may be a democrat, but Islam is not democracy – the Muslim masses are not to create for themselves divine law: that is the sole prerogative of the divine in the Islamic tradition. As such, Islamic law – as crafted by the absolute sovereign – is difficult to reconcile with a political system that takes as its authority the popular sovereignty and will of its citizens. In other words, reconciling two very different forms of legitimation and two very different worldviews within one culture, especially when they're as divergent as the libertine culture of the Netherlands and the traditional conservative religious culture of the immigrants would never be an easy endeavor. The social trauma created by men like Theo van Gogh, with his anti-Semitism, miso-Islamism, and anti-Christian provocations, and men like Mohammed Bouyeri, who was willing to murder to protect the dignity of his beliefs, makes sure that the multitudes of citizens who see both the importance of respect for the beliefs of the other as well as the imperative to maintain the freedom of the individual, never enter into a meaningful dialogue.[64]

Again, we return to the original question: what did Theo van Gogh die for and is he a martyr? A look at a conversation soon after Theo's death may give us a better understanding of how Van Gogh thought of himself and his work, which may provide an answer to our question. Upon seeing Ayaan Hirsi Ali blaming herself for his death, Van Gogh's best friend stated,

---

63 Ayman al-Zawahiri, *The Al Qaeda Reader,* ed. and trans. Raymond Ibrahim (New York: Broadway Books, 2007), 130.

64 Buruma, *Murder in Amsterdam,* 90–91.

No, Ayaan. If he were alive Theo would be hurt, hearing you say that. He wouldn't have wanted to die in his bed. He felt like a knight on horseback about *Submission*. He died in a battle for free expression, and that's what he lived for... This was a meaningful death.[65]

Although we may credibly state that Theo van Gogh was murdered for the freedom of speech, he was not however a committed revolutionary who wanted to *expand* the bounds of freedom beyond what they already were. What Theo van Gogh did profess to was his desire to *conserve* the liberal freedoms already established by Dutch democracy. As stated before, Theo van Gogh was a Dutch nationalist who believed that the presence of Muslim immigrants in the Netherlands was a threat to the secular liberal values of the open society. For him, Muslims represented an attack from the *religious-right* – a force that traditionally wanted to confine the autonomy of the individual within the strictures of religion. Thus, he believed the Muslims represented a religiously "conservative" threat to such secular liberal values; that they would attempt to impose an oppressive and restrictive *sharīʿah* law upon the non-believing Dutch population; that they represented an aggressively backwards and un-enlightened *weltanschauung* (worldview); that they were a threat to the rights of homosexuals, and that they were a threat to the rights of blasphemers. Theo van Gogh believed that Islam would attempt to reestablish a religious morality on a population that had previously emancipated themselves from the burdensome moral codes of religion. Against all statistical data available, he believed Muslims represented a population that receives benefits from the state but only contributes to society via petty crime, sexual assault, religiously inspired misogyny, and terroristic condemnation of their host society. In other words, echoing Geert Wilders, the Muslims wanted to Islamize Europe starting with its most tolerant nation, The Netherlands, thus delivering it to what he believed was a barbaric and unenlightened way of life. For Theo van Gogh, no matter if the Muslim immigrants were Dutch "citizens," they were not culturally Dutch unless they abandoned Islam and their native culture and adopted a secular-liberal worldview and lifestyle. They were Dutch by citizenship, but not by culture, and in Europe's post-racial and post-nationalist society, culture was more important that ethnicity.[66] Unexpectedly, Van Gogh's objection

---

65   Ali, *Infidel*, 323.

66   I do not say that ethnicity is not important at all in Europe for indeed it is. The different *ethnos* of most of the Muslim population remains a problem for many within Europe. However, it is the culture of Islam that most European critics of Islam object to; this separates them from the *demos* of any given nation more radically than their *ethnos*.

was not the "race" of the immigrants, but their beliefs and cultural practices. He accepted Ayaan Hirsi Ali's Dutch citizenship (and her right to become a member of the Dutch parliament) despite her African heritage. He would have seemingly been accepting of a Moroccan prostitute but not a Moroccan Imam, not because of their North African ethnicity, but because of their values and lifestyle.[67] The values of the Enlightenment, which shuns the judgment of individuals based on the "accidentals" that they had no control over, i.e. race, national origin, gender, sexual orientation, etc., was thoroughly entrenched in Van Gogh's psyche, but he could not avail himself of those characteristics that were not accidental, especially the deliberate binding of oneself to unenlightened religious systems and worldviews. In a free Dutch society, Muslims had the choice to continue with their "backwards" religious positions or join the forward-thinking enlightened European society as Ayaan Hirsi Ali had done. In accordance with his liberal views, those who chose the former earned his scorn and condemnation and those who chose the latter he accepted as his own.

Although Van Gogh's position may not be the most progressive stance to take, especially in terms of tolerance and multi-culturalism, it is however an example of a growing movement within European thought: the Enlightenment is under attack by conservative Muslim immigrants and it needs to be defended by the real Europeans who are not afraid to stand against the growing Muslim population in Europe. For Van Gogh and others, the demographic growth of the Muslim community represents a serious challenge to the secular ethos of Europe. Their fears are fueled by the high birth rate of Muslims, the seemingly never-ending flow of immigrants (both legal and illegal) into Europe via Greece and the Mediterranean, and the fact that Muslims often fail to "assimilate" (or integrate) fully into European society.[68] This antagonism has brought a shift in thinking towards the Enlightenment: where once the Enlighteners

---

67   Theo van Gogh's attitude towards immigrant women who embrace the sexual ethics of
       Europe is not unique among European leaders. For example, despite his anti-immigration
       politics, which were congruent with Italy's *Northern League* (a right-wing anti-immigrant
       group), Silvio Berlusconi, the former Prime Minister of Italy, demonstrated his hypocritical stance towards foreigners by proclaiming that they have no place in his country, unless
       they're "bringing over beautiful girls." See Nick Squires, "Silvio Berlusconi says immigrants not welcome but beautiful girls' can stay." February 13, 2010. http://www.telegraph
       .co.uk/news/worldnews/europe/italy/7223365/Silvio-Berlusconi-says-immigrants-not-
       welcome-but-beautiful-girls-can-stay.html (Accessed 11/11/2014). We should also bear in
       mind the Berlusconi was put on trial for his sexual relationship with a Moroccan teenager
       named Karima El Mahroug, a.k.a "Ruby the Heart stealer."
68   According to the Instituut voor Multiculturele Vraagstukken (Utrecht, Netherlands), the
       Muslim population in the Netherlands is 6% of the total population, just over a million

saw the values of the Enlightenment to be "universal," because they were based in autonomous reason which all of humanity has access to regardless of religion, race, age, etc., these new defenders of the Enlightenment take a more "relative" stance; they now see those values as being particularly "European," as they, and not any other religion or political philosophy, are solely responsible for the creation of the most modern, free and democratic society in human history.[69] Ian Buruma explained this new development within Enlightenment thought stating that,

> The conservative call for Enlightenment values is partly a revolt against a revolt. Tolerance has gone too far for many conservatives. They believe, like some former leftists, that multiculturalism was a mistake; our fundamental values must be reclaimed. Because secularism has gone too far to bring back the authority of the churches, conservatives and neo-conservatives have latched onto the Enlightenment as a badge of national or cultural identity. The Enlightenment, in other words, has become the name for the new conservative order, and its enemies are the aliens, whose values we don't share.[70]

The German Chancellor Angela Merkel echoed the feeling that multiculturalism had failed in Europe in October of 2010. In light of Germany's inability to cope with the problems associated with Muslim immigrants, she stated decried that 'this [multicultural] approach has failed, utterly failed.'[71] However, in the summer of 2015, Germany was the main destination for half a million Muslim refugees and immigrants fleeing war and instability in Syria, Iraq, Pakistan and Afghanistan, and ironically, she was the public face of the policy to let them into Germany. In Britain, Prime Minister David Cameron echoed Merkel's assessment of multiculturalism in February of 2011; believing the state had not adequately addressed the root cause for radicalization within his country, he denounced "state multiculturalism" as a failure. Promising greater scrutiny of Muslim organizations that profess views outside of the mainstream, Cameron declared,

---

Muslims in a total population of 16.8 million. http://www.forum.nl/Portals/Res/res-pdf/Moslims-in-Nederland-2010.pdf (Accessed 11/29/2014).

69   Buruma, *Murder in Amsterdam,* 27–29.

70   Buruma, *Murder in Amsterdam,* 27–29.

71   Matthew Weaver, "Angela Merkel: German Multiculturalism has 'Utterly Failed,'" October 17, 2010. http://www.theguardian.com/world/2010/oct/17/angela-merkel-german-multiculturalism-failed (Accessed 11/30/2014).

> Let's properly judge these organizations: Do they believe in universal human rights – including for women and people of other faiths? Do they believe in equality of all before the law? Do they believe in democracy and the right of people to elect their own government? Do they encourage integration or separatism?[72]

In light of the growing ghettoization of disaffected Muslim youths in Britain, who do not view Britain as the object of their loyalty, Cameron suggested a stronger commitment to a "British identity," one that is rooted in the values of the Enlightenment. Although these values were tacitly juxtaposed to the "backward" values of Islam, the point of Cameron's speech was not missed by the Muslim community, who understood that their worldview and way-of-life had become even more suspect in light of a Europe attempting to sort out its own fractured identity.

Echoing Buruma's previous point, the Critical Theorist Jürgen Habermas speaks of "interlocking processes" in his discussion of the contestation between conservative stances of the Enlightenment – its particular "European-ness" – and those who defend multiculturalism as an integral part of the Enlightenment.[73] He says,

> The multiculturalist party appeals to the protection of collective identities and accuses the other side of 'Enlightenment fundamentalism'; the secularist, by contrast, insist on the uncompromising inclusion of minorities in the existing political culture and accuse their opponents of a 'multiculturalist betrayal' of the core values of the Enlightenment.[74]

Theo van Gogh undoubtedly understood his position to be within the camp of the Enlightenment fundamentalists, which he believed created the freedoms that allowed him to live the life that he lived within a secular nation unencumbered by religious dogmas and restrictions. Knowing the history of religious Europe, Theo van Gogh understood that he could not have lived in pre-Enlightenment the Netherlands and and survived being who he was and how he lived – he would have been subject to attack by the church or other conservative forces for his libertinism. Van Gogh therefore saw the rapidly growing Muslim community as an ominous threat to those same liberal

---

72 Laura Kuenssberg, "State Multiculturalism has Failed, Says David Cameron," February 5, 2011. http://www.bbc.com/news/uk-politics-12371994 (Accessed 11/30/2014).

73 Habermas, *Europe*. 70.

74 Ibid., 70.

values that made him free. It was personal for him. Consequently he accused the multiculturalists of the Netherlands of aiding in the future destruction of enlightened European values, a position taken up by many Europeans on the anti-religious left and the xenophobic right, including Anders Behring Breivik, the anti-Muslim and anti-left mass terrorist of Oslo and Utøya island (2011).

The case of Theo van Gogh's possible status as a martyr, as has been demonstrated, is extremely complex. If Theo van Gogh is determined to be a martyr, then he is a martyr for what he believed to be the defense of the secular Enlightenment; he was a secular Enlightenment-fundamentalist, who wished to *conserve* the *progressive* political and cultural values of the Netherlands and European society from a religiously conservative minority population. But, like many of his critics suspected, did he functionalize the values of the Enlightenment to justify his xenophobia and miso-Islamism? Like Geert Wilders, Van Gogh was not prepared to surrender Europe to what he believed was an invasion of a foreign people and hostile religion, but does that alone make him a bigot? Although he wasn't attempting to augment freedom through revolutionary praxis, he was a defender of liberal freedoms; in the face of religious fanaticism, he wished to preserve and conserve such freedoms as a peculiarly European way-of-being-in-the-world against what he believed were forces that were attempting to diminish the freedom that distinguished the West from many other parts of the world. In a post-nationalist Europe, such Enlightenment values became the basis for a new European identity, one more fully integrated: the United States of Europe. He may have ultimately been mistaken concerning the intentions of the majority of Muslims in Europe, but his sincerity, even to his harshest critics, seemed genuine and was not simply for fame or profit. Unfortunately his intentions were clouded by an irrational miso-Islamism – especially exemplified by Ayaan Hirsi Ali – that prevented him from engaging the broader Muslim community in meaningful discourse. It is ironic that the immense freedom within Dutch society was not taken advantage of by Van Gogh and the Muslim community to engage in a self-critical and inter-subjective discourse with the other, as the Netherlands is particularity unique in providing a venue for such a discourse. In this sense, the freedoms he wished to defend were sorely underutilized.

Yet, on the other side, the disrespect that Muslims felt when viewing the movie *Submission* was authentic and painful, and it did not contribute to future reconciliation between differing communities. For the Muslims, this attack on what they held most sacred was a rejection of them as a people; a denunciation of their core values; and was done in complete disregard for their sensibilities and out of ignorance of Islam's core values of social justice and ecumenism. Clearly, in democratic societies, such offensive language is tolerated and even promoted in some ways, but for the majority of the Muslims, it was the height of *disrespect*, the opposite of *recognition* – the basis from which dialogue can occur.[75] For many Muslims, Van Gogh's movie was a poignant example of secular extremism and had to be rejected and fought against, as nothing seemed sacred to it. Likewise, the majority of the Muslim community also rejected the murderous nature of Bouyeri's religious extremism; it was a *transvaluation of Islamic values* that could not be justified via the Qur'an and Sunnah. For the believers, it is a radical distortion of the character of Muhammad to say he was a terrorist, violent, and misogynist, as the 2005 Danish cartoons of *Jyllands-Posten* depicted him.[76] Although Bouyeri's murder of Van Gogh did nothing to legitimate the claim, many Muslims in the Netherlands, seemingly to no avail, continued to maintain that Islam was a religion of peace, just as Prophet Muhammad himself was a man of peace. As many Muslims proclaimed, whether it be a Muslim or a non-Muslim that distorts the image of the Prophet to justify their own purposes, it is the responsibility of the Muslims, and especially Islamic authorities, to denounce and teach against it, but not to murder the critical voice, as that only legitimates their bigotry. It furthermore suppresses that which could be a legitimate critique of Islam and the Muslim community.[77] Many Muslim scholars, including the Turkish Imam Bediüzzaman Said Nursi (1887–1960), believe that violence in the name of Islam demonstrates not the perpetrators sincere belief, but their lack of belief; because their faith in Islam is weak, they tacitly believe it is incapable of defending itself with its own theological, moral, and philosophical resources. When it is attacked, the Muslim of weak faith feels the need to extinguish the attacking voice as the dissent threatens their faith. For Nursi, strong faith fears no critique, but rather welcomes it. It is not authoritarian, but is open to opposing voices. In this way, Bouyeri should not be viewed as a champion of Islam, but a misguided Muslim who killed for what he did not truly believe in.

Je ne suis pas Charlie et je ne suis pas avec les terroristes[78]

In Europe, France is the nation where the extremes of secularism arrive at their clearest apex, where secular culture and secular politics converge most

---

75   Axel Honneth, *Disrespect: The Normative Foundations of Critical Theory*. Malden, MA: Polity Press, 2007.

76   Klausen, Jytte. *The Cartoons that Shook the World*. New Haven: Yale University Press, 2009.

77   It is clear from both Islam and Islamic history that Muslims are not above critique; the Prophet often told his followers that to "help their brother" when he is doing wrong is to stop him from doing wrong. Critique then is an integral part of becoming a more faithful Muslim.

78   "I am not Charlie and I am not with the Terrorists."

forcefully. It also has the highest percentage of Muslims per capita in Europe. Being mainly from former North and West African colonies of the French Empire, Muslims now make up nearly 10% of the overall French population. A majority of Muslims reside in impoverished neighborhoods on the outskirts of the major cities (*banlieue*) and constitute an overwhelming majority of the inmates in French prisons. French secularity, while often being a haven for refugees and immigrants, has failed to adequately integrate the sons and daughters of those refugees and immigrants.[79] Exacerbated by the systemic poverty of their French ghettos, so many young Muslims have been left in cultural-limbo, not knowing where they belong – the religious world of Islam or the secular European culture of France. It is no wonder then it is also the country in Europe where the antagonism between religion and secularity is at its deepest. The reality of this situation was painfully neglected until it came to ahead in the first days of 2015.

In the face of the terroristic attacks on the "satirical newspaper" *Charlie Hebdo* on January 7th, 2015, in which twelve people in total were killed, including a Muslim police officer, many Parisians took to the streets with signs reading "Je suis Charlie" (I am Charlie). Expressing their solidarity with the victims of the terrorists of al-Qae'da in the Arabian Penninsula (AQAP), Saïd and Chérif Kouachi, and the ISIS inspired Amedi Coulibaly and Hayat Boumeddiene, the French symbolically made their nation synonymous with the racist, Islamophobic, and anti-religious bigotry of *Charlie Hebdo*, a small magazine that often derided and mocked religious groups, especially Muslims, Catholics and Jews. Consequently, many French Muslims, who also wanted to express their solidarity with the victims and affirm their belief in free speech, could not join their fellow citizens in exclaiming "Je suis Charlie," as they could not endorse *Charlie Hebdo*'s ridicule of sacred religious figures such as Muhammad, Jesus, the Trinity, etc. In a time when a traumatized society wanted to lionize the martyrs of "free speech," despite the fact that their satirical "journalism" was devoid of intellectual seriousness, but served only to enflame the antagonism between ethnic and religious communities, the false choice of making one group of people ethically pure and the other an absolute evil had to be rejected. And so many Muslims who were appalled by the murder of the *Charlie Hebdo* workers stayed home and did not join their fellow French in their rallies for the magazine.

---

79   Robert S. Leiken, *Europe's Angry Muslims: The Revolt of the Second Generation* (New York: Oxford University Press, 2012), 3–58; Emmanuel Todd, *Who is Charlie? Xenophobia and the New Middle Class,* trans. Andrew Brown (Malden, MA: Polity Press, 2015), 15–49.

It is of course ethically defensible to affirm the right to free speech without affirming the bigotry of a particular publication, and so many did so by criticizing the *content* of *Charlie Hebdo* while simultaneously respecting the *right* of the magazine to publish whatever it sees fit to publish. However, in the midst of national grief, those rational and ecumenical voices remained painfully muted. In addition, the right of the citizens (not all of whom were Muslims) to be offended by the bigotry of *Charlie Hebdo* had also to be respected, while at the same time they wished to criticize and reject the turn to violent terrorism in response to such Islamophobic bigotry.

Yet, from the perspective of Islamic inner-criticism and inner-reflexivity, instead of critically examining where the believers themselves "mock" the prophet by their own questionable actions in their daily life, which is a much more offensive in the Islamic view, they chose rather to focus their attention on those outside the faith who mock the prophet – seeking to pull the speck out of the other's eye before they pulled the beam out of their own. The degree to which the Muslim fundamentalists refuse to self-critically analyze their own failure ultimately impedes the ummah from pulling itself out of the ditch of history. This is not to exonerate the West for its destructive dealings within the Muslim world, but to exclusively lay blame at the feet of the West when the ummah itself suffers immensely from self-inflicted wounds must be taken into account. From a traditional Islamic position, attacks on Islam and Muslims initiated self-reflectiveness and inner-critique, which can give birth to better answers to the problems at hand. As Tariq Ramadan once publically argued, without such a radical reflection on those self-inflicted wounds, the Muslims will continue to be colonized (or neo-colonized) because they continue to be colonizable.

Unfortunately, instead of examining the real cause of the terrorist attack, i.e. the provocative *content* of *Charlie Hebdo*'s derisive cartoons within the context of a marginalized Muslim community, the dominant narrative became one about the *right* of free speech, which, like in the Murder of Theo van Gogh, was never really in question. From the statements of the attackers, *Charlie Hebdo* was not attacked because its authors bore the right to blaspheme; it was because of the blasphemous content of what they chose to publish. The terrorists that murdered the cartoonists and others also bore that same right to free speech and they did not attack themselves or others for having it. Additionally, some remembered that according to French laws, free speech is not an absolute right, as there are many reasons why speech in France is eclipsed or can end in prosecution, including the vocal or written support for terrorism. France is also one of many Western European countries that severely restrict the right of its citizens to deny the Holocaust. Passed in July of 1990, the *Gayssot Act*, also known as the *Law No. 90-615, to repress acts of racism, anti-Semitism and*

xenophobia, administers severe penalties for those who question the historical reality of the Holocaust.[80] Those who do so may be imprisoned up to five
years. The point here should not be missed; it is not that the Holocaust/Shoah
did not occur, for surely it did, or that the memory of the murdered Jews have a
protected status in Europe, as they do (and should), but rather that French society has a breaking point in terms of what can be said and what cannot, what
can be published and what cannot. If this breakpoint is transgressed, the French
state is willing to deprive the transgressor with up to five years of their lives.
In other words, they are willing to take action against those who they disagree with
simply because they write something outside of the accepted norm or dominant narrative. But this is not the case for those who mock the Prophet or Islam.
They are not protected in the same way. For many, this duplicity is hypocritical.

Unfortunately, this "breaking point" is too close to the logic of the terrorists
who attacked *Charlie Hebdo*; they too had their breaking point and were ready
to take action against those whom they disagreed and mocked the memory
of the Prophet, although, unlike the state, they do not possess access to the
legitimate "monopoly of violence" (*Gewaltmonopol des Staates*). France was
willing to take the issue of the Holocaust out of the public arena by passing the
Gayssot Act, so that the memory of the victims of fascism could not be mocked
by pseudo-scholarship. Although the Gayssot Act was meant to diminish the
possibility of 'racism, anti-Semitism, and xenophobia,' it failed to regulate the
mockingly crude material emanating from *Charlie Hebdo* that increasingly
heightened racist and xenophobic sentiments and actions.[81] Unfortunately,
and despite the law being able to remedy this, the insensitivity towards the
religious sensibilities of the French Muslim community led to tragedy. Where
once in the West satire was used to mock the powerful, in this case satire was
used as a weapon of derision against the most maligned and vulnerable segment of the French population, the Muslims, who are mainly of North African
descent – the sons and daughters of the formerly colonized.

The January of 2015, terrorists were willing to seek revenge for those who
they believed mocked the most sacred symbol of Islam: Muhammad – a man
whose honor millions are ready to defend, albeit in a variety of ways. As there

---

80   See the story of Robert Faurisson, a Holocaust-denier/academic who was prosecuted un-
      der the Gayssot Act in 1991. He was later (2012) given an award for "courage" by Mahmoud
      Ahmadinejad, then president of the Islamic Republic of Iran. Ahmadinejad cited his fight
      against censorship as proof that Europe does not have true "freedom of speech."

81   The issue of anti-Semitism in *Charlie Hebdo* has a history. In a couple different instances,
      the accusation that they were engaged in anti-Semitism resulted in the firing of individu-
      al employees. The magazine was sensitive towards these particular accusations. However,
      the idea that it was "Islamophobic" – because Islamophobism is swiftly become normal-
      ized in Europe – was of no concern for the editors.

was no discourse between the *Charlie Hebdo* community, who saw no compelling reason to "reason" with people they thought to be backwards and worthy of derision, and certain Muslims saw no reason to "reason" with those who disrespected their religion, a violent conflict was inevitable. Because the gulf that separates the two positions couldn't find a common point of agreement, violence was not limited to Paris. Despite the attempts of the President Francois Hollande to disassociate Islam from terrorism, reprisal attacks on Muslims and mosques occurred throughout the French Republic. 'Next time it will be one of your heads' read a note left with a pig's head on an Islamic prayer center in Corsica, as grenades and bullets flew at mosques and Muslim establishments.[82] Had Kant's *categorical imperative* been operative – which universalizes the acts of the particular – and therefore the Gayssot Act's ban on inciting xenophobia and racism had been extended to encompass the woeful provocation of Muslims, as it was extended to the memory of the deceased Jewish community, this form of violence may not have found enthusiastic support in Europe. However, because mutual-respect and mutual-perspective taking did not occur, the possibility of a peaceful rapprochment remained elusive.

From the very roots of the Bourgeois revolution, which established the political right of free speech of the individual in the West, no individual should be murdered due to their ideas regardless of how controversial and bigoted they are. No individual should be forced to shutter in fear because they voice opinions that are heterodox or heretical, as even once the bourgeois' political philosophy was criminal in the eyes of the feudal lords. In this sense, the murder of the *Charlie Hebdo* workers was not only a legal crime but also a crime against the values rooted within the Enlightenment itself. It was an attack on the West's civil "sacred symbol," its political and social freedom. However, post-event, the well-meaning French population claiming to be *Charlie Hebdo* overtly identified themselves with the most lowbrow forms of "journalistic" terrorism – the most vigorous forms of hates speech that emanated from the magazine of mockery and derision. They too have betrayed the values of the Enlightenment when adopting the phrase "Je suis Charlie," as if the revolutionary qualities of the French Republic can be reduced down to crude and xenophobic characters of many of its own citizens. Such mockery of a marginalized population only serves the purpose of dividing the Republic. In a time when political, religious, and ethnic reconciliation is desperately needed, as the post-secular conditions can either devolve into inter-community violence or create inter-community cooperation, the lampooning of a group of

---

82   Max Fisher, "This Map Shows Every Attack on French Muslims since Charlie Hebdo," January 10, 2015. http://www.vox.com/2015/1/10/7524731/french-muslims-attacks-charlie-hebdo.

people's most sacred symbols – Muhammad – only widens the gulf between non-Muslim and Muslim French and thus creates more distrust, suspicion, and gentrification in an already fractured and mutually-suspicious society. Additionally, if France and other western nations want to defeat Islamic extremism, it can only do so with the help of the Muslim community within the West. However, the West cannot expect to receive that assistance if powerful voices perpetually mock the deeply held beliefs of those it needs. As Habermas has pointed out, 'the basis of recognition is not esteem for this or that quality or achievement, but an awareness of belonging to an inclusive community of citizens with equal right in which each is accountable to everybody else for her political utterances and actions.'[83] "Je suis Charlie" is a small but powerful symbol of that continual mockery; it is an absence of *recognition* and an edifice of *disrespect*, which fails to recognize the inclusive community of equal citizens bearing equal rights.

Yet mockery has become the sign of an "enlightened" civilization that is moving into its retirement. As the British poet William Butler Yeats once wrote,

> Come let us mock at the great
> That had such burdens on the mind
> And toiled so hard and late
> To leave some monument behind,
> Nor thought of the levelling wind.
>
> Come let us mock at the wise;
> With all those calendars whereon
> They fixed old aching eyes,
> They never saw how seasons run,
> And now but gape at the sun.
>
> Come let us mock at the good
> That fancied goodness might be gay,
> And sick of solitude
> Might proclaim a holiday:
> Wind shrieked – and where are they?
>
> Mock mockers after that
> That would not lift a hand maybe
> To help good, wise or great

---

83   Habermas, *Europe*, 69.

> To bar that foul storm out, for we
> Traffic in mockery.[84]

We should bear in mind that after the terrorist attack, *Charlie Hebdo* could have portrayed Muhammad, Islam, and the Muslim community based on the actions of Ahmed Merabat, the Muslim police officer who was killed by the Paris terrorists, or by Lassana Bathily, the Parisian-Malian Muslim who saved the shoppers in the Kosher supermarket, but instead they chose to lampoon Muhammad through the lenses of terrorists, who represent a small fraction of the Muslim community.[85] Furthermore, those same terrorists attack Muslims in far greater numbers than they do non-Muslims. In the weeks just prior to the attack in Paris, Boko Haram, a Nigerian 'Islamist' terror group massacred approximately 2,000 Muslims in Baga, Nigeria; 61 Muslims were murdered in Yemen by al-Qae'da, and the Taliban executed 164 Muslim school children in their classrooms. Do these Muslims, who are also innocent victims of religious fanaticism, deserve to have their most sacred symbol comedically vandalized for the entertainment of those who live in relative peace and prosperity, who do not know what it is like to live without security, where religion is the only force that gives meaning and solace to one's endangered life?

In addition, the principle of political equality, also rooted in the Enlightenment, has been questioned by the French version of secularity: *laïcité*.

---

84   I have to thank Shaykh Hamza Yusuf of Zaytuna College for bringing this poignant poem to light during this time of crisis in the French society.

85   After the January attack in Paris, Lassana Bathily, the French-Malian Muslim man, who saved the lives of many Jewish customers in the Hyper Cacher (Kosher) supermarket by hiding them in the freezer, was hailed by many as a hero. However, *Charlie Hebdo* acknowledged his actions, which represented the ecumenical spirit of his Islamic faith, by again mocking the Prophet Muhammad in their next edition. Additionally, one of the three French police officers that were killed during the three-day ordeal was also a Muslim, Ahmed Merabat. Despite his heroism, *Charlie Hebdo* also mocked his faith. This has an additional effect: too often the dominant narrative *chooses* to define Islam by the actions of its misguided followers and not by those believers who embody Islam's ecumenical and merciful *geist* as displayed by these two men. When after the attempted assassination of the cartoonist Lars Vilks in February, 2015 in Copenhagen, Denmark, which was followed up by an attack on a Jewish synagogue, more than one thousand Muslims in Oslo stood shoulder to shoulder and created a 'protective human ring' around the Jewish center, shouting 'no to anti-Semitism, no to Islamophobia.' Unfortunately, this meaningful gesture of inter-religious solidarity garnished no major media coverage in the United States. Episodes like this, which can counter the prevailing stereotypes regarding the faith of Muslims, are routinely ignored, downplayed or dismissed. Again, its miscreants and not its most devout believers too often define Islam.

Although it presupposes the separation of church and state, this form of secularity extends the role of the government in civil society even further; it tasks
the government with protecting its citizenry from the influence of religion.[86]
This ideal takes on a particular object: Islam. In doing so, it restricts the freedom of religion of Muslims in France, as it sociologically and psychologically denies the legitimacy of their citizenship due to their religious identity, if
not legally. In other words, in an attempt to rescue secularity from the threat
of religion, it eclipses the right of expression of its own religious citizens. In
the private sphere all forms of religion are allowed. But in the public sphere,
citizens must submit around secular ideals, values, and identities – outward
traces of religion have to be thoroughly regulated if not abolished in certain
areas. As such, since 2004, headscarves, i.e. hijabs and other forms of religious
head-coverings, have been banned in government-operated facilities, including public schools.[87] In 2010, France enacted *Loi interdisant la dissimulation du
visage dans l'espace public* (Act prohibiting concealment of the face in public
space), which bans all Muslim women from wearing the *niqab,* the face-veil
that leaves only the eyes exposed. As there was estimated to be less than a
thousand Muslim women throughout the whole of France that wore the niqab,
this act was widely regarded as a form of discrimination against the religious
rights of French Muslim women to live their faith in public.[88] In the name of
secularity and security, France chose to selectively diminish the free right of
expression. Those claiming to defend secularity from religion do not woefully
ignore equality in matters of individual rights, i.e. "free speech" and "freedom
of expression." However, in the name of such secularity they mutilate the secular value of the government's neutrality in matters of religion. In this way, the
right of free speech is made nearly absolute for those who use it to antagonize
religious communities, to defame all that is still sacred in this secular world
and to unnecessarily widen the growing gap between religious voices and their
secular counterparts. While at the same time those who wish to be modest,
express their deeply held religious beliefs while still being an integral entity
in French society, to utilize their equal rights, and who have no sympathies for
terrorists, are forced to accept that their right to express themselves is worth

---

86   John R. Bowen, *Why the French Don't Like Headscarves: Islam, the State, and Public Space*
      (Princeton, NJ: Princeton University Press, 2007), 11–33.

87   In 2004, the United States Commission on International Religious Freedom issued criti-
      cal remarks regarding this law, believing it would be in fundamental disagreement with
      France's human rights commitments.

88   This law was condemned by Amnesty International and widely criticized in Europe, the
      Americas, and in International governing bodies as being inherently discriminatory to-
      wards Muslims.

less that the right of the cartoonist. In modern France, an infintile cartoonist has more rights than a religious citizen.

However, the often cited issue concerning whether or not an image of the Prophet can be drawn, painted, etc., is missing the point. Following a similar *bilderverbot* (image ban) of the Jews, images of Allah are expressly forbidden in Islam and have never been produced in Islamic history. However, Muslims have drawn images of the Prophet for centuries, and in some Muslims countries, especially those that are dominated by the Shi'a, one can still find images of the Prophet and other members of his family. Some of the most famous of depiction of Muhammad came from the Mongol and Ottoman Empires, albeit with Muhammad's face obscured behind a veil. However, most Islamic scholars believe the practice of depicting Muhammad to be misguided and a violation of Islamic law, even if these images were created out of devotion to – but not worship of – the Prophet. These are essentially devotional objects that are created out of the deepest reverence for the Prophet, and as such are generally uncontroversial (even if not recommended). Most Muslims prefer not to have them but will not react violently to seeing them. If they wish to "see" *Shamā'il Muhammadiyyah* (Muhammad's appearance), it must come through the "mind's eye." Rooted in the physical and spiritual description of Muhammad found within various *hadīth*, the *hilya* is an Ottoman form of literature and art that describes the Prophet through Arabic calligraphy without graphically depicting him through an image. The most famous hilya is the one narrated by Muhammad's cousin, 'Ali ibn Abū Ṭālib. It states,

> He was not too tall nor was he too short. He was of medium build. His hair was neither short nor curly, nor was it straight but somewhere in between. His face was not narrow, nor was it really round, but it had some roundness in it. His skin was white. His eyes were black. He had long eyelashes. He had a big frame and had broad shoulders. He had no body hair except on his chest. He had large hands and feet. When he walked, he walked at an angle, as if descending a slope. When he looked at someone, he looked at them directly in their face. Between his shoulders was the seal of prophecy, the sign that he was the last prophet. He was the most giving of men, the most truthful, the most mild-tempered, and the noblest of men in lineage. Whoever unexpectedly saw him was in awe. And whoever knew him intimately loved him. Anyone who ever described him would say, 'I never saw, before him or after him, the like of him.' Peace be upon him.[89]

---

89   My translation.

For the majority of Muslims, this linguistic depiction of Muhammad has sufficed to satisfy their curiosity concerning his appearance. So why is this important for *Charlie Hebdo*?

The satirical magazine's depiction of the Prophet is not done out of reverence, but out of derision. It is not a misguided form of devotion, but an attempt
to mock, dishonor and ridicule the sacred in Islam. The intention of the creator
of the image is the deciding factor as to whether the image is a misguided attempt at devotion or a mean-spirited attempt to provoke religious sentiments
by slandering the sacred. It was this form of free speech that Pope Francis
spoke about when he said, 'You cannot provoke. You cannot insult the faith of
others. You cannot make fun of the faith of others. There is a limit.'[90] Although
many rejected the Pope's appeal for respect of religious beliefs, believing that
he underhandedly legitimated the attack on *Charlie Hebdo* – which he actually condemned but gave an explanation why religious people would attack –
his comments betray his clear understanding of the post-secular conditions
of Europe. Through his speeches, actions, and discourses, he had shed light
on a very real phenomenon; there are two forms of being that are occupying
the same space: one secular and one religious.[91] There is no option other than
coexistence at this time, and that must be mediated through forms of *mutual
perspective taking*. Both *Charlie Hebdo* and the terrorist attack against it contribute to the retreat into pure identity, and as Adorno warned in his *Negative
Dialectics*, pure identity is pure death, as it allows for nothing outside of the
totalizing concept.

As religion is fully privatized in the French Republic, it can play no meaningful role in the national will formation, i.e. it rarely gets a public platform
by which it can express itself. However, the secular citizens right to free expression is not eclipsed, thus the secular atheist and libertarian persuasion
of *Charlie Hebdo* was free to "blaspheme" without legal repercussions, while
young Muslim girls are excluded from public education because they wish to
express their religiosity (and modesty) by wearing a *ḥijāb* to school. As such,
witnessing and professing a religion in the public is limited, while blasphem-
ing and provoking are protected speech. These laws, and many other regulations to curb the influence of Islam in France, have only increased the Muslims
community's alienation from mainstream French society. They are often left
feeling unwelcome in their own country – a country that they often adopted

---

90   BBC News Europe, "Paris Attack: Pope Francis Say Freedom of Speech has Limits," January
      15, 2015. http://www.bbc.com/news/world-europe-30835625 (Accessed 1/15/2015).

91   We do have to bear in mind that not all Muslims are religious and that not all westerners
      are secular. However, in general this distinction holds some weight.

by choice. Without any legitimate avenue to express one's identity, and achieve genuine recognition in doing so, the fundamental need for human recognition turns against itself and society; it becomes aggressive, demanding and often violent. Recognition through violence routinely comes through acts of terrorism. If one cannot feel respected in one's society, then one forces respect – or at least recognition – through the act of destruction. It is no wonder that terrorism has recently taken on the aura of "spectacle"; with the mass media's 24 hour news cycle, where every aspect of the terrorists' life and ideology are analyzed, where the apocalyptic feel of a rather small and unimportant event is manufactured and augmented by dramatic and ominous light and sound productions within news studios, the terrorists receives precisely what they're denied in life: recognition.

The growing tension between the Muslim and non-Muslim French population bolsters the claims of al-Qae'da and ISIS, who peddle the narrative that the West is fundamentally anti-Islam; even when Muslims integrate into western society, they are still unwelcome because of their faith, they say. *Fitnah* (divisions) within the European community – especially between Muslims and non-Muslims – plays into the hands of those who are the purveyors of "civilizational" conflict, both in Europe and in the *dar al-Islam*. Because *Charlie Hebdo* chose to print another cartoon of Muhammad less than a week after the January 7th Paris attacks, demonstrations and riots throughout the Muslim world were launched. Disgusted with the publication's unrelenting attack on the most sacred figure in Islam, which further diminished the potential for reconciliation and unity against post-secular barbarity, many of the protesters held signs saying, 'You are Charlie, I am Muhammad.'[92] For the radical clerics and Islamists who wish to further the hatred between communities, *Charlie Hebdo* had become their most effective publication, more effective than al-Qae'da's *Inspire* magazine and ISIS's *Dabiq*.

However, all did not join in the manufactured consent; many critical Europeans were uneasy with the phrase "Je suis Charlie," as they were already aware that *Charlie Hebdo* was a publication that echoed a questionable history. Albeit satirically, *Charlie Hebdo's* mockery of the Muslims resembled the Nazi newspaper *Der Stürmer*, the anti-Semitic publication produced by the rapacious Nazi Julius Streicher, whose love for the Fuhrer was only eclipsed by his

---

92   Simon Tomlinson, "#noapology: Muslims stage angry protests over Charlie Hebdo's Mohammed cartoon as Boko Haram terror leader hails Paris massacre," January 14, 2015. http://www.dailymail.co.uk/news/article-2910126/Muslims-stage-angry-protests-Charlie -Hebdo-s-Mohammed-cartoon-Boko-Haram-terror-leader-hails-Paris-massacre.html #ixzz3OpojSdsC (Accessed 1/14/2015).

hatred for the Jews.[93] Cartoons of the Jews were often depicted as being greedy, untrustworthy, genetically poisonous, destructive to German culture, and under the suspicion of blood libel. As was the method of *Der Stürmer, Charlie Hebdo* constantly published the most crude and stereotypical depictions of Muslims, ones that prepare the conditions for systemic bigotry, prejudices, and discrimination, as they helped cement all stereotypes about the "backwardness" of Muslims. As stated before, they "satirically" attacked the most marginalized and vulnerable segment of the French population, one that had very little political and social power to defend itself. This controversial but lucrative *modus operandi* increased after the magazine began to go bankrupt in late 2014. Inciting scorn and mockery of Muslims and their religious beliefs was a profit generating activity for the magazine. Unfortunately, it contributed to the growing normalization of Islamophobia in the French public sphere. As history shows us, such mockery and derision is the precondition for hatred, especially when it is already coupled with pervasive suspicion of the "other." As such, Islamophobia is the necessary precondition for miso-Islamism – the pathological *hatred* for Islam and Muslims.

As the far-right continues to gain popularity among the populace, these terrorist counterattacks against secular French society likewise prepares the conditions for the mainstreaming of the once marginal anti-immigrant right, especially the French *National Front* led by Marine Le Pen, the daughter of Jean-Marie Le Pen, a neo-fascist politician who made his career by taking an ultra-conservative stance against immigration, the European Union, and other *kulturkampf* issues. Those who would be at the forefront of a new conflagration between Muslims and the West have much to gain politically by the continual polarization of French society, as their poll numbers continue to rise as social strains become worse. Ironically, *Charlie Hebdo* was published by a group of people who identify themselves as left-leaning atheists, who frequently attacked the French *National Front* party, but their work helped solidify the miso-Islamism of the political right wing in France. Unfortunately, as many French move farther to the right, following a general trend throughout Europe, they run the risk of cementing the view among the Muslim population, including their own, that France had taken the lead, not against terrorism, but against Islam itself.

---

93   Julius Streicher was later tried and executed at the Nuremberg Trials. I do not claim that *Charlie Hebdo* advocated the extermination of Muslims or other crimes against Muslims that *Der Stürmer* did against the Jews, only that it contributes to the stereotyping of a minority community.

It would be a misreading of *Charlie Hebdo* to think it was only critical of "Islamic terrorism"; it was not. It was staunchly against Islam itself (as well as many other religions), but did so behind the disarming veil of crude humor. Multiculturalism, despite all its failures in Europe, is its current reality, and this context should not be forgotten when discussing the issue of "free speech." The last time the conditions were created by which the pluralism of Europe was challenged led to genocide, the likes of which had not been experienced before in western history. If European society wishes to forestall any possibility of returning to the barbarity of the Second World War, in which many French died to preserve the freedoms established by the Enlightenment, including French-Algerian Muslims, they cannot so willfully identify with the new form of anti-Semitism: miso-Islamism.

Despite all the misguided attempts to show solidarity, there was one extremely meaningful gesture to come out of the aftermath of the attacks. Led by the French socialist President Francois Hollande, who also ordered the French attack against al-Qae'da in the Maghrib in 2013, the "unity" rally of January 11, 2015 demonstrated to the world that France, in all its diversity, would stand as one people against those who chose to attack it through violent means. Although walking behind Francois Hollande were many other world leaders, some of whom are also responsible for heinous crimes perpetrated by the states under their control, the people's show of unity in the face of terrorism was an important expression of national solidarity, even if it was incomplete.[94] This is precisely because the masses at the rally were comprised not only of native and/or ethnic French (*Français de souche*), but they were also Muslims, both French citizens and not, from all over the world. No doubt those particular Muslims did not agree with the content of *Charlie Hebdo's* publication, but nevertheless they refused to allow their religious beliefs to be reinterpreted through the lenses of al-Qae'da and ISIS terror. The most devout of French

---

94 The fact that many of the Presidents and Prime Ministers who were in Paris for this rally were themselves perpetrators of violence, demonstrates the very hypocrisy of countries that is so often pointed out by jihadists. While individual and group terrorism, such as that perpetrated against Charlie Hebdo, are universally condemned, the terrorism perpetrated by states, such as by Israel, is tolerated and their representatives are honored guests of the state. The presence of Benjamin Netanyahu, whose 2014 "Operation Protective Edge" killed over 2,200 Palestinians (around 70% of which were civilians according to the U.N.), forced many French Muslims to stay home from the rally. They could not bring themselves to rally alongside someone who denies the fundamental right of existence to Palestinian men, women and children. Even Petro Poroshenko, the Ukrainian President who ordered the attacks on hundreds of thousands of innocent ethnic Russians in eastern Ukraine in 2014, joined the "unity" rally against terrorism.

Muslims stood with their fellow secular French citizens in a display of inter-religious, inter-denominational, inter-national, inter-ethnic, and inter-cultural unity. If from this historical tragedy can come forth a meaningful and lasting national will, united against barbarity, which values the beliefs of all its citizens, is yet to be determined. However, what was demonstrated most clearly through the rally is the revolutionary potential for the secular state if and when religions can find a meaningful place within the equal tapestry of voices. In other words, the unity rally briefly demonstrated to the world what is possible if the conditions of post-secularity are acknowledged and if the citizens are allowed to freely express themselves equally (both religious and secular) but within the framework of mutual-respect. It may be the case that the attack on *Charlie Hebdo* increases the awareness of Islamophobia's systemic violence experienced by French Muslims, and that the sensitivity towards the plight and predicament of Muslims living in a post-secular society comes to the forefront of the discussion. By embracing French Muslims as being an integral part of modern French culture and society, as the German Chancellor Angela Merkel did when she boldly stated, 'Islam belongs to Germany,' the French may be able to undermine the intellectual and spiritual drift towards religious extremism that Islamophobia inevitably creates. It was also an encouraging sign that there was a clear attempt by many left-wing and liberal voices warning against "amalgame" – or the conflation of the Muslim community entire with the actions of the few terrorists, nor were the personalities that usually peddle the inflammatory and Islamophobic line, such as philosopher Alain Finkielkraut and writer Eric Zemmour, allowed a public voice – a form of national self-censorship post-hoc, or "repressive tolerance" as theorized by Herbert Marcuse. What is clear is that the problems of post-secularity, of which modern terrorism is a symptom, cannot be repaired through the dogmatization of old and defunct forms of secularity. France today has an old form of secularity (*la-ïcité*) imposed upon the new reality of post-secularity, and no true solutions will come unless this is understood and worked through in a truly democratic and inclusive manner. This must include the free expression – the witnessing and professing – of one's faith, just as much as it must include the critique of the faith that is witnessed and confessed. Both blasphemy and public expression of religion are vital components in the post-secular condition.[95]

Yet the prognosis in Europe – and the West in general – is grim.[96] At the moment there may not be an adequate resolution to the problems of post-secular

---

95   Habermas, *Europe*, 66–70.

96   Since the attacks on *Charlie Hebdo* and the 13 November 2015 attacks on Paris in general, physical violence and discrimination against Muslims in the United States has risen

multiculturalism within the West today, especially in Europe where the Muslim community has a much harder time to integrate than in the United States and Canada. On the contrary, I expect relations between Muslims and Europeans to grow worse within the coming years due to (1) the social-political pressures felt by the European states to curb mass immigration, (2) the increasing alienation Muslims feel in secular, and seemingly anti-Islamic, Europe, and (3) the potential polarization that can be initiated through acts of terror, such as the attack on *Charlie Hebdo*, the "Je suis Charlie" aftermath, and the 13 November 2015 attacks on Paris by ISIS. However, there are invaluable historic episodes of Muslims and Christians peacefully breaking bread together that may serve as a template for a different future. As we'll see, the highly improbable encounter between a Christian saint and an Enlightened Muslim ruler amidst the vicious violence of the Crusades makes clear that discourse between the Muslims and westerners is not impossible, but requires and immense amount of bravery, fortitude, and a commitment to peaceful living together through mutual-recognition and respect.

---

sharply, culminating in the Presidential candidacy of Donald Trump, who has repeatedly stoked the fire of Islamophobia in the American electorate. Trump has publically called for a ban on Muslims coming into the United States, greater monitoring of Muslim communities, mosques and gatherings. He made headlines again in March of 2016 by emphatically stating, 'Islam hates us.'

Finding a Common Language

In today's post-secular society, the struggle to find a common language by which peoples of Islamic faith and secular citizens of the West can enter into a discourse remains frustrated. The post-metaphysical language through which democratic deliberation realizes itself fails to penetrate the theologically saturated language of Islam. The de-legitimization of religious language, especially its appeal to, and rootedness in, divine revelation, bars language that is cemented in autonomous reason from interacting on an equal footing. However, if we look in the distant past, in an age where religious violence was much greater than it is today, when the antagonisms between Christendom and the *dar al-Islam* were at their zenith, we find not only potential for inter-religious discourse, but an unlikely and therefore powerful example of what inter-religious discourse can entail. Yet, we cannot be satisfied to triumphantly cite the example of the interactions of the Catholic St. Francis of Assisi and the Muslim Sultan Malik al-Kamil as if the example itself mysteriously provides a way for discourse between civilizations and cultures. We must ask, *what are the conditions under which such a fruitful discourse is made possible*. What did St. Francis of Assisi and the Sultan Malik al-Kamil share that served as the basis for their inter-faith discourse?

13th Century Witnessing: Saint Francis of Assisi and Sultan Malik al-Kamil

In light of the present condition, where western powers remain deaf to the Muslim world's concerns, and where fear of the "other" is a stronger impulse than the willingness to engage in a friendly discussion, we can look to the past in a future oriented remembrance of a historical event that occurred in the 13th century between a living Catholic saint and an enlightened Islamic ruler: the Italian St. Francis of Assisi and the Ayyubid Sultan and nephew of the famous Muslim Amir *Ṣalāḥ ad-Dīn Yūsuf ibn Ayyūb* (Saladin), Malik al-Kamil. The example that this encounter has provided is one that has been thoroughly neglected, systematically written out of history (by the church), and/or conveniently forgotten by those whose interest it was to forget the ecumenical nature of Christianity and Islam.[1] However, in our age, where the religious

---

1 Paul Moses, *The Saint and the Sultan: The Crusades, Islam, and Francis of Assisi's Mission of Peace* (New York: Doubleday, 2009), 197–217. Out of the numerous biographies of St. Francis

passion of one of the discourse partners (the West) has abated, and the other is still open for discussions but is leery about the sincerity of their partner, we need clear precedents of individuals of courage, individuals of moral clarity, and individuals of deep faith to engage in an intense and respectful discourse.

Although most of the history of the West and the Muslim world has been antagonistic, every now and then a small breakthrough occurs. In the year 1219 CE, in the midst of the Fifth Crusade, which was taking place in the northern Egyptian city of Damietta, Francis of Assisi arrived in the Crusader camp to preach the love and peace of God. However, he was resoundingly rejected by his co-religionists, who saw no use for Francis. They were motivated out of greed and lust for war, not the weakness of peace and prayer.[2] After pleading with the Crusader Cardinal for permission, Francis and his companion Illuminato eventually crossed the battle lines that separated the Crusaders from the Muslims and with the prayerfulness of a living saint, walked into the camp of the adversary.[3] One would assume that he'd be met with complete hostility considering that his fellow Christians had invaded Muslim lands and where slaughtering the inhabitants mercilessly; a practice that had been going one for over two hundred years when Saint Francis arrived in Egypt. Indeed, Francis himself witnessed some of the most appalling acts that harkened back to the trauma of his days as a young soldier: the Crusaders mutilated captured Muslim soldiers. According to his biographer, the Crusaders 'cut off the hapless Muslim's noses, lips and ears and then gouged out one of each man's eyes. Thus hideously mutilated, the victims were sent back to their own side.'[4] In light of such brutality, the behavior of the Muslim army was surprising to Francis and his companion. After a brief moment of suspicion, the soldiers of Islam (*mujahideen*) were most welcoming, hospitable, and eager to hear from what they surmised to be a holy man from Christendom.[5] Without shrinking away from his Christian faith, Francis explained to the Muslim soldiers that he was a "follower of Jesus" and requested that he be taken to the Sultan.[6] This was an act of tremendous courage and faith, as the Sultan had been thoroughly demonized by the Christians authorities for years. In Europe, his image was one of systematic violence, a devilish Saracen, a living anti-Christ, who would

---

available, this one is the most comprehensive when discussing St. Francis' experience with the Sultan.

2   Augustine Thompson, *Francis of Assisi: A New Biography* (Ithaca: Cornell University Press, 2012), 67.

3   Moses, *The Saint and the Sultan*, 79–196; Thompson, *Francis of Assisi*, 68.

4   Spoto, *Reluctant Saint*, 158.

5   Ibid., 160.

6   Moses, *The Saint and the Sultan*, 128.

have to be defeated on the battlefield, not talked to in a tent. Up to that point, Francis had no reason to believe that the accusations weren't true, as he had already witnessed firsthand the devastating cost of war between the Christians and Muslims. However, he soon found this description of the Sultan to not only be misguided, but to be devoid of any truth, for the Sultan not only failed to exact revenge on this poor pilgrim, but had showered him with praise and brotherliness and showered him with quintessential Arab/Islamic hospitality. In doing so, the Sultan also ignored the advice of his advisors who encouraged the Sultan to decapitate Francis and Illuminato for attempted to convert them to Christianity.[7] But the Sultan recognized the sincerity of Francis and afforded him prophetic mercy and compassion, saying 'I will never condemn you to death – for that would indeed be an evil reward to bestow on you, who conscientiously risked death in order to save my life before God, as you believe.'[8] Additionally, what Francis may have not been aware of, and what the Sultan's advisors may have forgotten in their passion for war, is that: it is forbidden by the Qur'an for Muslims to attack clerics, monks, and other holy religious figures. Rather, Muslims are enjoined to respect them for their dedication to learning and faith. It says in the Qur'an, *sūrah* 5:82,

> Worst among men in hatred for the believers you will find Jews and Pagan; and those with the most love for the believers you will find those who say 'we are Christians': Because among them there are those dedicated to learning (priests and monks) and they are not arrogant.[9]

Indeed, it was Waraqa ibn Nawfal, the Christian monk and cousin of Khadīja, Muhammad's first wife, who embraced Muhammad as the long awaited Prophet who would descend from Abraham's oldest son Ishmael (*Ism'ail*). Muhammad's respect for holy men of the Abrahamic faiths would never leave him and he passed this on to his nascent followers. This stance would later be codified in Islamic law (*sharī'ah*).

Not only was the Sultan familiar with the Christians living in the Muslim world and their theology, their devotion to Jesus' message of "loving your enemies" and the holiness of their saints, he was also a dedicated follower of Islam, which privileges the "learned" amongst the Christians, especially monks, with special admiration. Although the Muslims believe monks and priests (especially in their celibacy) have gone too far in what God has called his faithful

---

7   Spoto, *Reluctant Saint*, 161.

8   Ibid., 161.

9   My translation.

to do, they nevertheless appreciate the extensive devotion these monks maintain in their lives. On the day St. Francis arrived in Damietta to speak with the Sultan, the Muslims recognized Francis as being one of the "learned" among the Christians and no harm was done to him.[10] On the other hand, according to St. Francis' biographer, Paul Moses, Francis himself was especially moved by the dedication that the average Muslims had towards their faith and their God and wished to see the same kind of commitment in the Christian lands.[11]

Similar to the Islamic greeting of *As Salaam 'alaikum* (peace be upon you), Francis would have greeted the Sultan in the way he greeted everyone: 'May the Lord give you peace.'[12] Francis did not reserve this greeting only for Christians, nor only for those he believed were holy, but rather he sincerely wished that all would be given the peace of his lord, especially those Muslims whom he now wished to speak to. Again, according to Paul Moses, Francis' words and demeanor with the Sultan demonstrated his disagreement with the Pope's Crusade against the Muslims. Francis wished a *friendly-being-with* type of relationship with the followers of Muhammad, one that would be anchored in peaceful recognition and not Crusades and *jihāds*.[13] Although he first left Italy expecting and hoping for martyrdom, Francis later saw himself as "God's ambassador" of peace and not the ambassador of the very earthly Popes (Innocent III and Honorius III) who initiated and advanced the hostilities against the Muslims in Egypt and other parts of the Muslim world.[14] The Sultan was impressed by Francis' sincerity, even when Francis was explaining to the Sultan that if he were to die as a Muslim he would be lost to eternal damnation; the Sultan rightfully understood this not to be a threat, nor even a vengeful warning, but as an invitation to salvation by one who was genuinely concerned about the fate of the Sultan's soul. Despite his commitment to the Qur'anic injunction banning violence against innocents, there was nothing in the political-military context that surrounded the Sultan that would have stopped him from murdering the one that just questioned the veracity of his faith, a faith that is very clear on the role (as prophet) and status (only a human) of Jesus. Nevertheless, the Sultan found the little ragged monk to be engaging, friendly, and committed to the

---

10   Certainly we can think of Francis as being "learned" in spiritual matters; indeed he was a master in this field. However, he was not a learned man in matters outside of the spiritual realm and was suspicious about his followers acquiring too much earthly knowledge.

11   Moses, *The Saint and the Sultan*, 130–155.

12   Ibid., 129.

13   Ibid., 130.

14   Ibid., 130.

one thing that was completely lacking among the Crusaders: *a commitment to peace through discourse, understanding, and respect.*

Amidst bloody battles, where thousands of Muslims and Christians were engaged in the most barbaric forms of butchery, the Sultan and the Saint broke bread and talked to each other about theology, morality, and *Adamic* fraternity.[15] Instead of inflaming the situation by verbally defacing the most cherished beliefs of the other, the two attempted to search for truth as brothers, as kindred spirits, as friends. The enmity that was displayed by the Pope against the Muslims, and the hatred for the barbaric Christians from Europe that spirited the tongues of many Muslim poets, ceased to drive the conversation between the two; theirs was a mission of peace and reconciliation. From the example of Francis the Sultan came to understand a substantive meaning of the *imitatio Christi* (imitation of Christ), as Francis would later be frequently called an *alter Christus* (other Christ). From the Sultan Francis learned that Islam wasn't a religion of violence, depravity, and hatred, but was a religion of spiritual reflection, intellectual curiosity, and sincere devotion to the creator. Via their open and honest discourse, by setting aside the preconceptions and totalizing conceptions that hindered the rest of their communities from looking upon the other without judgmental eyes, and from their courage to be with the "threatening" other, they came to understand each other and their religions, thus gifting later generations an example of the potential for peace that resides in an open, honest, and equal discourse.

But the real danger may not have been with the "other." Both Saint Francis and the Sultan risked offending their own peoples by talking to the enemy. Their contravening actions exposed themselves to the accusation of being a traitor to their communities and to their religions. Treason against one's religion, for both the Muslims and the Christians, at this time was viewed as a capital offense, yet both defied the possibility of death in the name of interreligious peace. The Muslims could have easily seen the Sultan's welcoming of the "Crusader monk" as an insult towards all the *mujahideen* who had been killed defending the *dar al-Islam* from Christian aggression, while those on the Christian side could have accused Francis of being a Judas to the holy cause and of consorting with the devil's Saracen. The threat of retaliatory violence against Francis, and therefore his achieving martyrdom at the hands of his

---

15   Both the Judeo-Christian and the Islamic traditions believe in a mono-Genesis, that all humans have descended from Adam and Eve, and thus all humans are connected as ancestors of the first humans created by the divine.

own fellow Catholics, was a risk he willfully undertook.[16] Francis understood the danger; he knew the Muslims could have killed him immediately or the less-enlightened Christians could have upon his return to the Crusader camp. His brave attempts to live the Gospel command to "love your enemies" and to be a "peacemaker" meant he must risk his life for his ideals. Although the possibility of violence against the Sultan from his own men was less than the risk Francis was subject to, it was nevertheless a real possibility for him as well. Any sense of weakness among the Sultan could have been cause for his removal; although the Qur'an instructs Muslims to obey they authority put over them, there is no "divine right" in the Islamic tradition and so the removal of a Sultan is not necessarily a direct act against God, but maybe one of historical necessity or ethical demand.[17]

The Saint and the Sultan engaged each other by witnessing to and professing their faith in a friendly discourse with the practical goal of ending the war (which would have been against the wishes of the Pope), and in doing so created a precedent for Christian-Muslim dialogue that has only recently been reinvigorated in light of the wars of the 20th and 21st century.[18] After days of penetrating discourse concerning the nature of religion, belief, reconciliation, and peace, both men returned to their respected camps, moved by the depth of faith of the other and with a new-found understanding of our common humanity and spiritual brotherliness.

As often happens when the fate of individuals of great spiritual and religious importance collide, the impact of this encounter with the Sultan wore on the mind of Francis for the rest of his life. According to Paul Moses, Francis was especially 'taken by the *adhan*,' the Islamic call to prayer, which is heard five times a day throughout the Muslim world.[19] After hearing it, devout Muslims pause their daily activities and direct their attention to their *rab* (Lord). Integrated within the everydayness of the lifeworld (*lebenswelt*) is religious

---

16 Although some have argued that Francis went to Egypt seeking martyrdom, Paul Moses' biography discounts that tradition based on literary evidence and Saint Francis' own words against intentionally seeking martyrdom. See Moses, *The Saint and the Sultan*, 162–163.

17 The Qur'an states in *Sūrat Al-Nisa*, (4:59): 'O believers, obey Allah and his messenger (Muhammad) and those who are in authority.' My translation.

18 Moses, *The Saint and the Sultan*, 218–242. It's interesting to ponder whether Francis understood clearly that he was engaged in an activity that contradicted the will of the Pope, especially considering that the Pope's will was understood to be identical with the will of the divine, being that the Pope was, and still is, believed to be the "Vicar of Christ" on earth. Was Francis the saint in opposition to Jesus' Vicar?

19 Ibid., 160.

devotion and the remembrance the divine, and for the purpose of beseeching the divine for peace, blessings, and mercy. According to many biographers of Francis, he may have even attempted to incorporate such a "herald" (*muezzin*) into his own community, which would call the faithful to prayer, as public and routine prayers would have been a great blessing for a society that had already drifted far away from their Christian ideals.[20] Later, in 1224, as the call for yet another Crusade emanated from Rome, in despair St. Francis retired to his mountain heritage in La Verna for forty days of fasting. During those days of spiritual and physical isolation, St. Francis received his first stigmata: the wounds of Christ. Was it out of grief and despair for the coming bloodbath that the wounds of his savior inflicted Francis? According to Roman Catholic Priest Michael Cusato, Professor of Franciscan Studies as St. Bonaventure University,

> Given the news [of Crusade preparations], I am convinced that Francis went with a few of his closest companions to the hermitage of La Verna profoundly discouraged, perhaps even depressed, over the events about to unfold. Once again, unable or unwilling to resolve human problems peacefully and fraternally through dialogue and mutual respect, the leaders of the Christian world were mobilizing their military might to engage in actions which would inexorably lead to yet more bloodshed and death. More personally still, Francis stood in danger of seeing the death of a man he had come to view as an *amicus* [friend] and, even more importantly, as his *frater* [brother]: someone he had come to know and apparently respect during that famous encounter with him under the tent of Damietta.[21]

After Francis received the stigmata, seemingly through *divina inspiratio* (divine inspiration) he penned a prayer that resembles the traditional Islamic meditation on the Ninety-Nine Names of God. Commonly known as the "parchment given to Brother Leo," He wrote,

> You are holy, Lord, the only God, You do wonders.
> You are strong, You are great, You are the most high,
> You are the almighty King.
> You, *Holy Father*, the King of *heaven and earth*.
> You are Three and One, Lord God of gods;
> You are good, all good, the highest good,

---

20   Spoto, *Reluctant Saint*, 156.

21   Michael Cusato, as quoted in Moses, *The Saint and the Sultan*, 180–181.

Lord, God, living and true.

You are love, charity.

You are wisdom; You are humility; You are patience;

You are beauty; You are meekness; You are security;

You are justice; You are moderation, You are all our riches

[You are enough for us]

You are beauty, You are meekness;

You are the protector,

You are our guardian and defender;

You are strength; You are refreshment.

You are our hope, You are our faith, You are our charity,

You are all our sweetness,

You are our eternal life:

Great and wonderful Lord,

God almighty, Merciful Savior.[22]

According to Father Cusato, after writing his Islamic-inspired prayer, St. Francis drew a picture of the Sultan underneath his favorite sign: the *tau* – signifying God's protection (Book of Ezekiel 9:4).[23] Francis' concern for the suffering of the finite individual in a world that despises weakness and glorifies strength, that resorts to violence before peaceful discourse is given an opportunity to be realized, extended to those whom Christendom considered to be less than deserving of mercy, compassion, and brotherly love: the Muslims. In an ecumenical way, his "Christ-like" love for others included the despised Muslims, who today, still look upon Francis as being the best (*ihsan*) of the Christian tradition.

In the later repressed *Earlier Rule*, written by Francis in 1221 CE, which was meant to guide his fledgling community in communal life – including a life of radical poverty – Francis used some "startling" language about the Muslims.[24] Chapter XVI of the *Earlier Rule*, entitled 'Those who are going among the Saracens and other nonbelievers,' states,

> The Lord says: *Behold, I am sending you as lambs in the midst of wolves.* 2. Therefore, be *prudent as serpents and simple as doves* (Mt 10:16). 3. Therefore, any brother who, by divine inspiration, desires to go among the Saracens and other nonbelievers should go with the permission of

---

22 St. Francis and St. Claire, *Francis and Claire: The Complete Works*, trans. Regis J. Armstrong and Ignatius C. Brady (New York: Paulist Press, 1982), 99–100.

23 Moses, *The Saint and the Sultan*, 184.

24 Ibid., 162.

his minister and servant. 4. And the minister should give permission and not oppose them, if he shall see that they are fit to be sent; for he shall be bound to give an account to the Lord (cf. Lk 16:2) if he has proceeded without discretion in this or in other matters. 5. As for the brothers who go, they can live spiritually among [them] in two ways. 6. One way is not to engage in arguments or disputes, but to *be subject* to every human creature for God's sake (1 Pet 2:13) and to acknowledge that they are Christians. 7. Another way is to proclaim the world of God when they see that it pleases the Lord, so that they believe in the all-powerful God – Father, and Son, and Holy Spirit – the Creator of all, in the Son who is the Redeemer and Savior, and that they be baptized and become Christians... 10. And all the brothers, wherever they may be, should remember that they gave themselves and abandoned their bodies to the Lord Jesus Christ. 11. And for love of Him, they must make themselves vulnerable to their enemies, both visible and invisible...[25]

Francis did not believe that provoking Muslims or offending their faith was a prudent way of gaining their trust and friendship. In fact, this type of behavior, displayed by some in his religious order, ended in their martyrdom and hardened the hearts of some Muslims. Additionally, Francis rejected the use of force against Muslims because (1) violence was against Jesus' message of peace and pacifism, and (2) it failed to convert anyone to Christianity; it only made life as a Christian in Muslim lands more difficult as it closed down the door to peaceful discourse. Instead, Francis wanted his Christian brethren to "be subject" to Muslims, live amongst them peacefully, engage them with kindness and to 'avoid quarrels or disputes' with them.[26] In the end, Francis wanted his brothers to be *Christ-like* towards Muslims; to be an example of what Christ's followers are meant to be – not war-mongering monarchs, Popes, and Knights, but men of gentle spirits, concerned for the poor, the weak, the suffering, and the excluded, regardless of their confessional commitments. This meant the Christians had to respect the Islamic tradition itself, for within Islam the biblical patriarchs, the Prophets, Jesus and his mother Mary, are all revered, and in this reverence common ground could be found. Francis knew this and was aware that Muslims cannot speak ill of Jesus and continue to remain within the fold of Islam, as the Islamic tradition regards all prophets as equals and their followers as 'Ahl al-Kitāb (people of the revealed scriptures).

---

25   Saint Francis, *Francis and Clare: The Complete Works*, 121–122. My emphasis on "be subject." Other emphases are from the original document.

26   Moses, *The Saint and the Sultan*, 162–163.

The outrage against the 2005–2006 Danish Cartoons printed by the small newspaper Jyllands-Posten, which depicted Muhammad as a terrorist, pedophile, misogynist, and imbecile, as well as the 2015 *Charlie Hebdo* attack, was often explained by Muslims to be a reaction to the West's disrespect for their sacred figures, a practice that all Muslims are forbidden by Islamic law to engage in.[27] By the command of Muhammad via the the Qur'an, Muslims are required to show respect to those "holy" figures of Judaism and Christianity, but that same respect for Muhammad has rarely been reciprocated. Francis understood that offending Muslims by denouncing their deeply held beliefs could not establish the conditions for peaceful discourse, but would rather make it impossible, as the Crusades had already nearly done. Therefore, in his *Earlier Rule* he wished his community to 'be subject to every human creature for God's sake, so bearing witness to the fact that they are Christians.'[28] For Francis, to be Christian was to be humbly subject to every human including the "enemy." Because of this position of humility, Francis opened up the geography necessarily for honest discourse, which may be why St. Francis is still remembered with fondness in the Muslim world today. Unlike the western powers of today, which project their influence into the Muslim world with blind arrogance, Francis' insistence on subjecting oneself to others and being humble in their presence, as well as honoring their religious beliefs, is an embodiment of sincere Christian belief that is easy for devout Muslims to recognize. It also lays the foundation for reconciliation, a space wherein peoples of different faith can find common ground.

Following Bonaventure's official biography, St. Francis' contemporary biographer Donald Spoto sees his mission to the Muslims in 1219 to be a complete failure; he had failed to convert the Sultan; he failed to make peace between the Muslims and Christians; and he had not become a martyr for Christ.[29] The Fifth Crusade would end in a disaster for Christendom and would remain just a footnote in the history of medieval Islam. Nevertheless, from the perspective of critical religiology, this episode established the possibility of interreligious discourse in the face of overwhelming hatred and war. What Francis and the Sultan accomplished was not realized within their lives, but the painful ecumenical "learning process" between religions was set in motion. Additionally, the Muslims gained a new understanding of their traditional religious rivals; the embodiment of Christ on earth can be achieved – as seen in

---

27   See Jytte Klausen, *The Cartoons that Shook the World*. New Haven: Yale University Press, 2009.

28   Ibid., 2009.

29   Spoto, *Reluctant Saint*, 161–162.

St. Francis – and in its achievement there exists a discourse partner. In the embodiment of the prophetic model of Jesus, who is recognized by Islam as such, reciprocity demands Muslims embody the prophetic model of Muhammad, who never denied the opportunity to enter into a substantive discourse with the other. In other words, when Muslim and Christians sincerely embrace the ecumenical and humanistic spirit of both traditions, the traditions themselves demand discourse.[30]

According to Father Donal O'Mahony, an Irish Capuchin friar who has worked with Muslims in Africa for decades, Muslims 'relate to Franciscans more closely than to the Catholic Church' for this very reason.[31] If we were to explain this phenomenon, we would point to the idea that deep within the Islamic tradition resides the respect for all things sacred and holy, especially when they are *identical to themselves*: they embody the humble and pious values they publicly and personally commit themselves to. In the case of Francis and the Franciscans, many Muslims see a person and/or religious order attempting to live the gospel of Jesus himself, which includes "being subject" to others who do not share the same religion, but are of similar faith. Being subject to others disarms the others, sets them at ease, and lays out the space for mutual respect and brotherhood/sisterhood. Because Islam already posits a concrete idea of who Jesus was, and Muslims recognize him as being fundamentally holy and good, those who are sincere in their attempts to live as a true *imitatio Christi* are seen also as holy and good. From the Islamic perspective, it is because Franciscans embody the ecumenical and humanistic spirit of both Francis and Jesus that they are most appreciated among the Muslim community, who often sees the West as being deficient in humility and openness towards the religious "other." Francis' courageous example can serve as a model for nations in our modern age to also live closer to the suspicious others, learn from others, and break bread with others. Additionally, his example of loving the outcasts – the lepers of his time – can serve as a catalyst to bring the Abrahamic faith traditions together as they are all tasked with taking care of those who are less fortunate in this world's means.

Another powerful example of *being-with-others* can be found in Francis' attitude towards lepers. The assumption that Francis, being a saintly character, found it easy to be with those stricken with lepracy is entirely wrong. It was precisely because he was appalled and horrified by the lepers that he forced himself to follow the *imitatio Christi* into a close *being-with* relationship with the outcasts. In other words, Francis' spontaneous attitude towards the hated

---

30   *Al-Qur'an* 3:64.
31   Moses, *The Saint and the Sultan*, 225.

other had to be overcome by a radical turning away from his own inclination; he had to embrace that which he feared: the social outcast, the existential enemy, and the seemingly entirely "other." Again, in his "overcoming" the stigma of otherness we can identify a model for social and political discourse among nations and religions. Although we may despise the other for their perceived inequities, nevertheless we embrace them as part of the human family and as subjects worthy of recognition.

Returning to our original question; what makes the discourse between St. Francis of Assisi and the Sultan Malik al-Kamil possible? First, the precondition is mutual respect and mutual recognition.[32] Both sides of the discourse allow the other to be who and what they are, accept their differences as being invitations to enter into a relationship, and are sincerely open to reconciliation. This was demonstrated both by St. Francis and the Sultan when they met and spent the days together in discussions while war between their peoples raged around them; they did not hurl insults and condemnations at each other for all their perceived faults, their perceived mistakes in theology, but rather appealed to both reason and faith in their attempts to come to an understanding of each others' position. Additionally, they both were humble in the sight of the other and therefore did not engage in a *strategic* communication, which is an attempt to win the other over to one's side through manipulative discourse, but rather they conversed in a way that expressed their solidarity, their honesty, their openness, and their eagerness to learn from the other. Secondly, both St. Francis and the Sultan spoke a similar language. Obviously we are not talking about Francis's Italian or French (which he spoke) and the Sultan's Arabic; the idiom (ἰδίωμα) by which meaning within a given religion is expressed can be overcome by appropriate translations. The language that they shared was not the explicit languages of Europe and the Middle East, but the common language of a religious worldview, especially ones that share similar backgrounds and therefore theological presuppositions, i.e. the monotheistic faith of Abraham. Both St. Francis and the Sultan Malik al-Kamil shared a worldview that was permeated by religiosity, a certain divine-centered metaphysics that provided shared concepts such as the veracity of divine revelation, the nature of revelation, the necessity of theologically guided reason, the spiritual importance of prayer, fasting and pilgrimage, the central notions of sacred time, sacred space and sacred figures, and the utmost importance of religiously-inspired ethics and moral codes that are predicated on both heavenly and earthly justice and compassion. In other words, a shared spiritual

---

32   See Axel Honneth, *The Struggle for Recognition: The Moral Grammar of Social Conflicts* (Cambridge, MA: The MIT Press, 1995), 92–139.

reality served as an incubator for their friendly discourse. Although they expressed these religious concepts within difference languages and within differing religious systems, the broader similarities and shared intellectual ancestry still provided a basis by which they could speak to each other in a way that was intelligible and recognized as being legitimate even if they differed on how such concepts are articulated in dogma, law, and spiritual practices. As such, a metaphysical worldview that included the centricity of the divine, revelation, and the possibility of the divine's interjection into history, served as the fertile soil for inter-religious discourse. What St. Francis and the Sultan discovered in their brave discourse was that the differences between Christianity, especially as it is practiced by saints like Francis, and Islam, when practiced by men and women who embody the *sunnah* (way) of the Prophet, diminished in the face of their common humanity, their common concerns, and their common religious and worldly goals. The reconciliatory geography that was created by St. Francis and the Sultan bore a small piece of fruit in the 20th century, when the Trappist monk Thomas Merton engaged in a robust study of Islam and Sufism, its mystical side. In a letter written in the spirit of St. Francis to a Pakistani Sufi name Abdul-Aziz, Merton wrote,

> Personally, in matters where dogmatic beliefs differ, I think that controversy is of little value because it takes us away from the spiritual realities into the realm of words and ideas. In the realm of realities we may have a great deal in common, whereas in words there are apt to be infinite complexities and subtleties which are beyond resolution. It is, however, important, I think, to try to understand the beliefs of other religions. But much more important is the sharing of the experience of divine light, and first of all of the light that God gives us even as the Creator and Ruler of the Universe. It is here that the area of fruitful dialogue exists between Christianity and Islam.[33]

Merton believed that by de-emphasizing the particulars within each religious tradition, and focused rather on the spiritual reality that each tradition attempts to articulate through its own language, *that which is divisive* can be overcome by *that which unites.* Dwelling within that which unites paves the way for the discovery of commonalities. These commonalities may set the stage for inter-religious discourse.

---

33   Rob Baker and Gray Henry, eds., *Merton and Sufism: The Untold Story – A Complete Compendium* (Louisville, KY: Fons Vitae, 2005), 1.

But does the inter-religious discourse of Francis and Sultan Malik al-Kamil adequately address the post-secular condition that we find ourselves in today? The post-secular condition in the West and a growing secular condition in the Muslim world pose new challenges for *all* religious voices: whether or not they are divided amongst themselves or in communion. Although they are out of step with secular modernity, some contemporary religious voices, as we will see, still speak a language that is steeped in religious semantics and semiotics, and continue to employ such language when discussing modern and sometimes very secular issues. Pope Francis is the most poignant western example of this form of recalcitrant faith. In an age of increasing secularity, where even the Vatican is surrounded by all the trapping of Roman modernity, with its jungle of capitalist consumerism, he addresses not only his faithful via the language of the saints, popes, and prophets, but also speak to, with, and for the Muslims who look to him as a new St. Francis with whom they can talk. This change in tone from the Roman Pontiff has itself opened up productive and warm relations between Christianity's largest denomination and the second largest religion in the world: Islam.

Different Francis, Same Mission: Witnessing with and for Muslims

On July 10, 2013, the recently elected Pope Francis released a letter to the Muslims in celebration of the end of Ramadan (*'Īd al-Fiṭr*). In it, the Pope of the poor and the disenfranchised, who adopted his papal name from the Catholic Saint most associated with poverty – the aforementioned Saint Francis of Assisi – reflected on the need for Christians and Muslims to engage in "mutual respect" as a way of building bridges between communities. Defining "respect" as an 'attitude of kindness towards people for whom we have consideration and esteem,' Pope Francis emphasizes that it must be "mutual," a relationship where both peoples, regardless of their religious differences, 'share [in the] joy' of the other.[34] The Pope, remembering the love that Saint Francis showed when he journeyed to the Islamic lands to share the Gospel with his Islamic brothers, wished to avoid augmenting the growing antagonism between Muslim immigrants in Europe and their secular (and religious) native counterparts, a dynamic one can daily witness firsthand just outside the walls of the

---

34   Pope Francis. "Message from Pope Francis to Muslims Throughout the World for the End of Ramadan ('Id al-Fitr)," July 10, 2013. http://www.vatican.va/holy_father/francesco/messages/pont-messages/2013/documents/papa-francesco_20130710_musulmani-ramadan_en.html (Accessed 3/22/2014).

Vatican, where Muslim immigrants line up to sell their wares and the *Cara-binieri* (Italian military police) chase them off.[35] Through education, the Pope states, we must 'bring up our young people to think and speak respectfully of other religions and their followers, and to avoid ridiculing or denigrating their convictions and practices.'[36] Pope Francis reiterated this sentiment after the attacks on *Charlie Hebdo*, which continually mocked and ridiculed religious believers, including the Pope and his predecessor Pope Benedict XVI. Disrespect, again, the opposite of *recognition*, is a deep source for conflict and violence, the growth of which can lead to future catastrophes between peoples.[37]

Despite the growing hatred for illegal immigrants from Northern Africa, whose gateway into Europe is often through the small Mediterranean island of Lampedusa, the Pope prophetically challenged Catholics to recognize the pain and suffering of the immigrants who flee from brutal conflicts, entrenched poverty, and the rampant devastation of their homelands, and to see them not as a threat to European culture, but as "neighbors" in search of a helping hand and a better future for their children, whom the Pope often reminds are also God's children. In accordance with these sentiments, the new Pope's first trip outside of Rome was to the island of Lampedusa, where he honored those who had died attempting to seek a better future in Europe.[38] The Pope's sensitivities for the suffering other, who finds themself in a foreign land, has its roots not only in his own biography (as a son of immigrants), but the experience of exile within the furtile soil from which Christianity sprang: Judaism. The book of Leviticus 19:33–34 states,

> When a stranger sojourns with you in your land, you shall not do him wrong. The stranger who sojourns with you shall be to you as the native among you, and you shall love him as yourself; for you were strangers in the land of Egypt: I am the Lord your God.[39]

For Pope Francis, who has demonstrated repeatedly that his solidarity with others transcends confessional boundaries, referenced the 2013 "Lampedusa

---

35   Moses, *The Saint and the Sultan*, 2009.

36   Pope Francis. *Message from Pope Francis to Muslims Throughout the World for the End of Ramadan*.

37   Axel Honneth, *Disrespect: The Normative Foundations of Critical Theory* (Malden, MA: Polity Press, 2007), 99–194.

38   Austen Ivereigh, *The Great Reformer: Francis and the Making of a Radical Pope* (New York: Henry Holt & Co., 2014), 1–3.

39   *Holy Bible*, (New York: Thomas Nelson Inc., 1972), 105.

Tragedy" – where hundreds of refugees from Eritrea and Somalia drowned in a fire at sea while attempting to reach the safe shores of Europe – as being the result of the 'inhuman global economic crisis, a serious symptom of a lack of respect for the human person.'[40] In his empathy for the suffering of those involved in the Lampedusa tragedy, Pope Francis instructed the Vatican Almoner to give away 1,600 phone cards so the survivors of the tragedy and other immigrants who'd been cut off from their families could call home to their loved ones.[41] This was only a small gesture – but a meaningful one – towards what Pope Francis has repeatedly called for: the transformation of the church into a 'field hospital.'[42] This field hospital church, Pope Francis has iterated, bandages the wounds of all humanity, not just faithful Catholics. It is an ecumenical hospital, which sees its mission as one that must 'heal the wounds' of society, the broken, the abused, the neglected, and the excluded, and not just focuses all of its attention to doctrinal and catechismal obedience.[43]

Pope Francis also remembered the importance of the teachings about Muslims in *Nostra Aetate* (In our time), the 1965 *Declaration on the Relation of the Church to Non-Christian Religions* by Pope Paul VI. In this modernizing and ecumenical document, Pope Paul VI declares,

> The Church regards with esteem also the Moslems. They adore the one God, living and subsisting in Himself; merciful and all-powerful, the Creator of heaven and earth, who has spoken to men; they take pains to submit wholeheartedly to even His inscrutable decrees, just as Abraham, with whom the faith of Islam takes pleasure in linking itself, submitted to God. Though they do not acknowledge Jesus as God, they revere Him as a prophet. They also honor Mary, His virgin Mother; at times they even call on her with devotion. In addition, they await the Day of Judgment when God will render their deserts to all those who have been raised up from the dead. Finally, they value the moral life and worship God especially through prayer, almsgiving and fasting.[44]

---

40   Catholic Herald. "Pope Francis Offers Prayers for the Victims of Lampedusa Boat Sinking," October 3, 2013. http://www.catholicherald.co.uk/news/2013/10/03/pope-francis-offers -prayers-for-victims-of-lampedusa-boat-sinking/ (Accessed 3/22/2014).

41   Howard Chua-Eoan and Elizabeth Dias, "The People's Pope," *TIME*, 23 December 2013, 54.

42   Pope Francis, *A Big Heart Open to God: A Conversation with Pope Francis* (New York: HarperOne, 2013), 30.

43   Ibid., 31.

44   Pope Paul VI, "Declaration on the Relation of the Church to Non-Christian Religions: Nostra Aetate," October 28, 1965. http://www.vatican.va/archive/hist_councils/ii_vatican _council/documents/vat-ii_decl_19651028_nostra-aetate_en.html. (Accessed 11/2/2014).

Looking towards a more-reconciled future relationship between the Catholics and Muslims, *Nostra Aetate* states,

> Since in the course of centuries not a few quarrels and hostilities have arisen between Christians and Moslems, this sacred synod urges all to forget the past and to work sincerely for mutual understanding and to preserve as well as to promote together for the benefit of all mankind social justice and moral welfare, as well as peace and freedom.[45]

Yet, despite the embracing and compassionate tone of the declaration, the relationship between the church and the Muslim world has grown more estranged within the conditions of modernity. As he is most troubled by the suffering of the weak, vulnerable, and broken, the Pope tearfully witnesses the way in which Muslim refugees in Europe are often met with indifference or derision; they are un-welcomed, unwanted, and greeted with hostility and suspicion. For the Pope, all human life is sacred, and *Christian* morality, according to Pope Francis – which is only one articulation of *human* morality – must reclaim its sense of solidarity, especially with those who are most vulnerable, most cast-aside, and most victimized. In his first exhortation, *Evangelii Gaudium* (The Joy of the Gospel), he wrote ecumenically that,

> Our relationship with the followers of Islam has taken on great importance, since they are now significantly present in many traditionally Christian countries, where they can freely worship and become fully a part of society. We must never forget that they 'profess to hold the faith of Abraham, and together with us they adore the one, merciful God, who will judge humanity on the last day.'[46]

Against those who claim that Islam's divine being is fundamentally different than that of Judaism's and Christianity's, and whose sense of ethical life (*sittlichkeit*) cannot be reconciled with Judeo-Christian ethical norms, he writes,

> The sacred writings of Islam have retained some Christian teachings: Jesus and Mary received profound veneration and it is admirable to see how Muslims both young and old, men and women, make time for daily prayer and faithfully take part in religious services. Many of them also have a deep conviction that their life, in its entirety, is from God and for

---

45   Ibid.

46   Pope Francis, *Evangelii Gaudium*, 121.

God. They also acknowledge the need to respond to God with an ethical commitment and with mercy toward those most in need... We Christians should embrace with affection and respect Muslim immigrants... in the same way that we hope and ask to be received and respected in countries of Islamic tradition.[47]

For those who are most opposed to the immigration of Muslims into Europe, Pope Francis proposes a more Christian and hopeful way of looking at their presence, one that emphasizes the universality of human experience and the potential for creating new and more vibrant pluralistic culture. He writes,

Migrants present a particular challenge for me, since I am the pastor of a church without frontiers, a Church which considers herself mother to all. For this reason, I exhort all countries to a generous openness which, rather than fearing the loss of local identity, will prove capable of creating new forms of cultural synthesis. How beautiful are those cities which overcome paralyzing mistrust, integrate those who are different and make this very integration a new factor of development! How attractive are those cities which, even in their architectural design, are full of spaces which connect, relation and favor the recognition of others![48]

The Pope's statements and actions are controversial for many who do not see these Muslim immigrants as victims but as a lingering threat: a dangerous *Trojan horse* in the midst of Europe. Many on the political-right, both religious and secular, accuse the Pope of contributing to the destruction of Europe via his soft hearted "Americano" stance towards immigrants, pointing out that there are already millions of Muslims residing in Europe, which is too many in their opinion. For groups such as the German based *Patriotic Europeans against the Islamization of the West* (PEGIDA), the *National Front* in France, or the *Lega Nord* (Northern League) in Italy, Muslim immigration is not an issue of solidarity, Christian compassion, or respect, but the survival of Europe as Europe. The threat of "Eurabia," they believe, is real, and the Pope, with his "solidarist" positions, puts Europe in great danger by calling for an acceptance of even more immigrants, especially after ISIS threatened to conquer Rome and the Vatican and its attacks on Christians, including the February, 2015, beheading

---

47   Ibid., 121.
48   Ibid., 105.

of twenty-one Coptic Christians in Libya.[49] Unlike the Pope, they emphasize *le piège de la société pluriculturelle* (the trap of the multicultural society), not its *potentiels positifs* (positive potentials). This sentiment has only been exasperated by the knowledge that ISIS (Islamic State in Iraq and Syria) are smuggling their operatives into Europe as immigrants, and those immigrants have attacked Paris and Brussels.[50] However, Pope Francis, echoing Pope Gregory the Great's *Letters on the Treatment of Jews*, (591 and 598 CE) which barred Christians from harming Jews while affirming their responsibility to protect the Jews, disagrees vehemently with those who view Muslims simply as an inherent threat. For him, they are fellow believers whose presence in Europe warrant Christian *agape* (ἀγάπη – "unconditional love") and should not be abused by the citizens of Europe nor individual states, regardless of whether some in the immigrant communities commit crimes or are attracted to radical Islam. In this sense, the Pope courageously attempts to maintain the "humanity" of those who are "dehumanized" simply because of their religion.[51]

From the beginning of Pope's Francis' tenure as Pope, he has continuously rejected the material privileges of being the Vicar of Christ and has embraced a more humble attitude towards the world. On one such occasion, March 28, 2013, on Holy Thursday (a.k.a. *Maundy Thursday*) – the day Christians remember Jesus' last supper – Pope Francis forsook the tradition of washing the feet of fellow clerics and instead washed the feet of twelve detained juveniles, among them were women and Muslims.[52] Although the media coverage of his

---

49   Dabiq, No. 4, 1435 Dhul-Hijjah; Ahmed Tolba and Michael Georgy, "Sisi Warns of Response after Islamic State Kills 21 Egyptians in Libya," February 15, 2015. htttp://www.reuters .com/article/2015/02/15/us-mideast-crisis-libya-egypt-idUSKBN0LJ10D20150215. (Accessed 2/16/2015).

50   After the Charlie Hebdo attack in January of 2015, the problem of radicalized immigrants became even more pronounced, especially concerning the second generations, who have an intimate knowledge of European society and travel on European passports. Mike Giglio and Munzer al-Awad, "Smuggler: I Sent ISIS Fighters to Europe," November 11, 2014. http://www.buzzfeed.com/mikegiglio/smuggler-i-sent-isis-fighters-to-europe?utm_term =4ldqpia (Accessed 11/12/2014).

51   David Livingstone Smith, *Less than Human: Why we Demean, Enslave, and Exterminate Others*. New York: St. Martin's Press, 2011.

52   NBC News, "Pope Washes Feet of Detainees in Holy Thursday Ritual," March 28, 2013. http://worldnews.nbcnews.com/_news/2013/03/28/17502522-pope-washes-feet-of-young -detainees-in-holy-thursday-ritual?lite (Accessed 3/23/2014). "Maundy" Thursday is a most appropriate word to describe what Pope Francis was trying to accomplish. "Maundy" derives from the Latin "Mandatum" ("mandate" in English), the first word in the phrase 'Mandatum novum do vobis ut diligatis invicem sicut dilexi vos' or 'I give to you a new commandment, that you love one another; as I have loved you' (John 13:34).

deeply symbolic departure from papal protocol was extensive, it nevertheless failed to adequately articulate the radical importance of this singular act. In one person, Francis honored (1) women, (2) Muslims, and (3) immigrants. The Vicar of Christ, the successor to St. Peter, the Bishop of Rome, the bearer of papal supremacy, and heir to the many popes that came before him that ordered Muslims to be massacred in Crusades, Inquisitions, and through the burning of women thought to be in league with Satan, who had a 1,400 year conflict with Islam, this Pope lowered himself, washed her skin, and kissed her feet in an act of humble atonement which recognized the pain and suffering of the poor, the immigrants, and women. This gesture of humility symbolized Pope Francis' desire to reconcile the church – without dissolving the church – to those it has previously thought to be heretical, outside the bounds of Christian love, and destined for an afterlife of hellish torment. Humanistic compassion outweighed eschatological judgment if only for a brief moment. Just as Francis of Assisi had done, the Pope's actions once again demonstrated to the world the ecumenical vitality of embodied Christian ethics; that not all of Europe was anti-Muslim, and that the very center of the Christian world was holding open the doors to an inter-subjective dialogue with the Muslim world. The common humanity of both the Pope and this one young Muslim woman was enough motivation for him to honor her, recognize her hardship, and pray for her. Through that simple gesture, the Pope demonstrated the church's *potential* to reconcile itself to its own ethical commitments.

In many ways, Pope Francis has been a unifying figure among the world religions, so much so that the immigrants of Rome, who are often socially maligned in the streets while peddling plastic trinkets, laser lights, purses, etc., turned to him when they felt they were being abused by the Italian state in their detention centers for illegal and undocumented workers. In a letter pleading for intervention by the Pope, they wrote, 'we came to seek a better life, but we've only found the bars of a jail cell... Holy Father, we are the new poor, but we're not meat for a butcher shop.'[53] After hearing the Pope's challenge to never let a "Lampedusa Tragedy" happen again, watching him embrace the dispossessed, the poor, the sick and the marginalized in society, these detainees, exclusively Muslims from countries such as Tunisia and Morocco, saw hope within the Pope's turn towards social justice and compassion and away from ecclesiastical dogmatism, sectarianism, and Roman elitism. Just as Muslims sought refuge with the Christian King Negus in Abyssinia in the year 615 CE,

---

53   John L. Allen Jr., "Mad at Everyone Else, Muslim Immigrants in Rome Trust the Pope," December 27, 2013. http://ncronline.org/blogs/ncr-today/mad-everyone-else-muslim -immigrants-rome-trust-pope (Accessed 3/23/2013).

knowing he was a man of Christian compassion, Muslims now sought intervention from the highest of Christian authorities, the same seat of power that once called for their destruction. Pope Francis demonstrated that he was the antithesis of his predecessor, Pope Urban II, the initiator of the Crusaders in 1095 CE. Francis wished to win over the Muslims with love and compassion instead of the sword and mace; he had no active agenda to "convert" the Muslims but rather "respected" the dignity of their religious beliefs. This kind of cooperation with and for the benefit of Muslims, let alone immigrants in Europe, would have made martyrs out of many before him at the hands of the Inquisition. The Pope's actions, echoing the views of the martyred "heretic" *Menocchio*, a.k.a. Domenico Scandella (1532–1599 CE), who read the biblical passage to "love one's neighbors" as meaning to also love his Islamic neighbors, have opened up a door towards healing the deep-seated wounds that exist between the *dar al-Islam* and Christendom.[54] Indeed, the fact that Pope Francis seems sincere in his faith and in his attempt to live the life of a humble servant of the poor – as Jesus himself commanded his followers to do – have led many to recommit themselves to their Catholic faith and others to convert, despite the ever-increasing secularity of society. This phenomenon has been dubbed the "Francis effect," and it is easily witnessed whenever he has a public engagement in Rome or abroad.[55] It should be noted that even non-Catholics,

---

54 Spellberg, *Thomas Jefferson's Qur'an*, 41–47; also see Carlo Ginzburg, *The Cheese and the Worms: The Cosmos of a Sixteenth Century Miller*. Baltimore, MD: The Johns Hopkins Press, 1992.

55 John Gehring, *The Francis Effect: A Radical Pope's Challenge to the American Catholic Church*. Landham, MD: Rowman & Littlefield, 2015; Tracy Connor, "Francis Effect? Popular Pope has Catholics Praying More, Polls Find," March 6, 2014. http://www.nbcnews.com/ news/religion/francis-effect-popular-pope-has-catholics-praying-more-poll-finds-n43451 (Accessed 3/26/2014). However, according the Pew Research Center, there has been no meaningful "Francis effect" among U.S. Catholics. Those who identify themselves as Catholics have not increased nor has attendance in mass increased. It appears that the American population is immune to the charismatic leadership of the new Pope in Rome. See Conrad Hackett. "No Clear 'Pope Francis Effect' Among U.S. Catholics," http://www .pewresearch.org/fact-tank/2013/11/25/no-clear-pope-francis-effect-among-u-s-catholics/ (Accessed 3/26/2014). It can be argued that the Protestant inspired and capitalist nurtured individualism has rooted itself so deep in the American consciousness that Francis' calls for solidarity with the poor falls upon deaf ears in the United States where there is little sympathy for the poor. While some parishes report a slight rise in mass attendance, other wealthy Catholics have made it known their displeasure with the Pope's condemnation of 'unbridled capitalism.' For example, Ken Langone, the co-founder of Home Depot and Republican party supporter, announced to Cardinal Dolan of New York that the 'multi-million dollar restoration of St. Patrick's Cathedral might run into funding

including many Muslims, can be spotted in the St. Peter's square whenever the Pope is in general audience; this is a powerful reminder of the ecumenical spirit that he embodies, especially in contrast to his predecessor who, unintentionally, antagonized Muslims worldwide through his 2006 Regensburg Address and other mismanaged moments.

From a critical sociological perspective, one can see the growing thirst for *real, prophetic,* and *humanistic* religiosity – authentic professing and witnessing – in our secular age that has, since the Enlightenment, industrialization, urbanization, and materialization, been depleted of its spiritual values and optimism about the future. Because the void is so vast – to the extent that it cannot be filled by consumerism, materialism, sex-car-and-career – any genuine return to the religious values that still linger within small moments of authentic morality in the secular public sphere – those values that we professed but rarely practiced – reminds many that religion is not entirely worthless, out-of-date, and socially irrelevant. It reminds many critics that religion may still play a positive role in society. Therefore, if the right religious values are rescued, emphasized, practiced, and fulfilled, religion may still have a positive future (especially in the West). Indeed, the faith and actions of Pope Francis have done a lot to make religion "respectable" once again in the post-metaphysical society.

Because of the Pope's new ecumenical orientation, which has become the cornerstone of his papacy along with his emphasis on poverty, he has been able to work with the Anglican Church and the Islamic authorities in al-Azhar University – the foremost authority in Sunni Islam – on a project to rid the world of modern-day slavery and human trafficking.[56] Historically, European Christians as well as African and Arab Muslims cooperated *within* the slave trade.[57] Now, cooperation *against* the slave trade among some of the world most powerful religious authorities may prove to be a radically transformative force for good in today's society. About human trafficking, The Pope says,

---

difficulties if wealthy Catholics keep getting their feeling hurt by 'exclusionary' papal remarks.' See Mark Binelli, "Pope Francis: The Times They Are a-Changing," *Rolling Stone.* 13 February 2014, 41.

56   Reuters, "Christians and Muslims Join Forces to Combat Modern Slavery," March 17, 2014. http://www.reuters.com/article/2014/03/17/us-religion-slavery-idUSBREA2G19N20140317 (Accessed 3/24/2014); Reuters, "Pope, World Religious Leaders, Pledge to Fight Modern Slavery," December 2, 2014. http://www.reuters.com/article/2014/12/02/us-pope-slavery -idUSKCN0JG1KM20141202 (Accessed 12/3/2014).

57   Ronald Segal, *Islam's Black Slaves: The Other Black Diaspora* (New York: Farrar, Straus & Giroux, 2001), 177–197.

Where is your brother or sister who is enslaved? Where is the brother and sister whom you are killing each day in clandestine warehouses, in rights of prostitution, in children used for begging, in exploiting undocumented labor. Let us not look the other way. There is greater complicity than we think. The issue involves everyone![58]

Indeed, Pope Francis' ecumenical faith and call to prophetic action does the opposite of the war of words articulated by Islamophobes such as Ayaan Hirsi Ali, Theo van Gogh, Geert Wilders, etc. His words do not embolden Muslims to think of Europe as the next frontier to "Islamize" but rather as a potential space to build the preconditions for reconciliation, understanding, and peace. The potential for ecumenisms is not alien to Islam either. The Pope's faith echoes the Qur'anic statement found in *Sūrat al-Hujurat*, 49:13,

O mankind, We have created you from a male and a female and made you nations and tribes so that you may know one another. Indeed, the most noble of you in the sight of Allah is the one most righteous. Indeed, Allah is all-Knowing and acquainted with all.[59]

For Pope Francis, like the Qur'an, the differences within mankind are not reasons to hate each other, but invitations to enter into a discourse and learn about each other, and work towards a more reconciled future society. We can only wait and see if the Roman Curia will finally appear from behind the tall walls of the Vatican and embrace their immigrant Muslims brothers just on the other side of those imposing edifices. Will the church take seriously Pope Francis' call to poverty – to make the church a "church of the poor" and a "field hospital" for the victims of history? Will the church take seriously his call for reconciliation with other religions, or, like so many other calls for a better more humane and dignified world, will his voice go unheard by the rank-and-file believers?[60] This is the challenge that the Pope has given all of mankind but most especially the Christians that remain recalcitrant within the post-secularity countries.

As the Pope begins to travel more frequently outside of the Vatican, he frequently returns to the issue of inter-religious discourse, respect, and recognition. In a speech to Albanian civil authorities in September, 2014, the Pope praised the nation for being one that can peacefully live together despite their

---

58   Pope Francis, *Evangelii Gaudium*, 105.

59   My translation.

60   Ibid., 100; Pope Francis and Antonio Spadaro, *A Big Heart Open to God*, 30–35.

mixed religious heritage while also warning the world against any religious communities' fortifying themselves with the "armour of God." He stated,

> There is a rather beautiful characteristic of Albania, one which is given great care and attention, and which gives me great joy: I am referring to the peaceful coexistence and collaboration that exists among followers of different religions. The climate of respect and mutual trust between Catholics, Orthodox and Muslims is a precious gift to the country. This is especially the case in these times where an authentic religious spirit is being perverted and where religious differences are being distorted and instrumentalized by extremist groups. This creates dangerous circumstances which lead to conflict and violence, rather than being an occasion for open and respectful dialogue, and for a collective reflection on what it means to believe in God and to follow his laws.
>
> Let no one consider themselves to be the 'armour' of God while planning and carrying out acts of violence and oppression! May no one use religion as a pretext for actions against human dignity and against the fundamental rights of every man and woman, above all, the right to life and the right of everyone to religious freedom![61]

For many Catholics and non-Christians, Pope Francis represents the hope that what remains of religion within the ever-increasing secularity of our age is a form of religion that embodies peaceful cooperation, transcendence of historical enmities, and a religion that faithfully commits itself to the possibility of a more-reconciled future society. If religion in the post-secular society limits itself to its reactionary-potentials, as opposed to its prophetic, Socratic and liberational potentials, then that which is left of religion will soon be a matter of history; rejected as a force for evil and division. Religion, if it is to be a force for human flourishing – the realization of humanity in-and-for-itself – then it must actualize its potential to aid in the creation of the conditions by which humanity thrives on the basis of cooperation, unconditional love, recognition, and reconciliation. The future of religion depends on the religious; it can either be forgotten because it cannot be realized, or it can be remembered because it's too destructive to be forgotten.

---

61   Pope Francis, "Apostolic Journey of His Holiness Pope Francis to Tirana (Albania): Meeting with the Civil Authorities," September 21, 2014. http://w2.vatican.va/content/francesco/en/speeches/2014/september/documents/papa-francesco_20140921_albania-autorita.html. (Accessed 9/28/2014).

Translation Proviso: Can We Witness and Confess in the Same Language?

For the critical theorist Jürgen Habermas, the Muslim community, and religious communities in secular societies in general, have a two-fold problem. First, religions are understood to be comprehensive worldviews that often locate themselves within "semantically closed universes" which do not allow for a free and undistorted communication with others outside of that semantic universe.[62] Since religious vocabulary is saturated with theological presuppositions it inadvertently stifles the necessary *shared* vocabulary and epistemology that is needed to enter into a discourse with their secular counterparts. Thus, citizens that do not have access to such religious language find it difficult to *reason* with those that cannot reason without an appeal to revelation or divine authority. Their vocabularies are rooted in two different authorities; one finds its arguments based in revelation and the other in autonomous reason – one heavenly and the other earthly. A solution to this entrenched problem is needed in a post-secular pluralist society *if* it wants to be both (1) inclusive, and (2) democratic. The answer to this problem cannot be to disregard religious voices; they must be considered within the democratic processes of secular societies. Additionally, despite the immense problem of semantics and reasoning, Habermas is insistent that religious communities not be *forced to abandon* their religious beliefs or be integrated into the discourse community through a coercion, but rather should express their autonomy in the way they see most fit and congruent with their religious sentiments. Habermas does not agree with those critics of religion that insist that religious voices must retreat into the private domain because their faith is an obsolete *Gestalt des Geistes*.[63] The forced privatization of religion only stifles the legitimate contributions that religious voices can offer in the public discourse and contributes to reactionary forms of religiosity that disassociate it from the broader community altogether. On the contrary, speaking explicitly about Muslims, he says 'Muslim immigrants cannot be integrated into a western society in defiance of their religion, but only together with it.'[64] Islam and Islamic values have to be enlisted into the discourse if devout Muslims are going to engage in national discussions as equals who have a unique perspective to offer the broader community. In this way, Islam itself is a motivational factor for Muslims participating in the unlimited discourse community; their religious beliefs provide sufficient reason to enter

---

62   Habermas, *Europe*, 72.
63   Ibid., 73.
64   Ibid., 71.

into the broader discourse community and it spares them the need to justify their action via reasoning that is alien to their worldview. According to his discourse theory, religious communities, in this case Muslim immigrant communities, are (1) able to both preserve their religious views in the public sphere, but (2) they equally must find some way of translating those same religious views into secular language so that they are made accessible to all participants via discursive reasoning. In this way, religious voices are not excluded from the democratic deliberation process, but are included, albeit via the translation of their thoughts and ideas into democratically accessible language. This process will open up the closed semantic system to the public. If religious communities living in secular societies can achieve such a translation proviso, then their principles, values, and ideals can be fully included in the national discourse, they can be debated, and if they gain democratic consensus, they can even be enacted (in secular form). In a world that has become deaf to religious and metaphysical thought, translation presents itself as the key to the locked door of religiously garbed semantic potentials.

If religious communities do not find such a translation proviso acceptable, then they risk their ideas being blocked from consideration in the democratic process in secular states. This would ultimately diminish both the democracy and the ability of the particular religious communities to contribute their unique perspectives to their particular societies. This self-ghettoization also has the consequences of creating a "parallel society" within a nation, one that is often perceived to be suspicious due to its failure to integrate, cooperate, and contribute to the health and wealth of the nation.[65] The status of the perpetual "other" can be imposed by the religious communities themselves if they cannot find a way of making their religious claims publicly accessible to those who do not belong to the same religious community but are of the same state/nation. Again, this self-imposed ghettoization through semantic and cultural isolation is a real threat to the survival of Islam and other minority religions in the secular West, as it bars them from politically, economically, and culturally integrating into their societies. Yet in the case of the Muslim communities in Europe, this often occurs by the actions of many conservative Muslims who fear that integration will lead to assimilation and a loss of their Islamic identity. This fear is not entirely irrational, as there is a certain measure of truth to the claim that immigrant communities tend to eventually assimilate the values and cultures of their adopted societies the longer they remain a part of that society. However, the consequence of self-imposed isolation is that if they cannot contribute to the construction of the overall political reality, such reality

---

65   Ibid., 71.

will be made for them without their input. This is a very precarious state to impose on one's religious community while living in a society that has yet to accept the identity, values, and religious beliefs of the particular religious immigrants. If those values cannot be expressed in such a way that the society can understand – in a language that is comprehensible to all – then such a society can easily adopt the age-old stereotypes of the religious community as they lack the first-hand experiences to overcome such historical biases. This is especially true for Muslims in Europe, whose religion has been demonized by European writers, Protestant preachers, and the Catholic Church for over a millennium with few exceptions. If Muslims fail to demonstrate the progressive nature of the Islamic tradition – the same progressive nature that made Islam so appealing in the first place – then a sizeable number of Europeans will maintain their already negative views of Islam and Muslims. The Muslim community will not be able to blame the West for their failure to make their religion understood and respected within the post-secular society when they fail to actively contribute to changing those views through discourse and the prophetic example that is sensitive to the concerns of the broader society. As they did in the past, Muslims should always seek to contribute their talents to the care and betterment of society, no matter which one it happens to be.

Yet, if Habermas insists we translate religious potentials into secular language, we have to ask him precisely what aspects of religion are to be translated and is there a specific form or content that he suggests be translated?

Cognitive-Instrumental Reason, Moral-Practical Reason and Aesthetic-Expressive Reason in Religion

According to the Critical Theory of Religion, religion has three specific components. They are (1) *cognitive-Instrumental*, which is religion's language, theory, theology, and values, (2) its *moral-practical* component, which both explains the motivational aspect of the religious life and constructs a collection of moral norms and a system of thought that legitimates and justifics them. (3) The *aesthetic-expressive*: this aspect of religion articulates itself in ritual, sacred music, architecture and fine art. These three components are integrated within traditional, i.e. religious worldviews, and thus create a substantive wholeness. But according to Habermas' *Theory of Communicative Action*, they are artificially separated under the conditions of modernity, which compartmentalizes and neutralizes the capacity for integrative wholeness that they once embodied. Nevertheless, he returns to these categories in his thoughts on translating aspects of religion into secular philosophy.

Habermas' analysis of religion in the post-secular society is not specific as to what would have value in a secular society if religion were to be thoroughly translated into publically accessible reasoning. Clearly an understanding of all three aspects by the broader society would be a benefit to all, but that would burden the citizen beyond what is reasonable for each individual to know about every religion. While the Critical Theory of religion would like to see all aspects of religion translated into secular semantics, it is also aware that some are simply not translatable. What is translatable above others is the *moral-practical reasoning* of any given religion. It is also the most useful to a multi-cultural and multi-religious society to be able to harmonize moral sentiments with other communities' moral values and principles. Therefore this element, which provides the believer with an interpretation of reality and therefore their orientation of action, would be the most pregnant with possibilities if it were to enter into public discourse with the non-religious citizenry.

The expressive aspect of religion is hardly taken seriously in secular society where devotional works of art, whether they are paintings, status, architecture, which were originally meant to provoke devotion, prayer, and contemplation, are *experienced* today as autonomous art: art for art's sake.[66] According to their own *notion*, such pieces of religious art are not autonomous, but rather serve a purpose beyond itself: the worship and contemplation of the divine. In today's Rome, the tourists meandering through the many beautiful cathedrals are more likely to hear a lecture on the various artists' biography than the devotional purpose of the art itself or the religious meaning it expresses. Or worse, they'll experience the art *de-contextualized,* i.e. in coffin-like museums, where the sacred art's natural connection to the given architecture, the smell of incense, and the sound of sacred music is absent, thus leaving the sacred art without its natural home. For Muslims, Islamic art is meant to invoke wonder at the world that the divine created, not itself to be the object of wonder. Nevertheless, within the modern secular world, the secularization of the expressive side of Islam will occur in the West as it is inclined to appreciate the culture "artifacts" of various peoples. However, such *appreciation* will not lead to Islamic *devotion,* just as viewing Michelangelo doesn't necessary lead to greater Catholic faith. As such, the sacred art of Islam will go the way of sacred art in Christianity: it will become detached from its original purpose,

---

66   Jürgen Habermas, *The Theory of Communication Action: Reason and the Rationalization of Society.* trans. Thomas McCarthy (Boston: Beacon Press, 1984), 160–161. This experiencing of devotional art as autonomous art is due to the rationalization process that has developed within the western world. Even though such devotional art is securely tied to the church through its history and intent, it is experienced by the secular citizen as being detached from its own history and purpose.

i.e. devotion, and will become a *profane* (desacralized) thing of beauty in a gallery or museum, enjoyed by nullifidians.

As for the *cognitive-instrumental* component of religion – the rationality of work and tool, calculative thought and mathematics, functionalizing logic, technology and the cold rationality of *strenge ordnung* (strict order/ discipline) – it doesn't have a substantive export for philosophical theory, i.e. it fails to supply adequate concepts and notions that can be properly appropriated within a secular system. As praxis or a way/attitude towards life within a faith, it is beneficial, but this attitude towards a faithful life is not what Habermas is interested in.

In the end, the *moral-practical* element of religion is the element most suited for translation; for it provides the moral and ethical categories out of which translation can occur most affectively. These categories are the most saturated with social-ethical potentials and therefore are the most likely to be found fruitful to discuss via public debate as most citizens can easily engage in discussion about morality and the demands of goodness on various social issues. Translating concepts such as piety, virtue, compassion, mercy, love, and justice from their religious contexts to a secular context is one that can be done both on the level of the intellectual as well as the general public, if we can assume that they would have at least a cursory knowledge of both secular and religious values and the philosophical imagination to do so. It is true that the particular coloring of the Islamic articulation of common or "universal" values may make the discourse partner (the westerner) unsure as to whether they are speaking about the same concept. However, the universal or humanistic component – that is deeply imbedded within the common human condition and human experiences – should reveal itself through the dense particularity of the language and thus establish itself as the subject of discourse. If the Roman playwright Terrance is correct in saying *homo sum, humani nihil a me alienum puto'* (I am human, nothing human is alien to me), and this statement is universally true, then all are capable of discerning the humanistic universals within their religious traditions that can serve as the basis for discourse and friendly relations. In this sense, the universal has to be parsed out of the particular by both the religious and the secular so that it can emerge as the neutral – and therefore debatable – common value.

Translation Dangers

The attempt to translate religious semantic and semiotic materials into secular language is not without its potential perils. In effect, it is asking a lot of

a religious community to risk entering their values into democratic deliberation. Such open and free deliberation is often brutal, odious, and dismissive
of religious sensitivities. Religious values can expect no reverential treatment
once they've entered into this combative arena. However, the translation of
the sacred into the profane – if not anxiety inducing already – may prove to
be even more disastrous if the religious voices are casually discredited and/or
perceived disrespected on the part of the discourse partner. One does not willfully offer the sacred to secular slaughter, which is precisely what Habermas'
proposal asks religious communities to do. Despite the fact that most claims
are given no special treatment due to their origin, care must be taken that the
sacredness of the values that are being expressed, even within the secular language, are seriously considered and extended respect. Muslims especially are
sensitive to disrespectful attitudes towards their sacred figures and beliefs. It is
often understood that the value of "freedom of speech" does not give one the
right to insult the prophets; somethings are simply more sacred than others. In
light of the continual attack on religion in our recent history and the systematic undermining of religion in our contemporary secular society, the Habermasian argument insists that recognition of the risk taken by the religious
communities should be honored by secular voices if a place for discourse is
to be established where all feel comfortable and safe to put forward their own
contributions. If religious voices do not feel secure offering their positions via
secular language, they inevitably will retreat into dogmatism, obscurantism,
and reactionary orthodoxy – all religious "defense mechanisms" that protect
the sacred from the rapacious onslaught of the secular.

If we assume that we are not going to return to a religious state any time
soon, that secular society is permanent in the West, while also recognizing the
continued existence of religious communities despite the ever-expanding secularization process, then a solution to this vexing problem must be found, one
in which both the religious and secular are secure and respected in their values. Habermas' suggestion – his *translation proviso* – is one possibility. It may
be the only viable possibility at this time in history. Nevertheless, the obligation of the religious communities to translate their theologically saturated semantics into the secular language is not the only obligation Habermas assigns;
he believes that secular voices have a substantive burden to perform as well.

Being-with-others who are in opposition to one's own worldview, such as
the case between many secular and religious citizens in any given country, is a
difficult matter when it comes to democratic deliberation on the future of one's
nation. If we accept the idea that democracies intrinsically have to make difficult compromises between competing factions, and that this is done under the
conditions of post-secularity, then both the religious and the secular will have

to carry a specific burden in order for democracy to be both *inclusive* and representative of the *will of the people*[s]. For Habermas, the translation proviso that the religious communities have to burden is balanced by the burden that the secular citizens have to carry; they have to go through a *learning process* similar to the religious voices.[67] For Habermas, secular citizens must (1) learn to allow religious voices to participate within the 'political will formation' even if they cannot separate their 'moral convictions and vocabulary into profane and religious strands.'[68] This religious participation in the political will formation is inevitably done within the public sphere where ideas can be contested by the citizenry before or simultaneously with the political discussions within the governmental institutions. Although such religious vocabulary cannot be a part of the institutional discussion of a political matter, due to the neutrality of the state towards religion, it can however be part of the overall discussion within civil society and the public sphere. Therefore secular citizens must allow for the articulation of religious sentiments within the public sphere, even if those sentiments remain stubbornly rooted within a sacred text or tradition. Although the secular state cannot introduce such religious language into its legislation, it nevertheless cannot bar such voices from expressing themselves, their concerns, and their values within the public sphere, which remains the open arena for information and idea exchange. (2) As a part of allowing the freedom of expression with the public sphere, the state, according to Habermas, should not 'over-hastily reduce the polyphonic complexity of the range of public voices, for it cannot be sure whether in doing so it would not cut society off from scarce resources for generating meanings and shaping identities.'[69] This is a curious statement by Habermas for those who fall within the secular-fundamentalist camp, for they often believe that an expansive notion of freedom of speech within a secular society provides the protection for those who wish to ultimately reduce and or destroy the very freedoms they invoke while expressing their displeasure with such broad freedoms. An expansive concept of "freedom of speech" allows too much space for those who would denounce "freedom of speech," as Islamic fundamentalist are often accused of when they articulate their disgust for the West's irreverence of religion and religious figures – which is speech protected by the freedom of speech. Nevertheless, Habermas is not attempting to diminish the ability for citizens to contest certain ideas in the *public sphere*, he is concerned with the *state's* attempts to 'over hastily reduce the polyphonic complexity of the range of public voices' precisely

---

67   Habermas, *Europe*, 73–77.
68   Ibid., 76.
69   Ibid., 76.

because he believes that religions still have the capacity to 'provide convincing articulations of moral sensitivities and solidaristic intuitions' that could be of great benefit to a secularized society that has been depleted of unconditional meaning, motivation for solidarity, and moral legitimation for revolutionary and progressive values.[70] In the end, secular citizens, despite their weariness and *unbehagen* (uneasiness) with their religious counterparts, must accept the fact that shared citizenship is not predicated on adjustment to and acceptance of a secular worldview, but on shared commitments to a constitution, a shared quest for national health and well-being, and the ability for secular and religious citizens to encounter each other 'face to face as equals.'[71] Both religious voices and the secular voices can learn from one another and together advance causes that would benefit all citizens within society.

The translation proviso and the burden of accepting the right of religious voices to express themselves in the public sphere are both challenges that have to be met for the benefit of our post-secular society if the perpetuation of the status quo, the non-discourse and non-recognition between the secular and the religious, which only distorts and diminishes the polyphonic nature of our modern and pluralistic democracies, is to be transcended. Habermas explains in the last paragraph of his essay,

> Secular citizens who encountered their fellow citizens with the reservation that the latter cannot be taken seriously as modern contemporaries because of their religious mindset would regress to the level of a mere modus vivendi and abandon the basis of mutual recognition constitutive for shared citizenship. Secular citizens should not exclude *a fortiori* that even religious utterances may have semantic contents and convert personal intuitions capable of being translated and introduced into secular discourse. Thus, if all is to go well, *each side must accept an interpretation of the relation between faith and knowledge from its own perspective*, which enables them to live together in a *self-reflective manner*.[72]

Although I find myself in agreement with Habermas concerning the complementary learning processes that each community has to undergo in order for a post-secular society to remain stable, free, and democratic, there are some important problems that his analysis does not fully consider in this particular essay. From the religious side, especially as it pertains to Islam and the Muslim

---

70   Ibid., 77.

71   Ibid., 77.

72   Ibid., 77. My emphasis.

community, substantial problems with the translation proviso can be seen in (1) the legitimacy of the "translated Islam," (2) the problem of who represents this translated Islam, and (3) who has the authority to enforce democratically agreed upon decisions within the Islamic community.

As was stated before, the Islamic tradition understands itself to be a "perfected religion" (*Sūrat al-Ma'idah* 5:3). With this in mind, any addition and or subtraction from the religion is often accused of being *bid'a*, or "innovation." All 'innovation,' it is said, is 'misguidance, and all misguidance leads to the hellfire.'[73] For traditionally devout Muslims, to interject an innovated thought, idea, or practice into a religion that the divine "perfected" during the time of Muhammad is an existential threat, for it threatens the believer with a very unpleasant afterlife – a possibility that devout Muslims take seriously.[74] The Qur'an's *Sūrat al-Baqarah* 2:42 reminds the believer not to 'mix the truth with falsehood,' which for many Muslims, is a prohibition against incorporating any kind of novel ideas and practices into Islam. Therefore, to take an Islamic ideal, divorce it from its prophetic, Qur'anic, and religious vocabulary, and articulate it within secular language, as a secular idea or secular value, for many Muslims, would be to deplete its legitimacy as "truth," as it would then be presented in a false way, which is devoid of the Allah's legitimation. It would no longer be a divinely commanded *absolute* value, but only a humanly *preferred* value. Habermas himself rejects this kind of religious abandonment – for the religious voices have to come to an agreement with their secular counterparts 'under the premises of their own faith' and therefore cannot be impelled by the secular state or society to violate their most basic religious convictions for political expediency.[75] Yet it is with the secularized value that Habermas believes the Muslims should enter into the national discourse. Is Habermas asking religious communities to offer up arguments that are in essence still religious but only appear to be secular for the sake of their non-religious discourse partners? Is that not deception, and is not an agreement made on the foundation of deception an invalid agreement?

Complicating the issue is the reality that "fact" and "value" are not often separated within the Islamic tradition as they have been since the secular-scientific

---

73   This was reported to have been said by the Prophet Muhammad by Abu Dawud and al-Tirmidhi.

74   It is often shocking for westerners to think that Muslims genuinely still believe in and fear punishment in the afterlife. There is very little *securi adversus Deum* (indifference towards God) in the Muslim world, whom, despite the growing secularization of the ummah, retains a good deal of *taqwá* (God consciousness or "fear of god").

75   Ibid., 75.

Enlightenment in the West. Therefore, the value of the ideal is predicated upon it truthfulness (not correctness) – as being approved of by the divine and *not* from whether it is democratically decided upon by an elected committee.[76] The *fact* that the consent of the governed and the agreed upon results of democratic deliberation does not decide the legitimacy of an Islamic *value*; only Allah and the *sunnah* of Prophet Muhammad have the legitimate and absolute authority to do that within the Islamic tradition. Whether a democratic institution chooses to approve of a *value* – translated into secular language – does not affect whether or not it is a moral *fact, imperative,* or *truth* for Muslims. Again, only the divine has the legitimate and absolute authority to justify and sanctify an absolute value of a given ideal, principle or law. If a democratic society chooses to enact and enforce a piece of legislation that is not in accordance with the Islamic tradition, the Islamic tradition itself does not alter its claims because a plurality of voices decided it was socially desirable to do so. This can be said of all religious traditions that are not rooted in democratic consensus, but upon divine revelation, sacred example, and ongoing revelation/religious experience. Thus the problem is this: how can one translate an Islamic argument into secular form if that secular form consequently de-legitimates the Islamic argument – in the eyes of Muslims – because it is divorced from its Qur'anic basis which is its sole true legitimation? Is it a matter of what I've called the "two perceptions theory," that the non-religious citizens who are considering the secularized Islamic argument perceive it to be secular while the religious voices secretly know it's still religious? It is *secular in name only – religious in intent and origin?* Or is this problem deeper than Habermas anticipated? Can Islam be translated into secular language at all without threatening the arguments legitimacy among the ones who would be making the secularized Islamic argument? If the answer is no, then the translation proviso may be dead on arrival from the Muslim perspective. If the answer is yes, then it may only be a matter of *political pragmatism* by which the two perceptions theory in concealed.

The second problem may be even more intractable then the first, being that it has a long history within the Muslim community. Representation – who speaks for Islam – has been a divisive issue since the death of Prophet Muhammad in 632 CE. Indeed, the question of who is the rightful representative of the Islamic tradition, who is authorized to lead the *ummah* in temporal

---

76   I make a philosophical distinction here between truthfulness and correctness. For Islam, correctness is mundane, a matter of protocol sentences, as in a theory of correspondence. "Truth," however, has to do with ultimate reality, not the appropriate correspondence of A and B.

and religious matters, led to the first great schism within Islam – the division between the *Shi'at al-'Ali* (Shi'a) and the *ahl as-sunnah wa l-jamā'ah* (Sunni) – an antagonism that has yet to be reconciled and has only grown more deep and complex with today's geo-political issues in Iraq, Iran, Syria, Saudi Arabia and Lebanon. Additionally, the Islamic tradition, despite the many western perceptions about it, is hardly monolithic. It is a dynamic religious tradition that holds within its ranks conservatives, progressives, liberals, Islamists, extremists, pacifists, mystics, secularists, intellectuals, Imams, Ayatollahs, lay believers, revolutionaries, capitalists, socialists, Marxists, etc. Who then should speak for the Muslim community: the Imams (they may have trouble secularizing their thoughts), the westernized Muslim Intellectuals (they may have a hard time finding legitimacy in the Islamic tradition itself), the Muslim masses (they may not be able to come to any kind of meaningful consensus due to their diversity and lack of theological and philosophical education)? On top of the already intractable problem of representational leadership, who would take the lead for a "secularized" Islam? Which scholars would want to be the ones responsible for introducing what many are sure to proclaim as being *bid'a*? Does anyone want to speak for the "virtues of *bid'a*"? The Muslim community may be stifled by the idea that Islam is a perfected religion if in its perfection it doesn't allow the Muslim community to adjust itself adequately to life within a post-secular and democratic society.

Furthermore, this problem is complicated by Islam's lack of hierarchical authority akin to the Catholic or Orthodox Church. Although the Shi'a community has an established religious hierarchy, the Sunni world, which comprises approximately 80% of the world's Muslims, has been without temporal authority since the demise of the Ottoman Caliphate post-WWI, which has left the community in an anomic situation by which the nation-state has practically replaced the Caliph as the source of practical authority. The *supra-nationalism* of the Ottoman Empire has been replaced by *petit-nationalism* that undermines the Islamic notion of the organic wholeness of the *ummat al-Islamiyah* (Islamic community). Furthermore, although many Sunni scholars' opinions on matters of *fiqh* (jurisprudence), *ihsan* (religious perfection), *'Ilm al-Kalām* (systematic theology), and *'ibādah* (forms of worship), etc., can be considered authoritative, they are only binding on those who choose to bind those rulings to their own personal religiosity and ethical life. Not all Muslims will accept the validity of any given cleric, religious authority, or scholar, nor does the Islamic tradition force them to do so. Unlike Catholicism, there is no infallible authority such as the Pope in Islam. However, what is universally agreed upon, minus the few "heretical" outliers such as the 'Alawites and Ahmadiyya, is that Allah is the only God and that Prophet Muhammad was his last and final messenger. Although the remaining four pillars of *ṣalāh* (prayer), *zakāt* (almsgiving), *sawm* (fasting), and *hajj* (pilgrimage to Mecca), have an overwhelming consensus among all variants of Muslims and schools of law (*maḏāhib*), even these "agreed upon" practices have substantial variations and interpretations among different sects. The diversity of thought, practice, and political-economic orientation among the Muslims make it almost untenable to reach some form of consensus as to who would represent Islam when making a secularized-Islamic argument – the kind that Habermas calls for if Muslims are to fully enter into the discourse community of the post-secular society. In order to avoid sectarian disputes, the same kind that plagued Europe throughout its religious history, the Muslim representatives would have to be the bearers of near "universal consensus" – even if only within one nation-state – and that would have to be legitimated through agreed upon Islamic authorities. If the so-called representative could not obtain such "universal consensus," then whatever resulted from the discussion within a secular constitutional democratic discourse, even if it was perceived to be in favor of the Muslim community, would maintain little to no legitimacy and could not be made binding on the community unless it was binding in the laws of the given nation state, in which case it is a matter of state and not religion. In other words, it is not the governing nature of the religion that would bind the adherents to the value or principle that was enacted into law, but the secular state. Being such, many Muslims could simply return to the bi-furcated position of "man's law is not God's law," and therefore has no *real* authority over the believer.

The only way to make such an agreement binding would be to take the discussion back to the Islamic community, having a universal discourse that excludes no one that would be affected by the decision, and entering into a robust dialogue, discourse, and debate, with the expressed intent to win a "universal consensus" *ex-post facto*. To by-pass the debate about who should be the legitimate representative of the Muslims *ummah* within a given nation state, engage the secular society in a discourse concerning a secularized-Islamic ideal, then return to the community to garnish its blessing, maybe the only way to avoid the inevitable entanglement concerning Islamic authority. However, what this process would not do is necessary import the legitimation of the Islamic tradition itself, but it may import the consent of the Muslim community. Yet, it is possible that the appeal of having a Muslim voice within the process of democratic deliberation may be enough of a motivation for many to overlook the question of representation and therefore take a more intra-religious ecumenical stance. The simple fact is that we just don't know because it has never been tried.

An additional factor that must be considered is the complexity of the Muslim communities within the West. There you find an even more dense concentration of diversity than in the traditional Muslim world itself. In one mosque, one may find the community divided between country of origin, ethnicity, immigrant and native believers, and those who've assimilated and those who haven't, those who are devout and those who attend the mosque only on the *'Eids* (holy days), etc. On the other hand, Muslims often belong to "ethnic" mosques; those mosques that cater exclusively to a given ethnic or national community and therefore tend to be more socially and politically homogeneous and isolated from the broader Muslim community. Furthermore, at least in America, there is an underlying tension between African Americans, who came to Islam precisely because it was liberating from their experiences with American racism, and immigrants, who came to America because they wanted to take part in the "American dream," which is predominately associated with white America. Where African Americans have often embraced the more militant and revolutionary aspects of Islam, their immigrant counterparts are often likely to compromise those same revolutionary ideals in the process of assimilation. In order to become more "mainstream," Muslim immigrants, especially "middle class" Arabs, are more likely not to engage in a radical critique of American culture and political policy as not to elicit suspicion concerning their loyalties. Sociologists have dubbed this later phenomenon the "whitening of Arabs/Muslims." This is often a serious source of tension between immigrants and their African American co-believers, the later tending to be poorer, less educated, and having a more militant *belief attitude* in their practice of Islam. For them the "American dream" has always been what Malcolm x often said it was: an "American nightmare." Consequently, an attempt to find one universally accepted representative within the polyphonic nature of Islam in the West might prove to be extremely difficult given the historical development and demographics of the Muslim communities.

The third problem I identified is the problem of enforcement. A consensus that is established by the discourse between the secular citizens and their Muslim counterparts may both garnish (1) democratic legitimacy, and even (2) Islamic legitimacy (via its own traditions), but who should enforce such a decision among the Muslims themselves? Through a democratically elected constitutional state, the citizenry recognizes the legitimacy of a piece of legislation even if they do not agree with its particular stance; the "democratic process" by which the legislation came to pass – if it is enacted without corruption – is not in question even if the goals and outcomes of a particular piece of legislation may be. The state, being neutral towards religion, but accepting the legitimacy of the democratically agreed upon value that was devised by the universal discourse community, has the sole legitimate function of enforcing the law upon its citizens; the administration of justice cannot be in the hands of private citizens themselves, but must reside within the apparatus of the state which represents all citizens, or the "common good," via constitutional norms. Nevertheless, those democratic consensuses that would have been argued for by the Muslims via secularized Islamic language would inevitably be once again understood through the lens of Islam in order to garnish broader Muslim support. In other words, in order to prove the legitimacy of the agreed upon decision to the average Muslim – those affected by the decision itself – those arguing for the decision would inevitably do so in Islamic language. Thus the ideal, value, or belief would migrate first from Islamic language, then to secular language for the purpose of democratic discourse, and then back to Islamic language for the consensus of the Muslim community. However, one cannot expect the average believer to be able to master the political-economic-philosophic language that is necessary to translate religious ideals into secular political thought. Therefore the ideal must once again clothe itself in religious semantics in order to engender the desired consent of the Muslim community.

Once the law is established, are we now asking the secular state to enforce upon its citizens a religious value dressed in secular garb, or does the "overlapping consensus" between the secular and religious voices generate its own legitimacy in terms of enforcement? Or are we asking the secular state to enforce a secularized religious value on other religious communities that may not have lent their support to the decision? This may seem like we are splitting hairs – fussing over hypotheticals that do not yet exist. However, the suspicion that religion lurks behind certain social programs, or that secular-humanism is thinly veiled behind social legislation, is enough to make different religious communities – as well as the secular – withdraw their support from the legislation, as it can be viewed as an underhanded attack on the secularity and neutrality of the state. If this is done on a national scale, the bitter divisions that are already entrenched within the multicultural society can widen even further, as both sides of the divide accuse the other of ulterior motives for their political decisions. In this way, enforcement of the decision can lead to animosity, distrust, and suspicion of the other's motives. These feelings can derail the whole intent of the democratic discourse and lead to a situation worse than the *modus vivendi* that is already the defacto reality.

Secular Entrenchment

Yet, for all the problems that must be surmounted for the post-secular society to come to any promising reconciliation between the religious and the secular, we must recognize that the most intractable objection of Habermas' attempt to establish the conditions for the post-secular society may not be found with the Muslims at all, but rather with their more militantly secular counterparts. Among the professional Islamophobes in Europe and America, such as Ayaan Hirsi Ali, Robert Spencer, the neo-Randian Pamela Geller, Glenn Beck, Geert Wilders, Bat Ye'or (Gisèle Littman), and Marine Le Pen, there is a common argument that expresses the fears of many in the West: that the immigration of Muslims represents an "Islamic Trojan Horse." They believe that lax immigration and asylum policies of liberal America and Europe are the camouflage under which the "silent" invasion of the West is taking place. They believe that because of the "bleeding-heart" nature of cultural liberals, multiculturalists, and progressives, radical Islam has snuck into the back door of the West; where the invading forces of the Ottomans and Moors once failed to conquer all of Europe, contemporary Europeans have let open the doors to their successors, who are just as committed to conquering "Christian" Europe as their predecessors. Although the relationship between Europeans, Americans and their Islamic immigrant communities haven't always been peaceful – witness the French riots of 2005 – the integration process has been relatively peaceful. It has yet to devolve into an apocalyptic *Crusade vs. Jihad* scenario that the professional Islamophobes have suggested as being inevitable. When conflicts have broken out, it has often followed the anti-Muslim factions having made "controversial" something that would not be controversial if it involved any other religious community.

Remember the unfortunate 2009–2012 mosque debacle in Murfreesboro, Tennessee, where a group of concerned citizens – nearly all working class Caucasians – filed a lawsuit to halt the building of a mosque in their city, even to the point of arguing in an American court that Islam was *not a religion* and therefore did not warrant the protections that religious communities are afforded under the U.S. Constitution, in particular the prohibition clause of the 1st Amendment: *Congress shall make no law... prohibiting the free exercise* [of religion] *thereof.* Although a federal judge disagreed with their ridiculous claim, and allowed the Muslim community to continue to build their new mosque and community center, the Muslims were continually harassed, subjected to violent threats, their construction equipment set ablaze, and they were shot at from the adjacent woods. Led by members of the *Tennessee Tea Party*, many irate citizens of Murfreesboro feared the mosque would serve as a terrorism-training center, a recruitment station for jihādists, and believed it was ultimately designed to infect middle Tennessee with extremist beliefs. Ironically, it was some of the most secular voices that demonstrated in favor of the mosque. They viewed the entire issue as one of equal rights for all citizens – the right of Muslims to build a mosque was no less than the right of an Evangelical Christian to build a church, or a Jewish community to build a synagogue. What was important was *citizenship*, not the pre-political foundation of religion.[77]

Another example of a manufactured "crisis" concerning Islam in the West was the *Park51* or *Cordoba House* debacle.[78] Here, Muslims of Manhattan wished to build a YMCA-like community center just two blocks away from the site of the World Trade Center. As well as having a space for prayer (to be used by members of any faith), much of the building would have been dedicated to inter-faith dialogue – an attempt to heal the wounds cause by the 9/11 attacks on New York City. However, many "Tea Party Patriots" objected to this plan, referring to it as the *Ground Zero Mosque*, which, in their minds, represented Islam's victory over the United States on September 11th, 2001. Stirred by conservative FOX News and other right-wing media outlets, the Park51 project became the object of protest as thousands of ill-informed citizens believed it was to be a terrorist recruitment center and victory monument.[79] Although the building of the community centered was motivated out of the idea of reconciliation, it quickly became a flashpoint between the Muslim community, their liberal supporters, and the Islamophobic and miso-Islamist right. Spearheaded by the Sufi leader Imam Feisal Abdul Rauf, who was also an FBI asset (according to Wikileaks), the idea of the center became so politically toxic for the Muslims that the project was eventually abandoned, the prayer center and community halls were never built, and reconciliation remained a dream of the ecumenically inclined. Those forces that saw no reason to peacefully communicate with their Islamic neighbors skillfully avoided such a discourse between Muslims and non-Muslims. For many, healing the wounds of 9/11 can only

---

77   See Jürgen Habermas, *Between Facts and Norms* (Cambridge, MA: The MIT Press, 1996), 494–495.

78   By naming the mosque *Cordoba House*, the planners were intentionally invoking the legacy of Cordoba, Spain, where in the 8th to 11th century Muslims lived peacefully with their fellow Christians and Jews. However, for critics such as Newt Gingrich, the name *Cordoba* invoked the Muslim conquest of Spain, a formerly Catholic territory.

79   During this "scandal," the anchors of FOX News regularly attacked the planned community center as being funded by Saudi Arabia, specifically Prince Waleed bin Talal, the billionaire Saudi prince, who shares the same nationality and Wahhabi orientation as the nineteen highjackers who attacked the United States on 9/11. This fact was used to show that the proposed community center was indeed funded by terrorist sympathizers like the prince. However, to the surprise of many of the FOX anchors, it was publically disclosed that the prince was the second largest stockholder in News Corp., the parent company of FOX News. When this information was made public, those same FOX News anchors quickly fell silent as they were in effect accusing their boss of funding terrorism.

come from the dropping of bombs on more Muslims; it does not come from entering into a conversation with the other, understanding the vulnerabilities and concerns of the other, or even engaging in a friendly dialogue with others, even if those others are citizens of the same country.

Nevertheless, this anti-Islamic sentiment, although only articulated in the public sphere by those generally of the right-wing nationalist persuasion, is uneasily felt by many more regular individuals who lack the courage and/or fortitude to state their concerns in public because they fear being ostracized as bigots, racists, anti-immigrants, and/or neo-Nazis both in the United States and Europe.[80] Their fear is often real and should not be easily dismissed, especially not in a post-secular democratic society. Yet one should remain vigilant in the detection of manufactured fear, which occurs often with right-wing demagogues. On the other hand, if Habermas' program of secularizing Islamic values for purposes of national discourse is recognized by those that are already weary of the influence of religious minorities within their secular country, a backlash is more than likely to occur. Again, the "Islamic Trojan Horse" appears to them to be not only a theory, but also a reality that is slowly undermining the western way of life. Indeed, in the Murfreesboro case, it became a constant refrain to 'look to Europe' when discussion the encroachment of Islam upon a secular and/or Christian population; 'they are about 20 years ahead of us,' said Bill French, a local anti-mosque critic.[81] The fear of Islamization may be real for many, even if those who profit off such fear have ulterior motives.

Although he seems unaware of it, the nationalist-right views the real *Trojan horse* in Habermas' theory as being the secular language itself. It is the vehicle by which Islam roots itself in the state via its carefully camouflaged secularized-Islamic language. The fear is rooted in the idea that Europe and the West can be *Islamized via secular language* instead of *Islam being neutralized via secularism*. The end result, they fear, is that they will be living in a nation that has been thoroughly transformed by the imposition of religious values that only "appear" to be secular in nature, but are in fact born out of "foreign" and antithetical religion. This Habermasian approach, if adopted by the political-Left

---

80   The 2015–2016 Republican presidential candidate Donald Trump, who openly gave voice to the fears and anxieties that many within the American electorate were feeling, alleviated this fear in the United States. However, his blatant demagoguery, race baiting, anti-immigration and nationalistic rants exposed the widespread miso-Islamism that infected much of the American populace.

81   Bob Smietana, "Religious Conflict isn't New to Murfreesboro: Catholic Immigrants Plan Fueled Protests in Murfreesboro in 1929," October 24, 2010. www.tennessean.com/article/20101024/NEWS01/10240382 (Accessed 10/7/2014).

of Europe (which doesn't have a counterpart in the U.S.), could also lead to a backlash against the multiculturalist Left as being the accomplices of the "Eurabianization" of Europe, as it's their insistence on a compassionate immigration policy, multiculturalism, and tolerance that leads to the influx of Muslims in Europe.[82]

This may seem farfetched, even conspiratorial to some, but we must be willing to read the present trends. The 2011 attack on Oslo and Utøya island in Norway by the right-wing miso-Islamist, Anders Behring Breivik, stands as a testament to the idea that the political-Left, i.e. socialists and communists, are the gatekeepers for the Islamic takeover of Europe, of which they have been accused of swinging the door wide open.[83] According to this theory, because of their ill-informed philosophical universalism and misguided compassion for third-world peoples, the Left is willing to destroy its own civilization by welcoming in an unending number of foreigners, whom they see as the historical "victims" of western colonialism, imperialism, neo-imperialism, and now today expansionist capitalism (globalization).[84] Additionally, the political-right sees the influx of Muslims as being the product of "cultural Marxism," a result of the Frankfurt School and other leftist theoreticians who wish to undermine the indigenous culture and national values through multiculturalism, political correctness, and class struggle. The ideology of multiculturalism – born out of a traditional universalist interpretation of Enlightenment values – in the estimation of Breivik and others, is the ideology that dumbs down the masses, makes them complacent in seeing their nation-state overrun with foreigners, and will eventually hand the once racially homogenous nations over to the uncivilized multi-ethnic Muslims. It is also the ideology that is espoused by the multiculturalist Left, in the political-right's view, which cares little for its own national culture and heritage. This is a familiar argument; it is the same accusations leveled at the communists decades ago when they expressed

---

82   The role of capitalism's need for cheap labor, and therefore immigrant labor, is often forgotten within the discussion as to why there are so many immigrants in Europe.

83   See Aage Borchegrevink, Aage. *A Norwegian Tragedy: Anders Behring Breivik and the Massacre on Utøya*, trans. Guy Puzey. Malden, MA: Polity Press, 2013; Jeffrey D. Simon, *Lone Wolf Terrorism: Understanding the Growing Threat* (Amherst, NY: Prometheus Books, 2013), 49–53.

84   This is a very ironical sentiment that the right-wing has concerning the political-Left and Islam, especially considering that Hitler himself believed that the history of Europe would have been better had the Muslims conquered it. See Albert Speer, *Inside the Third Reich: Memoirs by Albert Speer,* trans. Richard & Clara Winston (New York: Macmillan Company, 1969), 114–115; Adolf Hitler, *Hitler's Table Talk: 1941–1944*, trans. Norman Cameron and R.H. Stevens. New York: Enigma Books, 2000.

their solidarity for the working class regardless of what nation they found themselves in. *National* solidarity, favored by the political- and cultural-right because it preserves the class order and the "purity" of the race/culture, was rejected in favor of *international* solidarity, which cut across national boarders by emphasizing the co-fraternity of workers regardless of what nation they originated from. Communists, emphasizing *international solidarity*, argued that workers in all countries had more in common with each other than with the ruling class of their own nations, and therefore should band together in one "internationale." Therefore *international* solidarity was a threat to *national* cohesion. Here again this plays a role in Breivik's thinking; the political-Left of Europe cares more for the working class, the poor, and the immigrants of other nations and religions than they do their own pre-political ethnos/demos/nation, and are willing to sacrifice the later for their liberal, overly-compassionate and universalist interpretation of the Enlightenment. Breivik and others have no intention of participating willingly in what they viewed as national-suicide at the hands of misguided immigration and multiculturalist policies. In his attempt to arrest and/or abate the influx of Muslims into Norway, Breivik murdered 77 innocent individuals, most of which were the sons and daughters of Leftist members of the Norwegian parliament.[85] Fortunately, he was in a Norwegian prison during the summer months of 2015, when the war in Syria and Iraq brought millions of Muslim refugees to the doors of Europe, especially to Germany and Scandanavia, where they were promised better living conditions than in the poorer southern European states. Nevertheless, after the numerous incidents of rape and harassment by refugees and asylum seekers in Cologne, Germany, on New Years Eve, 2015, many Europeans who would normally not have followed Breivik's line of thinking, reconsidered his anti-immigrant and anti-Muslim stance. Although they continued to reject violence as an answer to the problem of immigration, they recognized that Breivik might have had a legitimate point, even if it was hidden under a mountain of racist ideology.

As stated before, the "Islamic Trojan Horse" theory may be far-fetched at the moment, but the perceptions among the populations in Europe, especially Western and Southern Europe, is growing at an ever-increasing pace with every Muslim attack on the West. Recall the backlash against Muslims in Britain after the brutal murder of Lee Rigby, an off-duty soldier in the British army. Rigby was killed in the city of Woolwich by Michael Adebolajo and Michael Adebowale, two British Muslim converts of Nigerian decent – sons of immigrants – who were protesting Britain's treatment of Muslims in Muslim lands. Not only did these two men run Rigby over with their car, they then

---

85   Like Geert Wilders, Anders Behring Breivik also harbored far-right Zionist views.

proceeded to stab him repeatedly and barbarically dismember him with a meat cleaver; this appalling site was witnessed by numerous pedestrians in the middle of the day. The murderers then proceeded to give invective lectures to the bystanders about the Islamic victims of Britain's policies in Muslim countries. These impromptu speeches were recorded and later broadcasted that evening through national and international news outlets to the disgust of the British public (and later the world audience). Without pause, the Islamic Society of Britain expressed their sincere sympathy for the victim and his family and vehemently condemned the action of the two men. A spokesman said 'This is a truly barbaric act that has no basis in Islam and we condemn this unreservedly... Muslims have long served in this country's Armed Forces, proudly and with honour. This attack on a member of the Armed Forces is dishonourable, and no cause justifies this murder.' However, the English Defense League, a right-wing nativist organization – sometimes labeled a neo-fascist group – attacked mosques and Muslims in various neighborhoods in Britain. They saw no distinction between the two assailants and the Muslim community at large.[86] Neither did they see this as an isolated act of individuals, but rather it was an act perpetrated by Islam itself; to be a Muslim was to be guilty of this crime. It is certainly possible to claim that the English Defense League is a fringe group on the edges of British society, but how long will that charge hold when average British citizens continue to see such acts of pure barbaric violence on their streets?[87] Can the average British citizen of Muslim faith, who patriotically holds his country dear to his heart, overcome the increasing suspicion that Muslims in Britain, and Europe in general, are not there with only peaceful intentions, but are rather a "forward operating base" for the future takeover of Europe by Muslims? Or will the acts of small minorities of Muslims and their

---

86 Ross Lydall. "Woolwich Killing: A Plea for Calm as Mosques are Targeted and English Defense Leagues Clash with Police," May 23, 2013. http://www.standard.co.uk/news/crime/woolwich-killing-plea-for-calm-as-mosques-are-targeted-and-english-defence-league-clash-with-police-8628387.html (Accessed 3/26/2014).

87 From a Muslim perspective, the question is slightly different: when will those who are responsible for the mass killings of Muslims in Iraq, Afghanistan, and other Muslim countries ever be brought to justice? When will Bush and Blair find themselves in the Hague for their crimes against humanity? The barbarity of watching innocent men, women, and children die at the hands of "smart bombs," drones, and Marines is too much for many Muslims to bear. Indeed, the inability of the West to confess its own sins, seek forgiveness, and mourn the loss of the dead other, motivates extremist Muslims to seek revenge for the suffering imposed on the ummah. Lex Talionis, or the "law of retaliation," becomes the normative tool of communication when peaceful discourse is non-existent.

right-wing nativist counterparts push the center of European society towards the politics of hate and divisiveness?

In light of the anti-immigrant/anti-Muslim attitude arising throughout Europe, in May of 2014, the Europeans elected an unprecedented number of anti-immigrant parties and candidates to the European parliament, including in France where Marine Le Pen's ultra-right-wing anti-immigrant Nationalist party took a record 25% of the vote, an ominous turn-of-events for Muslims in Europe.[88]

Yet the other side of the coin is equally violent (if only more mechanized). From the perspective of many war-weary Muslims, they ask how long can the Muslim community watch the nations of the West attack their countries, bomb their people from fighter-planes and drones, ravage their lands, leave behind legacies of broken promises, broken bodies, exploited markets and workers, and history of environmental destruction? For the purposes of our study, we must ask whether or not Habermas' theory of the mutual learning process, the secularization of Islam, and the acceptance of religious voices within secular society, alleviate the turn towards cultural dysfunction, cultural antagonism, and violence? That question is still open. At the present moment, it appears that history is plunging the world closer to confrontation rather than reconciliation, despite the example of St. Francis of Assisi and the Sultan Malik al-Kamil, and the recent ecumenical work of Pope Francis.

---

88   IBTimes UK. "EU Elections: Anti-Immigrant Wave Sweeps Europe," May 26, 2014. http://www.ibtimes.com/eu-elections-anti-immigrant-wave-sweeps-europe-1590035 (Accessed 6/3/2014).

Witnessing and Professing in Prophetic and Positive Religions

In light of the dominant trend to condemn all forms of religion within "vulgar" Marxism, as well as liberalism's thorough attempts to privatize and/or functionalize religion in the post-secular society, the Critical Theorists Theodor Adorno and Max Horkheimer, as well as the Frankfurt School in general, have made an important distinction between prophetic – or critical/negative/humanistic – religion and what they define as affirmative-positive and/or authoritarian religion. The prior form of religion, through its negativity, escapes positivism's semantic deflation of religious potentials and its priestly upholding of the world-as-it-is found in the positive religious traditions. The act of witnessing and professing by way of a negative theology, a negative religion that roots itself within the prophetic and Socratic soil, is qualitatively different than it is within positive religions. In order to understand these competing trends within the Abrahamic religious traditions in the context of the post-secular society, we must first return to Marx, who represents the second push towards secularization after the ascendance of the Bourgeoisie.

Affirmation and Negativity: Marx

Marx's analysis toward religion was dialectical in nature; while he understood, following Voltaire, that religion often allied itself to those who had the biggest battalions, i.e. those who held temporal power, he also understood that religion preserves within itself the genuine hopes, desires, and longings of the oppressed, exploited, and denigrated masses; it was at once the record of suffering and at the same time the illusion that anesthetized of such suffering. This dialectical understanding can be witnessed in Marx's most famous definition of religion, found in his *Contribution to the Critique of Hegel's Philosophy of Right,*

> Religious suffering is at the same time an express of real suffering and a protest against real suffering. Religion is the sigh of the oppressed

creature, the sentiment of a heartless world, and the soul of soulless conditions. It is the *opium* of the people.[1]

If one refuses to translate Marx's philosophy of religion into a simple anti-religion slogan, one can read within this passage the true nature of Marx's observation; religion is both a *protest* against an oppressive and violent world and a source of *affirmation* (or at least a subjective acquiescence) of that world. For Marx, it is the distorted and oppressive conditions of the world that create the need for a religion that dulls the consciousness, to make life bearable, to anesthetize the wound of a damaged life, but those conditions simultaneously produce the need for resistance to that damaging and crippling world. What Marx observed was that religion has within itself certain potentials that can either aid in the liberation of mankind or can reconcile mankind to his oppression, although he believed the later to more accurate in terms of the history of religion.

Marx was not the first to reject a form of religion that would dull the conscience in favor of one that would sharpen it. Following the great enlightener Immanuel Kant, he applied such a critique to the realm of political economy, whereas Kant confined it to personal morality. In his book *Religion within the Boundaries of Mere Reason,* Kant writes,

> The aim of those who have clergyman summoned to them at the end of life is normally to find in him a comforter, not on account of their physical suffering brought on by the last illness or even by the natural fear in the face of death (for on this score death itself, which puts an end to life, can be the comforter) but because of the moral sufferings, the reproaches of their conscience. At such time, however, conscience ought rather to be stirred up and sharpened, in order that whatever good yet to be done, or whatever consequences of past evil still left to be undone (repaired for), will not be neglected, in accordance with the warning, 'Agree with thine adversary' (with him who has a legal right against you) 'quickly, while thou art in the way with him' (i.e. so long as you still live), 'lest he deliver thee to the judge' (after death), etc. But to administer opium to conscience instead, as it were, is to be guilty of a crime against the human being himself and against those who survive him, and is totally contrary

---

1   Karl Marx, "Contribution to the Critique of Hegel's Philosophy of Right: Introduction" in *The Marx & Engels Reader,* ed. Robert C. Tucker (New York: W. W. Norton & Co., Inc., 1978), 54.

to the purpose for which such support given to conscience at life's end can be held necessary.[2]

Despite the bifurcated conception of religion, which Marx accepted, it does not mean that Marx himself *believed* in the metaphysical claims of religious traditions. Indeed, he believed that Feuerbach's "projection" thesis had already answered the question of the origins of religion, which were entirely within the psychological and material conditions of man himself. He states, 'the basis of irreligious criticism is this: man makes religion; religion does not make man. Religion is indeed man's self-consciousness and self-awareness so long as he has not found himself or has lost himself again.'[3] For Marx, man creates god in his own image and not the other way around, but that consciousness is itself a creation of the material world; a world in which suffering and oppression is created and/or exasperated by the condition imposed on humanity by modern capitalism and other historical forms of oppression.[4] Nevertheless, religion, as a social phenomenon created by the unjust conditions of society, not only expresses a protesting voice of man, but also has the potential to impel him towards action against the very conditions that oppress him. The inherent – but often neglected – negativity within religion, especially the Abrahamic traditions of Judaism, Christianity, and Islam, stresses the "fallenness" – the "it is not as it should be" – of this world. It is not a world that manifests justice, equality, and fairness, but a world that is driven by lust, greed, wickedness, and unwarranted violence, and therefore it is a world that demands its own negation via a conditions-changing nemesis: a messianic figure, group, or movement.

Yet for Marx, the negativity of Judaism and Christianity (he wasn't too familiar with Islam) was negated when religion reconciled itself to the world, when it became "of the world," thus it legitimates the world and the unjust powers that ruled the world. In this sense, religion, as it is reconciled to the world as it is, became the ideological mask that veiled the class interests of the ruling elites; it legitimated their rule, it sanctioned their actions, and it absolved the sins of their transgressions. That is why he believed that 'the criticism of religion is the premise of all criticism,' as one must first tear asunder religious legitimation from the terror of history's oppressors that it often sanctifies.[5] Temporal power must be evacuated of its divine legitimation as to liberate mankind from the religio-existential anxiety and fears about social and political rebellion. In

---

2   Immanuel Kant, *Religion within the Boundaries of Mere Reason,* ed. Allen Wood and George di Giovanni (Cambridge, MA: Cambridge University Press, 1998), 93.

3   Marx, *Contribution,* 53.

4   Ibid., 53.

5   Ibid., 53.

order to move towards universal emancipation, the equation of state and the divine had to be broken to unleash the liberational potential of the masses. Additionally, the identification of religion with power – as opposed to the powerless in Abrahamic thought – inevitably repressed religion's emancipatory potentials in the cage of conformity, as it shifts the divine's blessing from the *victims* of nature and history to the *victors* within nature and history. For Marx, in order for human emancipation to be achieved, religion had to be transcended as it had been perversely transfigured into a *positive-affirming* force in the world, i.e. it affirms and upholds the torturous status quo and rejects any radical attempt to overthrown the world as it is. Positive religion is religion that has abandoned its essential negativity, i.e. its ability to determinately negate the world of suffering, the world of antagonisms, and the world of oppression. For Marx, religion's insistence on suffering peacefully the injustices of the world, and not radically transforming them, is a powerful tool in the hands of those who do not want political-economic and cultural opposition, whose fortunes are tied to the status quo, and whose existence are affixed to the ruling elites. Therefore, mankind must be unshackled from its religious chains if it is to once again become acquainted with its true human nature, which is free. Marx says,

> The abolition of religion as the illusory happiness of men, is a demand for their real happiness. The call to abandon their illusions about their condition is a call to abandon a condition that requires illusions. The criticism of religion is, therefore, the embryonic criticism of this vale of tears of which religion is the halo...
>
>   The criticism of religion disillusions man so that he will think, act and fashion his reality as a man who has lost his illusions and regained his reason; so that he will revolve about himself as his own true sun. Religion is only the illusory sun about which man revolves so long as he does not revolve about himself.[6]

This sense of religion's abandonment of his its own humanistic and liberational potentials is also echoed in the writings of Max Horkheimer, the intellectual initiator of the Frankfurt School for Social Research. He writes in his *Thoughts on Religion,* which is his reformulation of Marx's "opiate of the masses" passage, that,

> The concept of God was for a long time the place where the idea was kept alive that there are other norms besides those to which nature and

---

6   Ibid., 54.

society give expression in their operation. Dissatisfaction with earthly destiny is the strongest motive for acceptance of a transcendental being. If justice resides with God, then it is not to be found in the same measure in the world. Religion is the record of the wishes, desires, and accusation of countless generations.

But the more Christianity brought God's rule into harmony with events in the world, the more the meaning of religion became perverted. In Catholicism God was already regarded as in certain aspects the creator of the earthly order, while Protestantism attributed the world's course directly to the will of the Almighty. Not only was the state of affairs on earth at any given moment transfigured with the radiance of divine justice, but the latter was itself brought down to the level of the corrupt relations which mark earthly life. Christianity lost its function of expressing the ideal, to the extent that it became the bedfellow of the state.[7]

For Horkheimer, learning from Marx, the 'image of a perfect justice' that early Christians embraced – and so often died for as martyrs – in the face of the injustice of the Roman Empire and nature itself, evaporated when it was legalized by Emperor Constantine via the *Edict of Milan* (313 CE), and later transformed into the official ideology of the state by the Roman Emperor Theodosius in his imperial decree *Cunctos Populos*, also known as the *Edict of Thessalonica* (380 CE). Constantinian Christianity – the strange reconciliation of Christ and Roman (state) power – depleted Christianity's potential for revolutionary change as well as its ability to substantively express the real possibility of a future reconciled world.[8] What came from this marriage of religion and state was not the long-awaited messiah and the messianic age, but only the institution of the Roman Catholic Church – the priestly administration of a once revolutionary but now *politically* conservative message. For the first generation of Christians, the *Kingdom of God* was not the *Empire of Rome*, but for later Christians,

---

7   Max Horkheimer, *Critical Theory: Selected Essays* (New York: Continuum, 2002), 188.

8   See James A. Reimer, "Constantine: From Religious Pluralism to Christian Hegemony" in *The Future of Religion: Toward a Reconciled Society,* ed. Michael R. Ott. Leiden: Brill Publishers, 2007. One should remember that even in Constantine's time, Christianity was still marginalized if not oppressed within the Roman Empire. By merging their religion with the power of the state, Christians gained not only gain a legal status but also the protection of the state. The more *corrupting* moment of Christian history is when Emperor Theodosius made Nicene Christianity the official religion of the state, in the year 395 CE. At this moment Christianity downed the power of the state and therefore betrayed its critical-prophetic role. After this, Christian authorities, including the Emperor, set about the systematic destruction of pre-Christian religions as well "heretical" forms of Christianity.

Augustine's "City of God" became the consolation for the *parousia*-delay ("God with us" delay) – the fact that Jesus had not yet returned.[9] The church as an institution of worldly power, for Marx and other critical religiologists, has the been primary purveyor of positive religion, as it itself became the object of faith, the crafter of dogma, the teacher who extolls the values of passive-suffering, and the final source of legitimation for the status quo. In his simple Christology, Marx accused the church of abandoning the 'carpenter whom the rich men killed' and thus perverting the revolutionary potential of Christianity's essential negativity towards the world.[10] Yet, such disappointment with the church was not his final word on religion. Marx could still see something of value within the church even if it was a flawed and corrupt remembrance of the revolutionary Rabbi Jesus. Marx, most sympathetically, taught his children 'we can forgive Christianity much, because it taught us the worship of the child.'[11] We can ruminate on the many things that the "child" may symbolize, but it seems for Marx to represent something within religion that must be preserved, emancipated from its dogmatic shackles, and be fulfilled within secular praxis. The "child" cannot be abandoned by revolutionary praxis even if religion has historically done so. The symbol of the child – the potential for goodness, innocence, and arguably even reason – is the very potential for Hegel's notion of reconciliation: the 'rose in the cross of the present.'[12] Negative religion refuses to abandon this potential but rather preserves it at the core of its thought and praxis.

Affirmation and Negativity: Lenin

Marx's Russian heir, Vladimir Lenin, also understood religion – in his case Russian Orthodoxy – to have abandoned its 'image of perfect justice' and had

---

9   Saint Augustine. *The City of God*, trans. Marcus Dods. Peabody, MA: Hendrickson Publishers Marketing, LLC, 2014.

10   Erich Fromm, *Marx's Concept of Man* (New York: Frederick Ungar Publishing Co., 1981), 252–253.

11   Fromm, *Marx's Concept of Man*, 252–253.

12   G.W.F. Hegel, *Elements of the Philosophy of Right*, ed. Allen W. Wood (New York: Cambridge University Press, 2010), 22. Hegel states that 'to recognize reason as the rose in the cross of the present and thereby delight in the present – this rational insight is the *reconciliation* with actuality which philosophy grants to those who have received the inner call *to comprehend*, to preserve their subjective freedom in the realm of the substantial, and at the same time to stand with their subjective freedom not in a particular and contingent situation, but in what has being in and for itself.'

hence reconciled itself to this world's injustice, represented by the corrupt oppression of the Russian Czars. Echoing Feuerbach's "projection" thesis, as well
as Marx's identification of positive religion's function within society, Lenin understood religion to be recalcitrant obstacle in the path of human liberation.
In his 1905 *Socialism and Religion* essay he wrote,

> Religion is one of the forms of spiritual oppression, which everywhere
> weighs heavily upon the popular masses, crushed by their perpetual work
> for others, by want and loneliness. The impotence of the exploited classes
> in their struggle with the exploiters inevitably gives rise to the belief in
> a better hereafter, just as the impotence of the savage in his battle with
> nature gives rise to the belief in gods, devils, miracles, and the like. Those
> who toil and live in want all their lives are taught by religion to be sub-
> missive and patient while here on earth and take comfort in the hope of
> being rewarded in heaven. But those who live by the labour of others are
> taught by religion to practice charity while on earth, and thus religion of-
> fers them a very cheap way of justifying their entire existence as exploit-
> ers and sells them at a moderate price tickets to heavenly bliss. Religion is
> opium for the people. Religion is a sort of spiritual home-brew [*sivukha*]
> in which the slaves of capital drown the image of man and their demand
> for a life more or less worthy of human beings.[13]

Lenin did not dedicate much time to religion, as he believed it was a subject
matter that was already resolved in the works of the Young Hegelians Feuerbach and Marx. Yet Lenin's 1905 article expressed an important distinction: the
two different messages religion sends to the two competing classes, i.e. bourgeois and proletariat. First, the proletariat was to be 'submissive and patient' in
dealing with the absurdity of class domination and they were to 'take comfort
in the hope' of heavenly reward for their complacency with the status quo. In
other words, they were to be passive in the face of human suffering and retreat
into metaphysical 'illusions' and 'delusions' to numb the pain of human existence, especially the pain exacted by class exploitation. Secondly, for the ruling elites, the only demand placed upon them was to practice "charity" – not
solidarity – with those suffering beneath them. They were not to recognize the
exploitative nature of their rule, on which they lived, to recognize it as an issue of morality, but rather as an opportunity to appear beneficent, i.e. to give

---

13   As quoted in *Lenin and Religion* by Bohdan R. Bociurkiw. *Lenin: The Man, The Theorist, The*
      Leader: A Reappraisal, ed. Leonard Schapiro and Peter Reddaway (New York: Frederick A.
      Praeger, Publishers, 1967), 108–109.

charity. This 'cheap way of justifying their existence as exploiters' offers them a way of gain absolution for their "tainted" wealth; it offered them a way to ease the guilt that they *may* have had for their exploitation of the poor, the workers, and peasants. Additionally, this peculiar bourgeois form of "charity" is a *functionalization* of poverty. It is crassly utilized for their own purposes but contributes nothing to its systematic alleviation. As such, it buys them the opportunity to appear pious in front of their peers (although secretly they all know it's only for appearances). For Lenin, this guilt removing "charity" allows them to have what Hegel calls a "happy conscience" (*glückliche Bewußtsein*) – a conscience reconciled to the state of the world despite the destruction, violence, and misery it imposes.[14] This happy conscience delivers an untroubled psyche to the ruling class in this life and allows them to purchase a ticket to "heavenly bliss" in the next. Even Pope Francis, who is deeply critical of globalized capitalism, in agreement with Marx and Lenin, deemed this form of charitable giving as fraudulent, it offers money but no real solidarity or love.[15] Peaceful endurance of unnecessary pain is the avenue for the poor and workers to obtain salvation; cheap bourgeois charity is the course by which the exploiters gain salvation. For Lenin, this was essence of bourgeois religion and it was a fraud for its victims.

Unlike Marx, who believed religion would disappear with the revolutionary transformation of the material conditions, for Lenin, this dichotomy had to be first removed before a revolution could occur.[16] Religion, and its removal from the social consciousness, had to be a primary concern for the communists if they ever wanted to steer society towards the ideal classless society. Unlike other leftist intellectuals, and even reformist clerics like Gregory Gapon (Гео́ргий Аполло́нович Гапо́н) – the Orthodox Priest that led the 1905 *Bloody Sunday* uprising against Czar Nickolas II – religion had no part to play in the modern emancipation of humanity for Lenin; it's positive nature, and therefore its obstructionism, was absolute.[17] The liberational potentials of the Abrahamic faiths could no longer be rescued, as he believed that history has terminally negated them through their institutionalization and total identification with

---

14   G.W.F. Hegel, *Phenomenology of Spirit*, trans. A.V. Miller (New York: Oxford University Press, 1977), 104–138.

15   Jorge Mario Bergoglio (Pope Francis I) and Abraham Skorka, *On Heaven and Earth: Pope Francis on Faith, Family, and the Church in the Twenty-First Century* (New York: Image, 2013), 170–1. Also see Andrea Tornielli and Giacomo Galeazzi, *This Economy Kills: Pope Francis on Capitalism and Social Justice.* Collegeville, MN: Liturgical Press, 2015.

16   Bociurkiw, *Lenin*, 110.

17   Ibid., 115–116. Also see Roland Boer, *Lenin, Religion, and Theology* (New York: Palgrave MacMillan, 2013), 60–63.

the ruling class, as well as through modern science. The only thing that could be done with religion was its complete negation from the minds of men. In the place of their formerly held religious beliefs, Lenin – following Marx and Engels' *dialectical materialism* – advanced the notion that a scientific form of socialism, not a *utopian* or religious version, had to be inculcated into the working classes' consciousness.[18] Socialism had to be rooted in reason and science and not in passé revelation. There could no longer be a religious consolation in the face of human despair, rather science and reason had to propel the working class towards its utopian future. As such, religion's ability to provide motivations for revolutionary change was exhausted; it was now time for science and rational thought to provide such motivations.

Affirmation and Negativity: Horkheimer and Adorno

The critical theorist Theodor Adorno expands on Marx, Horkheimer, and Lenin's suspicion about religion's incapacity to serve the liberation of mankind because of its own self-imposed class constraints. For Adorno, modern religion – especially since the Enlightenment period, with its subsequent industrialization and secularization – suffers from an inherent problem that cripples its emancipatory potentials; it is no longer socially necessary as a motivation for revolutionary change; rather it persists because of man's psychological *needs*. It is only because man turns toward religion to comfort him within his *damaged life*, that it remains an active component in modern society. The post-secular society, in which religion remains a social force despite the advancement of the secular society, is the product of man's need to ease his mind in the face of suffering. In his essay *Reason and Revelation,* he states,

> In the best case, that is, where it is not just a question of imitation and conformity, it is *desire* that produces such an attitude: it is not the *truth* and *authenticity* of the revelation that are decisive but rather the *need for guidance*, the *confirmation* of what is already firmly established, and also the *hope* that by means of a resolute decision alone one could breathe back that *meaning* into the disenchanted world under whose absence we have been *suffering* so long, as though we were mere spectators staring at

---

18   Bociurkiw, *Lenin*, 118; Also see Frederick Engels, *Socialism: Utopian and Scientific.* New York: International Publishers, 1989.

something *meaningless*. It seems to me that the religious renaissances of today are philosophy of religion, not religion.[19]

Adorno points us in a very important direction: we see that since the "death of god," heralded by Friedrich Nietzsche – as an observation of the zeitgeist in which he lived and not as god's assassin – the core content of religion, its theological premises, have become untenable in our post-metaphysical age. Science, technology, and autonomous reason all contributed to the destruction of the *veritas* of religious claims, and because of this the truth-element within religion has become superfluous. Despite this, secularity, as Habermas has articulated, has failed to adequately address those existential questions that religion once answered and as such leaves unattended an open flank by which religion either stubbornly remains with humanity, or returns after secularity's deficiency is made abundantly clear.[20] The current rise of religious fundamentalism, despite secularity's colonization of the lifeworld via globalization, attests to the fact that secularity has failed to answer many of humanity's most recalcitrant questions, and therefore has provided the opportunity for man to once again returned to sacred texts, traditions, and personalities for guidance, answers, and comfort, often in defiance – not just simple rejection – of science and reason. In the Muslim world, globalization has caused a supra-territorial communicative consciousness to occur – a thinking that emphasizes a return to a primordial community, the *ummah*, as a way of escaping the enclosed jaws of secularity. To little avail, this consciousness is both defensive and utopian in nature as it attempts to arrest or reverse the secularization and westernization process. Because of the social, cultural and psychological chaos that has occurred with the process of globalization, an intense *longing* for the idealized days when the *dar al-Islam* was ruled by the *khalīfah* (successor) has developed, thus contributing to the appeal of ISIS and other jihādi groups, who promise to restore the now defunct Caliphate. However, and despite the failure of religion to disappear in the modern age, as Adorno stated, it is not the truth content of religion that has convinced many to "return" to religion, but man's subjective needs, which have become all the more entrenched as the secular world's meaninglessness and anomic conditions. In other words, Adorno does not claim that the return of religion is motivated by a newly acceptance of religion's truth claims – as if secularism's defeat somehow proved the truth content of religion all along. No, Adorno states the opposite,

---

19   Theodor Adorno, *Critical Models: Interventions and Catchwords* (New York: Columbia University Press, 2005), 137. (My emphasis added).

20   Habermas, *An Awareness of What is Missing*, 15–23.

If religion is accepted for the sake of something other than its own truth content, then it undermines itself. The fact that recently the positive religions have so willingly engaged in this and at times compete with other public institutions testifies only to the desperation that latently inheres in their own positivity... As soon as religion abandons its factual content, it threatens to vanish into mere symbolism and that imperils the very existence of its truth claim.[21]

Adorno became aware that the contemporary retreat into sacred tradition is connected to the failure of secular reason to provide for the essential spiritual, existential, and transcendental needs of humanity. Nevertheless, he is skeptical that a post-Enlightenment and post-secular form of religion truly believes in its own claims, believing that it had mistakenly become intellectually ataraxic with its post-Enlightenment remainder. Since the scientific revolution and the Enlightenment, it had already capitulated its most fundamental truth claims about ultimate reality to the triumph of autonomous *ratio*. Consequently, when it attempts to defend itself, it is forced to do so via autonomous reason, and as such its very defense proves the triumph of such reason over mere revelation. That being so, the modern turn towards religion – as a system of thought that provides sophistic answers and artificially comforts the alienated and suffering man – is a return to a phenomenon that is ultimately pragmatic in praxis and symbolic in meaning.[22] For example, the existential anxiety that was produced during the atomic standoff between two competing ideologies, two competing empires, and two competing nuclear powers, motivated many rational people to seek solace within the comforting arms of religion. Adorno states,

> The real determining model of this behavior is the division of the world into two colossal blocs that rigidly oppose and reciprocally threaten one another, and every individual, with destruction. The extreme innerworldly fear of this situation, because there is nothing discernible that might lead beyond it, is hypostatized as an existential or indeed a transcendental anxiety. The victories that revealed religion gains in the name of such anxiety are Pyrrhic.[23]

For Adorno, if any other motive other than the truth claims of a given revealed religion is the core reason as to why an individual or nation turns toward

---

21   Adorno, *Critical Models*, 139–141.

22   Ibid., 141.

23   Ibid., 139.

religion, then it undermines itself, as truth can be easily divorced from need. Human needs are not dependent upon ultimate truth and knowledge; as such, *veritas* can be liquidated as an essential component of religion.[24] Ultimately, religion need not be *true* to provide comfort to suffering man, just *believable* based on whether or not it pragmatically slays the chaos and/or anxiety within. But this comforting religion can be replaced by other phenomena, i.e. patriotism, nationalism, cult of personality, or whatever else works. The kind of religion that has a function and not a truth – as a "pattern maintenance system," and not as a way-of-being-in-the-world that expresses some universal truth claims – is a religion that has been hollowed out of it truth, as its foundational principles lack a theologically grounded objectivity. They have become relativized: mere conjecture, opinions, individual preferences and tastes that correspond to individual needs. As such, they are completely unjustifiable within themselves and outside of those particular needs.[25] Nevertheless, according to Adorno, that hasn't stopped contemporary religion from capitalizing on the anxiety of modern man. He says, 'the fact that recently the positive religions have so willingly engaged in this and at times compete with other public institutions testifies only to the desperation that latently inheres in their own positivity.'[26]

For Adorno, both religion and the secular modern world find themselves in a precarious position. To abandon all religion is to abandon another avenue by which the possibility of another reality beyond the world-as-it-is is made possible. In other words, abandoning religion shuts the believer off from the very real thought that another existence beyond the given is a real possibility, thus resigning the believer to the status quo. That not only undermines religion, but would undermine a strictly philosophical project for a utopian situation as well. Horkheimer saw the danger in the complete defrocking of religion, as it undermined the possibility of philosophical metaphysics. He stated,

> The philosophers of the Enlightenment attacked religion in the name of reason; in the end what they killed was not the church but metaphysics and the objective concept of reason itself, the source of power of their own efforts.[27]

---

24   Ibid., 139.

25   Ibid., 140.

26   Ibid., 139.

27   Max Horkheimer, *Eclipse of Reason* (New York: Continuum, 2004), 12–13.

For the critical religiologist, we cannot return to a subjectively rooted religiosity as an objective way of comprehending or engaging the world; autonomous reason, and not revelation must guide our existence in the modern world. But, as Horkheimer and Adorno intuitively understood, instrumental reason cares little for the real suffering of people which the Abrahamic religions in their original impulses have committed themselves to arresting, abating and negating, and thus as long as reason cannot adequately address the existential anxieties and fears of humanity, religion will continue to find a place in secular societies.[28]

In light of this situation – between a ruthless world of instrumental rationality and an irrational world of religious subjectivity – how do we infuse reason with the concern for the suffering of the finite individual and at the same time imbue religion with autonomous reason? For Adorno, the answer lies in an imageless negative dialectical philosophy: the 'extreme loyalty to the prohibition of images, far beyond what this once originally meant.'[29] Religion, especially Judaism and Christianity, for Adorno and the Frankfurt School, calls to be *determinately negated*; the emancipatory and liberational aspects of religion must be rescued through their translation into secular philosophy and praxis.[30] If, he says, religion is to survive, it must invoke Walter Benjamin's *Theses on the Philosophy of History* and 'wizen up' and must 'keep out of sight.'[31] In other words, it must be translated into historical materialism, or at least make allies with it. In the conjunctions with historical materialism it can fulfill its *this-worldly* prophetic mission, albeit from within or with secular language and praxis. As stated early, in a post-secular world, one that no longer speaks the language of religion, the only way certain semantic and semiotic meaning and moral material can enter into the public discourse is through its translation into a secular idiom.

Confronting the Post-Secular Condition

Clearly what Adorno has argued in this essay is more applicable to the western post-secular situation than it is in other parts of the world that still embrace their religious traditions and worldviews. The radical separation of church and

---

28   Theodor Adorno, *Critical Models*, 142.
29   Ibid., 142.
30   Ibid., 136.
31   Ibid., 135–136; Walter Benjamin, *Illuminations: Essays and Reflections* (New York: Schoken Books, 2007), 253. I will return to this theme later in the book.

state – which began with the Bourgeois revolutions, culminating in the establishment of secular political constitutions as opposed to divinely sanctioned
monarchies – liberated the West from its outdated, irrational, and dogmatic
religious authorities that had crippled the minds, spirit, and freedom of men
and women alike. Although it ultimately depleted the West of any sense of unconditional meaning, the demythologization process was an emancipatory development that attempted to make mankind the masters of their own lives.[32]
With the rationalization and consequent demythologization of man's relationship with nature came the disenchantment of the world; the metaphysical
heritage of Christianity was no longer privileged as ultimate reality.[33] Science,
technology, and autonomous reason, especially instrumental reason, replaced
revelation as the core sources of knowledge of the world, mankind, and the
cosmos. However, this secularization of the lifeworld never took place in any
meaningful measure in much of the Muslim world, nor did the antagonism
between faith and science, reason and revelation, ever develop to the degree to
which it did in the West. For the Muslim world – outside of those fundamentalists whose understanding of religion was often limited to the literal or casual
– science and reason were tools for the understanding and discovery of the
divine and his cosmic architecture. As such, the same "return to religion" for
the placation of humanity's needs never really occurred in the Muslim world,
although there has been some "return to religion" as a form of defiance of westernization.[34] Nevertheless, Muslims by-and-large have remained faithful to the
truth content of the Qur'an, *ḥadīth*, and Sunnah, even if, to a smaller degree,
their *religiosity* mirrors some of the same pragmatic traits as western religiosity, i.e. the functionalization of religion for what it can do for human needs, or
what Bediüzzaman Said Nursi, an important 20th century Islamic intellectual,
describes as *taqlīdī-Islam* (Islam as imitation of forbearers, or Islam without
investigation).[35] In other words, there was no *civilizational* shift towards demy-
thologizing the world within the Muslim community, and therefore religion
and metaphysics remained a core component in the life of the ummah, even
after the loss of the Caliphate in Istanbul.

32   Max Horkheimer and Theodor Adorno, *Dialectic of Enlightenment: Philosophical Frag-
      ments,* ed. Gunzelin Schmid Noerr. Trans. Edmund Jephcott (Stanford: Stanford Univer-
      sity Press, 2002), 1–34.

33   Giovanna Borradori, *Philosophy in a Time of Terror: Dialogues with Jürgen Habermas and
      Jacques Derrida* (Chicago: University of Chicago Press, 2003), 69–70.; Max Weber, *From
      Max Weber: Essays in Sociology,* ed. and trans. H.H. Gerth and C. Wright Mills (New York:
      Oxford University Press, 1976), 155.

34   Weber, *Essays in Sociology,* 155.

35   Colin Turner and Hasan Horkuc, *Said Nursi* (New York: I. B. Tauris, 2009), 47.

Yet this seems to contradict common thinking, as one of the most important phenomena the modern individual witnesses in the contemporary situation is the *fundamentalist* "return of religion." But this apparent contradiction may not be so simple. If Adorno thinks the West is once again rediscovering the ability of religion to address human needs, and that explains its reemergence in the western world, it is not necessarily identical to why religion within the Muslim world has so often dressed in the cloak of a resurgent fundamentalism. Fundamentalism, according to Jürgen Habermas, is a 'peculiar mindset, a stubborn attitude that insists on the political imposition of its own convictions and reasons, even when they are far from being rationally acceptable,' and as such constitutes a *belief attitude* that is independent of the content of the beliefs.[36] Although this can be equally applied to various secular philosophies and political movements, it 'holds especially for religious beliefs,' were the legitimation of belief through rational – as opposed to revelational – argumentation can be problematic.[37] When a religious believer, group, or even nation, refuses to separate the political and religious, autonomous reason and divine revelation, they are perceived in the West as being essentially fundamentalistic, a mindset that insists on the implementation of their dogmas without democratic and/or reasoned deliberation. For Habermas, fundamentalism is the result of the 'repression of striking cognitive dissonances' that come about in a multicultural world – a world that approaches the religious believer with the attitude that their particular faith is no more valid or privileged than another.[38] Furthermore, in the Muslim world in particular, there is a political-cultural-economic component to the advancement of fundamentalism; in light of the overwhelming power of secular modernity, capitalism, and cultural liberalism, there is a 'defensive reaction against the fear of a violent uprooting of traditional ways of life.'[39] There is a sense of humiliation, disrespect, and dishonor, which must be remedied through a retreat into a fundamentalist mind-frame, which not only reinforces the perceptions of being wronged, but also provides an abundance of thought and praxis material by which the fundamentalist can oppose his supposed oppressor. *Restorative conservatism* is understood as a vehicle to once again regain the lost honor of the *dar al-Islam,* because only a strict adherence to Islam can save the Muslim world from the moral chaos of secular modernity and bring about its own civilizational renaissance. These two contemporary phenomena – the relativism of the modern multiculturalist

---

36 Borradori, *Philosophy in a Time of Terror,* 31.
37 Ibid., 31.
38 Ibid., 32.
39 Ibid., 32.

world and the attack of secular modernity on the traditional religious world – have become the fuel for the fire of Islamic fundamentalism.

As stated above, the Muslim world has not gone through the advanced stages of the secularization process, even if there are isolated pockets of secularity within the Muslim world, i.e. intellectuals, states, political parties, etc. For the West, the painful awareness of what's missing, as Habermas has described the state of secular emptiness in the face of human existence, has motivated many to once again come into contact with the Judeo-Christian tradition, as well as eastern forms of mysticism. They search for the answers that secularity has failed to provide. Although secular modernity has adequately answered many of the material problems that have afflicted mankind for millennia, it has not been able to adequately address the spiritual and existential issues that continually preoccupy mankind. In many Muslim societies, the answers that Islam provides to those questions are still relatively operational, accepted, and faithfully believed in. Thus, the appearance of fundamentalism – what appears to many as a violent return to religion – has a different genesis. Where fundamentalism in the West is often the result of the damaged life created by secular modernity, in the Muslim world, fundamentalism is an attempt to safeguard the Islamic society from having to go through that same form of damaged life created by that secular modernity. Or, it is to arrest the modernizing and secularizing processes that have already begun in the Muslims world. Either way, it is defensive in nature. Many Muslims see the social chaos, deficient and/or distorted morality, the "leveling down" of the human to base animal desires and instincts (*nafs*), and the rise of *al-jāhilīyah al-jadīd* (the new age of ignorance) values that come with commodification, marketization, corporatization and commercialization of the consumer society, and are horrified by it. These Muslims want to stay clear of the zeitgeist of the secular "having" life of *homo consumens* that they witness predominately in the West. In wanting to avoid this fate, many Muslims retreat into a reactionary stance that makes Islam impenetrable to the positive aspects of modernity, reform, and/or western culture. This retreat into itself poses a difficult problem for many Muslims; to retreat inward is to find safety, but it is at the expense of the overall health of the ummah. To confront the world through fundamentalism is equally as destructive, for it depletes the communicative core of Islam by becoming as cold-hearted and calculative as the western ruling class: the Bourgeoisie – those who brought secular modernity to the Muslim world. This is hardly acceptable for most Muslims. With this in mind, we must ask what kind (or orientation) of Islam is most adequate to engage the modern post-secular world, enter into a discourse with its representatives, learn from it, but also retain the Muslim communities' Islamic identity?

Prophetic and Priestly Religion

If we accept the claim that religion is either ascending within the framework of the post-secular society, or has simply failed to dissolve into history, we should determine what sort of religion is being produced through this religious resurgence in the West as well as in the fundamentalization of Islam in the Muslim world? In order to answer this problem, we turn to the social-psychologist and early member of the Frankfurt School, Erich Fromm, to help us understand the nature of two important forms of religion, both of which appear in today's world just as they have been in the past, but take on a new meaning and significance within the context of the modern post-secular society.

In Fromm's 1967 essay *Prophets and Priests*, he develops two sociological/political categories of authority, both of which are historically important for the evolution of mankind. Although both concepts are inspired by religion and are derived from religious vocabulary, they are not exclusively religious concepts, but can be applied to all forms of authority, both religious and secular.[40]

Citing the modern dilemma of the theory/praxis disconnect, where those with knowledge and truth fail to live a life guided by such knowledge and truth, and those devoid of such intellectual and moral proclivities, set themselves up as the masters of intellect and morality, Fromm states that 'those who announce ideas – and not necessarily new ones – and at the same time live them we may call *prophets*.'[41] From Fromm's secular-philosophical perspective, it is clear that he does not believe such people are necessarily "commissioned" by the divine to deliver revelation to the people as one has in Judaism, Christianity, and Islam, but rather believes those voices that 'announce' ideas that stand within the social, political, economic, cultural, and philosophical lineage of those biblical and Qur'anic prophets, even if their message is now secular, can be considered a "prophet." However, we have to realize that he is using this term in a purely secular way. His "prophet" can be either secular or religious, which is a wholesale departure from the strict religious understanding of what a prophet is in the Abrahamic traditions. Indeed, he cites Buddha, Christ, Socrates, and Spinoza as being historical representatives of the prophetic.[42]

---

40   See my book *Ayatollah Khomeini and the Anatomy of the Islamic Revolution in Iran: Toward a Theory of Prophetic Charism.* Lanham, MD: University Press of America, 2011. Also see my article "Fromm's Notion of Prophets and Priests: Ancient Antagonism, Modern Manifestations" in *Reclaiming the Sane Society: Essays in Erich Fromm's Thought*, ed. Miri, Lake and Kress. Rotterdam: Sense Publishers, 2014.

41   Erich Fromm, *On Disobedience and Other Essays* (New York: The Seabury Press, 1981), 42.

42   Ibid., 43.

Yet for the religious believer, it is a necessary condition that an individual be commissioned by the divine in order to be considered a prophet, anything less than a divine commission disqualifies their claim. Yet for Fromm, our secular age is devoid of directly commissioned prophets, but can, and sometimes still does, have prophetic voices who lead people in the direction of the prophetic life. Fromm states that,

> The Old Testament prophets... announced the idea that man had to find an answer to his existence, and that this answer was the development of his reason, of his love; and they taught that humility and justice were inseparably connected with love and reason. They lived what they preached. They did not seek power, but avoided it. Not even the power of being a prophet. They were not impressed by might, and they spoke the truth even if this led them to imprisonment, ostracism or death.[43]

He continues,

> They were not men who set themselves apart and waited to see what would happen. They responded to their fellow man because they felt responsible. What happened to others happened to them. Humanity was not outside, but within them. Precisely because they saw the truth they felt the responsibility to tell it; they did not threaten, but they showed the *alternatives* with which man was confronted.[44]

We can see from this passage in Fromm's essay a few constitutional categories of his understanding of prophets. First, the prophet's message is one with liberational intent; the prophet guides and encourages the development of man's reason and love in order to emancipate his from the smallness of irrationality and hatred; the prophet's message is meant to liberate him from the irrational fears that bind him to violence, animosity towards others, and competitive greed; it is meant to emancipate him from self-destructive nihilism, crippling pessimism, and hopelessness; and is meant to cultivate a way-of-being-in-the-world that is rooted in humility, solidarity, compassion, and love for oneself and others as one seeks perfect justice in this unjust world. Secondly, Fromm's prophet takes a principled stance against oppression, injustice, and those who impose needless suffering on the innocent. It is not without fear that they take on this task, but the prophets accept the possibility of their own painful

---

43   Ibid., 42.
44   Ibid., 42.

demise by the hands of the opposition. The prophet's role in this world is to advance the cause of justice without the demonization of the unjust, without losing track of the humanity of the oppressor, without dehumanizing the already dehumanized victims and victimizers. The prophets are aware of what Hegel would later describe as the *Master–slave Dialectic* – that in various ways both are victims, and therefore both are in need of liberation.[45] Thirdly, the prophet claims no temporal authority, does not wish for temporal authority, and would not accept temporal authority if it were offered to him. The prophets are given authority based on the perceptions of those the prophet leads. By the force of their argument, the legitimacy of their cause, and the altruistic core of their mission, spiritual authority is granted to them *by the people*. Although this authority bestows upon them immense power, the prophets willfully relinquish it when it is no longer needed. It is not a possession but only a temporary trust from their followers. Their power therefore is not autonomous, but contingent on the will of their community. As such, he cannot take for himself power, nor give it to another, as it can only be given and taken by and through the consent of the masses.

Fourthly, Fromm's notion of the prophet is one that rooted in self-identification with the suffering of finite humanity; they are *of* the masses and *sympathizes* (συμπάθεια: "feeling together") with the other because they share a common humanity. Differences in class, race, gender, etc., do not block the prophet's *being-with* others. The prophet has radically transcended such sources of historic animosity while at the same time does not pretend that such differences do not matter or are not continual sources of social animosity. As Fromm implies, the prophet feels responsible for those around them and out of that responsibility, is impelled to engage the world in a prophetic manner, to lend their talents and abilities towards the cause of their emancipation, and to risk their life for their emancipation. The prophet, unlike the tyrant, is martyr material. They are people of *being* and not *having*; therefore if all their possessions are taken from them, if their material wealth evaporates, if their status in life diminishes, their reason for *being* remains. For the tyrant, who lives for the "world and all it contains," the temporal stuff of wealth, the *necrophilia* (νεκροφιλία: "love of what is dead") of the market society, then their reason for *being* – rooted in his *having* – is gone; without it they are nothing and live for nothing.

Finally, the most important mission of the prophet – in Fromm's analysis – is that they clearly present the *alternatives* to the already existing society. A vision of the way society *ought* to be is their most powerful contribution towards

---

45   G.W.F. Hegel, *Phenomenology of Spirit*, 111–119.

the emancipation of society from the chains that bind it. They, in a way that is most uncharacteristic of temporal politics, offer up a *utopian* expression of society. Utopia (ουτοπία), although by definition is "that which has no place," is the philosophical *sum of all that ought to be*, and thus provides a powerful conceptual critique of *all that is the case*, i.e. present day antagonistic society. The prophet's mission is to present what humanity could be, how society should be, how relations between communities should be, and to guide humanity as close to that ought as possible, knowing full well that it may never materialize to its fullest extent. For Fromm, the prophet's showing of the clear alternatives confronts mankind with a decision; no longer can they hide behind a veil of ignorance and willful blindness, they must abandon their automaton lifestyle and decide their fate. Fromm writes, 'it is his [the prophet's] function to call loudly, to awake man from his customary half-slumber,' and in doing so forces man to choose either to live prophetically, priestly, or apathetically.[46] It is precisely the *negativity* of both the prophet and their utopian vision for society that makes their critique powerful. Their critical stance towards the world-as-it-is expresses their disobedience towards the current system of domination. Their negativity refuses to confuse *that which is* with *that which can and should be*; the conceptual *ought* remains non-identical to what *is*. Between the *"ought and what is"* is the space for revolutionary thought and praxis; its very non-identity creates the coordinates from within which prophetic contestation can occur. Therefore, the prophets and their vision is the opposite of *positive religion*, which recognizes, embraces, and upholds the current status quo. Positive religion inherently lends its power and prestige to the already existing relations and systems of domination; it sanctifies and often times reifies the power differential between the classes, the oppressed and the oppressors, the exploited and the exploiters, making that which is a product of history – and therefore can be historically undone – into a the "natural" state of relations, and therefore presenting the status quo as being inalterable. For the prophets, the concrete negation of such power relations is an essential goal of their prophethood. Their recalcitrant disobedience, as Fromm states, ironically expressed their complete obedience towards a higher value, principle, and ideal: a dialectical commitment *to what ought to be the case* through the determinate negation *of what is the case*. Their 'disobedience, then, in the sense in which we use it here, is an act of affirmation of reason and will. It is not primarily an attitude directed *against* something, but *for* something.'[47] Ultimately, every act of disobedience is an act of obedience to a higher demand, and no demand

---

46   Erich Fromm, *On Disobedience*, 43.
47   Ibid., 48.

remains higher for the prophets than that of human emancipation, liberation, and realization of mankind's full capacitiy for good and justice.

One simply cannot claim to be a prophet. According to Fromm, the historical situation 'makes prophets,' and thus they only appear when the times call for a prophetic voice.[48] In times of social tensions, economic collapse, war, civil strife, international aggression, or even within the banality of the affluent society – where everything is managed and regulated by corporations, PR firms, and liberal politics – the prophetic voices emerge to offer a more rational and sane alternative.

After the prophet makes their mark on society, it is the priest that is left to represent the voice of the prophet, which he often does in the most unprophetic way. Fromm states,

> Prophets appear only at intervals in the history of humanity. They die and leave their message. The message is accepted by millions, it becomes dear to them. This is precisely the reason why the idea becomes exploitable for others who can make use of the attachment of the people to these ideas, for their own purposes – those of ruling and controlling. Let us call the men who make use of the idea the prophets have announced the *priests*.[49]

While exploring the function of the priest, Fromm delivers a pessimistic analysis of the role of priests in society. He states,

> The prophets live their ideas. The priests administer them to the people who are attached to the idea. The idea has lost its vitality. It has become a formula. The priests declare that it is very important how the idea is formulated; naturally the formulation becomes always important after the experience is dead; how else could one control people by controlling their thoughts, unless there is the 'correct' formulation? The priest use the idea to organize men, to control them through controlling the proper expression of the idea, and when they have anesthetized man enough they declare that man is not capable of being awake and of directing his own life, and that they, the priests, act out of duty, or even compassion, when they fulfill the function of directing men who, if left to themselves,

---

48   Ibid., 43.
49   Ibid., 43.

are afraid of freedom. It is true not all priests have acted that way, but most of them have, especially those who wield power.[50]

The conceptual model of "the priest" that Fromm constructs is one that, as he himself recognized, cannot be universalized, as there have been many actual priests that have acted prophetically in their opposition to irrational and oppressive authority; priests like the American brothers Daniel and Jerry Berrigan, the Franciscan priests and monks that helped the Italian cyclist Gino Bartali save Jews during WWII, the Protestant Pastor Dietrich Bonhoeffer, the Orthodox Priest Gregory Gapon, El Salvadorian Archbishop Óscar Romero, the Nicaraguan Priest and poet Ernesto Cardenal, the American civil rights leader Rev. Dr. Martin Luther King, the German Protestant revolutionary Thomas Müntzer, the Muslim Malcolm X, and many other nameless and anonymous clerics that chose to side with the victims of history, believing that the divine was on the side of the oppressed, the exploited, and the murdered, and not on the side of those who oppressed, exploited, and murdered. These clerics – most prophetically – chose to side themselves with the innocent victims, those who had been left in the ditch of society, crucified on world-Golgotha, and were massacred on the slaughterbench of history. For Fromm, these "priests" are prophetic, regardless of their institutional title.

What Fromm conceptualized when he constructed the priestly model was any form of authority that speaks in the name of a once-revolutionary individual (or movement), who codified the revolutionary thought, transformed it into a dogma, and proceeded to functionalize the teaching of the revolutionary as a means of manipulating and controlling the people and or gaining power, prestige, wealth, etc. For these particular clerics, the 'priestly' model would not have appealed to them as all of them in different ways committed themselves not to controlling the masses, but rather to liberating them; nurturing their sense of reason and capacity for love; building up their ability to *be* for themselves and others and removing the obstacles that oppressed and exploited them. Nevertheless, history is full of these kind of non-prophetic "priests" – whether they be religious or secular, economic or political – who have killed off the dynamic nature of revolutionary religion and philosophy and replaced it with an stagnant edifice of cold dogmas and platitudes that are devoid of the liberational spirit that once gave them life. Fromm reminds his readers that,

> the priests usually confuse the people because they claim that they are the successors of the prophet, and that they live what they preach. Yet,

---

50   Ibid., 43–44.

while a child could see that they live precisely the opposite of what they teach, the great mass of the people are brainwashed effectively, and eventually they come to believe that if the priests live in splendor they do so as a sacrifice, because they have to represent the great idea; or if they kill ruthlessly they only do so out of revolutionary faith.[51]

This kind of priest is satisfied to gain converts based on what Adorno claimed was humanity's *need* for religion; the revolutionary and prophetic priest wants his followers to be convinced of the *truth* behind his claims; the *truth* behind his praxis, and the *truth* behind his mission. The prophetic priest truly does speak in the name of the prophet, often times against his own religious tradition or authorities, as was the case for the liberation theologians in Latin America who found themselves in opposition to the Vatican's official neutrality (or sometimes complicity) with the political right's attacks on socialists, peasants, and left-wing priests during the 1980's, which were supported – or simply ignored – by the church in the name of anti-communism. The priestly authorities in Rome, despite their theological differences with the liberation theologians, abandoned the prophetic liberational intent of the message of Jesus of Nazareth, which included a very earthly liberation, for a quietist policy that would allow the church to remain on the fence or in the good graces of the powerful. In this case, the prophetic was transfigured into the priestly once again while fascism created more victims for the benefit of North American capitalism.

If we look strictly at religion, the model of the priest that Fromm constructs is the model of the cleric within *positive religion*. Echoing Marx's definition of religion – the *opiate of the masses* – we see that Fromm's priest is one that confirms, justifies, and sanctifies the very conditions that call for opium religion. In this way, the priestly cleric is the opium-dealer, anesthetizing the masses from the pain of their condition, making them complacent, content, and accepting of their oppression. He may give lip-service to the language of the prophetic and revolutionary, but ultimately he is the one that blesses the existing world-as-it; implores the oppressed to "bear their cross" silently and patiently; and weaves a vision of the good life to be obtained only in the afterlife, while this life is abandoned to unnecessary socially-induced suffering. Through the enforcement of dogma, he bends the words of the original prophetic stance towards the preservation of the unjust class and power relations. As Kant pointed out, his form of religiosity is the religion that's called in to comfort the dying; it dulls the conscience of the masses, lulling them back into their

---

51   Ibid., 44.

half-slumber, their hypnotic automaton state, and their complacency with the "fallen" and corrupt world that oppresses them.[52] His priestly religion reconciles the victims to the victimizers, thus liquidating their inherent potential to revolt, to make a revolution, and to emancipate themselves from their oppressors. For Fromm, Marx, and Horkheimer, his religion is the adhesive that binds the masses to their chains, as it no longer 'expresses the ideal' of the prophetic/utopian vision, but rather convinces them that such chains are either the product of nature or their supernatural 'fate.'[53] However, the prophet takes seriously the 'sigh of the oppressed creature, the sentiment of a heartless world, and the soul of soulless conditions,' and demonstrates to the masses that this is not the natural state of man; this is not *Deus Volt*; and this is not the way of the biblical and Qur'anic prophets, no matter how much the priest insists.[54]

As we can see in history, professing a negative religious and secular way-of-being in an unjust world is dangerous; it calls for sacrifice and the risking of one's life, resources, and wellbeing, but for the prophetic there is no other option. Unlike what many anti-Marxists believe, Marx and the Frankfurt School never directly criticized Rabbi Jesus of Nazareth, but only the positivity that lurks within religion, most especially Emperor Constantine's form of Christianity that betrayed its original revolutionary nature. Both Marx and the Frankfurt School recognized within Jesus' mission a revolutionary moment – one that they saw fit to be translated into secular revolutionary politics in the 20th century. Indeed, they were not anti-religious at all, but wished to rescue religion from the cage of positivity and allow that which still remains prophetic to migrate from the depth of the mythos into secular revolutionary thought and praxis. Unlike those intellectuals, such as Ayn Rand, who wish to relieve the world entirely of religion, the critical theorists, who learned from the philosophies of Kant, Hegel, and Marx, attempted to exorcise the Abrahamic religions of their criminal histories and tendencies and preserve their negativity in critical philosophy and praxis. Religion, even in the modern period, may still find a role in revolutionary movements.

---

52   Immanuel Kant, *Religion*, 93.

53   Horkheimer, *Critical Theory*, 188.

54   Marx, *Contribution*, 54.

After Auschwitz: Islam in Europe

The mass immigration of Muslims into post-secular Europe has caused many to reflect on the state of religion in a society that once believed in the Christianity, moved through the Age of Enlightenment and now finds itself in a mixed society where religious and secular citizens cohabitate. This rapid change in demographics has been a destabilizing factor in a culture that sees itself as thoroughly secular, both politically and culturally.

There are two important factors that have contributed to the West's idea of itself as being without religion, which in turn make the transition to a post-secular society, in which the Muslim community is a dominant factor on the religious side, very difficult. The first can be found within the works of three philosophers, Freud, Nietzsche and Marx. The biological claim of Freud, that religion belongs to the infancy of the human species and that religion is an *interpretative* way of understanding humanity without possessing empirical truth, remains operative in many quarters of the secular society. Just as the natural sciences had already begun to do, Freud's psychological reductionism attempted to demonstrate that religion was a product to man's mind and/or biology, which furthered the separation of religion from metaphysical truth. Following this, I argue that the philosopher Friedrich Nietzsche, who heralded the death of God and the metaphysical reality that was associated with it, plays an abiding factor. According to him, a life beyond good and evil, beyond the slave ethics of Christianity, would give rise to nihilism and the age of the *übermensch*, which came to fruition in the modern period with the ideologies of nationalism and fascism. Nihilism was the future of Europe, and with all of its inherent meaninglessness, nihilism is what Europe received. For many, Marx devastating critique of religion would hammer the last nail in its coffin, a coffin that his contemporary Feuerbach had already begun to build by demonstrating the anthropological genesis of God.

In light of the modern western world's move away from religion, the most traumatic event that has affected the overall worldview of European society originates from the horrific unfolding of fascism in Europe and the absolute destructiveness of Auschwitz. The post-secular society is a society in which most of the population find it impossible to seek solace or comfort in a divine being that allowed for the systematic destruction of the Jews, the mass murder of twenty-seven communists, and millions of western soldiers, without any attempt by such a divine being to intervene into history. Theodicy, in this case, makes religion unintelligible for many, and therefore loses its place in the modern secular society. Following this catastrophe of the mid-twnetieth century, many ask *how can Europe return to their Catholic, Protestant and Orthodox prayers after the barbarism of World War II?* If Adorno once believed *poetry* after Auschwitz was no longer possible, how then is *prayer?* Already recognizign the difficulty for Christians, we must ask: how can Jews return to their prayers after Auschwitz?

Like the biblical Job, many Jews still pray today precisely because the victims of fascism continued to pray despite the nonappearance of the divine in Auschwitz. This recalcitrant devotion to God after the god of history, religion, and theology is dead, and the hope for the Messiah, animated the late religio-philosophical work of the critical theorist Walter Benjamin, who found a way to rescue certain semantic and semiotic material from the depth of Judaism by caccooning it in historical materialism. His work, in the face of the "single catastrophe" that is history, points in a poignant direction that the Muslims of Europe may read as a way of rescuing Islam from the snares of the post-secular society. Can Muslims follow Walter Benjamin and translate their messianic, prophetic and revolutionary ideals, rooted in religion, into secular philosophy, and thus rescuing it from the onslaught of neo-pagan secular society, or will Islam share the same evaporative fate as Christianity?

Violence and the Post-Secular

According to the Harvard psychology professor Steven Pinker, the abundance of violence that permeated the life of the pre-modern man has drastically subsided in the modern period.[1] With the advancement of civilization, which includes the rationalization of the lifeworld, the divorce of revelation from law, the separation of church and state, the advancement of human rights, international institutions of law, the creation of war crimes legislation, the integration of economies, etc., civilization has been able to create the conditions by which violence would no longer dictate the parameters of the lifeworld. Daily life, which was once permeated with a low-level of direct violence against the individual and the family, has been lessened to a major degree in the modern West, where nearly all forms of direct violence contravene positive law and most people live in relative safety. Yet when we look into the world-as-it-is today, we seen a increasing amount of barbarity; whether it comes from western

---

1   Steven Pinker, *The Better Angels of our Nature: Why Violence Has Declined.* New York: Viking, 2011.

countries' continual attacks on smaller, weaker, and darker skinned nations, especially when they fail to submit to the conditions of global capitalism, or when Muslim extremists attack innocent civilians both in the *dar-al-Islam* or in the West, the increasing callousness towards human life leaves many in a state of fearful paralysis, unable to comprehend the descent into the chaos of violence, hatred, and death-friendliness. In order to understand the barbarity that continues within the relatively peaceful modern world, and especially the antagonism between the West and the Muslim world, we have to return to the beginning of modernity and the emergence of the modern state. In it lies the key to understanding the pathology of post-modern violence which plagues not only the West but the Islamic world as well. This violence, as often cited, culminated in the systematic destruction of the Jews of Europe: *die Endlösung der Judenfrage* (The Final Solution to the Jewish Question). This, I argue, has an important effect on the issue of Islam and Muslims in post-Holocaust Europe.

Violence and the State

The philosopher Thomas Hobbes pointed out in his book *Leviathan* the civilizing affect that a maturing and increasingly differentiated culture can have on a society. In order to prove his basic thesis, the necessity of the state, he engages in a thought experiment that wipes away the existence of a governing power thus leaving man in an anomic *state of nature*. He conceives of this ungoverned situation in his famous paragraph on the 'incommodities of such a war.' He states,

> In such condition there is no place for industry, because the fruit thereof is uncertain: and consequently no culture of the earth; no navigation nor use of the commodities that may be imported by sea; no commodious building; no instruments of moving and removing such things as require much force; no knowledge of the face of the earth; no account of time; no arts; no letters; no society; and, which is worst of all, continual fear and danger of violent death; and the life of man solitary, poor, nasty, brutish, and short.[2]

Without the state, Hobbes theorized that man would descend into chaos and war. *Bellum omnium contra omnes* (war of all against all) was the natural

---

2   Thomas Hobbes, *Leviathan: Parts I and II,* ed. Herbert W. Schneider (New York: The Bobbs-Merrill Company, Inc., 1958), 107.

outcome of such an anomic condition, as the absolute right to everything and anything is only limited by one's ability to take it from another by force and violence. But Hobbes does not stop at calling only direct violence "war," but rather extends the conditions of war into the lifeworld, the everydayness of being – the common disposition within which humanity would live. He writes,

> Hereby it is manifest that, during the time men live without a common power to keep them all in awe, they are in that condition which is called war, and such a war as is of every man against every man. For war consists not in battle only, or the act of fighting, but in a tract of time wherein the will to contend by battle is sufficiently known; and therefore the notion of *time* is to be considered in the nature of foul weather lies not in a shower or two of rain but in an inclination thereto of many days together, so the nature of war consists not in actual fighting but in the known disposition thereto during all the time there is no assurance to the contrary. All other time is peace.[3]

Contemporary fascination which such an imaged state can be witnessed in the popularity of television shows and movies that take place within a situation of complete civilizational collapse, such as *The Walking Dead, The Colony, The Road* and *The Book of Eli.* The post-apocalyptic situation is the absolutization of the aristocratic law of nature, where the strongest, most clever, and most prepared, and often times most ruthless and merciless individuals, survive the *totalen krieg* (total war) of all against all due to their unencumbered ability to do whatever it takes to survive, including the mass killing of others. Unlike others, Hobbes did not believe the situation of complete lawlessness would lead to a state of anarcho-bliss, that the masses would bind together in an altruistic solidarity, but would rather use the situation to their own personal benefit to the extent that they could – a seriously pessimistic idea about human nature indeed, but one that seems to be fairly accurate so far if we examine history. Today, the popularity of the shows that take place within such anomic situations betrays the unspoken yet perverse desire to return to such a state, thus giving credence to Freud's position that man harbors a deep resentment towards the normative imperatives of civilization – the social "superego" that limits our instincts, our freedoms, our natural inclinations towards aggression and the desire to impose our will on others.

Nevertheless, the lawlessness of a life within a context of continual fear and anxiety about one's survival would penetrate even into the most religious of

---

3   Hobbes, *Leviathan*, 106–107.

individuals. Their altruistic concern for the other would often surrender to suspicion about everyone that they are unfamiliar with for fear of the threat they may pose. In such a society the masses become *totally atomized* – in a state of absolute concern for oneself. This is similar to the ideal state idolized by Ayn Rand and other advocates of hyper-individualization (albeit within the content of modernity with a modern state and police force). An atmosphere of paranoia, which would be most appropriate for survival, would drown any religious sense of solidarity with victims, as one's primary concern is making sure that they and their family are not the next victims. Social bonds, the adhesive that binds communities together in common projects and concerns, dissolves before the power of individualistic survival: the absolute reduction of man to his most basic animality.

In order to remedy this situation, Hobbes believes that society enters into social contracts, which is the process by which every individual relinquishes some "natural rights" that they would otherwise have within the state of nature, and by relinquishing those rights they gain certain guarantees to protection, safety, security, and the rule of law. This creates a situation where *absolute* rights are limited, whereas *political* rights – rooted in the social contract – create a space for substantive and subjective freedom. For Hobbes, one cannot live a human life in an absolute state of freedom, as each person's freedom to engage in behavior harmful to others is a concrete eclipse of another's freedoms to exist without such impingement. The political boundaries of subjective freedom have to be positively constructed as to allow for the free development of society unencumbered by the absolute violence of nature – which destroys subjective freedom as much as it allows for objective freedom.

In modern society we do not live in a complete lawless situation, but are rather governed by a minimum level of law, social contracts, and reciprocal norms.[4] The growing complexity of culture and civilization, especially in the realm of law and government, has continued to sublimate the instinctual drives that would otherwise be necessarily utilized to survive within the state of nature. Marx, following a Rousseau-like line of thought, takes this line of argument a step further. He optimistically believed that if we could overcome the class structure, we could not only overcome our instinctual inclinations towards violence and destruction, but we could also create a utopic society of equality. Marx posits a vision of a post-capitalist society that is classless and stateless, with common ownership of the means of production – a society

---

4 There are instances of complete breakdown of otherwise universal governing norms. The systematic destruction of Europe's unwanted, i.e. Jews, homosexuals, communists, etc., during WWII, opened up the floodgates to the most perverse spectacles of violence.

beyond the realm of necessity – where each gives according to their abilities and receives according to their needs.[5] This just society is a free association of individuals that expresses solidarity with all, have been liberated from labor exploitation, and have overcome the problem of alienation. Marx theorized that the revolutionary working class, itself a product of, and response to, the Bourgeoisie, would serve as the agent of historical change – transforming a society that is rooted in exploitation, injustice, imperialism, and the private accumulation of collective surplus value, into one that would be governed by the interests of the universal. Nevertheless, Marx's vision of the just society, which ends the exploitation of one part of humanity by another, is not without criticism. From a Freudian psychological analysis, Marx's vision of a just society may be predicated upon an overly optimistic understanding of human nature that cannot be reconciled with Freud's idea of the death-drive (*Todestrieb*), often referred to as the *Thanatos* (θάνατος).[6] Taken from the *daemon* of death in Greek mythology, the drive towards death within mankind was seen by Freud to be a major impediment to the peaceful and utopic dreams of social philosophers, artists, and religious believers. Utopia would always be stunted by man's inner-daemon.

Freud's Unbehagen mit Marx

To say the least, Freud is pessimistic about the chances for the kind of civilization that Marx wishes to bring about. In *Civilization and its Discontents,* Freud proposes a theory that attempts to explain the continual aggressiveness and destructiveness that he sees throughout history. This instinct towards death directly contravenes his prior belief in man only having an instinctual will to life (*Eros*), a realization that he was initially unwilling to accept. He wrote, 'I remember my own defensive attitude when the idea of an instinct of destruction first emerged in psycho-analytic literature, and how long it took before I became receptive to it.'[7] Nevertheless, his study of history and his clinical work with neurotics compelled Freud to adopt the idea that 'the inclination to

---

5 Some scholars of Marx, especially Liberation Theologians, believe Marx's notion of a society that gives according to needs and receives according to abilities is mirrored after the early Christian community, as described in the book of Acts 4:32–35.

6 Freud did not use the word Thanatos to describe the death instinct, but later Freudians titled it as such.

7 Sigmund Freud, *Civilization and its Discontents,* ed. and trans. James Strachey (New York: W.W. Norton & Co., Inc., 1962), 67.

aggression is an original, self-subsisting instinctual disposition in man...'[8] For Freud, man's tendency to destroy that which he has built, his continual antagonistic attitude and behavior towards others is rooted not necessarily in socially constructed edifices of civilization, i.e. class antagonisms, religious antagonisms, national antagonisms, as phenomenon like these are just the manifestations of a more primal cause. For Freud, the drive towards death and destruction is an instinct that is *within* mankind regardless of their social, political, and economic situation (although some social conditions are more conducive for their manifestation). Freudian theory rejects the idea that if only we had the proper education, laws, rituals, philosophy, social construction, etc., mankind could invent the *totally reconciled society* – a society where aggression, war, competition, etc., would cease to be part of man's existence. Man's inherent instinct towards death (Thanatos), is co-determinate with his inherent instinct towards life, and this inclination for aggressiveness is the 'greatest impediment to civilization' in Freud's view.[9] Even if we could resolve the problem of alienation, as articulated in Marx's *Economic and Philosophic Manuscripts of 1844*, in which man is estranged from other men, Freud believes man would remain hostile to others due to his instinctual drives, and no amount of social changes could empty man of such a disposition.[10] One is a social construction created *within* history, which can be transcended. The other is nature and is a permanent aspect of mankind's psyche.[11]

Freud defines the "death drive" as the particular instinct that's 'aim is to lead what is living into an inorganic state,' to return the animated to the inanimate.[12] This internal drive often operates tacitly within the organism in routine daily life but manifests itself in destruction and aggression when it's directed outward. Although Freud believed that the death instinct could in some cases be put in the service of Eros – destroying things as not to destroy the self (eating, sexual activity, etc.) – it nevertheless opposes the work of Eros most vehemently in the world. He believed that 'civilization is a process in the service of Eros,' that civilization 'combine[s] single human individuals, and after that families, then races, peoples and nations, into one great unity, the

---

8   Ibid.

9   Ibid.

10   Karl Marx and Friederich Engels, *Economic and Philosophic Manuscripts of 1844 and the Communist Manifesto*, trans. Martin Milligan (Amherst, NY: Prometheus Books, 1988), 78.

11   The idea that man's nature is also a product of history and therefore can be modified via historical changes, thus disproving the idea of man's "fixed" nature, is not an issue Freud addresses adequately.

12   Sigmund Freud, *An Outline of Psycho-Analysis*, trans. James Strachey (New York: w.w. Norton & Co., 1989), 18; Freud, *Civilization and its Discontents*, 65–66.

unity of mankind.'[13] If Eros is meant to bring together that which is disparate, the death instinct's work is to do the opposite – it opposes all forms of solidarity. It is the 'hostility of each against all and of all against each,' which inhibits the 'programme of civilization.'[14] Marx, who has a more pacific view of human nature (when it's not distorted by the conditions of capitalism), still believes man is capable of wanton destructiveness, especially when it is pressed into the service of the Bourgeoisie, either through war, nationalism, imperialism, or the reproduction of capitalist economy. For example, capitalism continuously falls into crises situations, where there is an 'enforced destruction of a mass of productive forces' a 'conquest of new markets,' and a 'more thorough exploitation of the old one.'[15] This continuous destruction of the status quo in favor of an ever expansion of the capitalist production keeps man's destructive capacities employed as it destroys the old to usher in the new for the increasing benefit of the few. Where Freud saw the expansion of civilization, even within a Bourgeois society, as being in service to Eros, Marx saw it in service of the ruling class.

Marx's underdeveloped psychological analysis of the working class doesn't take into account the psychological insights that were later discovered by Freud's theory of Eros and Thanatos. His more optimistic attitude towards the realization of a society in which the interests of the Proletariat would determine the existence of social norms, laws, etc., didn't calculate into the overall picture in the instinctual drive towards aggression and destructiveness. Even if there was an ultimate triumph of the working class over the Bourgeoisie, even if the dictatorship of the Proletariat triumphed and brought about a transition from their rule to communism, even if social conditions were most optimal for social solidarity, the innermost drives of the human mind – the division between the "world-dominating" instincts of Eros and Thanatos – would continue to ensure that antagonisms, aggression and violence, would plague humanity. For Marx, the problem is not *solely* outside of the mind, as the social consciousness of the people has to be reformed in light of critical analysis, ideology critique, etc., it is however *primarily* outside of the mind – the material world – where the change has to be made most radically. Yet for Freud, it is the

---

13   It's telling that Freud did not include "class" as a unity that organically came from civilization. The ones he mentioned in this passage are all *libidinal unities*, and not a unity solely understood as being bound together by a particular "interest" such as class. This maybe a tacit critique of Marx's notion of *class unity* – that it lacks the libidinal adhesive that is characteristic of racial, national, and familial unity.

14   Freud, *Civilization and its Discontents*, 69.

15   Marx and Engels, *Economic & Philosophic Manuscripts*, 215.

inner-world – the 'struggle between Eros and Death' – that continues to drive the 'evolution of civilization.'[16] Any change to the material world that does not take into account man's conflicting instincts will suffer from a relatively benign surface-transformation and will not get to the root of the problem – humanity's own inherent psychological antagonisms. If Marx's vision of a communist society is true – as being the society most conducive to the actualization of the human potentials – then an adequate way of sublimating the Thanatos will have to be major part of the structure of society; for if it fails to adequately discover ways of channeling such instinctual aggression, then such a 'civilized society' will be 'perpetually threatened with disintegration' just as every other society has been before it.[17]

In Marxist theory, class solidarity is the adhesive that binds individuals together under the banner of their common interests. Yet Freud is skeptical as to whether or not common interests, or as he describes them 'reasonable interests,' are strong enough to resist the power of instinctual passions.[18] The highest ideals of mankind, such as *Liberté, Egalité, Fraternité*, are all supreme values to which mankind can aspire, but too often prove to be based on weak intellectual foundations when opposed by the instinctual passions. Following Rousseau, Marx's assumption that mankind is 'wholly good and well-disposed to his neighbor,' combined with the idea that private property had 'corrupted his [mankind's] nature,' Freud also finds to be an 'untenable illusion.'[19] Freud sees a mistake in Marx's anthropology. He says,

> Aggressiveness was not created by property. It reigned almost without limit in primitive times, when property was still very scanty... it forms the basis of every relation of affection and love among people... If we do away with personal rights over material wealth, there still remains prerogative in the field of sexual relationships, which is bound to become the source of the strongest dislike and the most violent hostility among men who in other respects are on an equal footing.[20]

Freud does not believe that the common ownership of means of production would lead to an existence free of hostility and aggression, as the most basic

---

16   Freud, *Civilization and its Discontents*, 69.
17   Ibid., 59.
18   Ibid., 59.
19   Ibid., 60; Marx and Engels, *Philosophic & Economic Manuscripts*, 209.
20   Freud, *Civilization and its Discontents*, 60–61. It is doubtful Freud had studied Marx thoroughly but was instead familiar with certain Marxist tenets.

of human relationships, i.e. love, sex, marriage, and family, would inevitability serve as the conduit in which the death instinct makes its presence known. Neither would the abolishment of the traditional family (or the Bourgeois family as Marx understood it) have the desired effect of eliminating aggression.[21] Wherever Marx's revolutionary changes would take society, Freud believed that the 'indestructible feature of human nature [would] follow it there' as well.[22] Furthermore, similar to Hegel's analysis of war and the impossibility of Kant's notion of *Perpetual Peace,* Freud believes that it is possible to bind some together in a common subjectivity as long as there remains an "other" that serves as the object of negativity, i.e. it 'receives the manifestations of their aggressiveness.'[23] For Freud, peace among some unavoidably means aggression with others – the "other" has to be there to allow the expression of man's negativity via his death drive. If the "other" is not present, the death drive will turn on itself and become self-destructive. Yet Marx believes that resolving the class conflict *within* a nation would end the hostilities *between* nations, a view of humanity's future that Freud's analysis of the inherent destructiveness of the death drives would reject as overly optimistic as it doesn't account for man's inherent negativity toward the other.[24] In the end, the death instinct will find its subject, regardless of the type of society that is constructed. Therefore for Freud, it is doubtful if there can ever be 'an association in which the free development of each is the condition for the free development of all' as long as human instincts remain the same.[25] Even within a fully realized communist society, with its liquidation of alienation, man's destructiveness will inevitably break through and sabotage the project of the fully reconciled future society.

Religion's role in the history of mankind's ability to sublimate their existing libidinous energies, including those of Eros and Thanatos, into something positive was questioned by the most radical of anti-religious thinkers: Friedrich Nietzsche. His ultimate verdict on religion was not a positive one; he did not believe it was a great accomplishment of religion that it sublimated and/ or repressed man's natural tendencies towards aggression, competition, and violence, but rather a crime against mankind and his true human potentials. To actively confess a religion was already transgressing the true nature of man,

---

21   Ibid., 61; Marx and Engels, *Philosophic & Economic Manuscripts,* 226–227.

22   Freud, *Civilization and its Discontents,* 61.

23   Ibid., 61. The 'other' for the Marxist, Freud says, is the Bourgeoisie. Yet he wonders what will happen when the Bourgeoisie is no longer in existence (Freud, 1962: 62). For certain, within his analysis, the Thanatos will find another 'other' to direct itself towards.

24   Marx and Engels, *Economic & Philosophic Manuscripts,* 228.

25   Ibid., 231.

to witness for such religion was to embody the evil that was inherent within religions that, for Nietzsche, denied the moral goodness of man's potential for heroism.

Witnessing and Professing in a Nietzschian Age of Nihilism

In the revolutionary year of 1848, Karl Marx and Friederich Engels published their *Manifesto of the Communist Party* that began by heralding an ominous development: 'a spectre is haunting Europe – the spectre of Communism. All the powers of old Europe have entered into a holy alliance to exercise this spectre: Pope and Czar, Metternich and Guizot, French Radicals and German police-spies.'[26] For Marx and Engels, the dialectics of class struggle had finally brought to the foreground of history the revolutionary potentials of the industrial working class. History was on the verge of a new epoch. Just as slaveholders were once overthrown; just as the feudal lords were once overthrown, now the Bourgeoisie would soon be overthrown. Communism, predicated on the radical of reason and dedicated to the notion of equality, would eradicate man's domination over man. However, another herald was soon to be on the horizon, and his insights into the nature of history and man's potentials would have a far more lasting effect in the West then Marx's communism.

Friedrich Nietzsche instinctively, intuitively, and philosophically witnessed the coming crisis of faith in Europe. Heralding it as the 'death of God' and the 'triumph of nihilism,' he saw that the impossibility of maintaining an authentic commitment to religion and traditional metaphysics, and therefore the morality that was historically legitimated by such religion and metaphysics, was becoming impossible to maintain. The advancement of modern epistemology, science, autonomous reason, the inability of religions to adequately address the questions of theodicy, unconditional meaning, and provide real consolation in the face of human suffering, all pointed to the fact that the West had moved into an age on nihilism. Like Marx's conviction that the historical inevitability of communism was soon to come, Nietzsche believed that nihilism was as equally the inevitable state of modern man. He writes,

> ... why is nihilism inevitable now? Because the very values current amongst us today will arrive at their logical conclusion in Nihilism – because Nihilism is the only possible outcome of our greatest values and

---

26   Karl Marx and Friedrich Engels, *The Marx-Engels Reader*, ed. Robert C. Tucker (New York: W.W. Norton & Co., 1978), 473.

ideals – because we must first experience Nihilism before we can realize what the actual worth of these 'values' was... Sooner or later we shall be in need of *new values*.[27]

For Nietzsche, man's traditional values, rooted in Judeo-Christian metaphysics, had been the guiding moral values within the West for nearly two thousand years. So strongly were those values held, that they once overthrew mankind's most natural values, the master morality of those who *overcome* their personal limitations, their social contexts, and achieve greatness in-and-of-themselves. Christian morality, with its worship of the poor, the broken, the weak, and the decadent, by sheer power of numbers, imposed on the strong their morality; that which was condemnable in nature was elevated to godliness, to virtue. Nietzsche thought these altruistic values to be a perversion of man's potential for greatness, for heroism, and for the will to power. Although the normal functioning of society failed miserably to embodying such "degenerate" values, and rather pursued the life of power, pleasure, greed, and gluttony, the moral values of Christianity were maintained as *truth*, deserving of admiration, and eternally good, a status that was rarely questioned since the establishment of Christianity in the West.

Because these values were so entrenched within the western psyche, within its civilizational superego, because they were held to be the supreme good by nearly all peoples, the clash against the scientific, rational, and secular values that was occurring during Nietzsche's lifetime was painful and deeply traumatizing. The trauma of this crisis of faith, brought by the accusations against religion from science, philosophy, and natural history, was increased by the depth of the commitment to those Christian values, and therefore he states that 'Nihilism harbours in the heart of Christian morals' itself.[28] They were considered eternally true even if the civilization failed to realize them. Now, the whole worldview that was built upon those metaphysical truths was crashing under the weight of its inability to defend its claims against modern knowledge. 'Nihilism is at our door' Nietzsche wrote, because the downfall of Christian morality left mankind ontologically adrift, detached from any firm metaphysical moorings and unable to find meaning within a world that was reduced only to physical matter and human will.[29] Where once Christianity assigned meaning to the world, value to each and every individual life, and an eschatological

---

27   Friedrich Nietzsche, *The Will to Power,* trans. Anthony M. Ludovici (New York: The Barnes & Nobles Library of Essential Reading, 2006) xviii.

28   Ibid., 3.

29   Ibid., 3.

telos for which the individual could strive, such gifts of religion were no longer available to the contemporary individual, leaving them to themselves, alone and abandoned by the once meaningful and expansive otherness of God. The clash between the absolute necessity of such metaphysics – both psychologically and socially – and the *thief of modernity* which robbed mankind of such comfort and certainty, is the historical condition of the western man. It is that condition which brings about nihilism. Nietzsche states that,

> The time is coming when we shall have to pay for having been *Christians* for two thousand years: we are losing the equilibrium which enables us to live – for a long while we shall not know in what direction we are traveling. We are hurling ourselves headlong into the *opposite* valuations, with that degree of energy which could only have been engendered in man by an *overvaluation* of himself.[30]

In Nietzsche's posthumous book, *Will to Power*, he defines nihilism in various ways. He states that nihilism is (1) 'the absolute repudiation of worth, purpose, and desirability,' (2) 'a yearning for non-entity,' (3) 'that the highest values are losing their value... there is no answer to the question 'to what purpose,' (4) that 'life is absurd,' (5) that 'we have not the smallest right to assume the existence of transcendental objects or things in themselves,' and (6) 'Nihilism is therefore the coming into consciousness of the long waste of strength, the pain of 'futility,' uncertainty, the lack of opportunity to recover in some way, or to attain to a state of peace concerning anything.'[31] To Nietzsche's keen mind, mankind is lost within himself, laboring only for himself, and confused about himself; he is without values, without meaning, without purpose, and therefore longs for a Buddhistic "nothingness" that would end his ontological misery. The connectedness of religion – that it provided mankind a feeling of *being-with* (both with God and others) – has been lost to a form of extreme atomization, isolation, and disconnectedness to the world. Man's "progress," his development of thought and technology, his advancement of a scientific and materialist form of being-in-the-world, drives man into a pathological condition, where purpose, unity and truth no longer remain valid – they are but meaningless verbiage in a meaningless world – a signifier that signifies nothing. Nietzsche realized, much like the religious fundamentalist today (at least since Luther), that the 'belief in the categories of reason is the cause of

---

30   Ibid., 15.
31   Ibid., 5–7.

Nihilism.'[32] Or, as Max Weber understood it, the rationalization of the world brings about the disenchantment of the world, wherein mankind no longer can find his place; he is a stranger, eternally hostile to the world around him as it has been demythologized and transformed into matter that lacks any form of moral consideration due to its ontological status that can no longer be experienced as having value in-and-of-itself. In such a world we come to realize that our most important desiderata, our highest values – unconditional meaning, unconditional love, hopefulness, and the certainty of truth – are only necessary illusions that exist for our own psychological wellbeing. But in realizing their non-existence – their lie – our knowledge undermines our being, our progress diminishes our capability for happiness, and we live a life *with* truth but *in* despair. We live in a *post-metaphysical world* were *becoming* leads to *nothing*. Reason cannot point us in the direction of the "totally other" and traditional metaphysics are no longer adequate to the psychological, social, historical, moral, and political-economic problems of the today. We are left alone on our global island: the world has become godless and God – if only as a postulant – is worldless.[33] 'Now,' Nietzsche says, 'everything is false from the root, words and nothing but words, confused, feeble, or overstrained.'[34]

According to Nietzsche, in the aftermath of losing a metaphysically justified existence, western man looked for replacement gods to fill the cipher for their once religious souls, to give consolation and to bandage the wounds that were inflicted.[35] The post-religious western society searched for authorities that would slay the chaos created by the descent into nothingness; that would pacify the ontological restlessness and would cancel the epistemological confusion created by the reality of meaninglessness. Instead of trying to

---

32   Ibid., 9.

33   As discussed before, this is an ontological condition that is understood in the West as being normative for the entire world. However, it is not the case that the Muslim world by and large has adopted such a nihilistic attitude towards religion or metaphysics. For most Muslims, the de-theologizing effects of the secularization process have not penetrated into the religious psyche of the believer. Islam has proven to be much more entrenched within the Muslim mind than Christianity was in Christendom, mainly, I believe, because the theological underpinnings of Islam were must more reasonable than in traditional Christianity. Additionally, Islam didn't have the same abuse by authorities – thus causing so much bloodshed – as it did in Europe. Europeans couldn't wait to abandon religion while Muslims are still holding on to it vigorously. In Europe, to leave religion behind was eventually to find a new and truer identity. For the Islamic world, the identity had to be found within Islam itself.

34   Ibid., 15.

35   Ibid., 12.

revitalize the necessary *illusions* of the past, western society deliberately settled for *delusions* (deliberately self-imposed illusions). The post-religious man was tempted by the new gods provides by racism, nationalism, consumerism, egoism (the deification of self via power, status, and wealth), and war. These false ideologies, these new consoling idolatrous deities, gave man an artificial sense of belonging, a new sense of identity, and a new sense of meaning. By losing oneself in the project of the big, the mass, the nation, the race, etc., the anxiety of existing in a world confronted by its own meaninglessness was alleviated and the individual gained a new sense of power – they were a part of something bigger than themselves, greater than their small existence, and they experienced themselves as being once again intrinsically full of worth. The isolation that came with the atomized society was momentarily anesthetized, as the big project absorbed the alienated into itself and transformed them into a congealed mass of power. The *fasces* blade, held together by the binding of individual rods, is a poignant symbol of the capability of these new gods to transcend the pain of severe individualism and loneliness. It brought together that which had previously disintegrated. By providing control, structure, and guidelines, they once again restored mankind to certain equilibrium; he knew his place within such a society and thus experienced himself as free within the confines of that role. Because the coordinates of his existence were clearly demarcated, he felt secure, having escaped the anxiety of rootlessness. Although the transcendence of isolation may sound like a net positive for the individual and society, we must, as critical religiologists, be keenly aware of the nature of the new god these projects were in service to. The gods of modernity, which were meant to slay the God of pre-modernity, failed to eradicate the values and principles anchored within the Abrahamic traditions, and the post-secular condition was the subsequent result. This clash of the modern gods and the pre-modern God of Abraham is at the core of the troubles within the post-secular conditions.

While Nietzsche himself advanced a *new* set of values, ones that embraced the *Dionysian* way-of-life – which emphasized embracing the will to life, the passions of human drama, and potential for overcoming – the rise of the *übermenschen* – he was also painfully aware that the advent of nihilism in the European context would lead those of lesser intellectual strength and fortitude to gravitate towards ideologies that he thought to be rooted within slave morality – the ethics of the *untermensch.* Either way, Nietzsche could already see from his late 19th century perch that the 20th century would be reduced to ashes via society's attempts to overcome nihilism. These instances were ultimately feeble (yet destructive) attempts to "escape from freedom," which was at the same time an escape from nihilism through the creation of nihilism.

In their desire to overcome the state of meaninglessness, rootlessness, insignificance, powerlessness, and disconnectedness – those conditions created by the "death of god" – modern man turned to various authoritarian systems – the new gods – that guaranteed man's liberation from the anxiety of freedom via the suppression of his autonomy. They became united with the big project and in doing so liberated themselves from the burden of individualization and their conscience.

In Erich Fromm's 1941 book *Escape from Freedom*, he identifies the 'mechanisms of escape' that are frequently found within modern man's psyche when confronted with the pain of freedom.[36] Witness the social, economic, and political chaos that ensued between the two world wars in Germany; the diminishment of a proud and industrious people to the level of paupers, the humiliation of defeat and the oppressive insult of the Versailles Treaty, the sense that the divine had left them in the ditch of history, the feeling of hopelessness for the future, the witnessing of their children's lives being wasted, and the resentment about those at the top of the social latter living a good life while the rest scavenge for their daily bread. Although it is an extreme, such a situation, where the individual finds no sense of meaning, purpose, or prospects for the future, leads many to abandon their personal freedom for the rule of the authoritarian, for "creative destruction," and for the newly formed identity of the congealed masses – who, by creative propaganda and conditioning, invest themselves into a larger project that they perceive conquers their sense of isolation and insignificance. Hitler provided the German people a way of regaining their honor, their integrity, and the respect they felt they had lost. In order to regain such qualities, the German population had to abandon their individuality, their autonomy, and their freedom, to which they gladly did. They joined a national project through which they received a new sense of purpose, a new sense of meaning, a new and powerful identity, a new "secondary bond" with the greater community, and a new sense of divine legitimation.[37]

Within the context of the recent Muslim immigration to the West, we are witnessing a similar situation, albeit not one situated within the absolute destruction of war. Second generation Muslims, the sons and daughters of immigrants to Britain, the Netherlands, Belgium, France, Germany, Italy, Norway, Switzerland, etc., have been raised within two cultural systems; first is the religio-moral system of the home and family, where religion and "home culture" governs the expectations of the individuals. This "home culture"

---

36   Erich Fromm. *Escape from Freedom* (New York: Henry Holt and Company, Inc., 1994), 135–204.

37   Ibid., 205–238.

determines the rights and responsibilities of the each family member, it teaches the individual how to live with others, to fulfill the traditional roles that the family expects of one, and inculcates a sense of belonging and an altruistic *geist* in regards to kin and religious community. The home culture is rooted in social norms that are still valid within a religious context; it is the result of both traditional cultural norms, stemming from Pakistan, Turkey, Egypt, Morocco, Libya, and other Muslim countries, as well as Islam as it is practiced in the "home country." In the formative period of the young Muslims life, during the process of *bildung* (moral formation), and familial acculturation, young Muslims are absorbing certain normative beliefs and practices that are deeply saturated with religious legitimation – they are good and correct because they represent the will and truth of the divine. Even if young Muslim do not become actively religious but rather enjoy the secular and often time morally questionable trappings of life in the West, the *belief* that such normative values and principles are true because they are from the divine rarely dissipates – they just happen to be "bad Muslims" at the time. Many Muslim parents, fearing they'll lose their children to the trappings of secularity, work very hard to inculcate such traditional values in their children, believing it will be a strong defense against the *hedonism* (which is itself an inadequate answer to the state of nihilism) of modern life. If we understand this first home culture as being the dominant source of values within the most formative *bildung* years, then we can see how and why it becomes so traumatic later in life for Muslims in the West face Nietzsche's nihilistic culture. Their pre-modern morality is in conflict with the modern world, yet simultaneously it is *of* the modern post-secular world and cannot totally retreat from it. Everything the home culture taught about good and evil, right and wrong, about the meaningfulness of the world, its purposivity and goodness, is confronted with a society that is full of crass consumerism, spiritlessness, relativism, atheistic idleness, drugs, extreme isolation and atomization, and the abandonment of religious truth for a spirit-crushing meaninglessness. The young believer sees the remnants of a meaningful world in the churches and cathedrals, but also witnesses that which was expressed by Nietzsche when he says 'what are these churches now, if they are not the tombs and monuments of God?'[38] Yet, from the perspective of the West, what the individual is truly confronted with is *freedom* – the possibility of determining oneself outside of one's heritage, culture, and historical baggage. This "freedom" to be that which what one determines oneself to be is an incomprehensible possibility for those who have been already predetermined through a religiously constrictive *bildung*. It means that one has to

---

38   Nietzsche, *The Gay Science*, 104.

consider the abandonment of the home culture for one that lacks theological legitimation – as it is conceived and constructed by the individual and their secular, individualistic and egoistic culture – as opposed to being inherited from generations of pious ancestors. This second culture, embodied in the notion of individual freedom, coupled with the culture of nihilistic narcissism and hedonism, is a major challenge for the young Muslim in the West as it confronts them with something religion has rarely gifted its devotees: a radicalized notion of personal autonomy.

Yet we are no longer in an age were secularity and post-metaphysics has confidence in itself. The secular world, which hardly believes in its own truth claims, no longer recognizes the "inherent" value in human life, is death-friendly and crass about direct, systematic and systemic violent, and is pathologically directed towards all the new and *false* gods of the market, has stepped fully into Nietzsche's nihilism, yet it has not determined a healthy way of *being-with* such nihilism. It has sufficed to simply anesthetize the pain of being in a meaningless and godless world by bandaging the wound with the necrophilic materialist *zeitgeist*. Consequently, it is no longer the case that modern man is valued because the Divine itself gave him worth, but man is valued based on his ability to consume, to purchase, to accumulate commodities. For sure he is the bearer of rights, but those rights are not justified by a divine being, rather they are advanced by a democratically elected governing institution – and therefore those rights are contingent upon such institutions: there is no *absolute* guarantee as there was within religious systems.

The difficulty in internalizing the values of two very different cultures is massive and extremely traumatic. According to the Dutch-Muslim psychologist Bellari Said, depression was most prominent in first generation immigrants to Europe – as they longed for their homeland – but schizophrenia was most common in the second generation, having never lived in a country outside of the country their parents immigrated to. According to Ian Buruma, who interviewed Bellari Said, 'a young Moroccan male of the second generation was ten times more likely to be schizophrenic than a native Dutchman from a similar economic background.'[39] The normative expectations of two very different cultures tear apart the psychological wholeness of the person who is attempting to be both Muslim and western. If this reconciliation does not occur at the individual psychological level, the non-amalgamation of both creates an intense neurosis in the individual and 'lead[s] to the disintegration of the personality.'[40] This disunity within oneself – the *house divided* – is a

---

39   Buruma, *Murder in Amsterdam*, 121.
40   Ibid., 121.

disintegration of the ego that forces the individual to seek out ways of over-coming the accompanying confusion, anxiety, and the schizophrenic identity.

Such a situation leaves many Muslims with two options: either fully adopt the "home culture" of Islam and abandon their parent's "accommodating" ways, or assimilate fully into the predominant culture of the nation-state in which the individual resides. Those who choose the former, who withdraw from the culture that they're alienated from, as it has often shunned them through rac-ism and Islamophobic bigotry, acquire the "zeal" of a convert, which further isolates them from the predominant secular culture.

Most people think of a convert as a person who has left one religion and has adopted another, but there's a different kind of conversion that happens when a nominal "cultural believer" leaves behind the "religion as official iden-tity" form of religiosity and enters into a "religion as complete lifestyle" form of religiosity. Religious norms, convictions, and ideals become intensified and take on a heir of immediacy – for the "convert from within," the attachment to religious thoughts, principles, and practices, stemming from the newly discov-ered "relevancy" of religion, are all the more intense because they no longer identifies themselves with the predominant cultural that has been abandoned. In this sense, their religious beliefs are infused into all aspects of the believer's lifeworld because that is all they have. From the perspective of Bellari Said, these 'converts from within' are looking for a 'paradise lost,' a sense of purity within religion by which they can cleanse themselves of the stain of secularity and nihilistic culture.[41] Consequently, the more hedonistic and nihilistic the West becomes, the more it drives these young alienated individuals into an equally as deep hatred for such culture.

Not all witnessing and professing is positive. Some forms of witnessing and professing are highly destructive because they are either integrated aspects of diabolic ideologies while others are functionalized to further the aims of nihil-istic violence. Just as the German of the 1930's looked to an ideology to over-come their current social and psychological challenges, many Muslims in the West, especially in Europe, look to radical Islam, often referred to as *Islamism*, as a way of overcoming their personal identity conflicts.[42] Through adoption

---

41 Ibid., 122.

42 I will only use the term Islamism as to denote the transformation of Islam into an ideol-ogy. I use this term "ideology" in the Marxian sense as "false consciousness" or the "mask-ing of specific interests behind a religious façade." I do not consider Islam or any other religion an ideology in-and-of-itself and I do not use that term in the non-critical sense of a collection of ideas, thoughts, and values. Islamism, in this sense is false – because "it is not identical to itself" – as it abandons certain aspects of Islam that are essential to

of an authoritarian version of Islam, one that cancels personal autonomy and autonomous ratio for the certainty of authority, the literalness of scripture, the security of absolute moral correctness and the "purity" of thought and deed, the individual alleviates himself of all confusion about the meaning of existence, all questions of his purpose in life, and all doubts about truth. He hands over his schizophrenic existence to a movement that will provide for him a single identity – a prefabricated schema in which he melts into. This form of authoritarian Islam is a radical cancelation of subjective freedom, which he confronted within the secular society but could not find a way to reconcile himself to. In handing over his subjectivity to the objectivity of the schema, he also intimately ties himself to the "big project" of radical Islamism – the attack on the West.

From looking at testimony from former Islamists, we see that this attack on the West is both socio-political and psychological. From the first perspective, it is true that the individual has witnessed many evils done by various western countries to Muslims. Whether in Afghanistan, Iraq, Chechnya, Bosnia-Herzegovina, Israel, etc., these young men have grown up with the twenty four hour news cycle, Facebook, Twitter, and YouTube, where such atrocities are witnessed seemingly as a normative practice (albeit denied as being intentional) at least since the 1950's, wherein American foreign policy took over the European colonial and neo-imperial projects in the Middle East. The witnessing of these atrocities invokes the notion of the ummah, the transnational "family" that all Muslims feel themselves a part of, and it increases the feeling of global victimization: as western countries victimizes the Muslims in Iraq and Afghanistan, they simultaneously victimize all of the global ummah. Injury done to some is injury done to all. The bombardment of images of Muslims being slaughtered at the hands of western governments and militaries, the powerful symbolic image of *Muhammad al-Durra* – the 12 year old boy hiding behind his father in Palestine who was brutally assassinated by the Israel Defense Force (IDF) for example, increases the humiliation and rage that is felt by the ummah which feels helpless and impotent to aid their fallen brothers and sisters in faith. They know that there is a moral imperative that impels the community at large to aid their fellow believers, but they are ashamed they do not. Nevertheless, the injustices of such actions are felt deeply and hearts are wounded.

---

it (such as substantive spirituality, intellectual inquisitiveness, and compassion for the other), without which it is merely formal and can be functionalized for the purposes of politics, economics, war, etc.

Consequently, the confrontation with the West from the perspective of the "convert from within" is also a psychological *jihād* (struggle) against himself. No matter how much he wishes to cleanse himself of his upbringing within a western society, which inevitably has an effect upon his psyche, language, customs, etc., he cannot fully eradicate it from his being. It is always there as a constant reminder that he *is* a westerner even if he hates that aspect of himself. The convert hates that part of him, loathes it very existence, and desires to extract it from his being, for it is seen as a cancer. He psychologically projects such hatred of himself at the abstraction deemed "the West" as a way of killing off that which festers inside of him. By attacking "the West" he attacks, suppresses, and attempt to assassinate a part of him that constantly reminds him of what he now believes is "evil" residing within. The West has become – beyond its own sins against the Muslim world – a symbol for his own self-hatred. Psychologically, that symbol must be destroyed in order to alleviate its own self-hatred. As long as the West survives, it survives in him and therefore his personality, his ego, remains intractably divided and schizophrenic. Islam as an *ideology* has not the capacity to transform the individual into a fully integrated Islamic personality, although it promises to do so, as itself lack an integrative wholeness. It is a distortion of Islam that has falsely liberated itself from its more powerful and transformative aspects in the name of political expediency. It was not the political-economic aspects of Islam that transformed Malcolm x into a true Muslim, but the integrated wholeness of its truth content which includes its spirituality, its social justice, its intellectual inquisitiveness, its boldness in the face of a cruel world, its compassion for the poor, sick, hungry, orphans, and widows, etc. In other words, it was not just its politics, but its spiritual aspects, its moral code, its epistemology, its history, its radical social claims and its theology. Islam, in-and-of-itself, as embodied by the Prophet Muhammad, may be capable of such a transformation, but an authoritarian distortion of Islam which merely serves as a political ideology can never serve as the catalyst for a revivification of the Muslim world, nor the complete conversion of the individual. *Islamism* is itself a modern form of nihilism, albeit one disguised in the clerical garb of religion. The death-friendliness of Islamism, the willingness to unjustly sacrifice self and others for a cause that cannot gain a consensus via intellectual contestation and discourse, is a sign of such nihilism. In an attempt to flee from Nietzsche's nihilism, the Islamist runs into a religiously camouflage nihilism: *nothing* is worth living for except the illusion of a restored caliphate, so the Islamist is ready to die for that illusion. However, dying for something is cheap as anyone can do it. As Prophet Muhammad once said, 'The ink of the scholar is more holy than the blood of the martyr,' living for something is the greatest of all *jihāds* as it is the most difficult to endure.

Witnessing and Professing after Auschwitz: Theodor Adorno's Poetics

One of the main concerns for the Frankfurt School's critical philosophy was the question of life after Auschwitz. How does one go on living in a God-filled world where the mass production of corpses, the idolization of death, and the systematic extermination of "life unworthy of life," is possible? How can one believe in any form of metaphysical truth or unconditional meaning, especially conceptions tied to a deity and or revelation, after the reality of Auschwitz? How can one witness and confess anything joyful, eudaimonic, and or hopeful in the shadow of absolute catastrophe; is this really a world that a loving and all-powerful God created? Or, as Adorno poetically questioned, can we really write poetry after Auschwitz?

In order to fully understand Adorno's philosophy as it pertains to what is often called the Holocaust or Shoah, we must first examine why Adorno prefers to neither describe it as "Holocaust" or "Shoah." The most commonly used phrase, "holocaust," coming from the Greek ὁλόκαυστος (holokautein), was first made popular by Elie Wiesel, who thought it a fitting term to describe the fate of the Jews in Europe. Nevertheless, this term is imbued with theological and historical problems that render it morally unacceptable. A "holocaust" is a "burnt offering," the word that was used to describe the Jewish ritual act of sacrificing animals to the divine in Jerusalem during the two Temple periods. When Wiesel appropriated the word from ancient history and used it to describe the mechanized mass destruction of Jews during the Third Reich, he inadvertently transformed Hitler into the high priest of Judaism – an unintended ramification of a poor choice of words. Hitler, who oversaw the near-complete annihilation of the Jews of Europe through gas (Zyklon B) and fire, was likened to the High Priest who oversaw the burning of the animal offerings to the God of Israel. This would be a perverse insult to the Jewish victims of fascism – an unfortunate insight that Elie Wiesel only realized after the word had already been well established in literature, etc. In effect, each utterance of the word "holocaust" in this context re-victimizes the victims of fascism as Hitler semantically takes his place at the center of Jewish temple worship.

Additionally, the Hebrew word "shoah," which can be translated as "catastrophe," finds itself substantively inadequate to describe what happened to the Jews by the Nazis; it remains too vague a concept to represent what Adorno calls 'the millionfold death [that] has acquired a form never feared before.'[43]

---

43   Theodor Adorno. *Metaphysics: Concept and Problems*, ed. Rolf Tiedemann. trans. Edmund Jephcott (Stanford: Stanford University Press, 2001), 106.

The systematic mass *extermination* of the unwanted "other," the mechanized production of corpses, the complete identification of the totalizing concept with those who are conceptualized, has no precedent in history, and therefore the word or phrase used to express this "new" development should also embody this particularity if it is going to be a meaningful term at all.[44] "Shoah" fails at this task.

It is needless to say that the Third Reich's own triumphalist title, which in itself expresses the eternal desire to rid Europe of its Jewish "pestilence," is also morally repugnant; *die Endlösung der Judenfrage* (The Final Solution to the Jewish Question) need not be considered for the task. It should most certainly be remembered as it expresses the instrumental rationality, mentality and ideology that intoxicated a people with the insatiable lust for racial purity, but should not be used to remember the victims. To do so allows the perpetrators to once again define who the victims: they're the pestilence that warrants a "final solution."

What Adorno, and hence many others following him, including Elie Wiesel, have understood to be the most proper term to carry the weight of the history and the singularity of the crime is the term "Auschwitz" itself, for "Auschwitz," according to Adorno, embodies the unthinkable beyond the unthinkable. History itself has burdened it with the culpability of the crime that had the capacity to changed metaphysics entire, to which no previous crime has ever acquired the capacity.[45] Adorno strips Auschwitz of its limited geographical understanding, and transforms it into a concept that embodies the worst that modern man is capable of. The little Polish city returns to its Polish name, *Oświęcim*, while the mass extermination of individuals that took place there congeals into a conception that represents the totality of human destructiveness (in general), that is so clearly articulated in the gas chambers and crematorium (in particular). In his analysis of society post-Third Reich, Adorno posits that Auschwitz is both the period of the mass extermination of the Jews, as well as the 'world of torture which has continued to exist after Auschwitz.'[46] He makes it clear that Auschwitz is *still with us* even after the liberation of the extermination camps. I mean "still with us" not as poetic phrase to sentimentally

---

44   Theodor Adorno. *Negative Dialectics*, trans. E.B. Ashton (New York: Continuum, 1999), 362. This is not to say that genocidal acts had never occurred prior to fascist anti-Semitism, but that the way in which the forces of industry, mechanization, political-state resources, etc., were mobilized to accomplish the stated task of complete annihilation of a group of people was new to history.

45   Adorno, *Metaphysics*, 101, 115–116.

46   Adorno, *Metaphysics*, 101.

memorialize the horror and terror that was exacted upon the innocent victims, but as a way of articulating Adorno's contention that the conditions that produced Auschwitz have outlived Hitler both in the social, political, and economic realities of neo-liberal capitalism, as well as in the psychology that is molded and conditioned within the parameters of capitalism – particularly among authoritarian personalities and those who wish to escape the anxiety and *unbehagen* (uneasiness) that is forced upon the individual while in a state of freedom. Just as we can express that Auschwitz is *still with us* (objectively), we may also be impelled to say it is *still in us* (subjectively).[47]

The fascistic conditions that remain post-Hitler produces both the rapacious aggressiveness and hatred for the Muslims just as it creates the desire within some Muslims to exact revenge upon the West for its crimes against the Muslim community. Indeed, the post-secular society, in which secular citizens are integrated with their fellow citizens who are still religious, contains within itself the potential for a fascist resurgence. However, unlike the first outbreak of fascism, in the early 20th century, in which religious and secular fascists (via nationalism) colluded against the secular critics of capitalism, the international communists, this outbreak could very well be between secular forms of fascism and religious forms of fascism. Either way, the failure of the left to integrate religious communities into the broader body politic, and improve their economic conditions, leaves the door open for such a barbaric confrontation.

History and Metaphysics after Auschwitz

In Horkheimer and Adorno's essay *Elements of Anti-Semitism* in the *Dialectic of Enlightenment*, there is an absence of a direct confrontation with Auschwitz in-and-of-itself, but instead they turn their critical analysis towards the phenomenon of anti-Semitism as a symptom within the process of enlightenment's reversion to barbarism. To reflect on what Auschwitz itself is and was, beyond the simple protocol sentences of the positivist social sciences that seek to understand the mere mechanics of the extermination camps, deportations, and systematic terror of the *Einsatzgruppen*, is a much more intense and troublesome sort of thinking to engage in. Writing the *Dialectic of Enlightenment* in 1943, Horkheimer and Adorno felt confident that they could offer a theory of anti-Semitism that explained National Socialism's perverse infatuation with the Jews, account for the growth of nationalism, and elucidate the increasing

---

47   Theodor Adorno, *Can One Live After Auschwitz*, ed. Rolf Tiedemann (Stanford: Stanford University Press, 2003), 13.

diminishment of the genuine and autonomous individual within modern society. But with their limited knowledge of the *Vernichtungslager* (extermination camp) – which they would later learn more about from Eugen Kogon's book *Der ss-Staat* – could they explain Auschwitz in-and-of-itself?[48] At the time of writing the *Dialectic of Enlightenment*, the full details of the camps had not yet been disclosed. Nevertheless, it appears that the optimism that Horkheimer and Adorno demonstrated in their ability to explain anti-Semitism in the *Dialectic of Enlightenment* was stunted when they were confronted with the full reality of Auschwitz's mass catastrophe. The actual conditions of the pathological logic of the lager proved their 1942–1944 theories of anti-Semitism inadequate even if it did confirm their notion that the Enlightenment was engaged in self-destruction.[49] Unlike their friend and colleague Walter Benjamin, whose direct experiences with fascism led to his own suicide in Portbou, Spain, Horkheimer and Adorno only tangentially experienced the totalizing pain, suffering, and horror that terrorized the Jewish individual under fascism, as they escaped the murderous clutches of fascism by immigrating to America.[50] Later, when confronted with the reality of Auschwitz itself – the catastrophe of history that Benjamin already anticipated in his *Angelus Novus* – they were impelled to ask a different set of questions: what does Auschwitz ultimately mean? What kind of ramifications does the industrialized production of corpses have on our previously held conceptions of history, theology, theodicy, and metaphysics? We can clearly understand the calculative and technological thought of the fascists, i.e. the logistics; how many Jews could be quartered within a barrack; how many Jews could be gassed and burned within a 24 hour period; how many cattle cars will be needed to deport the entire Hungarian Jewish population to Auschwitz – our positivistic sciences make this kind of knowledge available to us without reflection as to what it means. Their questions were more metaphysical in nature: how is ultimate reality different after Auschwitz with the knowledge that we live in a world were an Auschwitz is possible? As Adorno famously stated: can one really live after Auschwitz?[51] From firsthand accounts, Horkheimer and Adorno eventually became aware of the conditions in the camps, especially through his reading the previously mentioned Eugene

---

48   Theodor Adorno, *Critical Models: Interventions and Catchwords* (New York: Columbia University Press, 2005), 195–196; Eugen Kogon, *Der ss-Staat: Das System der deutschen Konzentrationslager.* München: Wilhelm Heyne Verlag, 2006.

49   Horkheimer and Adorno, *The Dialectic of Enlightenment,* xvi.

50   Rolf Wiggershaus, *The Frankfurt School: It's History, Theories, and Political Significance,* trans. Michael Robertson (Cambridge: The MIT Press, 1994), 127–148.

51   Adorno, *Metaphysics,* 110–111.

Kogan's *Der ss-Staat*, and only then could they direct their consciousness to 'think[ing through] the last extreme of horror' in order to understand what Auschwitz meant to metaphysics and history.[52]

In their attempts to imbue some form of ultimate reason and meaningfulness into the catastrophe that was Auschwitz, philosophers and theologians often posit metaphysical claims, both secular and religious, to gleam some kind of conciliation that Auschwitz happened for an understandable reason – a reason that may not be manifestly available to us in all its fullness but is in existence nonetheless. For some Zionists, Auschwitz was clearly a part of God's plan: the Isaac-like human sacrifice that brought about the state of Israel. For other theologians it was a "test theodicy," equivalent to the afflictions inflicted upon Job, to see if the Jews would remain faithful to their 'abusive God.'[53] For some philosophers, reading back into Hegel's optimistic metaphysics, it was the violent struggle of absolute spirit working its way through history towards its own self-realization. Adorno, in his *Negative Dialectics* resists all attempts to impart a positive meaning to Auschwitz. He writes,

> After Auschwitz, our feeling resist any claim of the positivity of existence as sanctimonious, as wronging the victims; they balk at squeezing any kind of sense, however bleached, out of the victims' fate. And these feelings do have an objective side after events that make a mockery of the construction of immanence as endowed with a meaning radiated by an affirmatively posited transcendence.[54]

In this passage Adorno prepares to defend the idea that Auschwitz is entirely *meaningless* – that we cannot extract any positive meaning out of the suffering of the victims no matter how much the human *need* for meaning impels us to. For Adorno, we cannot articulate such a meaning without re-victimizing the victim in the process – without producing absurd conclusions about their suffering. No construction of a meaningful history within which an active agent, whether it be a divine being or absolute spirit, neither immanent or transcendent, can be taken seriously in light of Auschwitz. In Adorno's *lecture 13 on Metaphysics (July 13, 1965)*, he states,

---

52   Ibid., 125.

53   David R. Blumenthal, *Facing the Abusing God: A Theology of Protest.* Louisville, KY: Westminster/John Knox Press, 1993; Richard L. Rubenstein. *After Auschwitz: History, Theology, and Contemporary Judaism.* Baltimore: Johns Hopkins University Press, 1992; Schweizer, *Hating God*, 2011.

54   Adorno, *Negative Dialectics*, 361.

To assert that existence or being has a positive meaning constituted with-in itself and orientated towards the divine principle (if one is to put it like that), would be, like all the principles of truth, beauty and goodness which philosophers have concocted, a pure mockery in face of the vic-tims and the infinitude of their torment.[55]

In light of his claim, any attempt of the theologian to claim Auschwitz as *Deus Vult* (God's will) inevitably articulates a theodicy that is *affirmative* in nature – it endorses the systematic and discriminate targeting of one ethnic group for extermination as being a part of the divine's plan; that the innocent had to suf-fer and die while the guilty remain alive and prospered. All answers to the theo-dicy problem remain untenable post-Auschwitz, including Jewish, Christian and Islamic answers. Additionally, any philosophical notion of a *telos* in his-tory makes the same mistake as the theologian. This kind of thought, whether intentionally or unintentionally, advances an affirmative notion that the Jews, and their suffering, have a positive meaning in history, which somehow justi-fies their extermination. All positive notions of history, that express the notion that historical events happen for a ultimate-purposive reason, display a certain callousness that once again victimizes those already exterminated. Adorno's philosophy finds no metaphysical justification in the suffering of the victim. He continues in his lecture to state,

In the face of the experiences we have had, not only through Auschwitz but through the introduction of torture as a permanent institution and through the atomic bomb – all these things form a kind of coherence, a hellish unity – in face of these experiences the assertion that what is has meaning, and the affirmative character which has been attributed to metaphysics almost without exception, become a mockery; and in face of the victims it becomes downright immoral.[56]

For Adorno, if we feel that we can return post-Auschwitz to any conception of history that has a metaphysical meaning, we are wrong. To think that the world is imbued with meaningfulness, that it's full of purposiveness and guided by absolute spirit or the divine, is to believe that Auschwitz momen-tarily suspended such trajectory, and then returned to it after the liberation of the dead-not-yet-dead. For Adorno, this is entirely impossible, 'there can be no one, whose organ of experience has not entirely atrophied, for whom

55   Adorno, *Metaphysics,* 101–102.
56   Adorno, *Metaphysics,* 104.

the world *after* Auschwitz, that is, the world in which Auschwitz is possible, is the same world as it was before.'[57] Adorno seems to suggest that the world in which Auschwitz happened, and is still capable of producing another Auschwitz, demonstrates the impossibility of a "return" to a world in which there is some objective meaning. A mind that comprehends Auschwitz for what it is – the death of positive metaphysics – resists all attempts to return to such innocence or naïveté. Auschwitz is the final nail in the coffin of metaphysical positivity, which had already been slowly lowered into its grave by the Enlightenment's secularization of the lifeworld. Indeed, if we take Adorno's thought even farther, Auschwitz demonstrated the lie that the world ever had objective meaning. As the advance of Golgotha continues, as the slaughterbench of time provides more corpses piling upon one another, the more Benjamin's prophetic image of *Angelus Novus*, who sees all of history as the accumulation of catastrophe, reveals to us its prophetic core, that any attempt to rescue meaning in the face of meaningless slaughter is a fanciful and ultimately fruitless endeavor.[58] For Adorno, any attempt to rescue or resurrect an imminent or transcendent theory of history that posits an intentioned telos, a positive metaphysics, or a meaningful explanation of historical suffering, can only be unmasked as ideology and false consciousness. It may console, but it is delusional. After Auschwitz, Adorno remains suspicious of any thinking that fails to take into account the suffering of the finite individual, the *muselmänner*, and the totality of terror in the extermination camps, as that suffering exposes the ideological nature of all positive metaphysical statements in light of suffering's ultimate meaninglessness.[59] Metaphysical assertions that are saturated with meaning only further the subordination and domination of individuals

---

57   Ibid., 104.

58   Benjamin, *Illuminations*, 257.

59   "Muselmänner" is a phrase that became part of the extermination camps' lexicon. It denoted those who were "walking dead," the "dead-not-yet-dead," as Primo Levi described them. Outside of humans turned specimens, they were the most original product of Auschwitz. The muselmann figures in our most vivid images of Auschwitz. Those survivors who were propped up before the Allied cameras so that the world could see the unspeakable horror of mass starvation, sadism, and extermination, rarely survived after liberation. Their spirit was broken after being forcibly transformed into a new species: a species utterly devoid of human contact, human empathy, or human meaning – the wholly depraved. The hatred for them by other Jews in the camps inspired Rudolf Hoess, the commandant of Auschwitz to say 'the Jews... lack solidarity. One would have thought that in a situation such as this they would inevitably help and protect one another. But no, quite the contrary.' See Rudolf Hoess, *Commandant of Auschwitz*, trans. Constantine FitzGibbon (London, Phoenix Press, 2000), 151.

to a system of complete domination by providing a sense of comfort and false reconciliation. He states,

> In view of them, the assertion of a purpose or meaning which is formally embedded in metaphysics is transformed into ideology, that is to say, into an empty solace which at the same time fulfills a very precise function in the world as it is: that of keeping people in line.[60]

In a world where there is clearly no metaphysical meaning to existence, a metaphysics that provides such a sense of purposiveness and ultimate reasoning for disaster, suffering, and catastrophe, does nothing for the individual but reconcile them to the socially manufactured horror and suffering of their lives. Post-Auschwitz, not only are metaphysical claims untrue, their continued annunciation creates more potential victims for the pyre, as they prepare the grounds for another Auschwitz: they are illusions that kill.

Only later, after further reflection, did a glimmer of redemption arrive on the horizon for metaphysics in the language of the "totally other." As expressed by Horkheimer,

> The appeal to an entirely other (*ein ganz Anderes*) than this world had primarily a social-philosophical impetus. It led finally to a more positive evaluation of certain metaphysical trends, because the empirical 'whole is the untrue' (Adorno). The hope that earthly horror does not possess the last word is, to be sure, a non-scientific wish.[61]

Even on Horkheimer's gravestone he had inscribed Psalm 91:2, 'In you, eternal one, alone I trust.' But after Auschwitz, did he really mean it?

Ethics after Auschwitz

The overwhelming catastrophe that was Auschwitz endowed it with a certain moral authority, and that authority, rooted in the experience of incomprehensible suffering, has a claim on our thoughts and actions. Hitler himself, according to Adorno, imposes a 'new categorical imperative' upon us, that we

---

60   Adorno, *Metaphysics,* 104.

61   Horkheimer's forward in Martin Jay, *The Dialectical Imagination: A History of the Frankfurt School and the Institute of Social Research, 1923–1950* (Berkeley: University of California Press, 1996), xxvi.

'arrange [our] thoughts and actions so that Auschwitz will not repeat itself, so that nothing similar will happen.'[62] Adorno refuses to subject this new imperative to any form of logic as to 'deal discursively with it' would be an 'outrage' that would degenerate into a 'bad infinity.'[63] Instead, he believes that this new imperative is rooted in the material, i.e. the sensitivity towards the suffering of the finite individual, and most importantly to bodily experiences of agony, pain, and misery, and not metaphysical speculation. He says, 'it is quite simply the moment of aversion to the inflicting of physical pain on what Brecht once called the torturable body of any person.'[64] Ethics should direct itself to the reduction of suffering in the world, that one should not contribute to a globe that is already agonizing with *weltschmerz* (world pain), and that society should engage in the task of furthering the goal of a more-reconciled future society which resists the one-dimensionality of the culture industry that integrates the consciousness of the individual into the totalizing system, as well as continues Auschwitz through napalm, torture, ABC wars, genocide, drone strikes, and all other forms of systemic, symbolic and direct violence. Adorno takes seriously Benjamin's notion of the *weak messianic power* that the present generation has to redeem the innocent victims of the past – so that the murderer shall ultimately not triumph over the innocent victim.[65] The redemption of past suffering, although it will never guarantee autonomous meaning, can only occur when the present generation overcomes the conditions that make Auschwitz possible.

Adorno advances practical suggestions as to how we should direct our thoughts and actions towards the concrete negation of a future Auschwitz: education. He begins his essay *Education after Auschwitz* with this exclamation: 'The premier demand upon all education is that Auschwitz not happen again... every debate about the ideals of education is trivial and inconsequential compared to this single ideal: never again Auschwitz.'[66] Although Adorno believes that the overall structure of society that enabled Auschwitz to happen remains firmly in place, and that the significance of the systematic and industrial murder of millions barely penetrates the consciousness of the individual, we must nevertheless infuse education with the means to combat that structure. Adorno rejects the idea of appealing to 'eternal values' to combat the advancement towards another Auschwitz, as those eternal values have been depleted

62   Adorno, *Negative Dialectics*, 365; Adorno, *Metaphysics*, 116.

63   Ibid., 365; Ibid., 116.

64   Adorno, *Metaphysics*, 116.

65   Benjamin, *Illuminations*, 254.

66   Adorno, *Can One Live After Auschwitz*, 19.

of their significance for those already 'prone to commit such atrocities.'[67] Furthermore, he believes those same "eternal values" that in popular usage are
understood to be unequivocally good, too often serve as the ideological legitimation for the evil that perpetuate Auschwitz.[68] Through their functionalization and abuse, they have lost their essential truth-content. Rather, he believes
that since the root of genocide to be in nationalism – the ideology of *blut und
boden* that ideologically binds the already atomized masses together – an education thoroughly reformed after Auschwitz must penetrate into the individual's constitution. He says,

> One must come to know the mechanisms that render people capable of
> such deeds, must reveal these mechanisms to them, and strive, by awak-
> ening a general awareness of those mechanisms, to prevent people from
> becoming so again.[69]

Critical self-reflection, thinking against thinking, resistance to identity
thought – the total identification of concept and those conceived, must all be
nourished, fostered, and taught, beginning at a young age.[70] Additionally, true
individualism, the autonomy of the self that allows for resistance towards the
coercive totalizing universal, must be recovered if the individual will have any
ability to resist the 'established authorities [when they] once again give them
the order.'[71] For Adorno, the autonomy of self is the only social power that has
the capacity to resist another nationalist hysteria that would result in another
Auschwitz. This autonomy is rooted in the individual's ability to think against
the universal, engage in self-reflection and self-critique, and act on conscience
and not out of social pressure. He says, 'I think the most important way to confront the danger of a recurrence is to work against the brute predominance of
all collectives, to intensify the resistance to it by concentrating on the problem
of collectivization.'[72]

    Adorno has no illusions about this struggle against barbarization. He under-
stands that the prevailing trajectory of history is on a path towards such a global calamity, thus making any struggle against this totalizing trend *contra mundi*
in essence. Bourgeois coldness, the instrumental rationality that animated the

---

67   Ibid., 20.
68   Adorno, *Metaphysics,* 171.
69   Adorno, *Can One Live After Auschwitz,* 21.
70   Ibid., 21–22.
71   Ibid., 22.
72   Ibid., 25.

plans, the production, and execution of Auschwitz, and the incestuous ideology of nationalism in service to and in cooperation with capitalism, and the loss of the autonomous individual, are the conditions that were necessary for Auschwitz to occur. Unfortunately, as Adorno understood, they are also the predominant conditions of the world today, and that despite our best efforts, we may 'hardly hinder the renewed growth of desktop murderers.'[73] Nevertheless, philosophy, thinking, education, and religion, must all be directed towards the total ban on Auschwitz ever reoccurring. If 'perennial suffering has as much right to expression as a tortured man has to scream,' not only can we write poetry after Auschwitz, we are impelled to give voice to the suffering through our words and deeds so that more victims of Auschwitz are not created.[74]

Witnessing the Messianic: The Case of the Martyr Walter Benjamin

The core of the Frankfurt School's critical theory of religion can be found in the sensitivity to the suffering of the finite individual who is threatened and plagued by both first and second nature, who is subject to the horror and terror of nature and history, as well as the modern form of exploitation through globalized corporate neo-liberalism, neo-colonialism, neo-imperialism, dictatorship, and class domination. The modern individual is also subject to the growing antagonism between the secular and the religious, the political right and political left, the polarizing politics of capitalism and socialism, as well as the struggle between various religions and non-religious philosophies. The pain of being against the grain of modern society, once acutely felt by Jews in Europe, is now what afflicts the Muslims in the post-secular West. Because of the alienation and suffering caused by the anachronistic tension of recalcitrant faith, the longing for messianic transcendence is strongest among them today. This comprehensive cage of anxiety, tension and despaire gives birth to a powerful longing: the longing for the messianic.

The idea of the messianic is born out of the notion that history is catastrophe and the idea that history is catastrophe is rooted in the experience of history as unbearable suffering. This sensitivity towards the horror and terror caused by the slaughterbench of history can be witnessed most profoundly in Walter Benjamin's messianic infused *Theses on the Philosophy of History* (1940). Written 'with the thoughts of death' ever-present, Benjamin's *Theses* provide momentary glimpses into his thoughts on the catastrophic nature of

---

73   Ibid., 33.

74   Adorno, *Negative Dialectics,* 362.

human existence.[75] The intensity of fascism, culminating in the Nuremberg laws, *Kristallnacht,* and the Molotov-Ribbentrop Pact (Hitler-Stalin Pact), engulfed his thinking about the nature of history, the role of the historian, the present-day accounting of past victims of history, and the potential for the messianic age. Although Benjamin was deeply influenced by the Marxism of Bertolt Brecht, the last worked he penned was saturated with theological and messianic content that has puzzled many as to why he consistently resurrected theological language that had already lost most of its social relevance in his secular age. Was Benjamin simply following Marx in his translation of religious semantic and semiotic materialism into secular philosophy, or rescuing philosophy in the form of theology? Was he returning to the religious views of his forefathers in light of the historic catastrophe of fascism as so many other hitherto secular Jews had done, or was he bringing the two very different and often antagonistic worlds together in an uneasy synthesis? Were theology, messianism and radical Marxist philosophy engaged in a détente in Benjamin's mind and working towards the same liberational goal? If so, can the Muslims of Europe and America today learn something useful from this alliance of theology and philosophy?

The Place for Theology

The debate between scholars of Benjamin's political theology have divided themselves within two different camps, (1) those who interpret Benjamin's theological language symbolically, arguing that Benjamin's religious language should be understood as revolutionary-Marxist language behind the persona of theology, always carrying a "materialistic intent" (Tiedemann, Žižek, Wolin, Boer, etc.), and that Messianism and Marxism are essentially incompatible, and (2) those who interpret Benjamin's theological language as both revolutionary-materialistic and theological (Rabinbach, Jacobson, Buck-Morss).[76] Battle

---

75   Walter Benjamin, *The Correspondence of Walter Benjamin: 1910–1940,* ed. Gershom Scholem and Theodor Adorno. Trans. Manfred R. Jacobson and Evelyn M. Jacobson. Chicago: University of Chicago Press, 1994. Adorno stated, "Insight into the objective conditions of that fate [private misfortune] gave him the strength to raise himself above it; the very strength that allowed him in 1940, doubtless with thoughts of death, to formulate the theses 'On the Concept of History.'"

76   Rolf Tiedemann, "Historical Materialism or Political Messianism? An Interpretation of the Theses 'On the Concept of History'" in *Benjamin: Philosophy, Aesthetics, History,* ed. Gary Smith. Chicago: University of Chicago Press, 1989; Slavoj Žižek, *In Defense of Lost Causes.* New York: Verso, 2008; Richard Wolin, *Walter Benjamin: An Aesthetic of Redemption.* New

lines are drawn over Benjamin's first thesis in his *Theses on the Philosophy of History*, where he conjures up an image of the symbiotic relationship of a puppet-automaton and a hunchback dwarf (the perennial image of a distorted life). He says,

> The story is told of an automaton constructed in such a way that it could play a winning game of chess, answering each move of an opponent with a countermove. A puppet in Turkish attire and with a hookah in its mouth sat before a chessboard placed on a large table. A system of mirrors created the illusion that this table was transparent from all sides. Actually, a little hunchback who was an expert chess player sat inside and guided the puppet's hand by means of strings. One can imagine a philosophical counterpart to this device. The puppet called 'historical materialism' is to win all the time. It can easily be a match for anyone if it enlists the services of theology, which today, as we know, is wizened and has to keep out of sight.[77]

A materialist reading is uncomfortable with Benjamin's image of a "wizened" theology that animates the puppet of historical materialism and the idea that theology is the force that allowed historical materialism to "win all the time." This seems to subordinate historical materialism under the authority and direction of theology, as it is the dwarf that remains in control of the string, which conjures up a feeling of *odium theologicum* among the materialists.[78] From a conventional Marxist perspective, theology, belonging to the realm of religion as opposed to science, has the function of dulling the consciousness of the masses partly by promising paradise in the hereafter for their quiet acceptance of the current system of domination. The Marxist does not want to wait to be rescued from oppression through death or by a promised Messiah, but rather is committed to actualizing a classless and just society in the present through revolutionary thought and praxis. Religion for many Marxists, as we

York: Columbia University Press, 1982; Roland Boer, *Marxist Criticism of the Bible*. New York: Continuum, 2003; Anson Rabinbach, "Benjamin, Bloch and Modern German Jewish Messianism" *New German Critique* Winter 1985, Number 34. 78–124; Eric Jacobson, *Metaphysics of the Propane: The Political Theology of Walter Benjamin and Gershom Scholem*. New York: Columbia University Press, 2003; Susan Buck-Morss, *The Dialectics of Seeing: Walter Benjamin and the Arcades Project*. Cambridge, Mass: The MIT Press, 1991.

77   Benjamin, *Illuminations*, 253.
78   'Odium Theologicum' – a feeling of disgust for theology.

stated earlier, is counterrevolutionary. And yet Benjamin positions theology as the grand strategist of historical materialism?

The theological reading suggests that (1) historical materialism has returned to its origins in religion – based on the notion that Marxism has secularized prophetic and messianic religion – especially with its insistence on the principle of equality. In the crisis leading up to 1940, historical materialists like Benjamin understood that the previous Feuerbachian negation of religion also negated its liberational potential – its ability to point to a possibility of life beyond the horror and terror of the already given. This action, stemming from a particular anti-religious reading of Marx's critique of religion, reduced Marxism to the point that it shared in the same *scientistic* qualities as fascism.[79] (2) Despite the social reality that "God is dead," theology can once again be an agent of change if rescued by historical materialism. (3) Due to the painful memory of religion and theology's criminal history in Europe, and the fact that its dictates appear absurd and authoritarian in the modern world, theology must hide its "ugliness" in the secular public sphere.

Those opposed to this kind of theological reading suggest that historical materialism 'enlists' theology, and therefore historical materialism is in fact the possessor of agency: 'it is in control.'[80] For Tiedemann and others, theology serves historical materialism and does the heavy lifting of revolutionary change, but does not possess autonomous authority. In this sense, the messianic moment is not a matter or theology or religion; the Messiah is not the redeemer of the world, but rather the agent of redemption is Marx's revolutionary working class aided by theology. The materialist readers of Benjamin reject the idea that he appropriated traditional Jewish apocalypticism and messianism within his Marxist critique of history; rather they read him as saying that secular historical materialism can cooperate with theology (maybe not the theologian) to win in all their struggles. Nevertheless, historical materialism doesn't resign its revolutionary potential when it enlisted theology, but forms a coalition but keeps itself at the helm. Ultimately *Theses I*, at minimum, reserves a place for theology in the struggle for human emancipation and does not retreat into a dogmatic "scientific" materialism that was characteristic of Soviet Marxism – even ardent materialists such as Tiedemann admit the validity of this interpretation, albeit uneasily.

Although it may make some secular scholars uncomfortable, one cannot deny that Benjamin's theological impulse permeates his work. He says in his *Arcades Project*, 'my thinking is related to theology as blotting pad is related to

---

79   Ibid., 259.
80   Tiedemann, *Historical Materialism of Political Messianism*, 190.

ink. It is saturated with it.'[81] Although his writing may be saturated with theology, which gives "orthodox Marxists" pause, he nevertheless understands that it must remain hidden behind the face of historical materialism: *hidden behind* the 'specter that is haunting Europe,' is wise but ugly theology. In this sense, Benjamin's philosophy of religion anticipates the post-secular society as both religion and secularity are operate in conjunction with each other just as both are prevalent within the conditions of modern western society. The question is whether or not they can form a mutually acceptable and beneficial alliance in bringing about a more reconciled future society as Benjamin's philosophy would suggest it could.

Messiah, Messianic and the Historian

Benjamin's three most important works for understanding his philosophy of history and messianism are his *Theologico-Political Fragment* (1921), *The Arcades Project* (1927–1940), and his *Theses on the Philosophy of History* (1940) – the last being the most substantial work on messianism. In these three works, three figures remain at the core of the analysis: The Messiah, the messianic, and the historian. Although all three are often woven together in Benjamin's analysis, there is enough space between them to see the three as distinct entities or "thought constellations." Benjamin is most explicit about the role of the Messiah in his Theologico-Political Fragment, where he makes clear the role of the Messiah in relation to history, which makes it the most impenetrable to a materialist reading. Benjamin writes,

> Only the Messiah himself consummates all history, in the sense that he alone redeems, completes, creates its relation to the Messianic. For this reason nothing historical can relate itself on its own account to anything Messianic. Therefore the Kingdom of God is not the *telos* of the historical dynamic; it cannot be set as a goal. From the standpoint of history it is not the goal, but the end. Therefore the order of the profane cannot be built up on the idea of the Divine Kingdom, and therefore theocracy has no political, but only a religious meaning.[82]

For Benjamin, no activity *within* history can claim to be of the Messiah, i.e. it cannot redeem or consummate history, nor can it redeem the dead, and no

---

81   Benjamin, *The Arcades Project,* 471.
82   Benjamin, "Theologico-Political Fragment" in *Reflections*, 312.

political attempt to bring about a more reconciled society can be legitimized via the "Kingdom of God." All of this culminates in Benjamin's political imperative: there can be no theocracy, where the state and religion are identical. The historical entrance of the Messiah, who reveals the *Deus Vult*, is the *end* of history and not the teleological culmination of history. The unredeemed world cannot bring about its own redemption according to Benjamin, who draws this notion from a certain Jewish understanding of the role of the Messiah.[83] What history is capable of doing is directing the order of the profane toward human happiness, i.e. the ideal goal of political economy. Nevertheless, he understands history as having a dialectical tension within it between the sacred and the profane,

> If one arrow points to the goal toward which the profane dynamic acts, and another marks the direction of Messianic intensity, then certainly the quest of free humanity for happiness runs counter to the Messianic direction; but just as a force can, through acting, increase another that is acting in the opposite direction, so the order of the profane assists, through being profane, the coming of the Messianic Kingdom.[84]

Benjamin isn't explicit by what he means by "happiness"; whether he has a *eudaimonic* conception in mind or an emotive form of temporary titillation that is prevalent within modern consumer society is not fully disclosed. Neither is he clear on what kind of "profane" society he has in mind: is it a socialist, communist, or capitalist society? If we can assume that Benjamin believes historical materialism is capable of bringing about the conditions for human flourishing (or *actualization* as he preferred),[85] and therefore true human happiness, then we must assume that historical materialism is the unintentional handmaiden of the Messiah, as its trajectory towards profane happiness "assists" the interjection of the Messiah into human history; the closer history actualizes true human happiness, the closer the messianic age comes into being. But would the opposite of this analysis consequently be equally as true: the worse the world gets is the time least likely for the Messiah to appear? When he is needed most is precisely when he will *not* come? At least in 1920–1921, the traditional notion of a Messiah, as a redeemer who ends history, was not a complete impossibility for Benjamin, even if it was a radically different understanding than can be found in Judaism, who understood the Messiah to

---

83   Scholem, *The Messianic Idea in Judaism*, 10–11.

84   Benjamin, *Theologico-Political Fragment*, 312.

85   Benjamin, *Arcades Project*, 460.

be more of a temporal figure who delivers the Jewish people from their trials and tribulations. Nevertheless, within Benjamin's philosophy he preserved the idea of a messianic break of history via means that were *outside* of history, something that revolutionary class struggle could not do as it is bound *within* history.

Although the ultimate goal of this fragmentary writing was to warn against the legitimization of human activity via the messianic, the Messiah he speaks of in this fragment is incapable – by definition – of being understood as symbolic language for revolutionary class struggle. At the time of writing, the Messiah and the messianic (as we can interpret later in the *Theses*) are wholly separate concepts. Only *the Messiah* can end history. The end of history cannot be brought out by the triumph of the working class as Marx would have it, or as the working out of absolute spirit as Hegel would have it, for both are *within* history. For Benjamin's 1921 essay, the historical process can only increase the dialectical tension that hastens the appearance of the Messiah (but cannot force it to come – not even the disaster of Auschwitz forced the long awaited Messiah to appear). It is apparent from history that the Jews, in all their agony and desperation, suffer from the same *parousia* (παρουσία) *delay* that Christians have experienced since the death of Rabbi Jesus of Nazareth: the non-appearance of the promised and severely needed Messiah.

Benjamin's notion of the Messiah is one that ushers in the *utopian* element of messianism as well as the violent destruction of the world as it is: the 'hell' of the 'status quo.'[86] The Messiah breaks into history through the gates of time, destroys the world characterized by the *aristocratic law of nature*, and ushers in a total reconciliation of the historical antagonisms that have plagued human and natural existence – the wolf will lie down with the lamb and eat straw like an ox.[87] Yet Benjamin's Messiah is not *restorative* and *nationalistic* in the traditional Jewish sense, i.e. restoration of the Kingdom of David in Israel, but rather takes the form of a universal *apocatastasis* (ἀποκατάστᾶσις – restoration of primordial conditions) – he is *tikkun olam* (world healing). Whether or not Benjamin, through the influence of Scholem, truly believed in a figure such as the Messiah is not truly possible to ascertain from his enigmatic writings. Nevertheless, the importance of the *Messiah* in his early writings seems to suggest that there remained a *longing* for a Messiah-like figure – one that would ultimately redeem a historically unredeemable world. This 'longing,' according to

---

86   Ibid., 473.

87   Benjamin, *Illuminations*, 264; Scholem, *Messianic Idea*, 17; Isiah, 65:25.

Horkheimer, 'unites all men so that the horrible events, the injustice of history so far would not be permitted to be the final, ultimate fate of the victims...'[88]

In Benjamin's *Theses on the Philosophy of History*, he once again preserves the idea of the figure of the Messiah as separate from the *messianic*, speaking of the later in terms of the "we," i.e. historical materialists historians, whose messianic purpose it is to 'brush history against the grain.'[89] The importance of the historian can be seen in Benjamin's most striking image: Paul Klee's painting *Angelus Novus*. In attempting to unravel the meaning of Benjamin's theses on the Angel of History, many interpreters fail to notice that the painting serves as the image for Benjamin's conception of the *historical materialist historian*. Benjamin is not making a theological claim but rather is constructing a dialectical image that discloses to those influenced by historical materialism the importance of seeing *history as catastrophe*. He writes,

> A Klee painting named 'Angelus Novus' shows an angel looking as though he is about to move away from something he is fixedly contemplating. His eyes are staring, his mouth is open, his wings are spread. This is how one pictures the angel of history. His face is turned toward the past. Where we perceive a chain of events, he sees one single catastrophe which keeps piling wreckage upon wreckage and hurls it in front of his feet. The angel would like to stay, awaken the dead, and make whole what has been smashed. But a storm is blowing from Paradise; it has got caught in his wings with such violence that the angel can no longer close them. This storm irresistibly propels him into the future to which his back is turned, while the pile of debris before him grows skyward. This storm is what *we* call progress.[90]

Those that see history as 'one single catastrophe' are those who have adopted the historical materialists conception of history (like the angel of history); they are those that see the catastrophic within the 'cultural treasures' before them; they honor the agony of those who toil – whose blood and tears are the precondition of modern 'progress'; they remember the suffering of those who built the skyscrapers, the castles, the bridges, those who have suffered alienated

---

88   Max Horkheimer, *Dawn and Decline: Notes 1926–1931 & 1950–1969*, trans. Michael Shaw (New York: The Seabury Press, 1978), 239.

89   Benjamin, *Illuminations*, 257. One must note that Benjamin himself never describes any historical entity as the Messiah, not even the revolutionary working class.

90   Ibid., 257. My emphasis.

labor and exploitation, those who have fought the wars started by others and for the benefit of others, etc. They are those who have suffered throughout history so that the few can have the spoils of life. They cannot rejoice in the triumphs of culture as they alone see the destruction that those triumphs are built upon. Like the angel of history, they see disaster where others see beauty; they see pain where others see joy; they see suffering where others see accomplishments; they see all of history as a monad of catastrophe where others see an unstoppable linearity of progress. Expressing this insight, Benjamin says, 'there is no document of civilization which is not at the same time a document of barbarism.'[91] It is the historical materialist who can see clearly the barbarism of history – the cross in the rose (to reverse Hegel). Furthermore, it is the role of the historical materialist historian to look back into history to give voice to the suffering of the victims of history – as proleptic solidarity with the innocent victims of history is the *weak messianic power* that the present generation has against the possibility that the murderer shall not ultimately triumph over the innocent victim. In the face of the Messiah's absence, that is all the living can do to rescue the dead. This future oriented remembrance of past victims allows the critical historian to reveal the 'depository of historical knowledge' that is embedded in the existence of those who have been relegated to the ditch of history. The present generation must be motivated by the past injustices done unto the 'enslaved ancestors,' which Benjamin understands as its 'greatest strength' in the face of fascism.[92] In remembering the dead and giving voice to their suffering, the critical historian prevents history from becoming a 'tool of the ruling classes' as the triumph of the victors is denied the ability to silence or functionalize the memory of their victims.[93] Conversely, in the hands of the historical materialist, history becomes the grand inquisitor of the victors and not its triumphal creation. This historical materialist approach to history aids in the bringing about a 'real state of emergency' that 'will improve our position in the struggle against Fascism,' as the real state of emergency is predicated on the full accounting of human suffering.[94] According to Benjamin's dialectical image, a storm that *we* [historical materialists] call progress is brewing, either in the form of the Messiah's breaking of the eternal cycle of suffering, or the final *messianic* triumph of the working class which is its own form of breaking the historical cycle of man's domination over man.

---

91   Ibid., 256.
92   Ibid., 260.
93   Ibid., 255.
94   Ibid., 257.

Benjamin's Critique of Progress: Witnessing History as Barbarity

'This storm is what *we* call progress' is the key phrase in Benjamin's theses on the *Angelus Novus*. Benjamin wants to contrast the historical materialist conception of progress to that of the Enlightenment's conception of progress as shared by liberals, social democrats, German idealists, vulgar-Marxists, and all others who see history in a linear fashion that is imbued with optimism concerning the perfectibility of man and society. What 'we' call progress is not the same as what 'they' conceptualize as progress, he says,

> historical materialism... has annihilated within itself the idea of progress. Just here, historical materialism has every reason to distinguish itself sharply from bourgeois habits of thought. Its founding concept is not progress but actualization.[95]

For Benjamin, the belief in the Enlightenments notion of progress has a heavy price. The Enlightenment posited the ideal that mankind and human society could be perfected through the mastery of the self and nature; that humanity could become the masters of their own fate; that we could bring about a society that is rooted in *Liberté, Egalité, Fraternité* within the bounds of the given: bourgeois capitalism; that it would produce an abundance of material goods beyond the realm of necessity; that industrial and technological advancements would increase the efficiency of the means of production, thus leading to a life lived more abundantly; that scientific knowledge would replace religious dogmas and provide better conditions for human flourishing. "Progress" was synonymous with *inevitability*, or what Benjamin described as 'something that automatically pursued a straight or spiral course.'[96] Yet Benjamin is aware that the 'technological progress' of humanity, the 'advance in men's ability and knowledge,' is not identical with man's moral advancement, or his actualization, or his ability to think and act in universally humanistic ways.[97] Technological advancements, i.e. instrumental rationality, had advanced beyond communicative rationality. Human "progress" had not brought about a more reconciled world, but a world gone mad (irrational ends) with better tools of destruction (rational means). What Benjamin rightly deems "progress," in the

---

95   Benjamin, *Arcades Project*, 460.
96   Benjamin, *Illuminations*, 260.
97   Ibid., 260.

messianic sense, is the 'first revolutionary measure taken' against such an optimistic world.[98]

The spirit of Benjamin's critique of progress can be seen most clearly in Horkheimer and Adorno's *Dialectic of Enlightenment* – which was deeply influenced by Benjamin's work – where the light of critique is shined upon the dark side of the Enlightenment's "progress." The Hegelian optimism that history is inherently on a trajectory towards its own resolution; that all events in history dialectically propel it towards a progressive final outcome; that the horror and terror of Golgotha serves a meaningful teleological end, cannot be maintained in light of the catastrophic 20th century – which is but the latest layer of historical debris piling skyward. In light of the perennial suffering of the oppressed, history seems more akin to Nietzsche's *eternal return*: a never-ending cycle of misery that lead to no resolution or reconciliation.[99] For Benjamin, if true progress can exist, it is within the historians' memory of the victims of 'progress' and the absolute cessation of such 'destructive' progress via the 'storm that is blowing from Paradise.' What remains to be determined is whether or not the Messiah or the messianic power of the working class is the true agent behind the storm or even if a storm is truly brewing. If we follow Horkheimer, Adorno, and Marcuse's pessimistic analysis of the diminished potential for revolutionary change via the working class, then the messianic power of the working class has already been abandoned in theory because it was absorbed into the prevailing system of domination by socially modified capitalism and nationalism. Consequently, WWI and WWII demonstrated that capitalism and nationalism have the power to subdue and neutralize the messianic qualities of the working class. If the materialist interpretation of Benjamin's philosophy prevails, then his political messianism plays very little if any role in Critical Theory today. What does remain is his method of translating religious semantic and semiotic material into critical social philosophy within the tradition of Critical Theory.[100]

If we remain loyal to the apocalyptic conception of the Messiah, then, as before, the world suffers from the pain of delay – the non-appearance of the Messiah. The *weltschmerz* (world pain) of the unredeemed world continues unabated through history as neither the Messiah nor the messianic revolutionary working classes have ended the continual slaughterbench. All that has come is the consolation of the historical materialist historian, whose calling it is to remind us of the victims of history who continue to press their claim

98   Benjamin, *Arcades Project*, 474.

99   Ibid., 115–119.

100   Adorno, "Reason and Revelation" in *Critical Models*, 136–137.

upon us, for it is he that 'invites the dead to the table.'[101] History, from the perspective of Benjamin, cannot redeem itself. That which transcends the given is not born within the given; that which makes past suffering meaningful cannot have as its genesis the same history that created the suffering. Redemption, if there ever can be such a thing, can only break the history created by man and nature – it must come from outside of the conditions of the given. Benjamin's hopefulness that such a time-continuum-stopping event could occur is among the most distinguishing elements of his theological-oriented form of historical materialism. Only through the eyes of the messianic, or through that which has the power and authority to redeem, was he given any form of hope about the future. For him, it was the only available option left when surrounding by history that appeared to him in its most honest form: a single event of catastrophe. The theological element in his thought, which cured him of the idealist's optimism, also forced him to witness the barbaric absurdity of history, simultaneously rescuing him from the despair through messianic hope.

---

101   Benjamin, *Illuminations*, 254; *Arcades Project*, 481.

Post-Secularity and Its Discontents: The Barbaric Revolt against Barbarism

The summer of 2014 revealed most brutally the pathological and violent stances that are often adopted by world religions. In moments of crisis, where the potential for the greatest forms of reconciliation are possible, they have chosen to embrace a deeply antagonistic attitude towards the other that has often led to destruction, mass murder, absolute brutality, and the deepening of distrust and disrespect, which has resulted in the widening of the gulf that already separates them. Whether it be Israel's war on Gaza's civilian population and Hamas' war on Israel – resulting in the deaths of over 2,200 people; the war perpetrated by Kiev's liberal-fascist coalition on ethnic Russians in Eastern Ukraine; ISIS's war on Yazidis, Christians, and Shi'a Muslims; the very un-Christian-like reception of immigrants fleeing from violence-infested countries in Latin America at the southern U.S. border, or the neo-Nazi response to Muslim immigrants fleeing into Europe from Iraq and Syria; or the racial conflict in Ferguson, Missouri, USA, in which aggressive police action was taken against violent street protests after the killing of 18 year old Michael Brown by the Ferguson police office Darren Wilson; in all these events, religion rarely played any reconciliatory factor, but either helped fuel the fire of division and violence. At best it remained mute and/or ineffective in seeking reconciliation. In some occasions, such as in Israel, Iraq, and the Ukraine, clerics blessed those who were killing (often indiscriminately) – offering them the legitimation and sanction of their religious authorities. In one summer, all these things pointed to the growing trend of rebarbarization. But why, if all the statistical trends point to a more peaceful world, has such violence become commonplace? What is it about the conditions of post-secular modernity that bring this level of violence to the forefront of history, and what has religion to do with it all?

In his *advocatus diaboli* essay, Prof. Morris Cohen wrote about the *dark side of religion,* stating,

> cruel persecution and intolerance are not accidents, but grow out of the very essence of religion, namely, its *absolute claims.* So long as each religion claims to have absolute, supernaturally revealed truths, all other religions are sinful errors. Despite the fact that some religions speak

eloquently of universal brotherhood, they have always in fact divided mankind into sects... Even when a religion like Christianity or Islam sweeps over diverse peoples and temporarily unites them into one, its passionate nature inevitably leads to the development of sects and heresies. There is no drearier chapter in the history of human misery than the unusually bloody internecine religious or sectarian wars which have drenched in blood so much of Europe, Northern Africa, and Western Asia.[1]

Although Professor Cohen's essay was meant to strengthen the arguments of those who are systematically attacked by the critics of religion, there is nevertheless some truth within their critiques, otherwise such critiques would not speak so forcefully to so many in today's world that have left religion out of disgust for either religion's dogmatic obscurantism or the seemingly warped moral compass of so many believers. According to the Frankfurt School's critical theorists of religion, such critiques of religion shouldn't be dismissed lightly, but should themselves be subject to critical interrogation, as such arguments may serve as a vital source of rethinking, self-reflexivity, and reform. So, we must ask, is the critic right? Has religion become the opposite of what many assumed it is supposed to be? Has it collapsed upon itself due to the weight of its own internal fears and anxieties, thus distorting its true nature? Is Horkheimer correct in thinking that religions, especially those that are rooted in the negativity of the *bilderverbot*, betray their cause and ideals when they become identical with state power?[2] These and many other questions about religion – especially the Abrahamic faiths – in the post-secular society as well as in pre-secular societies should be asked and asked repeatedly, for if the critics are right, and religion is simply a source of division and violence, the sooner we abandon religion the sooner humanity can achieve universal peace. If they are incorrect, and religion still can serve as a force for universal good, then we must explore how and in what form religion can be rescued.

---

1 My emphasis. Walter Kaufmann, ed., *Religion from Tolstoy to Camus* (New York: Harper & Row Publishers, 1964), 289–290.

2 Max Horkheimer, *Critique of Instrumental Reason*, 34–40; Roland Boer, *Criticism of Theology: On Marxism and Theology III* (Chicago: Haymarket Press, 2012), 33–42. Also see Michael R. Ott, *Max Horkheimer's Critical Theory of Religion: The Meaning of Religion in the Struggle for Human Emancipation*. Lanham, MD: University Press of America, 2001.

Absolutivity

We must begin to look at the problem of *absolutivity*, or the "absolute claims" that Cohen identifies as not only the essence of religion, but also the source of its sinful "persecutions" and "intolerance." From a critical perspective, the notion of absolutivity is *dialectical* in nature: it maintains within itself two natures that are in tension with one another. First, absolutivity – the idea that a particular value, belief, or practice, or cluster of values, beliefs, and practices, are infinitely correct, morally infallible, and without flaw, precisely because they – and only they – are the directives of the divine, and as a by-product of divinity, these absolute claims make identifiable 'sinful errors' in others. In this case, absolutism produces *exclusivity* in truth. For example, Christianity's claim for Christ's divinity can either be true or not, but cannot be both simultaneously. To enter into a *détente*-like status between these two absolute claims is to fall into the trap of relativism, wherein another form of "double truth" theory reigns: where (1) each individual is subjectively satisfied with the veracity of their own particular claim, and (2) individuals abandon any conception of objective universal truth.[3] While this relativist double truth may help reconcile the believers to each other on a social level, and therefore forestall tense and aggression, it fails to establish the veracity of the competing truth claims. Additionally, such exclusive claims to absolutes often migrate from the purely theological into the political, which often has diabolical consequences. An example of the most intractable conflict of absolutes resides in the Palestinian-Israeli conflict, especially over the "right" to the land. For many Israelis, the land of Palestine was given to the Jews by the divine as their homeland, and thus what God has given to them no man can rightfully take away or *give away* in a peace process. This absolutist stance aborts any meaningful prospect for peace that is predicated on "land for peace." On the other hand, some Palestinians, mainly those associated with more radical Islamist groups, in the face of systematic persecutions by the state of Israel, no longer believe that Jews have any rightful claim to the land of Palestine, even if Muslims throughout history have almost always defended the Jewish right to be within their ancestral lands, mostly as minorities. The absolute claims have impeded any meaningful attempts to overcome the increasingly entrenched bitterness and hatred for

---

3 We must remember that those who "abandon" a claim of absolute truth do so in such a passive way precisely because one cannot positively argue that "there is no such thing as absolute truth" without a performative contradiction. Arguing that there is no absolute truth is to make an absolute truth claim about the nature of reality and thus betraying the individual's belief in at least one absolutes truth – that there is no absolute truth.

the other as they do not allow for any room for *compromise* – the most hated word in the "politics of absolutivity." Compromise, in both matters of dogmatic theology, philosophy, etc., as well as in political matters, means a turning away from ultimate "Truth": the construction of half-truths that can hardly be tolerated or justified in absolutist discourse. As Cohen implies in his essay, when truth is saturated with the authority of the divine, because the particular claim is understood to be a directive of the divine itself, then compromise on the divinely-given truth is a rejection and/or insult against the divine itself. This is a prospect that many religious believers cannot bring themselves to accept. For them, the world must be reconciled and governed by the absolute truths and values that they adhere to or it is in a state of "sinful error" and therefore doomed. As Cohen remarked, absolutism has driven many religious believers and institutions to engage in some of the most barbarous activities throughout history and will most likely continue to do so in the future.

Secondly, there is the abiding issue of tolerance and relativism. In his discussion of the ills that plague Europe and the rest of the world, Pope Benedict XVI remarked that there were certain limits to tolerance within the post-secular societies; the danger being that near-absolute tolerance is predicated on the acceptance of the validity of various truth claims, or at minimum the acceptance of their existence. This may not seem like a very threatening development within society, but the consequence of such tolerance for a multiplicity of truth claims too often undermines the very truth claims that validate the belief in tolerance itself. If the state, and therefore the society, is not predicated on some normative values that are seen to be absolutes, such as the equal status of all citizens, the inherent integrity and dignity of all life, and the dedication to uphold all human rights, then the state itself relapses into a form of arbitrariness. The state, as understood since the Bourgeois revolution in France, America, and later other European state, is understood, in Hegelian terms, to be the embodiment of the spirit of the people – it is a manifestation of their commitment to certain values, principles, and beliefs. Additionally, the "pre-political" foundations of the pre-modern state, i.e. the necessity of shared history, shared language, shared race or ethnicity, have been forcibly removed. Constitutional norms have replaced these pre-political foundations. Normative values, most of which were first articulated in the Bourgeois revolution of the late 18th century, and later critiqued for their inadequate realization by the Marxists in the 19th and 20th centuries, now serve as the basis for the state. However, the fact of pluralism, i.e. the conglomeration of ideas, truth claims, and worldviews – many of which are not only *comprehensive* but also *exclusive* – within one country, if not predicated upon some normative and/or absolute beliefs about the equality of all citizens, becomes a dangerous disposition, as it fails to establish the required foundation by which such a diverse group of people can share the same conception of citizenry, statehood, etc. If the liberal-democratic state cannot rely on the pre-political adhesives of race, language, and history, but rather most replace them with shared thoughts on equality, freedom, liberty, and democracy, than the absolute tolerance of those who would undermine this new form of political foundation would lead to a certain undermining of itself. In other words, some form of absolutivity may be necessary for the modern nation-state, especially in the post-secular society, where both religious and secular people are equal citizens even if they disagree vehemently in worldviews, to remain healthy and thus able to produce the conditions for the flourishing of a multi-cultural society. An "overlapping consensus" on basic absolutes proves necessary for the social cohesion of a nation-state whose social reality is diverse and cosmopolitan. If the state is the agent for the common good of the nation, and is tasked with overseeing the interests of all, then it is an imperative that the citizenry recognize, accept, and internalize the normative values that underlie and give legitimation to the state as the institution tasked with the protection and furthering of that same common good. Without such a constellation of normative/absolute values, principles, or thoughts, at the core of society, which the citizenry are able to draw upon in times of discourse concerning the policies, etc. of their nation-state, then, as Habermas remarked, society can be transformed into 'isolated monads acting on the basis of their own self-interest, persons who used their subjective rights only as weapons against each other.'[4] Again, in order to avoid the degeneration of society into a conglomerate of 'isolated monads' who are only subject to their own self-interest – the realization of Ayn Rand's *Galt's Gulch* – or the utopia of *absolutized individualism* – some social and/or political worldview that commits itself to the shared values of human dignity, human sanctity, and humanity as a value in-and-of-itself – regardless of race, class, ethnicity, creed, etc. – proves necessary in the post-secular society. Again, if we assume the argument that the secular society has drained the pre-political adhesive of religion from the modern nation-state, then a secular philosophy that appeals and applies universally to all must take its place and be accepted. It must be made into an integral part of the society's overall norms and beliefs. In other words, the individual, regardless of their religious, racial, national origin, etc., must internalize the philosophy as their own and, through the process of "moral formation" (*bildung*), impart such values to the next generation.

Continuing with this line of thinking, the opposing side of the dialectical notion of absolutivity can be identified as the *negativity of absolutism*,

---

4   Habermas and Ratzinger, *Dialectics of Secularization*, 35.

i.e. the juxtaposition of absolute humanistic and liberational values against the world-as-it-is. As stated before, the secularization process has drained all forms of positive metaphysics from modern society. Those who continue to posit such metaphysics in the face of such contemporary developments stand out like relics from an ancient past, artificially refusing to accept that which is clearly present before them. This secularized zeitgeist, the meaninglessness of modernity, and ethos of consumption which has been the attempted replacement for religion within today's market economy, has left many people feeling isolated, alienated, without consolation, and hopeless. At least in times where religion still had a dominant presence in the thought and being of people, there was something that gave hope to the hopeless: an eschatological longing for absolute justice, true peace, and a utopian afterlife devoid of suffering.[5] Now, with the advent of science, natural philosophy, and atheism – all of which religion had to fight rear-guard struggles against (and lost) – such consolation has evaporated. In prior times, religion – especially the church – provided absolutes for society sanctioned by the divine. Now, the collective discovers its norms through political-economic and social discourse, and the individual has to discover their own personal moral positions independent of religion's absolutes. However, there is always a nagging doubt about the fallible rationale that produces such norms, i.e. there is a longing for the assuredness of divine absolutes. This longing is expressed in many religious forms, most especially in Jewish/Israeli nationalists, Christian (mainly Evangelical Protestants) politics, and Muslim fundamentalism. These groups often reject the historical developments that have brought society into the confusion of the secular age and wish to replace such democratically deliberated and rationally articulated norms with a divinely guaranteed morality. Even within the conditions of post-secularity, these divine absolutes take on two opposing forms; they are either *authoritarian* or *humanistic*.

Authoritarian Absolutes, Heteronomy, and the Islamic State in Iraq and Syria

An authoritarian form of absolutivity is often rooted in *romanticism* – the idea that the answers to the present and future are solely in the past. This expresses a certain desire for a "golden age" it is also rooted in *nationalism* – which augments a particular people to a status above others – and attempts to forcibly

---

5   Revelation 21:4.

place all others under the dictates of the power against their will (if needs be).[6] Furthermore, such nationalism emphasizes *obedience* to a given power and enforces *uniformity*. A modern example of this nationalistic romanticism can be found with ISIS (Islamic State in Iraq and Syria), which has ordained itself as the enforcers of Islamic morality within the territories that they have seized in the summer of 2014 and after.[7] Any form of "sin" or activities not endorsed by Islam, or that are explicitly condemned by Islam, e.g. use of alcohol, pornography, adultery, cheating customers, etc., are criminalized and punished according their particular understanding of Sharīʿah law. *Dura Lex, sed lex?*[8]

Despite the fact that forced morality is no morality at all, but is rather only *heteronomic compliance,* motivated out of fear of repercussions, and is therefore not an expression of one's deeply held beliefs, ISIS has tasked itself to be the judge, juror, and executioner – completely circumventing the established Islamic and/or state authorities to regulate and punish criminal activities.[9] Not only does this circumvent the internationally recognized state, it also circumvents the *will of the people* whose opinions were not taking into consideration when ISIS imposed their order on the population.[10] Additionally, some scholars may argue that the Qur'anic injunction '*la ikraha fii din*' ('there is no compulsion in religion') only pertains to forced conversion.[11] However, a more dialectical approach to *Sūrat al-Baqarah* 2:256 – which outlaws religious compulsion – reveals a deeper and much more important possibility; that any attempt to artificially force an individual to accept a moral precept without their truly accepting it as their own has no merit in the Islamic tradition, even if the individual is a believing Muslim. If we can say that any particular religion is a *system* of beliefs, rituals, interpretation of reality and orientation of action, and the traditional reading of the *āyah* ("sign" – verse) forbids Muslims from imposing their religion (as a system) on others against their will, then it is equally as valid to say that it also pertains to a given particular belief (as opposed to a whole system); where the universal is true, so too is the particular. In short, the forcing of any particular moral claim upon the individual who doesn't

---

6   See Adorno et al., *The Authoritarian Personality.* New York: Harper & Brothers, 1950.

7   Joby Warrick, *Black Flags: The Rise of ISIS.* New York: Doubleday, 2015.

8   'The law is harsh, but is it the law.'

9   Rudolf J. Siebert, *The Development of Moral Consciousness towards a Global Ethos* (New Dehli, Sanbun Publishers, 2012), 35–36.

10   This may not be the case entirely in some areas of Iraq where ISIS was seen as a preferable option to the chaos of the post-Saddam situation. See Warrick, *Black Flags,* 223–307.

11   One should note that this verse was revealed in Medina when the Muslims were in power. This verse was never abrogated and remains a normative sentiment within Islamic law and fiqh.

accept it as their own is in violation of the Qur'anic injunction and risks the possibility of creating injustice. The Qur'an in this matter respects the conscience (*Ḍamīr*) of the individual and clearly warns against its violation via heteronomically enforced religious pronouncements. Consequently, in the traditional understanding of this verse, those who were forced to openly pledge their alliance to a given religious belief under duress are within their rights to revert back to their original beliefs.[12] Historically, Muslims have respected the individual's autonomy when deciding whether or not they accept a certain matter of faith; it is not by force that the individual accepts Islam (or any other religion), but by convincing the individual of the correctness of the belief via free and uncoerced discourse.

With this Qur'anic prohibition, we can see that those who force conversion onto others, such as ISIS, betray their psychological secret: they have little confidence in Islam to be convincing, but rather force a situation where the individual must *pretend* to be Muslim just to stay alive so they may *secretly* retain and practice their true religious tradition or non-religion.[13] From the perspective of the *al-Sīra al-Nabawiyya* (biography of the Prophet Muhammad), these actions of ISIS fall well outside of the domain of the established *Sunnah* of the Prophet, and have been condemned by many important Islamic scholars as such.[14] In a sense, there was a certain level of civilization in the 7th century Arabia – with the birth of Islam – which ISIS in the 21st century has gone behind. As many critics of ISIS continually state that they want to return to that 7th century, their most brutal actions demonstrate that they have migrated to *al-jāhilīyah*, the *age of ignorance* prior to Islam, when human life had very little intrinsic value and when the early Muslims were forced to renounce their faith or face execution. Where forced conversions ended with Islam in the 7th century, they continued through the medieval period in Christendom. As such, ISIS embraces a medieval ethic more akin to the Spanish Inquisition than one that is associated with the Prophet of Islam. For Shaykh Muhammad al-Yaqoubi, a reknown Damascan scholar of Islam, ISIS is more akin to the *Khawarij* (the succeeders), who are vilified in the Islamic world for their

---

12 Surely Muslim have a right to legislate the laws of their lands over the objections of any particular individual or group, but they cannot force the individual or group to accept such laws and pledge fidelity to them against their conscience.

13 A similar historical analogy may be found in the *conversos* of newly Catholicized Spain in the 14th and 15th century. The crypto-Muslims (*Moriscos*) and the crypto-Jews (*Morranos*) were forced to publicly live like Catholics while they preserved their personal religious beliefs in private.

14 See Shaykh Muhammad al-Yaqoubi, *Refuting ISIS: A Rebuttal of its Religious and Ideological Foundations.* United States: Sacred Knowledge, 2015.

succession from the early Caliphate and the murder of the Prophet's cousin and son-in-law ʿAlī ibn Abī Ṭālib.[15]

As previously mentions, *heteronomic compliance* in issues of morality cannot be made normative within Islam as Islamic law forbids it, even against other Muslims.[16] Heteronomy (ετερονομίας), or the imposition of norms, values, and principles upon an individual by external force, robs the individual of their capacity to act morally according to their own conscience. It is a non-moral action when it is an action simply in compliance with heteronomic forces precisely because the actions do not originate in the individual's autonomous being – the inner source of an individual's moral commitments.[17] It is only when the individual self-regulates via the willful acceptance of the norms of a given society as their own, or through the realization of society's norms as being that which is identical to the norms that autonomously develop within the individual, that the individual can be understood a being moral. In other words, it is not sufficient for an action to be considered morally good if it simply *conform*[s] to the moral law – it must also be done for the *sake* of the moral law.[18] In an Islamic formulation, the action must be done *fisibillilah* (for the sake of Allah) and not simply in compliance with Islamic regulations. If ISIS wishes to create a moral society – a society that is not only *formally* guided by morality but is *substantially moral* because it is the result of man's autonomous moral development – then it cannot *heteronomically* impose its morality onto the society, but must create the conditions where individuals can realize their own autonomy *through* and in *conjunction with* moral social norms. From a pragmatic standpoint, ISIS may well be satisfied with a population that is compliant with their dictates and submits to their will. However, this does not make it an ideal Islamic society, which is a society that balances autonomy of the individual's will and solidarity with the collective will, and one whose strictures are identical with the morality of its people because the people – through their autonomous decision making – have chosen it to be thus. From the people – whose morality may be rooted in Islam – comes the positive articulation of law and norms of society, not the other way around. From the prophetic example, it cannot be imposed from above but must be freely chosen.

---

15   Ibid., pp. 8–9.

16   One always retains the right of objection towards certain laws on the basis of morality or a different interpretation of an Islamic principle itself.

17   Immanuel Kant, *Critique of Practice Reason* (New York: Cambridge University Press, 1997), Pt. 1.

18   Immanuel Kant, *Groundwork for the Metaphysics of Morals*, trans. H.J. Paton (New York: Harper Torchbooks, 1964), 442.

The heteronomic imposition of draconian laws upon a populace that doesn't share their interpretation of religion – in this case Islam – may very well have the opposite effect; it may fertilize the grounds of resentment towards ISIS and their interpretation of Islam by those very people who ISIS claims to represent: the Muslims. As such, heteronomy is dialectical: the more it is enforced and the more the autonomy of the individual's conscience is eclipsed, the more those individuals seek out their autonomy in non-conformist ways. The suppression of autonomy leads to either (1) *broken people* – their autonomy so thoroughly suppressed that they have completely surrendered to the dictates of the regime and thus remain reservedly compliant, (2) *rebels* – those who will express their autonomy in ways deemed unacceptable by the governing forces but do not direct their autonomy towards the overthrow of the authority, or (3) *revolutionaries*, who coalesce around an oppositional philosophy (which develops autonomously) and are determined to overthrow the oppressive regime. In the present time, ISIS is attempting to create the conditions of a society that will either be severely crippled; will indirectly encourage social deviancy (by their standards); or will end up being opposed by a countervailing force. Either way, the end result will be a brutal non-Islamic society.

The ability to impose heteronomically an interpretation of religion, law, social norms, etc., onto others without any hesitation is rooted in the confidence derived from the absolutization of one's own particular claims, especially when those sentiments are legitimated by a commonly agreed upon absolute, i.e. the divine. As stated before, the authoritarian personality believes that which the divine has made absolutely true, or morally correct, cannot tolerate critical examination, and is thus understood to be universally applicable to all peoples at all times.[19] The authoritarian personality reacts violently when their views are questioned, as they have become identical with what they feel or perceives to be absolute. Any questioning of their ideology is perceived as a personal attack against them. Psychologically, they have taken refuge within the absolute statement that gives them the ability to be in the world with confidence: the absolute is on their side. To question that dictate is to undermine their authority, which is something the authoritarian finds unacceptable.

Although some may agree with ISIS's enforcement of their interpretation of *Sharīʿah*, the authoritarian nature of their regime is witnessed in, (1) the absence of consent from the people who are under their rule, (2) the brutal imposition of a puritanical orientation of religion, and (3) their consolidation of power through the enforcement of draconian laws and regulations. This last quality can be seen most clearly in their relations with minorities. ISIS's attack

---

19   Adorno et al., *The Authoritarian Personality*, 727–743.

on Yazidis, Christians, Shi'a Muslims, and other Sunnis who do not agree with
their pseudo-Caliphate, has little precedent within Islamic history, as can be
attested by the fact that those communities have continued to exist within the
majority Muslim world (at least until the 20th century). Doubtless, the history of inter-religious relations is not without its challenging moments, but
when taking a larger historical view, the history of Islam in relation to other
religions is much more peaceful than in Christendom. Thus the religious and
ethnic pluralism of the Middle East is threatened by ISIS's current seizure of
churches, impromptu crucifixion of Christians, wholesale slaughter of Yazidi
men and forced marriages of their women and children to ISIS fighters, attacks
on the Kurds, and the frequent beheadings, including the American photo
journalist James Wright Foley in retaliation for the United States' bombing of
ISIS targets.[20]

Although it should not have, this "first terror attack" (as the Obama White
House described the execution of James Foley) on the United States by ISIS
provoked intense disgust around the world. Yet the United States was already
warned. In an August 12, 2014, email to James Foley's parents, ISIS articulated
their desire for retaliation (*lex talionis*),

> Now you return to bomb the Muslims of Iraq once again, this time resort-
> ing to Arial attacks and "proxy armies," all the while cowardly shying away
> from a face-to-face confrontation! Today our swords are unsheathed to-
> wards you, GOVERNMENT AND CITIZENS ALIKE! AND WE WILL NOT
> STOP UNTILL WE QUENCH OUR THIRST FOR YOUR BLOOD. You do not
> spare our weak, elderly, women or children so we will NOT spare yours!
> You and your citizens will pay the price of your bombings! The first of
> which being the blood of the American citizen, James Foley! He will be
> executed as a DIRECT result of your transgressions towards us![21]

---

20   Chelsea J. Carter, "Video Shows ISIS Beheading U.S. Journalist James Foley." August
      20, 2014. http://www.cnn.com/2014/08/19/world/meast/isis-james-foley/index.html (Ac-
      cessed 8/19/2014). Upon hearing of her son's death, Diane Foley, James's mother, posted
      the following on facebook: 'We have never been prouder of our son Jim. He gave his life
      trying to expose the world to the suffering of the Syrian people. We implore the kidnap-
      pers to spare the lives of the remaining hostages. Like Jim, they are innocents. They have
      no control over American government policy in Iraq, Syria or anywhere in the world.
      We thank Jim for all the joy he gave us. He was an extraordinary son, brother, journalist
      and person. Please respect our privacy in the days ahead as we mourn and cherish Jim.'
      https://www.facebook.com/FindJamesFoley (Accessed 8/19/2014).

21   GlobalPost, "Full Text of the Last Email the Islamic State sent to the Foley Family," August
      21, 2014. http://www.globalpost.com/dispatch/news/regions/middle-east/syria/140821/

In the video that depicted the beheading of James Foley, the masked British Muslim, popularly known as "jihad Johnny" – later identified as Muhammad Emwazi – took aim at President Obama. The jihadist said,

> As a government, you have been at the forefront of aggression towards the Islamic State. You have plotted against us and gone out of your way to find reasons to interfere in our affairs. Today, your military air force is attacking us daily in Iraq. Your strikes have caused casualties against Muslims. You are no longer fighting an insurgency: we are an Islamic Army and a state that has been accepted by a large number of Muslims worldwide, so effectively, any aggression towards the Islamic State is an aggression towards Muslims from all walks of life who have accepted Islamic Caliphate as their leadership. So any attempt by you, Obama, to deny Muslims their right of living in safety under the Islamic Caliphate will result in the bloodshed of your people.

The day after ISIS released the video showing the decapitation of James Foley, President Barack Obama, who is a Christian but also the son of a Kenyan Muslim, as well as the leader of the most powerful secular state, expressed his disgust, forcibly stating,

> Jim Foley's life stands in stark contrast to his killers. Let's be clear about ISIL [ISIS].[22] They have rampaged across cities and villages killing innocent, unarmed civilians in cowardly acts of violence. They abduct women and children and subject them to torture and rape and slavery. They have murdered Muslims, both Sunni and Shia, by the thousands. They target Christians and religious minorities, driving them from their homes, murdering them when they can, for no other reason than they practice a different religion.
>
> They declared their ambition to commit genocide against an ancient people. So ISIL speaks for no religion. Their victims are overwhelmingly Muslim, and no faith teaches people to massacre innocents. No just god would stand for what they did yesterday and what they do every single day. ISIL has no ideology of any value to human beings. Their ideology is bankrupt. They may claim out of expediency that they are at war with

---

text-last-email-islamic-state-sent-foley-family (Accessed 8/22/2014). Capitalizations and misspellings are in the original message.

22   The American government refers to the "Islamic State in Iraq and Syria" as ISIL, the "Islamic State in Iraq and Levant."

the United States or the West, but the fact is they terrorize their neighbors and offer them nothing but an endless slavery to their empty vision and the collapse of any definition of civilized behavior.[23]

For the parents of James Foley, who are devout Catholics, their son's work in Syria made him a 'martyr for freedom.' According to his father, 'James felt compelled to bear witness to people in conflict,' and for that commitment, that witnessing, he was murdered by ISIS as a symbol of their defiance against the United States.[24] Pope Francis, appalled by the brutal beheading of Foley, and seeing members of his church in agony, personally called the family and offered his sincere condolences, offering whatever comfort he could. Despite the mass killing of Christians in ISIS territory, the Pope continues to hold onto his Franciscan inspiration and routinely prays for peace in the region, both for Muslims and Christians, *ex animo*.[25] On the other hand, ISIS has in *praxis* rejected the ethos of inter-religious discourse and a peaceful living together that was expressed both by St. Francis of Assisi and by the Sultan Malik al-Kamil in Damietta, Egypt, in 1219 CE, and continues to viciously attack religious minorities who pose no threat to their pseudo-Caliphate. The only threat they pose is to the *absolutivity* of ISIS's faith. As long as there exists those who don't believe in their interpretation of Islam, then there exist alternatives to their fundamentalist worldview. Those options reveal, just by existing, the insecurities of ISIS's authoritarian faith.

In November of 2014, to the horror of the world, ISIS decapitated its third American, Peter Kassig. Peter was a former Army Ranger who had been deployed to Iraq in 2007. According to various reports, Peter was struck by the poverty, destitution, and suffering of the people he was sent to occupy, and later wished to return to the region to offer whatever help he could to alleviate the misery caused by the turmoil of the Syrian civil war. In 2012 he formed his own non-profit organization *Special Emergency Response and Assistance* (SERA) and began his work in Lebanon and Syria, giving medical aid to any and all in search of it. In an interview he stated, 'I am not a doctor. I am not a

23   Barack Obama, "President Obama's Remarks on the Execution of Journalist James Foley by Islamic State," August 20, 2014. http://www.washingtonpost.com/politics/transcript-president-obamas-remarks-on-the-execution-of-journalist-james-foley-by-islamic-state/2014/08/20/f5a63802-2884-11e4-8593-da634b334390_story.html (Accessed 8/20/2014).

24   Bev Ford and Rich Schapiro, "Pope Francis calls Parents of Slain Journalist James Foley to Give Condolences." August 22, 2014. http://www.nydailynews.com/news/national/pope-francis-calls-parents-james-foley-article-1.1912382 (Accessed 8/22/2014).

25   "from the heart."

nurse... I am a guy who can clean up bandages, help clean up patients, swap out bandages, help run IVs, make people's quality of life a little bit better. This is something for me that has meaning, that has purpose.'[26] Motivated out his deeply felt solidarity for those who had become victims of history, he traveled furthered in the contested areas of eastern Syria, where ISIS eventually captured him. Jailed, beaten, and tortured by ISIS, Peter would eventually convert to Islam, taking on the name *Abdul-Rahman* (servant of the most Merciful). Ironically, the mercy Peter showed to Muslims through his charity and medical work, even those believed to be members of ISIS, was not reciprocated. Neither was Peter's heartfelt conversion to Islam honored by ISIS.[27] Sometime in November, despite the pleas of a grieving mother, who desperately wanted her child home and safe, and despite the pleas from the al-Qae'da affiliate *al-Nusrah Front* (who remembered Peter as an honorable man who even gave them medical attention when needed), Peter was barbarically beheaded by ISIS; his head made into a prop for ISIS's latest anti-America propaganda video. To gain a convert to Islam was never the goal of ISIS, to kill an America, taunt the President of the United States, and strike terror in the hearts of all non-Muslims and Shi'a Muslims was their chief aim. To kill another Muslim such as Peter 'Abdul-Rahman' Kassig was of no importance; he was simply a means to an end. However for Peter, his mission was in stark contrast to that of ISIS. He wrote to his parents 'If I do die, I figure that at least you and I can seek refuge and comfort in knowing that I went out as a result of trying to alleviate suffering and helping those in need.'[28]

In another letter from Syria, Kassig wrote home saying 'I wish this paper would go on forever and never run out and I could just keep talking to you. Just know I'm with you. Every stream, every lake, every field and river. In the woods and in the hills, in all the places you showed me. I love you.'[29] His parent remained deeply proud of their son for living his beliefs. He had become identical in thought and praxis with those heartful beliefs and died as a martyr in the cause of humanity solidarity, empathy, and loving recognition.

---

26 Michael Pearson and Dana Ford, "Peter Kassig's Parents: 'Good will Prevail,'" November 17, 2014. http://www.cnn.com/2014/11/17/world/meast/isis-peter-kassig-remembered/ (Accessed 11/18/2014).

27 Although some may say he conversion was convenient – an attempt to escape execution – his family and friends have maintained that he was interested in doing so long before his capture.

28 Pearson and Ford, "Peter Kassig's Parents: 'Good will Prevail,'" (Accessed 11/18/2014).

29 Amy Davidson, "The Mystery of Abdul-Rahman, or Peter Kassig," November 17, 2014. http://www.newyorker.com/news/amy-davidson/mystery-abdul-rahman-peter-kassig (Accessed 11/18/2014).

In many ways Peter's life was a symbol for the potential for Islamic-western reconciliation; he began his life in the Muslim world as a Christian soldier, but like St. Francis of Assisi, chose to abandon the military life and love his former enemy. Like Francis, who traveled to the Muslim world and was deeply affected by the love and respect he received from Muslims of deep faith, so too was Peter; so affected that he later embraced the very faith of those who would murder him. Recognizing the mercifulness of the Islam tradition, he chose the Islamic name of mercy: 'Abdul-Rahman,' but was showed no mercy by ISIS. From the perspective of Islam, Peter Kassig is a martyr for his faith; an altruistic faith that motivated him to give freely to others and risk his life for others in attempt to alleviate their suffering. Rightly, Kassig's father, remembering and mourning the loss of his beloved son, quoted the Gospel of John 15:13, 'greater love hath no man than this, than to lay down his life for another,' a sentiment that the Qur'an is fully in agreement with. In a most ecumenical nature – rooted deeply within both the Islamic and Christian faiths – Peter's father asked the people of the world to not only pray for his son Abdul-Rahman, but also for the people of Syria, whom his son graciously served most faithfully and lovingly. Wheras Peter discovered beauty, mercy and compassion for the suffering of frail human beings in Islam, ISIS only found ugliness, hatred and violence.

ISIS's threat to civilization, their brutality in the name of religion, and their sheer cruelty towards the "other," led even the most conservative Wahhabi scholars to denounce them.[30] Saudi Arabia's Grand Mufti Sheikh 'Abdul-'Aziz Al al-Sheikh, the nation's highest religious authority, has condemned ISIS's actions calling them "enemy number one of Islam" and denied that they have anything to do with the religion of Prophet Muhammad.[31] With the full force of his authority, he stated to the Saudi Press Agency, 'Extremist and militant ideas and terrorism which spread decay on Earth, destroying human civilization, are not in any way part of Islam, but are enemy number one of Islam, and Muslims are their first victims.'[32] This statement is significant in the sense that many Saudis – raised on a very schizophrenic form of Islam, Wahhabism, which is morally obtuse and restrictive while languishing in the

---

30   According to many accounts, ISIS has also been denounced by al-Qae'da. What has motivate bin Laden's organization to denounce ISIS is still up for debate but it is most likely born out of competing ideologies, strategies, motivations, and goals.

31   Reuters, "Saudi Grand Mufti Denounces ISIS," August 19, 2014. http://www.dailystar.com .lb/News/Middle-East/2014/Aug-19/267697-saudi-top-preacher-blasts-isis-as-enemy-no1 .ashx#axzz3AqneMQkc (Accessed 8/19/2014).

32   Ibid.

house of luxury – are often accused of supporting some of the most violence and reactionary forms of Islam. Wahhabism, which is a "puritan" or "pietistic" form of Islam, is akin to Christianity's nascent "protestant" movement; it directed itself towards simplifying Islam by shedding cultural attachments that developed post-Muhammad; they declared a war against *bid'a* (innovations) and set about rejuvenating Islam through returning to its "roots."[33] In attempting to rescue Islam from the accumulation of non-Islamic practices, beliefs, and cultural norms, it developed a reactionary and dogmatic attitude towards other Muslims who did not adhere to their perceived need to purify Islam. This antagonism appears most often where Saudi petro-dollars support Wahhabi inspired clerics, architecture, education, etc., in areas of the Muslim world that are more influenced by Sufism or the other religions in the area.[34] However, simply because Wahhabi Islam is culturally and religiously conservative – minus its intense adjustments to the luxuries of global capitalism – it is not *inherently* terroristic as many critics in the West have claimed. It is an extremely conservative orientation within Islam, but conservatism does not equal religious violence, even if it does maintain a reactionary and dismissive attitude towards cultural modernization, secularization, etc. With his condemnatory statements against ISIS, the Wahhabi Mufti Sheikh has placed an important distinction between conservative Islam and those who'd justify their barbarity with a form of Islamism that is even beyond the pale of the most conservative of clerics.

Most interesting about Mufti Sheikh 'Abdul-'Aziz Al al-Sheikh's comments is that he agrees with Shaykh Muhammad al-Yaqoubi, and drew a historical connection from ISIS back to the *Khawarij*, the 7th century group of Muslims that first supported the Prophet's cousin and son-in-law 'Alī bin Abī Ṭālib's claim to succession (*khalīfah* – "successor"), only to abandon him and actively fight against him after the arbitration at the Battle of Siffin in 657 CE.[35] What was the crime that 'Ali committed that led to such a change in support: arbitration, i.e. the *compromise* between 'Ali and his foe Mu'āwiyah ibn 'Abī Ṣufyān. With the cry "only God has the right to decide," the Khawarij believed "Ali to be endowed with absolute authority from the divine and therefore didn't have the

---

33 Natana J. DeLong-Bas, *Wahhabi Islam: From Revival and Reform to Global Jihad.* New York: Oxford University Press, 2004.

34 Anecdotes about unwanted Wahhabi influences appear in places such as Chechnya, Bosnia-Herzegovina, Pakistan, Indonesia, Europe, and the U.S. See Hamid Algar, *Wahhabism: A Critical Essay.* Oneonta, NY: Islamic Publications International, 2002.

35 The Khawarij are sometimes known as "Kharijites." The term "khawarij" is generally translated to "seceders" or "those who have gone out."

right to negotiate with those who didn't accept such authority. It also demonstrated to them 'Ali's lack of faith that Allah would give a victory to the *Shi'at al-'Ali* (party of 'Ali). Again, the insistence of absolutizing his status, and therefore his authority as the successor of the prophet, coupled with the perception that he *compromised* that absolute authority, led to his murder. 'Ali was later killed by the Khawarij assassin Ibn Muljam in 661 CE, thus solidifying the early division (*fitnah*) between what would later become the Shi'a and Sunni branches of Islam.[36]

The Mufti's comparison of ISIS to the Khawarij is also appropriate on another level; ISIS, like the Khawarij, practices *takfīr*: the practice of declaring a fellow Muslim to be a non-Muslim (*kāfir*) or of engaging in apostasy (*riddah*) for the purpose of oppressing and/or killing them. As it is not lawful under Islamic law for a Muslim to kill another Muslim unless under extenuating circumstances, such as in self-defense, punishment for a crime, etc., *takfīris* (those who engage in *takfīr*) conveniently appropriate that which is understood in fiqh to be the sole prerogative of the divine, i.e. the judging of faith of any particular individual. *Takfīris* declare the other's faith to be fraudulent and therefore worthy of punishment or even death. However, even Immanuel Kant's *categorical imperative*, which began its pre-secular life as a religious imperative, applies within the Islamic context. When ISIS and other *takfīris* appropriate the right to unilaterally declare others believers to be *kāfirūn* (disbelievers), they are also tacitly endorsing the legitimacy of others to do the same to them; their particular actions become universalized. In this moment, the sole prerogative of the absolute to declare who is a believer and who is not, testified in the Qur'anic statement that Allah 'misguides whom he wills and guides to the straight path whom he wills,' saves humanity from augmenting themselves into a divine being with the capability of piercing into the inner-most sanctum of one's religious life: their conscience.[37] If the practice of *takfīr* can be rescued from the political, economic, and social realm of religious fanaticism, and returned once again to the sole realm of the divine, religious communities can return to a more honest and true state of religion; a realization of man's limited ability to know the *thing-in-itself*, whether that be divine will or the individual's conscience. In the case of Islam, through the rescuing the divine's authority from the hands of authoritarian fanatics – and therefore negating it as an effective way of dehumanizing the other based on their religious or non-religious

---

36   Heinz Halm, *Shi'a Islam: From Religion to Revolution* (Princeton, NJ: Markus Wiener Publishers, 1999), 6.

37   Qur'an 6:39. My translation.

conscience – the *ummah* can deprive the authoritarian believer both the legal and moral ability to render the "innocent other" fit for execution.

Humanistic Absolutes

When the humanistic core of the Abrahamic religions is coupled with absolute authority, such values are different in degree rather than in kind from their authoritarian counterparts. Humanistic absolutes have as their utmost concern the wellbeing of the finite human as opposed to the supernatural and/or divine being, and are prepared to subject their ideas, thoughts, and values to democratic deliberation and scrutiny. Many in today's religious communities believe that humanism is inherently separate from religion, in that it takes as its main concern the finiteness of the human subject as the measure of value as opposed to upholding religious traditions and/or dogmas, or by measuring all human activity by the standard of divine revelation. This is not entirely true. Desiderious Erasmus of Rotterdam, a Dutch humanist, Catholic priest and theologian, rescued the religion of his time by integrating humanist ideals within faith, as the humanistic ideals themselves were embedded within the theology of Jesus' very human suffering.[38] Erasmus' form of Christo-humanism could have reformed the church of its ills had not Luther's revolt taken hold of parts of Europe in the 16th century, driving the church into its reactionary Counter-Reformation. In addition to the "prince of humanism," Erasmus, there was also Nicholas of Cusa, and the Saint Thomas More, who were also deeply concerned with the *renovatio Christianismi* (renewal of Christianity) by recovering its humanistic potentials which had been long buried in forgotten history.[39] Their work, and the work of many others, was an attempt to rediscover the softer and more empathetic side of the Gospel tradition and reintroduce it back into Christendom as a way of realigning the church with the compassion and mercy displayed by Jesus of Nazareth.

---

38   We must admit that Erasmus' inspection of the Bible did cause quite the controversy for the church. For example, he discovered many Bible verses that served an important legitimation function for the church's authority were not in the original texts but were rather additions in the Vulgate. Such a humanist return to the Bible did undermine many of the church's most important claims. See Alister McGrath, *Christianity's Dangerous Idea*, 28–33.

39   Hans Küng, *The Catholic Church: A Short History*, trans. John Bowden (New York: The Modern Library, 2003), 118–120, 128, 132.

Religious humanism is a certain form of belief attitude and philosophy from within a religious tradition that directs itself towards the wellbeing of mankind as one of its primary goals. For instance, many of Dr. Martin Luther King's followers were not men of religion like himself. Nevertheless, their common goal was the advancement of certain rights and privileges for minority peoples in the United States, which later, during the 1967 *Poor People's Campaign,* took on, more sharply than the earlier Civil Right movement, the issue of class. Although they could not agree on theological matters, their common goals – the advancement of humanity and a just society – allowed them to cooperate most peacefully and productively. The values themselves transcendent any particular religions and could be found within the "American values" of *life, liberty, and the pursuit of happiness – freedom, justice, and equality.* Malcolm x's founding of the Organization of Afro-American Unity (OAAU) was also in this vein. It stressed the *common humanity* of African Americans regardless of their religious and/or philosophical traditions.

In August of 2014, Dr. Tariq Ramadan of Oxford University, one of the preeminent philosophers of Islam in the modern period, spoke to the very issue of values that transcend religious articulation. He said,

> As western Muslims and American Muslims, we need to understand that the values and principles we promote are not only Muslim values. American Muslims live in a country where justice, dignity, freedom and equality are essential values. The Muslim contribution to the future of America is to not only speak out as Muslims, but to also speak out as citizens in the name of our common values. Our main contribution is to reconcile the American society with its own values, those that are not in contradiction to Islam. We have a duty of consistency.[40]

From this understanding, it can be realized that humanistic values are in complete service to the flourishing of mankind, both in humanity's autonomy as well as its solidarity. As Erich Fromm, the psychoanalysis and Critical Theorist of society, stated in his essay on Humanistic Socialism,

> The supreme value in all social and economic arrangements is man; the goal of society is to offer the conditions for the full development of man's

---

40   Tariq Ramadan and Amina Chaudary, "Tariq Ramadan: My Absence Would Certainly Be the Most Powerful Speech I have Ever Give at ISNA," August 14, 2014. http://www .theislamicmonthly.com/tariq-ramadan-my-absence-would-certainly-be-the-most -powerful-speech-i-have-ever-given-at-isna/ (Accessed 8/19/2014).

potentialities, his reason, his love, his creativity; all social arrangements must be conducive to overcoming the alienation and crippledness of man, and to enable him to achieve real freedom and individuality.[41]

In other words, humanistic absolutes – which at its essence is the belief in the sacredness of mankind – attempts to create the conditions in which there can be a friendly living together predicated on the nourishment and actualization of man's potentials to create a more reconciled future society. Such absolutes are just as dogmatically maintained as the irrational absolutes of unjust power, the rightness of oppression, and the value of exploitation for the benefit of the exploitors. In the vacuous situation of modern civil society, where there is a deep-seated longing for values that are beyond those of simply having, such humanistic values are able to bind religious communities together in common projects for the benefit of all. Those religious movements, such as ISIS, right-wing Israeli Rabbis, Hindu nationalists, and Christian fundamentalists, that cannot transcend their own particularity and embrace the religious subjectivity of the other, are often those who either self-ghettoize or become violent towards the other, the common humanity of the other is simply ignored even when explicitly perceived. The weakness of fundamentalism and extremist faith positions are witnessed in the anxiety and fear that they have towards opposing religious claims; they experience the existence of other religions as threats to their own truth claims. Just as we've seen in ISIS, as long as there are others who are just as vehement about their faith and their beliefs as the fundamentalist, then there is always the possibility that the fundamentalists' faith isn't true in its *absolutivity* – the opposition remains the physical manifestation of the doubt that remains behind the veneer of absolute faith. Because of this, the fundamentalist, especially when they have power, often seeks to destroy the alternative that instills doubt: the Bamiyan Buddha in Taliban controlled Afghanistan, Christians, Yazidis, and Shi'a Muslims in Iraq, Sufi shrines and mosques under ISIS, Native American sites in Colonial America, the Babri Mosque in Ayodhya, India, and the *auto-da-fé* (acts of faith) of "heretics" and "unrepentant" Jews by the Holy Inquisition in Spain, etc. Although they appear to be ardent in their certitude, they are psychologically unstable of their beliefs, and thus take solace and comfort in the destruction of the alternative. In this light, we can see that these groups and others are not the true believers that they claim to be, neither are they the "doubting Thomas's" that critically and thoughtfully reflect on their own positions, but rather are those of weak faith who must destroy the other to bandage their own festering uncertitude.

---

41 Fromm, *On Disobedience*, 75–76.

ISIS: Same Problem, Different Manifestation

Upon a critical analysis, we can explain the rapid rise of ISIS and its success-es in the heart of the Middle East. The three key components that help the outside observer understand are (1) its motivation, (2) its ideology, and (3) its opportunity. A critical penetration of these aspects of ISIS helps explain why such a return to a barbaric and pre-Islamic way of life has been resurrected amidst the post-secular society; which is a society of relative peace, security and material abundance.

(1) Motivation: That which drives ISIS and other similar groups is abun-dantly clear when looked at through the lenses of recent history. It is their contention that the 20th century must be overcome. Its long shadow still casts a spell over the Muslim world and today's militants are attempting to break out of the shadow and develop what they think is a viable alternative to the western model of the nation-state and the destabilizing and culturally dam-aging process of western globalization. In today's increasingly secular world, groups like ISIS view themselves as breaking the chains of colonial and im-perial oppression, especially in the form of the 'Arab façade' – the Arab face that hides the West's involvement and/or interests within the nation-states' affairs.[42] Additionally, in the particular case of ISIS, they want to cancel the 1916 *Sykes-Picot Agreement* that was responsible for the artificial divisions in the Middle East between the French and British spheres of influence. They re-member that the Ottoman Empire and the last *Caliph* of Islam were destroyed at the end of WWI and they believe such destruction to have been a historic crime against the Muslim community. This agreement was itself already a step in the secularization process, as it wrestled power away from traditional re-ligious authorities in favor of secular governments – both collaborating and imperial. Where Islamic authorities once governed – or at least claimed to – via the Qur'an and Sunnah, in its place were imposed the western backed nation-states. In the mind of many ISIS members, their destruction of those artificially created boarders between what is now Iraq and Syria was not only a symbolic act, but also a concrete attempt to undue that which should have never been done to the Muslim ummah: *divide et impera* (divide and conquer) by western imperial powers. It is also a step in ISIS's primary goal: to estab-lish an Islamic state through the reintroduction of the Caliphate within the heart of the Muslim world. Partially to atone for the historical crime perpe-trated by Mustafa Kemal Pasha (Atatürk), who abolished the Caliphate in 1924,

---

42   See Noam Chomsky, *Fateful Triangle: The United States, Israel & the Palestinians.*
Cambridge, MA: South End Press, 1999.

ISIS has installed Abu Bakr al-Baghdadi (his *nom de guerre*) as the head of the Muslim community.[43] The recreation of the *caliphate* has been a long awaited desire of many Muslims, who believed the leaderless status of the Muslim world was one of the main reasons why the *dar al-Islam* had moved into the backseat of history, why it is no longer respected, and why it has become so weak. Additionally, it is the idea that the Muslims who were at the head of the ummah prior to the demise of the last caliphate were religiously insufficient, unfaithful, and corrupt. ISIS's brand of redemptive religiosity is one of "purification for fortification" – in order to protect the Muslims the caliphate must be restored; in order to restore the caliphate the Muslim world – especially the Arab Middle East – must be purified of all those who would oppose such a development, i.e. religious minorities, ideological opponents, and Shi'a Muslims. Purity of faith and community is seen as a pretext for the *tajdīd*, or the "rejuvenation"/"renewal" of Islam and the Muslim world, and such rejuvenation contains within itself the potential to overcome history and redeem the ummah. The historical crimes perpetrated upon the Muslim community via western powers as well as those within the Muslims world who collaborated with the West, must be overcome so that the Muslim world can once again live in dignity, and possibly expand the boarders of the *dar al-Islam*. Thus, transcending the 20th century – negating those developments that so crippled the Muslims – is an utmost concern for ISIS.

Ironically, the *symbolic* power of the Caliphate resides in its concreteness; it is a physical manifestation of the revenge motive – revenge against the West for its humbling of the Muslim world, i.e. the restoration of Islam to a place of honor and dignity, as well as the sincere desire of Muslims to live under divine law. Symbolically, the caliphate does violence against the dominance of western-style democratic capitalism; it provides an alternative possibility to the status quo by undermining its principles; demonstrating to the West that Muslims may have accommodated themselves to western values, which are understood to be universal, but remain first-and-foremost followers of a different metaphysics: a religiously permeated worldview that stands diametrically opposes to the world devoid of the divine, separated from divine law, and living in accordance to the will of the self as opposed to the will of the creator. Where proponents of the secularization theory would have it, religion should have disappeared by now, but ISIS reminds them that not only has it failed to evaporate, it continues on with a new sense of vitality and intensity.

---

43   Michael Weiss and Hassan Hassan, *ISIS: Inside the Army of Terror* (New York: Regan Arts, 2015), 114–130.

The caliphate is a symbol for resurgent religion in a secular and western dominated age. Indeed, it is the most poignant proof of the post-secular condition.

For Hans Küng and other critical historians of religion, this attempt to resurrect the Caliphate within the Muslim world represents a feeble attempt to
undue history; an act that's meant to restore Islam to a historical paradigm
that could only have existed within an entirely different set of historical coordinates.[44] For Küng, the paradigm of Arab empire is over; the classical
paradigm of the Muslim world is over; the paradigm of 'Ulamā' and Sufis is
over, and the modernization paradigm is also over. What's now before the ummah is the imperative to create a new paradigm, a vibrant, post-modern and
contemporary Islamic paradigm that doesn't reject the modern world for a
foolish attempt to return to a historical 'golden age' but rather embraces that
which it can and make into its own that which is beneficial in modernity while
not simultaneously abandoning its core characteristics and values.[45] From the
perspective of the Frankfurt School's critical theory of religion, just as Pope
Francis has made the rediscovery of the Jesus' humanistic gospel a primary
goal of his papacy, the recovery of Islam's humanistic core, those social principles that made it most attractive to the poor, the widows, the orphans, the
slaves, and the broken, is vital to the survival of Islam in the modern period.
A recovery of this kind will not only prolong its life, but also make it a vital
force for good in political economics and culture, precisely because those
same values can be articulated in a variety of conceptual languages, making
it understandable to a multiplicity of peoples outside of the Muslim community. Therefore the motivation of ISIS has to also be the motivation of those
who wish to rescue Islam both from post-secular modernity and from the violent reaction to such modernity: fundamentalism. The motivation to rectify
that damage of colonialism, imperialism, neo-conservative war and economic
exploitation – which was done for the benefit of western powers – must be
shared with progressive and humanistic Muslims, albeit their answers to such
a motivation must remain true to the humanistic core of the Islamic tradition
itself. It cannot return behind *al-jāhilīyah* as ISIS and other groups have done.

Ideology: It has often been claimed that after the 1991 fall of communism
in the Soviet Union that we live in a post-ideological era. It is said to be a time
where activism has no concrete goals, no guiding principles, and no thought
beyond the immediate condemnation of what is the case. In this state of
confusion, the "then what" questions have not been answered or really even

---

44   Hans Küng, *Islam: Past, Present & Future*, trans. John Bowden. New York: Oxford University
      Press, 2007.
45   Ibid., 433–662.

explored. Case-in-point is the Occupy Wall Street Movement; the sentiments were correct concerning the abuses perpetrated on the world by global capitalism, especially the banks, whose risky yet lucrative actions led to the economic collapse of 2008, which only furthered the suffering of those who were already the victims of systematic and systemic violence within the coordinates of neoliberalism. Along with those already suffering from the ravages of economic exclusion, the collapse created many new victims among the working class and poor.[46] Yet, how such problems where to be remedied was unfathomable to most in the Occupy Movement as it failed to articulate any form of grand project, normative philosophy, or even stated goals beyond minimal reformism. The masses were gathered simply to protest the crimes of capitalism without any concrete contributions as to how it should be overcome and what should replace it. As such, it never coalesced into a political force within American (or European) polity. The ultimate deficiency of the Occupy Wall Street movement that doomed it to the footnotes of history was that the problem itself – *capitalism in crisis* – defined the movement; it failed to define itself as a alternative to capitalism by only addressing the symptoms of capitalism. Here I agree, most regrettably, with the "radical for capitalism" Ayn Rand, who in a column entitled "Blind Chaos," written for the Los Angeles Times in September of 1962, stated, 'a majority without an ideology is a helpless mob, to be taken over by anyone.'[47] Does this not illuminate what is already suspected about our post-ideological claims: the lack of a coherent and systematic *ideology* (in the non-Marxian sense) is the core reason for the failures of good movements such as Occupy Wall Street, whereas groups like ISIS, who are well-entrenched within a system of ideological convictions, are able to bend history towards their goals?

To the minds of many, including the philosopher Slavoj Žižek, this post-Cold War zeitgeist is satisfied with modest adjustments to the overall system of political economy and therefore fails to demand radical change.[48] In other words, there is no dominant philosophy that serves as a countervailing force against the domination of global capitalism and neo-liberal "democracy."

---

46 I include the "middle class" in the description of "working class," as they may be prosperous, but that prosperity is based within their working hours and salaries. Simply because they often do not want to be identified as working class does not mean they aren't. I consider the term "middle class" as part of the overall ideology of capitalism – it is meant to hide a certain reality about political economy, that the majority of the population is still workers even if they've bought – or have been integrated – into the system.

47 Ayn Rand, *The Ayn Rand Column* (Irvine, CA: Ayn Rand Institute Press, 1998), 44.

48 Slavoj Žižek, *The Year of Dreaming Dangerously* (New York; Verso, 2012), 77–89.

Sadly, it seems to many that the right-wing Hegelian Francis Fukuyama's theses about the end of history – that history has come to the point where the largest and most important questions about what society should be – have been answered.[49] The apex of history has culminated in the very bourgeois ideals espoused by the American ruling class. Thus the utopian visions of an egalitarian society, predicated on the equal distribution of resources, freedom, and justice, that served as the Bourgeois revolutions' inner-criticism, have all but been forgotten as "daydreams," "fairytales," or "lost causes," and we have come to recognize the confluence of neo-liberal democracy and free market capitalism as being our fate because – it is claimed – it is most *natural* and, via utilitarian logic, it is argued to be the most beneficial to the most amount of people. However, this claim, in-and-of-itself, is *ideology*, or the clever masking of national, class, and racial interests, especially behind the veneer of *nature* – it is a *reification* (*Verdinglichung*) of ideology (false consciousness and/or necessary appearances) that is presented to the world as being self-evident and therefore beyond question. It is then presented to the world as being the standard that all other nations must aspire to embody, regardless of a nation's history, religion, language, culture, and normative conception of legality and morality.

It is clear that we are not in a *post-ideological* era, but in an era of *mono-ideology*, where one particular ideology prevails over all others because of its ruthlessness and cunning. Falsely, because it is perceived to be the "last man standing," it is presented as being without any alternative. Nevertheless, ISIS and its affiliates do not see it that way and thus their true – but often hidden – danger to the West. The *Caliphate* is seen as the "other" of western democratic-capitalism: it is the divinely sanctioned alternative that is, in their minds, bound to triumph over the substancelessness of western modernity.

On August 21, 2013, the then U.S. Secretary of Defense, Chuck Hagel, said ISIS was 'beyond just a terrorist group' and 'beyond anything we've seen.'[50] Hagel's dire warning about ISIS was meant to prepare the American public for another round of conflict against an organization that was believed to be not only a threat to our "allies" in the Middle East but also to civilization itself. ISIS, being not only a terrorist group like al-Qae'da, but an ideological movement with goals of not only *destruction* (like al-Qae'da), but with a goal to *construct* a society unlike one that exists in the world today, presents itself as a

---

49   Francis Fukuyama, *The End of History and the Last Man.* New York: Avon Books, 1992.

50   Jake Miller, "Chuck Hagel: ISIS 'beyond anything we've seen,'" August 22, 2014. http://www
       .cbsnews.com/news/chuck-hagel-defends-failed-james-foley-rescue-attempt/ (Accessed
       8/22/2014).

challenge to Fukuyama's thesis about the apex of history; clearly not everyone has accepted neo-liberalism to be the end of history. ISIS's attempt to create a modern *Caliphate* as a viable alternative model for national, social, and political-economic being within the Muslims world is a threat to ideological claims of global capitalism and democracy, which many Muslims themselves have accepted as being the de-facto state of the modern world. Being so, it is also a threat to the human rights, war crimes legislation, rights of religious freedom, etc., that were established since the Enlightenment, WWI, and WWII, as it articulates the moral and legal status of people through the eyes of their particular religious identities as opposed through internationally agreed upon norms and laws, especially those deriving from the western Enlightenment. ISIS, as a religious ideology, not only challenges political establishments, but the entire way the modern world as developed, as it returns these questions back to religion and away from international and democratic (and secular) institutions. *Democratic deliberation*, informed by the disastrous experiences of the 20th century, as a way of determining the validity of social laws and norms, is rejected in favor of the absolutes of divine law. *Sharī'ah*, for ISIS and others, is a divinely guaranteed system of government and administration of justice. The post-metaphysical age of the modern West is thoroughly rejected for the pre-modern faith in revelation. In order to create a just society that could be endorsed by the divine, arguments must be rooted in sacred text and not man's autonomous, yet faulty, reason. Although reason is not entirely negated by groups such as ISIS, it is subordinate to revelation, which takes precedence over human understanding. In western terms, the epistemology of Descartes, with its emphasis on reason as the sole source to determine truth, is replaced by the scholasticism of Thomas Aquinas, which takes the truth of revelation prior to that of reason.

As can be witness by their actions, ISIS takes their particular articulation of Sunni Islam as the organizing principle for all activities within their domains. Not only is Islam "perfected" and therefore *petrified* in that perfection, Islam's claim to be comprehensive is absolutized; nothing is outside of the purview of Islam according to ISIS, and therefore that which is legislated and governed by religion demands a religious enforcer. With the melding of religion with the notion of totality, ISIS rejects the idea of the separation of religion and state, as articulated by the Bourgeoisie – especially the American founding father Thomas Jefferson – but rather leaves intact what had been married prior to the secularization of the state: *what God has enjoined let no man tear asunder.*[51]

---

51   Although he is critical of the Bourgeoisie on a multiplicity of issues, Marx confirms his agreement with the separation of church and state in his essay *On the Jewish Question.* Marx, *Marx-Engels Reader,* 31–34.

Rejecting the idea that morality should be separated from legality, their ideology believes to enforce morality upon the people is to follow not only the legal norms as expressed in the Qur'an and Sharī'ah law in any particular case, but to make *identical* God's demands and "Islamic" society. Thus, an important factor in ISIS's thought is the instilling of Qur'anic norms within all aspects of the community; from marriage to courtship, banking to farming, eating to urinating – the *sunnah* (way) of Prophet Muhammad and the Qur'an must be made operational from the micrological to the macrological if such a society can be worthy of the descriptor "Islamic." But is this a *deus ex machina* in regards to the conditions of the Muslim world in a secular zeitgeist?[52] To answer this we have to return to recent history.

Since 1979, the West has been pathologically infatuated with the Islamic Republic of Iran and the figure of Ayatollah Khomeini.[53] The abolition of the Shah Mohammad Reza Pahlavi's secular western-oriented regime and its "foreign" cultural influences was the vision of Khomeini, a cleric of the highest order who advocated the political activism of the clergy and the overthrow of the monarchy. In its place he implemented the *vilayat-i faqīh,* or "rule of the jurist." This jurist, in the absence of the Mahdi, the 12th Imam that currently, according to the Shi'a, remains in occultation (*'ghayba*), has a duty to rule until his return. As such, society cannot be left without righteous guidance. Therefore those who are most familiar, experts in, and embody themselves, the laws and regulations of the divine, must stand in the place of the Mahdi until his return. In Khomeini's treatise on "Islamic Government," he explains his position on the need for a religiously rooted form of rule. He states,

> According to one of the noble verses of the Qur'an, the ordinance of Islam are not limited with respect to time or place; they are permanent and must be enacted until the end of time. They were not revealed merely for the time of the Prophet, only to be abandoned thereafter, with retribution and the penal code of Islam no longer to be enacted, or the taxes prescribed by Islam no longer collected, and the defense of the lands and people of Islam suspended. The claim that the laws of Islam may remain in abeyance or are restricted to a particular time or place is contrary to the essential credal bases of Islam.

---

52   *Deus ex machina* – "artificially contrived solution," literally "a god from a machine."
53   Dustin Byrd, *Ayatollah Khoemini,* 1–23; Baqer Moin, *Khomeini: Life of the Ayatollah* (New York: St. Martin's Press, 1999), 223–313.

He continues,

> Since the enactment of laws, then, is necessary after the departure of the
> Prophet from this world, and indeed, will remain so until the end of time,
> the formation of a government and the establishment of executive and
> administrative organs are also necessary. Without the formation of a gov-
> ernment and the establishment of such organs to ensure that through
> enactment of the law, all activities of the individual take place in the
> framework of a just system, chaos and anarchy will prevail and social,
> intellectual, and moral corruption will arise. The only way to prevent the
> emergence of anarchy and disorder and to protect society from corrup-
> tion is to form a government and thus impart order to all the affairs of
> the country.[54]

Although the Shi'a concerns about the absence of the Mahdi distinguish Khomeini's analysis from that of ISIS, the overall trajectory is very similar: the
abandonment of the revealed way-of-being-in-the-world as embodied by the
Prophet Muhammad was a historical mistake – one that was brought upon
the Muslim both by outside colonial powers and by the many religiously-lax
"cultural Muslims" within the ummah itself. This mistake must be corrected
if the Muslim world is going to drag itself out of the ditch of history and thus,
in the case of Khomeini, a righteous jurist – an Ayatollah (preferably a *marja-
i taqlīd* or "source of emulation") – should govern society until the return of
the Mahdi.[55] In the case of ISIS, it is the *Caliph,* not an Ayatollah, who must
assume the responsibility as the *Amīr al-Mu'minīn* (leader of the faithful) and
restore the spirit of Islam to a spiritually fallen ummah.

It would be a mistake to think, as some western scholar do, that because
ISIS and other affiliated groups emphasize the political – or the struggle for
recognition as Muslims – in Islam, that they are engaged in sheer ideology that
is devoid of "true" religion, as if "true" religion has no political component. This
is entirely untrue; religion has been involved in politic affairs from its earliest
forms, including the theocracy of King David, the political-theology of Jesus
of Nazareth, to the construction of the first Islamic city in Medina, in present
day Saudi Arabia. Religion is not simply spirituality devoid of socio-economic
and political concerns; it is not simply the establishment of a personal relationship between man and his god, but also one that is deeply entrenched in

---

54   Ayatollah Khomeini, *Islam and Revolution,* trans. Hamid Algar (Berkely: Mizan Press,
      1981), 41–42.

55   This is the Farsi rendering of the phrase. In Arabic, it is *Marja al-Taqlīd.*

the affairs of this world. In other words, religion impels the believer to engage this world in ways that are consistent with their religious beliefs. This is especially true for the Abrahamic faiths, which distort themselves when they artificially compartmentalize the various aspects of the human experience, making some "religious" and therefore "private" affairs and others public and therefore "secular." The ethical life cannot be "rendered unto Caesar" when it all belongs to God. Nevertheless, the strict apartheid of religion and polity opened up a space for the civilizational progress in the West since the Enlightenment; the suffocating strictures of authoritarian religion were lifted and the genius of European inquisitivity was let loose. However, the trend towards privatizing religion within civil society – that has predominated in the West since the Bourgeoisie guillotined the nobility of France – is precisely what ISIS is attempting to suture. Similar to Iran, if a Sunni state can be constructed with Islam as its organizing principle, it will potentially serve as an example of an Islamic alternative to western secularity. However, if it chooses to do this predicated upon ethnic cleansing, mass murder, and barbarity, it will fail, as such activities can hardly be justified by the constitutional norms of the Islamic tradition itself.

For all of ISIS's claims about fighting for the cause of Islam, the Qur'anic prohibition on murdering innocent civilians has been so ignored that one has to wonder what sort of Islam is ISIS fighting for. The Qur'an, in *Sūrat al-Anʿām*, verse 151 states 'and do not kill a soul that Allah has made sacred except by [legal] right.'[56] Nevertheless, ISIS continues to articulate their own interpretation of Islamic "legal rights" in order to justify their slaughter, but such imaginary "rights" have been rejected by Islamic authorities throughout the Muslims world to no avail.

Throughout history, as groups brought states into existence, their status as states was dependent on the recognition of others; they would ask: do other states recognize the newly formed entity as a state; do they have a legitimate system of justice; do they have a legitimate government; do they have a right to create the entity or is it disputed; do they have a continuous land mass; are there any extenuating reason why such an entity should not be recognized as a state? The process of recognition – which is the process by which one state accepts the sovereignty of another – is solely a *political* matter as there really is no absolute consensus as to what criteria an entity must achieve in order for a state to be recognized as such. Therefore, states recognize each other based

---

56   Qur'an, 6:151. My translation. Legal right excludes systematic mass killings of individuals and groups simply because they are from another religion. One's adherence or non-adherence to a religion has never qualified someone for summary execution in the Islamic tradition.

on their own interests. In the case of ISIS we recognize a new dynamic. Their struggle for recognition is not dependent upon western countries or any other countries per se. As they do not accept the "power" of non-Muslim states to grant them statehood, nor do they recognize the legitimacy of most of the governments that rule over Muslims; there is no authoritative "other" who can recognize them and thus officially impart legal statehood. Non-recognition, in this case, is entirely superfluous as the "Islamic state" only respects the determination of itself by itself – it grants itself statehood in the name of Islam, not international laws and norms. For international law this is clearly not enough to join the world community, but for those who remain within the framework of fundamentalist religion, the de-legitimized Muslim governments or non-Muslim states and their views of ISIS matter little. The *Calilphate* has been declared in the name of the ultimate sovereign, the divine, and that's all the recognition that ISIS requires in their estimation. In that sense, it is a "self-recognizing authority." Would it *like* the recognition of Muslims as being the legitimate caliphate: yes. From its own perspective, does it *require* it: no.

A robust critique of ISIS is certainly warranted, especially on the level of its abuse of communities within its domain, but in order for it to be meaningful to ISIS itself, such critique cannot be made from the standpoint of western values, laws, and legislation, as those do not hold any validity among ISIS-minded individuals. Rather, the critique must derive wholly from the Islamic tradition itself, for only an argument that is rooted in the ultimate source of Islam, i.e. the Qur'an and Sunnah of Muhammad, can persuade those who reject any other source of justification and/or legitimacy. *Inner-critique* – or critique from within the Islamic tradition – must be called for, as only Islam has the principles and conceptions that are normative, and therefore binding, on all Muslims. If ISIS is not to be destroyed, as the U.S. Secretary of State John Kerry says it will be, but rather reformed, it must make itself identical to Islam via Islam itself, not by force from the outside.[57] Nevertheless, at this moment in history, it does not appear that this process of becoming identical with Islam will be peaceful, as ISIS itself, through its very un-Islamic practices, has alienated most of the world, including millions of Muslims. However, the futility of killing those who hold certain beliefs without addressing the validity of those beliefs is well known, as beliefs have a longer shelf-life than those who articulate them. Therefore no amount of drone strikes, no amount of bombings by coalition forces, NATO and Russia will affect the resolve of ISIS. It will take a concerted effort by Muslims to eradicate such a barbaric and distorted

---

57   John Kerry, *Twitter – 8/20/2014*. (Accessed 8/22/2014).

interpretation of Islam through a concerted effort to *convince* them that they have deviated from Islam. Inner transformation via inner critique is what is needed.

Despite the ineffectiveness of critiquing ISIS from the standpoint of western values, one can engage in a sociological investigation of ISIS's likely future success and failures. Based on a Marxist reading of their ideology, it can be surmised that ISIS will ultimately fail as a movement to change the overall conditions of the Middle East and the broader Muslim world. It will not bring about a new caliphate that garnishes universal recognition, nor even recognition from the majority of Muslims (including the Sunnis). This is for one very important reason that Marx articulated in the introduction to his *Contribution to the Critique of Hegel's Philosophy of Right* (1843). When Marx set about identifying the class that possessed the potential to be the concrete agent of historical transformation, one that would replace Hegel's metaphysical *world spirit* (*weltgeist*), he looked for an entity that represented the universal interest of mankind. For Marx, those groups that solely represented a *particular* – their own interests at the expense of all others, and saw all others as opponents within a much larger competition for advancement – were disqualified as the true agents for substantive change. In mid-19th century Prussia, the nobility, state bureaucracy, and monarchy, were all competing factions within civil society. As such, they experienced the other simply as opponents with which they were locked in an eternal conflict as the interests of each limited the realization of the interests of all. To Marx, none of them could transcend their own particularity; because of this limitation they could not serve as the instrument for *universal* human emancipation. Systematically and constitutionally trapped within their particularity, the degree of real emancipatory change was severely limited if possible at all. What was needed was an agent that represented the *universal* interest of human emancipation. Marx writes,

> What is the basis of a partial, merely political revolution? Simply this: a *section of civil society* emancipates itself and attains universal domination; a determinate class undertakes, from its particular situation, a general emancipation of society. This class emancipates society as a whole, but only on condition that the whole of society is in the same situation as this class... No class in civil society can play this part unless it can arouse, in itself and in the masses, a moment of enthusiasm in which it associates and mingles with society at large, identifies itself with it, and is felt and recognized as the *general representative* of this society. Its aims and interest must genuinely be the aims and interest of society itself, of which

it becomes in reality the social head and heart. It is only in the name of general interests that a particular class can claim general supremacy.[58]

Just as the Bourgeoisie represented that emancipatory class during the French Revolution of 1789, the *proletariat* – those whose situation in society could only be advanced through the total transformation of all existing conditions – bore the burden of revolutionary change; they were Marx's concrete *absolute spirit* of history (at that historical moment). Thus revolutionary workers, for Marx, were the only faction within civil society that embodied the universal interest of all, and therefore they, and only they, could emancipate society entire.

However, in order for there to be a radical change in consciousness concerning the possibility of emancipation within the suffering classes, the oppressing classes have to be thoroughly identified and revolutionary action must be directed against them through a popular movement. He continues,

In order to attain this liberating position, and the political direction of all spheres of society, revolutionary energy and consciousness of its own power do not suffice. For a *popular revolution* and the *emancipation of a particular class* of civil society to coincide, for *one* class to represent the whole of society, another class must concentrate in itself all the evils of society, a particular class must embody and represent a general obstacle and limitation. A particular social sphere must be regarded as the *notorious crime* of the whole society, so that emancipation from this sphere appears as a general emancipation. For *one* class to be the liberating class *par excellence*, it is necessary that another class should be openly the oppressing class.[59]

From the perspective of critical religiologists, informed by the Frankfurt School, who learned from Marx his concrete dialectics of history, ISIS, and any other organization, group, class, or movement, that fails to embody the burden of the universal interest, but remains shrouded within the interest of a particular, who define themselves against the interests of all, will ultimately fail to transform society in such a way that it brings about a totally-reconciled and peaceful society. ISIS, as the present manifestation of militant Sunni particularity, like the nobility of 19th century Prussia, fails to transcend its sectarian limitations, may make history, but will fail to define it. Despite their attempts to overcome the oppression of other groups, their own particularity limits

---

58   Marx, *Marx-Engels Reader,* 62.

59   Ibid., 62–63.

their historical significance. Yet one could affectively argue that the uprising of Sunnis against the 'Alawiyyah in Damascus and the Shi'a led government in Baghdad takes the form of a liberating class struggling against the oppressing class that represents the "evils of society" and the "notorious crime." It is true that the Damascus and Baghdad governments systematically suppressed the Sunni population and failed to allow them to adequately realize their political-economic potentials within civil society and the state. This oppression, to some, legitimated the ISIS led uprisings. However, this line of argument is fundamentally flawed due to the fact that ISIS and the Sunni affiliates *cannot* represent the universal against the particularity of the ruling elites precisely because they themselves have clearly articulated that they are exclusively sectarian in nature: they are Sunni and for the Sunnis. Against this kind of particularizing thought, Marx defines this emancipatory class as such,

> A class must be formed which has *radical chains,* a class in civil society which is not a class of civil society, a class which is the dissolution of all classes, a sphere of society which has a universal character because its sufferings are universal, and which does not claim a *particular redress* because the wrong which is done to it is not a *particular wrong* but *wrong in general.* There must be formed a sphere of society which claims no *traditional* status but only a human status... a sphere, finally, which cannot emancipate itself without emancipating itself from all the other spheres *of* society, without, therefore, emancipating all these other spheres, which is, in short, a *total loss* of humanity and which can only redeem itself by a *total redemption of humanity.*[60]

In this sense, ISIS's attack on Damascus and Baghdad is not an attack by a liberating universal movement, but one sectarian group struggling against another. It does not wish to transform all of society by destroying those social and political strictures that limit human emancipation, but rather they simply wish to replace the rule of one particularity with the rule of another: the universal interest is wholly absent.

Opportunity: The 2003 American led attack on Iraq opened up a Pandora's box in the Middle East that had been suppressed by the various dictatorial regimes. Like Yugoslavia, which was held together by a socialism that emphasized communist universal equality over nationalist particularities, the decision of Bush and Cheney – rooted in Neo-Conservative ideology

---

60   Ibid., 64.

(the combination of Leo Strauss's political philosophy and the economics of Milton Friedman) – to remove the Ba'ath party from power and therefore de-emphasize the nation (the singular), set loose the violence of sectarian particularity. For decades the different sects and religions lived relatively peacefully under the secular regimes of the Middle East, but their removal, both by invasion (Iraq) and the Arab Spring (2010–2012), once again created a space for sectarianism. The particularity of tribe and sect overcame all thoughts of the solidarity among "Iraqis"; nationhood as the basis for *demos* was replaced by *ethnos* and religious identity as the signifier for "in" and "out" group. However, what did not occur was violence against rival sects based solely on their religion per se, but their identity as the "other" served as the motivation for violence. In other words, differences of opinion regarding *kalam, fiqh, 'aqēdah,* etc., did not animate the attacks, but rather the feeling that the other was (or would) gain the upper hand politically and economically provided the motivation for the violence. In the case of Iraq, the Sunnis were marginalized by the governing coalition (led by Ambassador Paul Bremer) after being in power for decades as a minority (via the Ba'ath party).[61] Consequently, the feeling of disrespect, dishonor and of being cast out ran deep among the Sunni which later fueled their resistance to the American led occupation of Iraq.[62] Although the Shi'a had much more to gain by cooperating with the American authorities, Muqtadā al-Ṣadr and his Mahdi Army led a fierce insurgence against the United States for the majority of time they occupied the nation. Although he remain steadfast in his opposition to the American occupation, he did encourage the Shi'a to participate in the elections which would eventually bring about a Shi'a led government under Nuri al-Maliki. As the United States withdrew their forces under President Barack Obama, Iraq was squarely in the hands of the Shi'a who systematically began to purge all Sunni influences from the state – once again advancing the particular over the universal. Consequently, the actions by the Shi'a led-government created a massive cadre of disaffected Sunnis who abandoned their allegiance to Iraq and embraced their Sunni identity more strongly than ever before.

In the spring 2011, protests against Syria's 'Alawite President Bashar al-Assad began nationwide, mainly by Sunnis and secular Shi'a. Unlike in Egypt, where President Hosni Mubarak relinquished power without resorting to an outright

---

61   We should be clear that the Ba'ath party was a secular party that held within itself member of various religions, tribes, and sects. However, the Sunni Arabs were by far the most dominant.

62   Warrick, *Black Flags*, 101–220.

war upon his people, Assad would resist capitulating at all costs.[63] He believed the 'Alawiyyah would be subject to genocide if the Sunnis were to gain control of the state. As such, he thought the fate of his people rested upon his ability to remain in control of his country, and thus he elicited the military assistance of his ally Vladimir Putin, the President of Russia, who entered the fight against ISIS and the Syrian rebels in the summer of 2015. Many groups determined to wrestle power from the hands of Assad developed in the rubble of Syria. Some of these groups were more secular in orientation, such as the Free Syrian Army, while others were clearly jihādist, such as Islamic Front, al-Nusrah Front, and the Army of Mujahideen. Among these was ISIS, who had begun as *al-Qae'da in Iraq* (AQI), but had taken on an even more sinister orientation.[64] Now that those same Sunni fighters and Ba'athists who were driven out of Iraq by the coalition forces had honed their skills in combat by fighting the Syrian army, resulting in their takeover of 1/3 of Syria, they turned their attention back to Iraq where the Shi'a led government was quickly showing itself to be incompetent, overly sectarian, and incapable of mounting a adequate defense of the nation.

Unable to find the motivation to fight for "Iraq," as nationalist sentiments had been drained in favor of sectarian ones, many Iraqi fights abandoned their posts, surrendered to ISIS, or fled to Baghdad, hoping for American intervention into the conflict. These soldiers for Iraq proved not to be martyr material – the state of Iraq could not instill in them any feeling of patriotic belonging, i.e. their personal identity and that of the state were fundamentally different and therefore many were therefore unwilling to die for something they could not identify with: the Shi'a led American manufactured Iraqi state. In the face of the Shi'a dominated state, many Sunnis in the western and northwestern provinces of Iraq, where the Sunnis are the majority, welcomed ISIS's redemptive mission – to restore Sunni pride and power.[65] They saw within ISIS the possibility of creating something better than the old Iraq, with its multiethnic and multi-religious complexion. They saw the potential to create a new caliphate. In their vision, 19th and 20th century style nationalism, an attempt to overcome religious sectarianism, as well as language, cultural, and historical divisions, under the banner of a secular state, was at an end in the Middle East.

---

63   See Dustin J. Byrd, "On the State of Islam: Thoughts on Revolution, Revolt and Reform," in *Global Future of Religion: Probing into Issues of Religion and Religiosity in the Postmodern World,* ed. Seyed Javad Miri (London: International Peace Studies Centre Press, 2012), 289–311.

64   Michael Weiss and Hassan Hassan, *ISIS,* 20–47.

65   Warrick, *Black Flags,* 223–307.

Now was the time for states to reflect the *religious* composition of the people. Against the grain of history, ISIS and their Sunni backers believed that the religious state – the new theocracy – had to be born within the modern period; that was the only true answer to both (1) western influence in the region, and (2) the dominance of the non-Sunni sects' rule: the 'Alawites in Syria and the Shi'a in Iraq.

The 20th and 21st century's attack on socialism, be it in Europe or in the Middle East, and the undermining of socialistic equality – that emphasized *humanity* and *class* over religion, ethnicity, race, and culture – bears immense responsibility for the descent of history into tribal barbarity. Where once the equality of peoples was slowly materializing, albeit often in less-than-desirable circumstances, capitalism's insistence on inequality within society, as well as the West's ruthless pursuit of its own interests within the Muslim world, led to the evaporation of egalitarianism. Now, in the 21st century, tribalism, sectarianism, and crass nationalism – predicated on the hatred of the other – has replaced the drive for the egalitarian; where once religion emphasized that which is common to all mankind, and thus the source for universal solidarity, it is once again in the service of those who see difference as a reason to destroy, a reason to fight, and a reason to annihilate. The failure of socialism and communism in the 20th century to create a society of equality – one that actualizes the empty promises of the Bourgeoisie – is partly to blame for creating the space by which modern religious fundamentalism thrives. But then again, socialism and communism can hardly be blamed for its own failures, as it was never allowed to emerge from its "siege mentality" due to the capitalist world's perpetual attempts to destroy it. The secular non-capitalist alternative to western globalization, which had begun to develop within the Muslim world, was systematically undermined by the West during the Cold War for fear that those countries would be more friendly to the Soviet Union. Furthermore, these newly liberated countries could not be allowed to create a functioning socialist alternative to both liberal democracy and/or Bolshevism.[66] The West was indeed correct; those anti-colonial and emerging nation-states mostly saw their future in socialism, either in conjunction with the Soviet Union or in cooperation with them, and near universally rejected the ideals of capitalism, seeing it as just another form of colonialism. NATO and the West in general, attempted to undermine and/or overthrow all attempts throughout the world to create such a viable secular alternative to western capitalism along the lines of Marxism or Marxist-Leninism; whether that be in Iran, Afghanistan, various

---

66 Mahmood Mamdani, *Good Muslim, Bad Muslim: America, The Cold War, and the Roots of Terror*. New York: Pantheon Books, 2004.

Latin American and Caribbean countries, etc. As such, secular-leftist governments, many of which were democratically elected, were the victims of coups d'états, assassinations, and invasions. The destruction of this alternative forced many, especially those in the Middle East, to retreat back into their religiosity as a form of defense against the neo-colonialism of the United States and its allies. In other words, religious extremism is the "blowback" for the defeat of socialism/communism. Just as the capitalist West functionalized religious voices against the Soviet Union, such as in Afghanistan, the ugly side of religion was later resurrected to fight against the ugliness of capitalism and neo-imperialism.[67] ISIS is just the latest manifestation of that phenomenon.

The term "religion" etymologically has to with "that which binds." However, the *dark side of religion,* as Cohen describes it, has to do with that which fails to be bound; for everything that is bound together must simultaneously be separated from something else. In other words, religion inherently and simultaneously binds as well as separates one group of people from another. Although this is the nature of religion, religious communities always have the capacity to *emphasize* one aspect or the other. They can either accept that they are bound together as one ummah (community) while also choosing to embrace the other in all their differences, or they can allow their particular identity to serve as a barrier against which the others may not cross, which inevitably leads to a fractured humanity. Religion, in all its singularity, can either transcend its sectarian nature or embrace the universal – which threatens to dissolve their singularity into the universal – or they can remain self-ghettoized behind their singular identity – and the whole remains antagonistic towards itself. Because religions always define themselves *against* something else: Christianity against Judaism, Islam against Christianity, Buddhism against Hinduism, all religions against secularity, etc., they are always in the business of constructing an identity for the other. The same dynamic can be found in sects, but because sects are so close in identity, and usually only separate themselves on minute details, such small differences take on a much more important meaning; the intensification of meaning does not augment the actual differences, only the meaning between the difference. This has the effect of communities having to intensify the antagonism between the rival identities even though those identities are overwhelmingly similar and share similar roots. In other words, the small differences between sects take on a much bigger meaning than the big differences between various religions, precisely because their differences are so slight. Being that the particularities between sects are minute, their hatred for the other has to be enflamed as to distinguish between the two. For example,

---

67   Mamdani, *Good Muslim, Bad Muslim,* 119–177.

the hatred between the Irish Catholics and Irish Protestant is deeply seated despite the fact that they both share Christian beliefs, a common ethnicity, shared language and customs, and a shared history. In a more reconciled society, those small differences would serve as a basis for discourse and hopeful reconciliation, not the intensification of hate. But in our present antagonistic, atomized and ego-centered society, the microscopic differences have to be augmented as not to reconcile communities to each other which would confuse the distinct identities, because reconciliation is the transcending of the inherent negativity of particular identities in favor of the universal identity: humanity beyond its differences.

Nevertheless, it is up to the religious believers to decide if their religious tradition will aid in the realization of a more-reconciled future society (universal solidarity) or if it will contribute to furthering the barbarity of war, violence, and mass death, the result of absolutized singularity. However, we must remember the sentiment of Adorno in his *Negative Dialectics* that was informed by the mass destruction of humanity in the *Shoah:* pure identity is death.[68]

American and Euro-Jihādis

Among the discourse concerning the descent into barbarity at the heart of the Middle East is the looming fear in Europe and the United States that many of ISIS's western-born fighters may return home to carry out attacks upon the West itself. Indeed, with the beheading of James Foley, Steven Sotloff, David Haines, and Peter Kassig at the hands of Mohamed Emwazi, a British Muslim, as well as the murder of the American aid worker Kayla Mueller, the West has become painfully aware that many of its Muslim sons have turned against their homelands and have adopted a very different ideology: *radical jihādism.*[69] According to published reports, thousands of ISIS fighters hail from Europe and a few hundred may be from the United States. ISIS has recruited fighters from at least 81 countries via the Internet – and sometimes even active headhunters – and swarms of young men, many of them disaffected by their lives in the West, have responded to the call. Additionally, many young

---

68 Adorno, *Negative Dialectics,* 362.

69 I agree with the defenders of the traditional sense of the word *"jihād,"* that it is first an inner struggle towards righteousness, and second, a war of self-defense, etc. However, I use the word *"jihādi"* to designate those who ideologically appropriate the term *"jihād"* in order to legitimate their un-Islamic actions. For those I think are engaged in a legitimate struggle for self-defense, etc., I prefer the term *mujahideen.*

western-Muslim girls have traveled to Syria to become "brides" of ISIS fighters. Overall, it is estimated that by the end of summer of 2014, over 12,000 ISIS fighters from countries other than Iraq and Syria have joined the fight. It is estimated that there are more foreign fighters in the Syrian-Iraqi conflict than those who fought against the Soviet Union in the 1980–1988 war in Afghanistan and these fighters makes up approximately one-third of ISIS's forces.[70] Additionally, according to the Canadian government, by the fall of 2014, approximately 130 Canadian "extremist travelers" have gone to Syria to fight with ISIS, including Damian Clairmont, brothers Collin and Gregory Gordon, and Farah Shirdon. Damian Clairmont was killed in action just one month after arriving while fighting in Aleppo against the Free Syrian Army.[71] All four of these jihādis were from Calgary and attended the same downtown mosque. It appears that Canada, despite its political differences with the United States, shares similar, if not the same, cultural problems that serve as fertile grounds for radicalism.

Unlike the West, which is engulfed within a hyper-atomized civil society that has few resources to bind people together in substantive solidarity, the concept of *ummah* and the establishment of a "caliphate" have immense power to attract fighters to its banner, a power that is almost inconceivable within the extreme atomistic civil society of the West. As Slavoj Žižek has remarked, the West is languishing in its Nietzschian "Last Man" stage of history – where we've become complacent in our material luxury, happy to engage in mindless busy-ness, and undisturbed by the existential crises that surround us; we are 'apathetic creature[s] with no great passion or commitment. Unable to dream, tired of life, [we] take no risks, seeking only comfort and security.'[72] The West's once powerful dreams of creating a society rooted in liberty, equality and fraternity, have given way to a life of materialist stupor; drunk on our own successes, we fail to commit ourselves to any vision of a more just society, and for this lack of vision beyond the given we tacitly accept our existentially empty status quo as our ultimate fate. However, this status quo is predicated upon the submission of other parts of the world to our capitalist imposed world-order,

---

70   Richard Barrett, *Foreign Fighters in Syria* (Soufan Group Report, June, 2014), 6. One should bear in mind that those Arabs that fought in Afghanistan against the Soviet Union later created *al-Qae'da* (the base).

71   Public Safety Canada, "2014 Public Report on the Terrorist Threat to Canada: Responding to Violent Extremism and Travel Abroad for Terrorist Related Purposes," Her Majesty the Queen in Right of Canada, 2014; David Fitzpatrick and Drew Griffin, "Canadians have Joined ISIS to Fight – and Die – in Syria," September 10, 2014. http://www.cnn .com/2014/09/10/world/canada-isis-jihadists/ (Accessed 9/10/2014).

72   Slavoj Žižek, "ISIS is a Disgrace to Fundamentalism," *New York Times*, September 3, 2014.

yet we rarely witness this fact as it is thoroughly camouflaged in the jungle of consumerist abundance. "We in the West," says Žižek, 'are… immersed in stupid daily pleasures, while the Muslim radicals are ready to risk everything, engaged in the struggle up to their self-destruction.'[73] The 'transcendental cause,' which animates ISIS and other jihādist groups, is a unifying force dedicated to the destruction of the status quo; the same status quo that the West has imposed on the world and has enjoyed since WWII. But Žižek's analysis is lacking in one important feature: because of the relative comfort the West currently enjoys, we are too often unaware that there are alternatives to day-dreams of a petit-bourgeois existence; we've come to believe that our way-of-life is normative throughout the world and thus all opposition to it is a gross violation of the natural order. Happy in our complacency, we rarely journey out of ourselves and into the lifeworld of the other where real transcendental causes still animate and motivate humanity beyond its simple social, economic, and political reproduction. The true danger of the "Last Man" is that in his automaton-like existence, he is unaware that his degraded life isn't universal, but remains within the trap he's found himself in, while at the same time he reflexively supports those that would export this automaton culture to other parts of the world in the name of "universal values." The globalization of the Last Man is both a goal and a hidden truth for the man languishing within Max Weber's "Iron Cage" (*stahlhartes Gehäuse*).[74] It may now be the case that the absolute barbarity of ISIS will either (1) disturb the iron cage of the western automaton, or (2) further enforce his false-consciousness concerning its truth and inevitability.

Hegel, War and Individualism

Since the fall of the Soviet Union, an additional problem has plagued the post-secular West. As stated above, despite its abundance of individual and formal political rights, its *common* projects have already been depleted; the bourgeois revolution survived its inner-critique, i.e. communism, and empty consumerism has become the new way of life. Or, as Walter Benjamin claimed, capitalism itself has become the western world's *new religion*. He writes, 'a religion may be discerned in capitalism – that is to say, capitalism serves essentially to allay the same anxieties, torments, and disturbances to which the so-called

---

73   Ibid.
74   Max Weber, *The Protestant Ethic and the Spirit of Capitalism*, trans. Stephen Kalberg (Los Angeles, CA: Roxbury Publishing Co., 2002), 123.

religions offered answers.'[75] Since the demise of religion as a way-of-being for western society, as well as the diminishment of its secular translation in socialism/communism, the West has failed to provide a new common project that could unify itself, other than its own militarized defense. Going back further, since Luther introduced the *individual* as a concept of upmost importance, detaching the individual's salvation from the salvation of the whole or the community, which was later secularized with the development of democracy and capitalism, the West has rarely been able to overcome its social atomization, it social fragmentation, and its inter-societal competitiveness, and when for a brief moment it has transcended its atomization, it has resulted in disasters such as WWI and WWII.[76] In the increasingly secular society, religion ceases to supply the sufficient motivation to galvanize the West into a project that points beyond itself at any given moment. As the aggregate masses of deteched individuals experience the "other" in society as their competition, their antagonist, and not as a fellow participant in the whole, a sense of a *friendly living together* in a particular cause fails to materialize. Indeed, even collective practices, such as electoral politics, are in service to the individual who purely votes for "his/her self-interests" and not the interests of the whole. The individual is led to believe that his or her own interests are identical with the interest of the whole. With this being the case, politics proves to be too divisive to motivate substantive solidarity, while at the same time free market economics augments and perpetuates these social divisions within democratic/capitalist nations. Given this situation, what then motivates the masses towards universal ideals?

Philosophy (despite its hidden pervasiveness) – no matter its overall weakness in the world – yields more social significance in Europe than in America, where its abstract vocabulary invokes suspicion of Euro-elitism. Yet even in Europe philosophy fails to motivate adequately, nor does it aid in overcoming the social ailments associated with atomization, but often serves to separate communities and nations instead of uniting them. Marx's idea that philosophy could take as its object the revolutionary working class, and therefore realize philosophy within history, failed to materialize as the revolutionary working class refused to embrace the revolutionary cause in much of the West.[77]

---

75   Walter Benjamin, *Walter Benjamin: Selected Writings Vol. 1: 1913–1926*, ed. Marcus Bullock
      & Michael W. Jennings (Cambridge, MA: The Belknap Press of Harvard University Press,
      2004), 288.

76   Herbert Marcuse, *A study on Authority* (New York: Verso, 2008), 12–34.

77   Marx stated in his *Contribution to the Critique of Hegel's Philosophy of Right: Introduction*,
      that 'just as philosophy finds its material weapons in the proletariat, so the proletariat

Additionally, the pre-political foundations of nations, i.e. their language, history, religion, and ethnicity, have all been formally negated as bases for the modern enlightened secular state and therefore their potential to bind the masses has been removed, unless the bureaucratic neutrality of the state is broken by nationalist negativity: xenophobia, racism, and Islamophobia (as one variant of religion-hatred). Through its negativity the state may be able to conjure solidarity among the atomized, and thus stabilize itself, but the consequences of such conjuring has proven to be diabolical in the 20th century.

However, this conjuring of the nation-states' negativity may adequately serve as a potential catalyst for overcoming the languishing political, economic and culture life in the West, but it may not be what the western world ultimately wants.

Hegel pointed out in his *Philosophy of Right* that there is a tremendous potential for social solidarity through ravishes of armed conflict. War, as a way of stirring civil society out of its automaton-like slumber, may instill in a society sufficient motivation to congeal around a given issue short of delivering a nation to a *perpetual* state of war. For Hegel, nations may have to risk doing "evil" in order to realize the *ethical moment of war.* He writes,

> For war should not be regarded as an absolute evil (*Übel*) and as a purely external contingency whose cause (*Grund*) is therefore itself contingent, whether this cause lies in the passions of rulers or nations (*Völker*), in injustices etc., or in anything else which is not as it should be... War is that condition in which the vanity of temporal things (*Dinge*) and temporal goods – which tends at other times to be merely a pious phrase – takes on a serious significance, and it is accordingly the moment in which the ideality of *the particular attains its right* and becomes actuality... The ideality which makes its appearance in war in the shape of a contingent external relationship is the same as the ideality whereby the internal powers of the state are organic moments of the whole. This is apparent in various occurrences in history, as when successful wars have averted internal unrest and consolidated the internal power of the state.[78]

---

finds its intellectual weapons in philosophy... philosophy can only be realized by the abolition of the proletariat, and the proletariat can only be abolished by the realization of philosophy.' Marx and Engels, *Marx-Engels Reader*, 65.

78 Hegel, *Philosophy of Right*, 361–362.

He continues,

> In peace, the bounds of civil life are extended, all its spheres become firm-
> ly established, and in the long run, people become stuck in their ways.
> Their particular characteristics (*Partikularitäten*) become increasingly
> rigid and ossified. But the unity of the body is essential to the health, and
> if its parts grow internally hard, the result is *death*. Perpetual peace is of-
> ten demanded as an ideal to which mankind should approximate. Thus,
> Kant proposed a league of sovereigns to settle disputes between states,
> and the Holy Alliance was meant to be an institution more or less of this
> kind. But the state is an individual, and negation is an essential compo-
> nent of individuality. Thus, even if a number of states join together as
> a family, this league, in its individuality, must generate opposition and
> create an enemy.[79]

For Hegel, war and the threat of war can potentially deliver enough motivation to congeal society into a common project, albeit predicated upon fear
(whether true of simply perceived) and aggression towards the other. WWI,
WWII, and the Cold War forced nations to think about their national commonality over and above the all-consuming peace-time concerns of individuals; the fact that all were targeted for nuclear destruction during the Cold
War forced them to become self-reflective about their own singularity and
mortality; they become conscious of the fact that their existence depends
on the existence of others and most importantly the *state,* which serves as a
common bond and an apparatus for self-preservation within a nation. In this
case, *singularity* dissolves into the concerns of *particularity* – the people of a
given nation as a whole, but does not rise to the level of *universal* – humanity
in its totality. However, as Hegel already knew, in peacetime, when the external pressures of war are not bearing down upon the populace, society
descends into isolated ghettos of selfishness and individuality, leaving behind
the concerns for collectivity. In the post-Cold War period, the West may be
completely depleted of its ability to sustain any substantive form of solidarity
with and for itself. War may even be exhausted of its social solidarity potentials that Hegel witnessed to, as the West – the United States in particular –
have continually been in war which has depleted the legitimacy of democratic
semantics. Not even Hitler's right-wing Hegelian political-theologian, Carl

---

79   Ibid., 362. My emphasis.

Schmitt, and his dictum, that the *essence of politics is the identification of the enemy*, can muster enough emotional sentiment against the external enemy to unite the West, even after the enemy has been identified as being radical Islam: the conceptualized "totally other society" against which the West defines itself.[80]

However, the lack of social solidarity may be a structural phenomenon within capitalist society that is steered primarily on the interests of multi-national corporations. Remember the American President George W. Bush's response to 9/11: he asked the American people to go about their business-as-usual, to "enjoy life," and not be afraid; in other words to "go shopping." It was a perverse but logical move by the President not to encourage the populace to think of themselves as being part of the war effort against al-Qae'da, but rather they were commanded to do their patriotic duty and consume while ignoring the war that the nation was now engaged in. Solidarity, or the congealing of a nation within a common project or common sentiment, was understood by Bush to be the death-knell of capitalism, especially because many Americans population perceived that – following the WWII example – they should sacrifice a part of their own economic happiness for the war-effort. Out of the residue of religious guilt, it did not appear to them to be appropriate to enjoy the "blessings of freedom" through consumptive activities while others were suffering, dying and killing to protect it. Nevertheless, for capitalism, the atomization and extreme individualism that exists within peacetime had to be maintained if the war was to be successful. Economic self-sacrifice for the common cause would hinder the already fragile economy and thus the nation's ability to pay for the war without selling more debt to communist China. The logical conclusion from this observation repeats what Max Weber (and Karl Marx) already knew: capitalism by nature depends upon the division of individuals – solidarity is its poison, and not even a massive foreign war can now dislodge the collective zeitgeist of individualism in the West. Culturally, we have all become collectively socialized to be radical individualists (with some exceptions). Additionally, if capitalism was going to be protected by the state against al-Qae'da, the workers of America had to continue to drive the engine of the economy via their purchasing prowess, which too often translates into massive personal debt to financial institutions who profit off the financial misery of working class people.

---

80   Carl Schmitt, *Political Theology: Four Chapters on the Concept of Sovereignty.* Chicago: University of Chicago Press, 2005.

ISIS and Western Alienation

Many young Muslims who have grown up in the West are alienated from the social freedoms that are normative within society; they yearn for a form of religious life that permeates all areas of being; they want to have a religious society that is governed not on the basis of individual freedom, but on God's law; they desire a society that abolishes that which their religion deems immoral, and makes pertinent that which God demands upon his creation. Islam, being a religion that is rooted in sacred law, and thus refuses to separate morality and legality, is seen as the only viable way of establishing a society that could be endorsed by the divine. True freedom, many of these young believers think, can only materialize within the bounds of God's laws. Cultural freedom, as articulated and practiced in the West – as *freedom to be autonomous from traditional religious morality* – for many of these young believers, cannot lead to a good life, a moral society, or a state predicated on the principles of absolute justice precisely because it lets loose the anomic nature of the *nafs* (ego, desires, instincts, etc.). The religiously-rooted moral component in secular society is missing and the anxiety of working through vexing moral questions and subjectively establishing moral commitments without scriptural guidance overburdens the individual's psyche and leads, he/she believes, to moral mistakes and social mischief. Certainly a society that dictates a preconceived moral system appeals to a certain form of religious authoritarianism, as it releaves the burden of the individual to engage in moral deliberation and coerces the individual to act in conformity with the beliefs of others. It's a form of *moral scholasticism:* one that starts with the moral truths (as already having been established by revelation) and works its arguments backwards to legitimate and prove those moral "truths." Consequently, societies that enforce religious morals, such as what ISIS has attempted to do, do not allow for sufficient living-space for an individual to actually *become* moral, but rather demands one *be* moral if only on the surface. In other words, there is no public space for trial-and-error in morality; the individual must simply *conform*: no *becoming*, only the *appearance of being*. On the other hand, in the moral vacuousness of the West, ISIS's brutal implementation of morality is a powerful magnet for those who wish to see the construction of a true *Islamic state* – political, economic, and cultural embodiment of Islamic morality. To quote Freud, 'where id was, there ego shall be,' or, 'where *enslavement to individual desires* is, there *religious law* shall be.'[81] From the perspective of ISIS, the *id* of the West must be

---

81   Freud, *Introductory Lectures on Psychoanalysis,* 100.

subdued by the *ego* of Islam, and that process starts with the abolishment of western values, practices, and culture in the Muslim world.

The magnetism of ISIS and other fundamentalist groups is made especially poignant when the alienation of Muslims in the West is coupled by a feeling of dejection, as if they are not wanted within those western countries, whether that feeling is the result of specific government policies, a cultural climate that cannot be reconciled with Islamic morality, or an overt Islamophobic or miso-Islamist environment. This feeling makes it easy for young Muslims to abandon any form of allegiance they once had to their home countries and adopt the rhetoric and lifestyle of the Islamic militant, even if cultural patterns of western society run deep within the individual. There is a sense of "coming home" even when that same young Muslim remains in the West but has spiritually migrates to the *dar al-Islam* (or what is imagined to be the *dar al-Islam*), often times through self-radicalization facilitated by the internet. The homecoming is even more profound when the young Muslim joins those who he believes to be fighting for an Islamic utopia-state as it gives him a sense of purpose, a sense of belonging, and a transcendent project, all that which was missing in the atomized West. The struggle to establish an Islamic state – and more importantly an Islamic society – is a common project within the Muslim ummah that, like Hegel remarked, wrestles the individual out of his singularity; it is a war that binds disparate individuals from various nations into a whole with common purpose. This 'redemptive' project disturbs the 'lasting calm' that makes society "stagnant."[82] Seemingly, ISIS's call for the rejuvenation of the caliphate has fundamentally disturbed the delicate balance within the Muslim ummah between those who long for Muslim liberation and those who accommodate themselves to the status quo. As such, ISIS is forcing Muslims to take sides: are you with the rejuvenation and restoration of Islam as a world force or are you with the western-backed world order as-it-is? Many Muslims simply reject this binary proposition, citing both sides to be fraudulent answers to the problems facing Muslims within the conditions of modernity.

Yet some have chosen sides. After an ISIS-inspired Algerian group beheaded Hervé Gourdel, a 55 year old French hiker on a tourist trip to Algeria in September of 2014, French Muslim youth took to the streets and to their social media in protests. Antagonized not only by the murder of Gourdel, but also by the insistence of ISIS's propaganda encouraging western Muslims to kill other

---

82   Hegel, *Philosophy of Right*, 361.

non-Muslim westerners, including the 'dirty French,' these youth courageously claimed 'We are also Dirty French.'[83] Joining their British counterparts in their *Not in My Name* campaign, the French Muslims insist on the authenticity of their religious identity as well as their faithful commitment to the French nation, even if that relationship has been strained in the recent past.[84] For ISIS and other extremist groups, such siding with a western nation, especially one that has shown aggression towards Muslims, both in and outside of France, can only be met by severe hostility and a declaration of apostasy (*takfir*). They understand the "we" in 'we are also dirty French' as being linguistically symbolic of the divided loyalties of the French Muslim community, which is unacceptable in their eyes. Consequently, it is so believed, they have divorced themselves from the greater Muslim community and allied themselves with those who seek to harm that same Muslim community. For ISIS, this is treason. For the other side, this isn't treason at all, but one of the highest forms of witnessing against tyranny and professing '*asabiyya* (Islamic solidarity) with others, even if they are non-Muslims.

Internationalism

The fact that thousands of western Muslims are making their way to the Middle East to fight with ISIS and the potential that they could eventually turn their jihādist expertise against western governments and societies, only gives credence to the claims of Islamophobes and miso-Islamists who have denounced Islam and Muslims as being 'inherently' violent, anti-democratic, and a fifth column within Europe and America. It also demonstrates the power of religious ideals over secular nationalism. From the perspective of capitalism, the internationalism of Islam, much like the internationalism of communism, is a threat to the established world order. Western governments often do not believe they can trust the allegiance of their Muslim citizens because they perceive that the Muslims too frequently have divided loyalties. For some

---

83   Sara Miller Llana, "French Muslims to Islamic State: We are also 'Dirty French,'" September 26, 2014. http://www.csmonitor.com/World/Europe/2014/0926/French-Muslims-to-Islamic-State-We-are-also-dirty-French (Accessed 9/28/2014).

84   See the insightful works of John R. Bowen, *Blaming Islam*. Cambridge, MA: The MIT Press, 2012; *Can Islam Be French?* Princeton: Princeton University Press, 2010; *Why the French Don't Like Headscarves: Islam, the State, and Public Space*. Princeton: Princeton University Press, 2007.

Muslims this is true; some Muslims choose to reconcile their religious opinions and practices with their national identity and remain faithful to both; they find some way of being Muslim and American, Muslim and British, Muslim and French, etc., while others find this compromise of Islam and national identity as being too distorting. Again, for them, there can be no compromise in the truth of Islam if it is a "perfected" and therefore a "petrified" religion – a religion of absolutes (in terms of identity). For these Muslims, Islam will always take precedent over the nation because national citizenship is less important to their identity than their religious faith. The metaphysical reality of Islam is a higher priority than the accidentals of history, including citizenship in any given country. Nationality is a matter of "this-life," while the adherence to the dictates of Islam is a matter of the "next-life," which for the believer is of utmost concern. As such, Islam and the ummah, which both transcend all political boarders, are the primary objects of loyalty, and not any particular nation-state. As stated before, all ideologies, philosophies, and religions that transcend the boundaries of nation-states are often times looked at with deep suspicion in the modern period.

During the early and mid-20th century, communism's emphasis on class solidarity, which cut across national boundaries, was perceived as an ideology that would create division *within* nations as it advanced working class solidarity over and above national solidarity and national identity. In other words, the working class of Germany, for example, had more in common with its fellow workers in Russia, Italy and France, than it did its own ruling class, and therefore they, the communists argued, should subsume or abandon their national allegiance in favor of their class allegiance. Although this was a powerful idea, the advent of WWI demonstrated just how weak and superficial it was. To the disgust of the Marxists, including the members of the Frankfurt School, workers almost uniformly chose to fight for their nations over their class, thus dividing the working class on national lines and forcing them to fight each other in the horrible trenches. The workers of the world failed to unite and so their class chains continued. It is feared by many that Islam, especially in its radical form, may be able to pierce through national loyalties and ferment solidarity on the basis of religious identity, just as communism once attempted to do.

Like their views on Islam, many right-wing politicians and activists in Europe and America today see the internationalism of the Catholic Church as being a threat to the West as well. Christian internationalism, which places the universality of humanity over the particularity of nationhood, when coupled with the desire to be merciful, charitable, and giving towards others, creates the conditions where the Catholic Church seems to be the open flank by which

Muslims can invade Europe.[85] They are perturbed by Pope Francis' conciliatory remarks about Muslims, calling them "brothers," and advocating on their behalf in Europe, all of which invokes the ecumenical spirit of Vatican II's *Nostra Aetate* – especially its remarks on Islam, which state,

> The Church regards with esteem also the Moslems [Muslims]. They adore the one God, living and subsisting in Himself; merciful and all-powerful, the Creator of heaven and earth, who has spoken to men; they take pains to submit wholeheartedly to even His inscrutable decrees, just as Abraham, with whom the faith of Islam takes pleasure in linking itself, submitted to God. Though they do not acknowledge Jesus as God, they revere Him as a prophet. They also honor Mary, His virgin Mother; at times they even call on her with devotion. In addition, they await the day of judgment when God will render their deserts to all those who have been raised up from the dead. Finally, they value the moral life and worship God especially through prayer, almsgiving and fasting.
>
> Since in the course of centuries not a few quarrels and hostilities have arisen between Christians and Moslems, this sacred synod urges all to forget the past and to work sincerely for mutual understanding and to preserve as well as to promote together for the benefit of all mankind social justice and moral welfare, as well as peace and freedom.[86]

For these right-wing commentators and politicians, the attempts of the church to be reconciled with Muslims, to engage in a friendly living together, has opened the doors for the Trojan horse; radical Islam – and ISIS's ideology in particular – will follow those Muslims into the West. Because the church, under Pope Francis, wants to reform itself in light of the Gospels' social teachings, it will increasingly emphasize Christian compassion for the poor, the suffering, and dispossessed, which includes the Muslims. For the political right, this is a western sign of weakness that radical Islam will exploit. It will, in their view,

---

85   Diversity Chronicle, "Pope Francis Invites the Homeless, Undocumented Immigrants and Prostitutes to Exclusive Catered Vatican Banquet," April 11, 2014. http://diversitychronicle .wordpress.com/2014/04/11/pope-francis-invites-the-homeless-undocumented -immigrants-and-prostitutes-to-exclusive-catered-vatican-banquet/ (Accessed 9/6/2014).

86   Pope Paul VI, "Nostra Aetate: Declaration on the Relation of the Church to Non-Christian Religions," October 28, 1965. http://www.vatican.va/archive/hist_councils/ii_vatican _council/documents/vat-ii_decl_19651028_nostra-aetate_en.html (Accessed 8/27/2014); Vatican Radio, "Pope Francis to Muslims: We Must Confront Common Challenges," http://www.news.va/en/news/pope-francis-to-muslims-we-must-confront-common-ch (Accessed 8/27/2014).

not reciprocate such compassion when it attacks Europe, but will rather use such conciliatory language to integrate into Europe in hopes of seizing the opportunity to engage in jihādi attacks, just as we witnessed in the 2015 and 2016 attacks on Paris and Brussels. In their thinking, the ecumenical and Argentinian Pope Francis himself is the gullible fifth column of Europe. Statements like the following enrage the European right: 'many people forced to emigrate suffer, and often die tragically; many of their rights are violated, they are obliged to separate from their families, and unfortunately, continue to be the subject of racist and xenophobic attitudes' once in Europe.[87] This sympathy for the ominous other does not go very far with those who believe that Islam itself is a threat to the existence of Europe and European culture. For these critics, immigrants from North Africa, Syria, Libya, etc., may not come into Europe as ISIS, but they may radicalize while in Europe and become future ISIS members camouflaged in the midst. Each immigrant, it is so believed, has a potential for the same kind of radicalization that occurred to the perpetrators of the *Charlie Hebdo* massacre, and so do their children, and thus the Trojan horse of immigration. They think that with each immigrant allowed to stay in Europe, generations of potential terrorists come about. Greeting them with Christian *agape*, as the Pope advocates, is the wrong attitude to adopt because it leaves Europeans exposed to the ever-growing threat of radical Islam. For these critics, it is not only a matter of Europe's identity, but of its survival as Europe.[88]

Seeking Heaven at the Barrel of a Gun

Attacks on the West by Muslims are already a source of deep distrust for many westerners. Since the rise of ISIS, the suspicion of Muslims living in western nations has only increased. Just in the year 2014, numerous stories of American and Euro-jihādis have surfaced, sparking intense measures by their governments to stem the flow of western fighters into Syria. Moner Muhammad Abusalha, a 22-year-old American of Palestinian and Italian descent from Florida, who was drawn to a deeper faith in Islam, became the first American suicide bomber to blow him up fighting against the forces of Bashar al-Assad. His attack on May 25th, 2014, killed 37 people on *Jabal Al-Arba'een*. Moner was

---

87   Elise Harris, 'Pope Denounces "Racist, Xenophobic" Attitudes towards Immigrants,' July 15, 2014. http://www.catholicnewsagency.com/news/pope-denounces-racist-xenophobic -attitudes-toward-migrants-84304/ (Accessed 9/10/2014).

88   Bruce Bawer, *While Europe Slept: How Radical Islam is Destroying the West from Within.* New York: Broadway Books, 2006.

recruited into jihādi ideology via the Internet by Anwar al-Awlaki, the American shaykh of Yemeni descent who was killed by a drone attack ordered by President Obama in 2011. Moner fought for *Jabhat al-Nusrah* (al-Nusra Front) after arriving through Turkey.[89] Before his death, he recorded numerous tirades against the American government, accusing it of attacking Muslims, calling it the 'capital of al-Dajjal (the anti-Christ),' and threatening 'we are coming for you.'[90] Reflecting his experience with the nihilism of American consumer society, he stated in his video testimony that,

> I lived in America. I know how it is. You have all the fancy amusement parks and the restaurants and the food and all this crap and the cars. You think you're happy. You're not happy. You're never happy. I was never happy. I was always sad and depressed. Life sucked. I had to walk from my work [to] home... and I begged Allah, cried to Allah, get me out of this land. All you do is work 40, 50, 60 hours a week, and then you go waste it on garbage... this is what you do your whole life.[91]

Moner overcame his alienation from western culture through a complete adoption of Islam; absorbing his autonomous subjectivity into an all-encompassing religious tradition that gave him direction, an interpretation of reality and an orientation in action, and a transcendental cause. Additionally, it instilled within him the longing for absolute and perfect justice, which he believed could only be realized through the revivification and conquest of Islam. However, Moner's religious immaturity, coupled by the zeal of the jihādi, led him to sacrifice himself unnecessarily in the process of killing others, who were also Muslims. As there is a dearth of qualified Muslim scholars in the West, Moner's potential to be become a bridge between the secular West and the *dar al-Islam* was great, but unfortunately ISIS's ideology distorted his sincere religiosity and led him into a form of religious nihilism – the twin sister of secular nihilism which he was attempting to escape via his *hijrah* (migration) to Syria.[92] Moner

---

89   Jabhat al-Nusra is an al-Qae'da affiliate and has been named a terrorist organization by the U.N., the U.S., and other nations.

90   Meg Wagner, "American Suicide Bomber Feared the FBI was Hunting him when he Fled from Florida to Syria," August 28, 2014. http://www.nydailynews.com/news/world/american -suicide-bomber-feared-fbi-hunting-article-1.1919902 (Accessed 9/2/2014).

91   YouTube. "Inside the Mind of a Terrorist: Moner Mohammad AbuSalha (Abu Huayrah al-Amriki)" https://www.youtube.com/watch?v=HSdtCcWTaSI (Accessed 9/02/2014).

92   In the video posted to youtube.com, Moner talks about Anwar al-Awlaki's lecture, stating "In a lecture, Anwar al-Awlaki said when you make hijrah (migration) it's like a cliff, jump off the cliff and you don't know if the water is deep or shallow. Don't know if there're rocks

was both the victim of post-secular modernity's meaninglessness – its reduction of human life to simple material possessions and the imperative to "enjoy" as way-of-being-in-the-world – as well as the ideological distortion of Islam by jihādi militants, who are more *necrophilic* than *biophilic* in their religious life.

Mona Muhammad Abusalha al-Amriki wasn't the only American fighting in the Middle East. In August of 2014, the world was introduced to African American Douglas McArthur McCain and his Native American friend Troy Kastigar, two men from Minneapolis who converted to Islam and chose to fight for ISIS in Syria and al-Shabaab in Somalia. After a life of petty crime in Minnesota, McCain moved to San Diego, California, where he became closer to the religion he was first introduced to by his Somali friends in Minnesota. By the spring of 2014, McCain journeyed to Turkey to study Islam but instead joined ISIS in Syria where he was eventually killed fighting the forces of Bashar al-Assad. His friend, Troy Kastigar, going by the name Abdal Rahim Muhammad, had a similar experience. In 2008 Kastigar told his family he was leaving to study Islam in Kenya but instead went to Somalia where he was killed fighting for al-Shabaab, the Islamist organization that effectively controls much of the country. In the summer of 2013, al-Shabaab released a recruitment video entitled *Minnesota's Martyrs: The Path to Paradise*, which featured Kastigar talking about his time in Somalia and extolling the virtues of jihādi warfare. With a mix of youthful immaturity and appreciation for religious solidarity, Kastigar said,

> This is the best place to be. I can only tell you that you have the best of dreams, you eat the best of food, and you are with the best of brothers and sisters who came here for the sake of Allah. If you guys only knew how much fun we have over here. This is the real Disneyland. You need to come here and join us.[93]

However, Somali Disneyland killed Kastigar soon after making the video.

Both men felt alienated by the American way of life; both men felt underappreciated, unrecognized, and seemingly without control of their own destinies, until they chose to abandon their American "freedom" and join a group

---

or if it's going to be very deep. You just have to jump and put your faith in Allah that it's going to be deep and you won't be harmed, that you're going to be safe after you land in the water." "Interview with Moner Mohammad Abu Salaha aka Abu Hurayra al-Ameriki Part 1: Hijra." https://www.youtube.com/watch?v=DvCUMagTiCo (Accessed 9/2/2014).

93   Alex Grieg, "Almost a Dozen Men from Minnesota are Fighting for ISIS in Syria, Say Officials," August 29, 2014. http://www.dailymail.co.uk/news/article-2737982/Almost -dozen-men-Minnesota-fighting-ISIS-Syria-say-officials.html (Accessed 9/2/2014).

that could furnish them with a sense of belonging, a sense of identity, and a sense of purpose beyond simple materialism. Islam filled the existential void that they had developed through their experience of American poverty, marginalization, and moral vacuousness. Like Moner Muhammad, these men looked for guidance in a post-religious society and found Islam being the most capable of instilling in them a sense of truth, purpose, and meaning. Subjective freedom, through which they chose their religion, left them existentially untethered, morally adrift, and without a transcendental cause. Unfortunately, their turn to Islam was distorted into a turn towards the jihādi ideology, which ended in their unnecessary premature deaths – or what they believed was their sacred martyrdom.

Moner Muhammad, Douglas McArthur McCain and Troy Kastigar were never able to return to their home country to engage in subversive or terroristic activities. However, others who did go to the Muslim world for training did return to deploy their crafts upon the unsuspecting. The Chechen-American brothers Tamerlan Anzorovich Tsarnaev and Dzhokhar Anzorovich "Jahar" Tsarnaev were both born in what was the Soviet Union, but came to the United States as asylum seekers between 2002 and 2004. After a life of struggle within the U.S., trying to create an hybrid American/Islamic existence in university, boxing, and various failed relationships, etc., the older of the two brothers, Tamerlan Tsarnaev, traveled to Russia (north Caucasus) in 2012 where he came into contact with various Chechen and Dagestani jihādists, including some family members, who furthered his resentment towards the West, especially the United States and its latest "war on terror." On April 15, 2013, the brothers planted pressure-cooker bombs in the audience at the finish line of the Boston marathon; once exploded, these bombs killed 3 people and wounded more than 250. What motivated the brothers, according to the testimony of Dzhokhar, was America's killing of Muslims in Iraq and Afghanistan. In other words, the attacks on Boston were understood to be a *retaliatory* strike against a nation that was guilty of killing thousands of innocent believers in the Middle East and Central Asia. While hiding from police in a boat stored in the backyard of a Boston suburb, Dzhokhar wrote the following,

> I'm jealous of my brother who ha[s] [re]ceived the reward of jannutul Firdaus [paradise] (inshallah) before me. I do not mourn because his soul is very much alive. God has a plan for each person. Mine was to hide in this boat and shed some light on our actions. I ask Allah to make me a shahied [shaheed] (iA) to allow me to return to him and be among all the righteous people in the highest levels of heaven. He who Allah guides no one can misguide. A[llah Ak]bar!

The US Government is killing our innocent civilians but most of you already know that. As a [UI] I can't stand to see such evil go unpunished. We Muslims are one body, you hurt one you hurt us all. Well at least that's how muhhammad (pbuh) wanted it to be [for]ever. The ummah is beginning to rise. [UI] has awoken the mujahideen. Know you are fighting men who look into the barrel of your gun and see heaven, now how can you compete with that. We are promised victory and we will surely get it. Now I don't like killing innocent people it is forbidden in Islam but due to said [UI] it is allowed. All credit goes [UI]. Stop killing our innocent people and we will stop.[94]

Like Moner Muhammad, Douglas McArthur McCain and Troy Kastigar, the Tsarnaev brothers had both expressed their alienation from American culture openly. For example, in a Boston University article entitled *Will Box for Passport: An Olympic Drive to Become a United States Citizen*, which was produced before the bombings, Tamerlan told the author that, "I don't have a single American friend. I don't understand them."[95] Furthermore, he found the American Muslim community's stance towards American culture and cultural icons, such as Dr. Martin Luther King Jr., too accommodating, believing that a local Imam's comparison of Dr. King to the Prophet Muhammad to be blasphemous.[96] In the midst of a *khuṭbah* (serman), Tamerlan yelled at the Imam, Yusuf Vali, exclaiming that he was a *kāfir* (disbeliever) and was polluting the minds of the Muslims.[97] For Tamerlan, more so than his little brother, the conditions of the western Muslims were indicative of a community trying to assimilate and integrate into a society that was radically different from the

---

94 This is a direct quote from the prosecutor's filings. The odd abbreviations seemed to have been added by the prosecutor and not explained in the document. However, the "UI" seemed to be the areas where damage was caused by the bullets fired into the boat. See the U.S. prosecutor's court filings against Dzhokhar Tsarnaev. Carmen M. Ortiz (United States Attorney), "The United States of America v. Dzhokhar A. Tsarnaev (Defendent), Case 1:13-cr-10200-GAO" http://c.oobg.com/rw/Boston/2011-2020/2014/05/22/BostonGlobe .com/Metro/Graphics/tsarnaev1.pdf (Accessed 3/14/2015).

95 Johannes Hirn, "Will Box for Passport: An Olympic Drive to Become a United States Citizen." *The Comment* 2010, 18–19.

96 Beth Daley and Martin Finucane, "Marathon Bombing Suspect's Disrupted Cambridge Mosque on Martin Luther King Day," April 21, 2013. http://www.boston.com/ metrodesk/2013/04/21/marathon-bombing-suspect-outbursts-had-disturbed-cambridge -mosque-goers/HUM4K1dm5IKWqRRKktFM9L/story.html (Accessed 9/5/2014).

97 Daley and Finucane, "Marathan Bombing Suspect Disrupted Cambridge Mosque." (Accessed 9/5/2014).

one they truly belonged to, and in doing so were diluting Islam. Islam could not be reconciled to American culture, not even the most prophetic within American history, Dr. Martin Luther King Jr. Additionally, Tamerlan believed the West had to pay for its immorality, for which Tamerlan blamed his own personal failures, temptations, and shortcomings. Had the United States been a proper religious state, one that understood that morality could and should not be separated from the *divinae legis* (divine law), then he would not have been able to engage in practices that are formally condemned by Islam. In this sense, not only was Tamerlan alienated from western culture, but blamed it for his own deviance from Islam. As Slavoj Žižek remarked in a New York Times Op-ed, one can feel that, in fighting the sinful other, they [*jihādi* terrorists] are fighting their own temptation.[98] In this sense, the April attack on Boston was a violent suppression of Tsarnaev's own struggle to be a devout Muslim amidst the hedonistic post-secular culture of modern American capitalism. Unfortunately his victims paid the price for his lack of faith.

Material Poverty or Poverty of Being?

Some thinkers have suggested that the motivational cause for the high numbers of European and American fighters in ISIS can be found solely within their economic conditions. Poverty, for these thinkers, has given birth to those who are willing to fight for a cause that, according to them, is not really their fight, but rather is a way of overcoming economic disparity. The answer to this problem is the rearrangement of the economic map that determines their class status within western societies. Echoing a simplistic Marxist sentiment, and one that fails to comprehend the existential and religious motivations for westerners to become jihādists, this analysis is woefully insufficient. Although poverty may be a factor within the radicalization of Muslims in the West, it is not the core factor that motivates them to join ISIS or other radical groups. Many young Muslims from prosperous families, including Mohammed Emwazi, also known as "Jihādi John" – due to his the famous British accent he had as he beheaded westerners on video – have come from prosperous and educated families.[99] Poverty, although it may in some cases play a part in the

---

98   Slavoj Žižek, "ISIS is a disgrace to True Fundamentalism." (Accessed 9/5/2014).

99   Mohammed Emwazi was born in Kuwait but raised in London. In 2009 he graduated from Westminster with a degree in information technology. After being suspected of Islamist activities in Tanzania and later at home in Britain, he joined ISIS in 2012 and become the famous British "spokesman" behind their gruesome beheading videos.

radicalization process, is neither a necessary nor a sufficient condition to explain the phenomenon. The answer to this problem goes much deeper into the spiritual and existential condition of Muslims, especially the second generation of Muslims living in the West.

In Angel Rabasa and Cheryl Benard book *Eurojihad: Patterns of Islamist Radicalization and Terrorism in Europe,* they studied the Muslim populations of various European countries only to find that the Muslims of Britain are securely within the middle class, have a high degree of education, and the majority of which are gainfully employed. On the other hand, the situation in France wasn't as positive; their study of converts to Islam in France demonstrated that they were disproportionately from lower socio-economic strata, education beyond secondary school was severely lacking, and a majority of converts were unemployed with a large percentage being under-employed (low-skilled, low-wage jobs).[100] Clearly, differences in socio-economical standings throughout Europe and North America should caution analysts to avoid making blanket judgments about poverty being a prime factor in individual's decision to join a radical organization. According to a University of London Study done in the summer and fall of 2014 demonstrated that 'financially stable British-born Muslims who take their security for granted are most at risk of radicalization by terror groups, according to new research' and that 'socially isolated and depressed Muslims are also identified.'[101] What the research demonstrated was that poverty was not necessarily a determining factor for radicalization, but rather psychological instability, stemming from a failure to integrate and assimilate, as well as social alienation stemming from the dual-identity phenomenon (being both European and Muslim), serves as a prime factor in whether or not an individual can resist the lure of radicalization. The individual who has no ontological and existential attachments to the West or western culture, nor has invested themselves in its ideals and values, but rather feels emptiness about life in a secular modern capitalist country, which is often times coupled with social rejection, are most susceptible to a worldview that provides a believable articulation about "ultimate concern."

What we can deduct from this insight is that no matter the socio-economic status of the given Muslim, the call for a radical jihād against the West, in defense of the ummah, or with the dream of building a caliphate, transcends

---

100 Angel Rabasa and Cheryl Benard, *Eurojihad: Patterns of Radicalization and Terrorism in Europe.* Cambridge: Cambridge University Press, 2014.

101 RT. "British-born, rich & isolated Muslims more likely to be radicalized – study," September 25, 2014. http://rt.com/uk/190588-british-depressed-muslims-radicalized/ (Accessed 10/11/2014).

the given economic misery (or non-misery) of the individual believer. Socio-economic status is not the determining factor in the decision to join ISIS and other terroristic groups, but is rather ancillary. What is more likely is that those Muslims within the middle class in Europe have identified a horrible truth about the secular world; that the religious lifeworld has been replaced with nothing that can adequately address the existential needs of humanity. As Jürgen Habermas has written: *something is missing*.[102] While submitting to the reality of the spiritual emptiness in the modern technological world, many Muslims also have a growing sense of victimization; they are watching attentively and in horror as the purveyors of that deflated reality continue to export their same spiritual emptiness to the *dar al-Islam,* often times at the barrel of a gun. The shock of watching western armies ravage the cities and homes of their co-religionists is overwhelming; the terror of watching the Islamic way-of-life being undermined by another way-of-being – which has caused much social chaos with very little beneficial return – is painfully poignant; the disillusionment with the West because of its theory-praxis disconnect – its insistence on democracy and freedom while propagating dictatorships and oppression – leads many to believe that the West's interference within the Muslim world is a one-sided proposition, i.e. only one side stands to gain anything. Islamist ideology, which is in part rooted in the reality of the Muslim world today and its relationship with the West, is the driving factor for young radicalized Muslims to join groups like ISIS. It is not simply the case that their socio-economic status drove them into the arms of the radicals., as the majority of poor Muslims do not become radicalized. However, Islamic radicalism is empowering among those who have experienced life through the prism of the *politically* powerless. Through their radical stance, they experience themselves as a redeeming power; they can cleanse the Muslims world of the corrosive effects of the western secularization and neo-colonial politics, and they can once again return the Muslim world to the forefront of history. Failure to achieve, maintain, and/or integrate into a petit bourgeois existence within Europe is not the root cause of their rejection of the West; the answer is much more

---

102   This critique of the West is not a defense of the Muslim world. I do not believe that what is missing within the secular zeitgeist of the western civilization is necessarily found within the Muslim world. There is a lot missing there as well, especially within those Arab countries that are ruled by brutal and repressive dictators. However, for many Muslims, that which is missing in the secular West can be found within Islam, especially in its more politically militant expressions. Additionally, Islam is not identical with the nation in which Muslims live as majorities, so often times this same kind of political Islam provides what the "Muslim countries" are missing as well.

accusatory than that. In some sense, the Muslims who abandon their western nations for the chance to fight against the West and its influence in the Muslim world are the strongest condemnation of the West; it is a failing project.

On the issue of poverty, what alienated Muslims in the West are experiencing more so that material poverty is a *poverty-of-being*. As stated before, this poverty takes the shape in meaninglessness, dejection, and humiliation, a life unguided by truth and virtue, and a sense of detachment from any true transcendental purpose. Material poverty, which the Qur'an teaches the Muslims as being a test from the divine, can be reconciled with Islamic values, an Islamic interpretations of history, and Islamic ideals – it is an affront to the divine if poverty is not fought against, but in-and-of-itself, it is not an insult towards the divine if Muslims are materially poor. As stated before, their poverty is the pre-condition that makes Islam possible, for without the poor, *zakāt* (almsgiving) and *ṣadaqah* (charity) become meaningless for those who give *zakāt* and *ṣadaqah*. However, the *poverty-of-being*, that is the by-product of secular-materialism and most poignantly capitalism, is, for the Muslims, a direct insult against the divine, because it denies the divinely created *entelechy* (ἐντελέχεια – "purposivity") for its creation, especially for mankind. This spiritual vacuousness drives many into a state of *kufr* (disbelief), as the neo-pagan ideals of western capitalist/consumerist society idolize money, power and status.[103] The purpose of mankind, according to Islam, is not the accumulation of commodities, i.e. *necrophilia* (νεκροφιλία), nor is it a simple "ticklish" form of happiness, but rather a form of spiritually induced *eudaimonia* (εὐδαιμονία – "human flourishing") within the confines of "Islam," i.e. the submission to God.[104] For Islam, the poverty-of-being must be overcome by the complete and total submission to the will of the creator, which reclaims divine entelechy for mankind. Additionally, the ummah is the protective vehicle by which the spiritual entelechy of mankind is safeguarded. When that ummah is infected by the secular value of capitalism, i.e. greed, competition, social antagonisms, social stratifications, and severe individualization, it cannot protect the spiritual wholeness of the community. As Marx already knew, under the conditions of capitalism, the community becomes fractured, the family becomes dissolved, and the society turns upon itself through the structural and sometimes direct violence that capitalist conditions impose. Therefore, when the instrumental values of secular capitalism overcome the communicative values of Islam; when the

---

103   See Erich Fromm, *To Have or To Be*. (New York: Harper & Row, Publishers, 1976), 15–64.

104   I use the term "ticklish" to describe a form of happiness that is fleeting, or impermanent, by nature.

markets socialize the following generation by advertisements; when there is an increased desire to own for the sake of owning; and an individual's worth and value is predicated on what they possess, substantive life is replaced by the empty-life of *commodities*. These fractures within society are reproduced within the family, which only serve to weaken society, thus allowing more space for capitalism to extend its tentacles.

Most ironically, in light of their poverty-of-being among western Muslims, many of the young have been socialized by capitalist optimism to believe that they can do anything if they direct their mental and physical energies towards achieving it; they are the pampered generation that has been sheltered from the reality of the true human condition, i.e. its frailty and limitations. Believing this pseudo-capitalist ideology, born out of the society of over-abundance, they have betrayed the original point of their ideological *bildung* and have directed that optimism towards supposedly "Islamic" goals. Even in the midst of combat in the Middle East and East Africa, the western foreign fighters are the most optimistic about their own future and the future of the "Islamic State" for which they are gladly giving their lives, realizing the optimistic spirit of liberal-capitalism which was taught to them by the market economy in the West. Either way they are existentially fulfilled by their radical-praxis; they will either achieve their goals and establish a so-called Islamic State or achieve martyrdom in the process.

Genealogy of Terror

When discussing modern terrorism, it is important to have a future-oriented remembrance of it genealogy, as it gives us a clear insight into the nature and purpose of terror itself. Against the common – in America – misconception that so-called Islamic terror began with al-Qae'da's September 11th attack on the United States or the establishment of the Taliban in Afghanistan, we should be aware that the original template for the westerner turned Islamic terrorist is certainly not John Walker Lindh, the American Taliban who was captured by American forces in Afghanistan in 2001, nor was it Jose Padilla, the American "enemy combatant" that planned a dirty bomb attack on the United States after receiving training in Pakistan and Afghanistan in 2001 and 2002; it was not Richard Reid, the "shoe bomber" who attempted to blow up an American Airlines flight from Paris to Miami in 2001, nor was the archetype Umar Farouk Abdulmutallab, the British-Nigerian "underwear bomber" who attempted to blow up a plane traveling from Amsterdam to Detroit on Christmas day in

2009.[105] In fact, the archetype for westerners turned jihādis was not the per-
petrators of the July 7, 2005 London bus bombings, Muhammad Sidique Khan,
Shehzed Tanweer, Germaine Lindsay, and Hasib Hussein, all British Muslims;
neither was it those responsible for the 2004 training bombing in Madrid,
Spain. Not even the western educated Arabs that perpetrated the attack on
New York and Washington D.C. on September 11, 2001 provide the template
for international terrorism. Indeed, the 2015 and 2016 attackers on Paris and
Brussels had a very differnet model to follow other than Usama bin Laden. The
original archetype for this form of jihādi was neither European nor a Muslim,
he was not an Arab or any other ethnicity commonly associated with Islam;
his name was Ilich Ramírez Sánchez, a.k.a. "Carlos the Jackal." "Carlos," who
has been all but forgotten in the modern history of terrorism, was born the
second son of a Marxist intellectual-lawyer in Venezuela. He was named, as
was his two brothers, after Vladimir Ilich Lenin, in whose philosophy his father
schooled him from a very young age.[106] After a brief and incomplete education
in Moscow, Carlos lent his talents to the Palestinian struggle via the *Popular
Front for the Liberation of Palestine* (PFLP), a Marxist-Leninist organization
determined to bring about the end of the Israeli occupation of Palestine as
well as the construction of a leftist secular Arab state rooted in Che Guevara's
notion of the "new man," who was the revolutionary humanist-socialist who
worked for the benefit of the masses through armed struggle against colonialism, imperialism, and capitalism primarily in Latin America and Africa.[107]
While there, he worked for and trained with Wadie Haddad, the commander
of the military wing of the PFLP. The PFLP was a secular "pan-Arabist" organization, believing that the basis for Arab independence resided in inter-Arab
solidarity, not on the basis of religion that would divide the Arab world.[108] For
Wadi Haddad, there was no going behind the fall of the caliphate; the *modern*
Muslim world needed a modern ideology to combat America and the West

---

105   Mark Kukis, *My Heart Became Attached: The Strange Odyssey of John Walker Lindh.*
       Washington D.C.: Brassey's Inc., 2003. The title of this book, the strange odyssey of John
       Walker Lindh, betrays the time-core of truth; what seemed strange in 2003 that a western-
       er from an affluent background would leave it all behind to join a terrorist organization,
       in his case the Taliban, has become all too familiar in 2014.

106   John Follain, *Jackal* (New York: Arcade Publishing, 1998), 1–18.

107   Michael Löwy, *The Marxism of Che Guevara* (Lanham, MD: Rowman & Littlefield Publish-
       ers Inc., 2007), 17–19. Also see Karl Marx's essay *The Jewish Question*, as it is this transfor-
       mation of man from a being of selfish particularity to a being of collective solidarity that
       he discusses. Karl Marx and Friedrich Engels, *The Marx-Engels Reader*, 26–52.

108   Follain, *Jackal*, 19–36.

during the Cold War and its smaller manifestation in the Israeli/Palestine conflict. Having fully adopted the Palestinian cause as his own, Carlos engaged
in various attacks in Europe, including attacks on prominent Israeli business-
men, banks, airlines, and media outlets that were supportive of Israel. He was
connected with the Baader-Meinhof group, the German Revolutionary Cells,
and other left-wing terrorist groups, that frequently engaged in violent activities against neo-fascists, the American military, and other pro-western Muslim groups in Europe. His most notorious action occurred when he kidnapped
the representatives OPEC during their annual meeting in Vienna, Austria, in
1975, resulting in the taking of 60 hostages and the death of three individuals,
among them a member of Libya's OPEC delegation. The goal of the attack was
to assassinate the oil minister from Saudi Arabia, Shaykh Ahmad Zaki Yamani,
as well as the Iranian oil ministers from Iran, Qatar, and the United Arab Emir-
ates, who Carlos and the PFLP viewed as traitors to the Arab/Palestinian cause
for their lifting of the 1973 oil embargo. He would later escape capture by demanding a flight to the Middle East (Iraq) but ended up in Algeria where he
was released in a deal brokered by the Algerian Foreign Minister Abdalazziz
Bouteflika. His inability to assassinate the intended victims led to Wadi Haddad's ejection of Carlos from the PFLP. After becoming a "freelance" terrorist,
employed by various Middle Eastern states including Hafiz al-Assad's Syria as
well as Saddam Hussein in Iraq, Carlos was eventually captured in 1994 while
recuperating from an operation on his testicles in Sudan.[109] French Domestic
Intelligence Services (DST), in cooperation with U.S. intelligence services, captured him and later tried him for the murder of two French policemen who had
been investigating his activities in France in 1975. Carlos has been in a prison
in France since he was captured in 1994. His official prison term began in 1997.
Despite his attempts to appeal his conviction, Carlos remains imprisoned in
France. Before Usama bin Laden's campaign of terror, Carlos the Jackal was the
leftist-Arab *cause célèbre* of the West. It is to no surprise to many of his detrac-
tors that he converted to Islam after being captured by the French (or possibly
earlier) and later, with the help of his French wife and lawyer, wrote the book
L'islam Revolutionaire (Revolutionary Islam), in which he argued for the mor-
phing of leftist-communist ideals into the Islamic tradition.[110] Reminiscent of
the works of 'Ali Sharī'ati, the 'Red Shi'i' intellectual of the Iranian Revolution
of 1979, Carlos believed that Islam was the carrier of the revolutionary spirit
in world history. For Carlos, Marxism's potential for radical change has been
exhausted in its manifest form, but could realize its potentials tacitly through

109   Ibid., 195–228.
110   Ilich Ramírez Sánchez, *L'islam Revolutionaire*. Éditions du Rocher, 2003.

its translation into prophetic religion, i.e. "revolutionary Islam." In a reversal of Walter Benjamin's philosophy of translating theological potentials into historical materialist revolution, Carlos argued that religion, more succinctly *revolutionary religion*, was the proper vehicle by which a true revolution could occur. If Marxism was to survive the triumphalism of capitalism, especially after the fall of the Soviet Union, it would be through radical Islam.

Although the memory of Carlos the Jackal, the Latin American *Che Guevara*-like revolutionary of leftist and Arab causes has abated in post-9/11 America and Europe, when he was alive the fear that he created in the governments of the West were driven by the fact that he was both a westerner himself – familiar with the culture, able to move around undetected, a master of languages – and completely committed to his transcendental cause: anti-imperialism. His willingness to become a martyr was only overshadowed by his uncanny ability to escape detection and arrest, frustrating authorities as he lived to fight another day.[111] Although they completely lack the *suave* demeanor of Carlos, who indulged himself in women, drink, frivolity, embodying the mystique of an anti-capitalist James Bond, the latest western jihādis are just as committed to their vision of a Muslim world renaissance, guided by the values of Sunni Islam. However, where Carlos the Jackal, despite his unjust attacks on innocent civilians, may hold a legitimate claim to the adjective "revolutionary," ISIS and its affiliates are hardly so. Revolutions, as Carlos himself would insist, are inherently in the service of humanity in its universal form, not in the service to a particular religion, religious sect, or ethnicity. Nevertheless, Carlos created the template for the international westerner-turned-terrorist that many would-be terrorist today aspire to, even if their memory of terrorism only goes back to Usama bin Laden.

What's more important than the template of an international terrorist that was established by Carlos was his dialectical method of war. Having studied dialectical materialism in Moscow and before with his father, Carlos introduced a more dialectical way of engaging the enemy that the West has never properly prepared for, especially since it was off the traditional battlefield. The ability to adapt to the conditions in which one is fighting as opposed to

---

111   Some biographers of Carlos accuse him of being too narcissistic and vainglorious to have given his life for the cause. I find this to be an extremely deficient reading of his life. Every operation he was engaged in risked his life and could have potentially made him a martyr. His perpetual enjoyment of luxury confuses their analysis; they assume all revolutionaries are religious ascetics (or secular ascetics) who, on principle, would refuse to indulge in the "goods" of capitalism. Carlos, however, was not an ascetic, but that should not be mistaken for narcissism or weakness in believing in his cause.

having a rigid and pre-conceived "form" of warfare allowed Carlos to evade capture for years; he was always "one step ahead" of his positivist-educated enemies, already anticipating their reactions and tailoring his movements and methods to account for their deficiency. Additionally, he made the everyday landscape, the world of business, skyscrapers, restaurants, banks, etc., into a new urban battlefield for which domestic "policing" was not adequate to counteract, often using the tools of modernity more creatively and effectively than the states and corporations that invented them. The same can be said about the insurgency in Iraq after the 2003 invasion; while the United States and its allies fought a war within a "traditional" military mindset, the insurgency dialectically adapted to the Coalitions strategies and weapons until the u.s. itself, under the Army General David Petraeus, educated in the u.s. Military Academy and Princeton University, learned the dialectical skills of counter-insurgency (which was never adequately learned in the Vietnam war). After Petraeus took command of the armed forces in Iraq and enacted his own dia-lectical form of war (the "surge" of 2007), the insurgency nearly disappeared. However, the dialectical method of warfare resurfaced again outside of Iraq, this time in Syria in the form of ISIS, led by the Soviet educated Ba'ath gener-als. At the present moment, those who've retreated back into a non-dialectical form of warfare that has proven to be unable to abate their advances are en-gaging ISIS. While I write this book, ISIS continues to gain territory despite the heavy bombing of the United States, United Kingdom, Australia, and the push-back by the Kurdish Peshmerga. Only the Russian forces, led by Vladimir Putin, the Soviet educated dialectician, have been able to make substantial advances in pushing ISIS back.

There may also be an important factor as to why the United States and its core allies have failed to defeat ISIS; unlike the Israelis, who see their fight with the Palestinians as a fight for survival, and therefore the Israeli state has very little regard for any form of Palestinian life, the American administration un-der President Obama either (1) sees itself, or (2) wants to be perceived as being a nation in service to the universal (humanity, civilization, etc.), as opposed to the particular (any given nation-state, as in the case of Israel). This may prove to the weakest point in the battle against the foes of the West. The United States and its allies do not want to be perceived as being against an authentic *tajdīd* (renewal) of Islam, nor does it want to be perceived as being the killer of Muslims, which would only enforce the *West vs. Islam* framework that so many in the Muslim world already suspect of being the case. No, the West, especially the United States, wants to be perceived as the protector of Muslims, as well as the minority faiths of the Middle East. Israel makes no apologies for its particu-laristic fight against the Palestinians; it serves no *altruistic* cause, but rather is done purely out of their own national interests, and there is no equivocation on this point.

Despite its attempt to prove otherwise, the United States is seen throughout the Muslim world as being a "wolf in sheep's clothing"; in the name of the universal it pursues its own interests. And after the unprovoked attack on Iraq by President George W. Bush, in which Iraq neither had weapons of mass destruction nor ties with Usama bin Laden and the September 11th, 2001 terror attack, but was rather a preconceived plot and desire of the neo-conservatives, led by the *Project for the New American Century* (PNAC), the idea that the United States represented the will of the world, the universal good, evaporated.[112]

In light of its assault on ISIS, it is most likely that the terrorist group will attempt to counter the airstrikes of the United States and its allies by disappearing within the *everydayness* of the Arab world in Iraq, Syria and Libya – and possibly every other post-Arab Spring country – by becoming, at least in the eyes of the populace, a legitimate state by addressing the social problems of health, education, retirement, property, etc.[113] In doing so, it will become nearly impossible to distinguish between ISIS and the average Arab/Muslim in the region, and thus perpetuating and facilitating the dialectical method of war – strike and retreat into society as camouflage – that Carlos "the Jakal" perfected in his insurgency against neo-imperialism.

This melding into the populace causes sever problems for those who claim to represent the *universal* interest of mankind (the United States and its allies), as killing innocent women and while hunting ISIS will undermine their claim to be in on the side of the common good. Those that do not share that claim, and represent the *particular*, such as Putin's Russia, who wants to aid the Syrian regime against its enemies, including both ISIS and the "moderate" rebels, do not share the same problem. However, with every bomb dropped on ISIS, with every attack on the so-called "Islamic State," with every monarchial and dictatorial Arab state that joins its coalition, the more sympathy there will be for ISIS, especially if it achieves its ends: the construction of a true Islamic state that adequately addresses the needs of its people. The dialectical dilemma for the West is thus: through their constant attacks on ISIS they can unwittingly increase ISIS's legitimacy, thus making them appear more "Islamic" to

---

112   Gary Dorrien, *Imperial Designs: Neoconservativism and the New Pax Americana* (New York: Routledge, 2004), 181–221; Philippe Sands, *Lawless World: America and the Making and Breaking of Global Rules from FDR's Atlantic Charter to George W. Bush's Illegal War* (New York: Viking, 2005), 174–204.

113   As of 2015, they have already begun to print their own currency and have taken on other functions associated with a legitimate state.

more people. Another way to delegitimate the terror group must be found, and that must be through Islam itself.

Symbolic Message

Just as the terror attacks of September 11th, 2001, were not only episodes of direct violence upon America – but were also meant to send a retaliatory message about American capitalism, militarism, and empire – so too is ISIS's violence not only directed towards certain individuals, but meant to broadcast a much broader symbolic message to the West and to other Muslims. Their message is clear if one can read the symbolic nature of their actions.

ISIS's flag is rich with symbolic meaning. First, their flag is black, which recalls the color that Prophet Muhammad preferred when engaging in *jihād bil-saif* (struggle of the sword); second, the top lettering of the flag is the first part of the *Shahada* (declaration of faith), i.e. *La ilaha ill Allah* (There is no god but God), and last, the round symbol on the bottom is the *seal of the Prophet* – a rendition of Prophet Muhammad's signet ring by which he signed his official correspondence. These, in-and-of-themselves, bear no inherent violent or jihādi intention, but taken within the context of ISIS's broader ideology and worldview, these symbols take on a new and perverse meaning. ISIS's flag uses an early form of written Arabic that was rudimentary during the time of the Prophet; it lacked diacritical marks and the artistic stylization that later came to be the hallmark of the Qur'an and a much more sophisticated – and therefore "this-worldly" – Islam. The simplicity of the flag's script anchors ISIS's claim of Islamic authenticity within the framework of Muhammad's life; the message being that ISIS is a legitimate return to the *sunnah* (way) of the Prophet established in Arabia within the 7th century, as if Muhammad himself set his "seal of approval" upon their worldview and actions. Many other jihādi groups, including al-Qae'da, various mujahideen groups in the Caucasus, Islamic Jihad, al-Nusrah Front, Hamas, and even the national flag of Saudi Arabia, use the *shahada,* but it's written in intricate calligraphy (generally in *Tuluth* or *Naskh* script). Symbolically, those scripts represent a form of Islam that, while increased in worldly and artistic sophistication, have conversely lost the purity and authenticity of Islam's original simplicity; this simplicity is represented in the uncomplicated nature of the Prophet's seal and the script used on ISIS's rendition of the *shahada.* In this simplicity resides the way Islam and Muslims *ought* to be for ISIS, while the more sophisticated and artistic (and therefore less purely religious) script indicates the corruption of later Islam – an Islam concerned with the trappings of empires, administration, wealth, etc. Although it became a necessity to develop the Arabic language beyond its simple beginnings, including the use of diacritical marks to preserve the original meaning from being distorted by non-Arabic speakers, it nevertheless distanced the believers experience of Islam and the Qur'an from that of the ṣaḥābah (Prophet's companions) who experienced the Qur'an in its most purest and primal form. For ISIS, the truth of Islam resides within its purest or most undiluted form, i.e. the form it took during the life of the Prophet, and they believe it is imperative to recover this so-called purity. Thus, the flag of ISIS conveys their desire to reform Islam back to what they believe is its most genuine form – the paradigm of Islam during the time of the Prophet. Nevertheless, this *being-towards-authenticity* does not mean they wish to "return to the 7th century" as so many western analysts claim. ISIS is a fundamentalist group by nature, which means it is perfectly satisfied to employ modern means of technology in service to pre-modern beliefs. This was not the *sunnah* of the Prophet Muhammad nor of the early Muslim community. Most naively, ISIS and other fundamentalist groups believe certain achievements of modernity can be utilized for the advancement of religion, without every carefully considering the corrosive effects such an ill-advised appropriation can have. *Instrumental rationality*, the rationality of efficiency, calculative thought, quantification, and bureaucracy, has a way of infiltrating and deflating the communicative nature of religion, especially that of the Abrahamic faiths.[114] This is the very reason why so many fundamentalists within other religious traditions, including Christianity and Judaism, shun the modern world in its entirety; the technological world, which is predicated on the instrumentalization of reason – the fetishization of calculative and cold reason – brings about an undermining of non-instrumental reasoning, including religious ethics, theology, and spirituality. It is the Trojan horse within the religious community.

In the propaganda videos that ISIS released showing the beheadings of James Foley, Steven Sotloff, David Haines, and Alan Henning, the men appear to be wearing orange colored prison suits. Again, this must not be over-looked, as it is no mere coincidence. ISIS is invoking the West's suppressed and shameful memory of the many crimes it has perpetrated upon the Muslims from 2001 to the present, especially when the victims were made to wear similar garb while in American custody. Seeking a symbolic retaliation, ISIS effectively resurrects the images of Muslims (supposedly al-Qae'da members) detained in Cuba's Guantánamo Bay and Abu Ghraib prison in Baghdad, wearing orange prison suits as they were interrogated, tortured, and imprisoned for years

---

114 Jürgen Habermas, *The Theory of Communication Action: Reason and the Rationalization of Society, Vol. 1*, trans. Thomas McCarthy. Boston: Beacon Press, 1984.

without due process.[115] The orange symbolized the shame and guilt that the West bears for engaging in crimes against innocent Muslims (and supposed *Mujahideen*), as well as the United State's practice of "extraordinary rendition," by which the U.S. government would outsource the torturing of "unlawful combatants" to friendly countries who were not bound by anti-torture treaties.[116] Additionally, some of these "detainees" were moved to CIA secret detention centers, also known as "black sites," in countries that either looked the other way or were unaware of the CIA's clandestine activities. In other words, the orange suits are a reminder that ISIS's violence against James Foley, Steven Sotloff, David Haines, and Alan Henning is a *retaliatory* strike against the U.S. and other western countries' abuse, torture, and murder of Muslims, both in Bush's "war on terrorism" and Obama's "war on terrorists."[117] Consequently, it is no mistake that the ISIS members that killed these men were dressed in black; the Islamic color of armed struggle against tyranny. Orange is the historical crime; black is its revenge.

Reign of Terror: Bourgeois and Muslim

As individuals, the murdered James Foley, Steven Sotloff, David Haines, Alan Henning and Peter Kassig (Abdal-Rahman Kassig) take on a symbolic meaning that is greater than the direct violence that was perpetrated upon them. Ironically, these violent murders are akin to a pivotal moment within western history: the Bourgeois Revolution. During the anti-monarchy evolution in France, the nobility was systematically beheaded through revolutionary violence via the *guillotine*: the "cross" of Bourgeois dominance. The beheading of the nobility, including King Louis XVI and his family, was a concrete message to the rest of Europe: the age of monarchy was at an end and a new era had begun. This dialectical moment in the history of class struggle had produced its new subject and the old has been determinately negated *saecula saeculorum*.[118] This is why the young French Republic adopted a new calendar; the *calendrier révolutionnaire français* was a physical representation of the cancellation of the old order

---

115   Sands, *Lawless World*, 143–173; Mohamedou Ould Slahi, *Guantánamo Diary*, ed. Larry Siems. New York: Little, Brown and Company, 2015.

116   The practice of extraordinary rendition began with President Bill Clinton and was further developed under President George W. Bush.

117   ISIS specifically mentioned Obama's air attacks on ISIS fighters as a motivation for their execution of Foley and Sotloff.

118   'For ever and ever.' Slavoj Žižek, *In Defense of Lost Causes* (New York: Verso, 2008), 415–416.

and the birth of the new: a starting point in a new history. Nothing could have been a more graphic and compelling sight to demonstrate the end of the reign of monarchs than to see the king of a nation – once secure in his "divine right" – beheaded in front of his own "subjects." According to Ruth Scurr, in her book *Fatal Purity: Robespierre and the French Revolution,*

> News of Louis XVI's execution spread like a stain across Europe. In England Prime Minister Pitt pronounced it 'the foulest and most atrocious deed which the history of the world has yet had occasion to attest.' In Russia Catherine the Great, shocked and grieving, took to her bed and decreed six weeks' mourning for her whole court. Spain immediately recalled its ambassador. Public opinion in all these countries turned unremittingly against the Revolution. The reaction in America was more ambivalent – distant support for the embattled new republic, mingled with sorrow for its regal victim, who, in his time, had supported the colonists in their struggle to found their own modern republican government on the other side of the Atlantic. 'As Americans we regret the loss of the life of the King,' wrote the religious minister and diarist William Bentley, 'but we remember the liberties of mankind are dearer than any life whatever.'[119]

The revolutionary message was clear; gruesome beheadings were to be the future of the European monarchy if they refused to relinquish power to the new subject of history. In Paris' *Place de la Révolution,* the political component of the age of the Enlightenment began with the systematic annihilation of the monarchy in France, and to a lesser degree in the United State of America. Revolutionary terror constructed a new world, a world that was fundamentally different than the one presided over by God's divinely appointed kings. This would be a world that was determined by the masses, not by the few who confused their prerogatives with that of God's. Society, religion, politics, economics, business, and all other manners of state, civil society and family, would be fundamentally changed forever, as the beheading of King Louis XVI began the downfall of European nobility and ushered in an era of Bourgeois dominance – a change of events that not even Napoleon – the self-declared Emperor – could overturn.[120]

---

119   Ruth Scurr, *Fatal Purity: Robespierre and the French Revolution.* (New York: Metropolitan Books, 2006), 257.

120   See Žižek's discussion of "revolutionary terror" or "divine violence" in *Robespierre: Virtue and Terror* (New York: Verso, 2007), vii–xxxix.

In the same vein as the French Revolutionaries, albeit for very different purposes, ISIS's beheading of Foley, Sotloff, Haines, Henning and Kassig was a message to the West: the era when the United States and its allies feel free to interfere in the affairs of the Muslims is at an end. However, this time it is religion that strikes back at secular modernity, against the first form of secular Enlightenment, the Bourgeois, as it had already perceived itself to have destroyed the second secular Enlightenment (Marxism) in Afghanistan (Soviet-Afghan war of 1980–1988) which precipitated the fall of the Soviet Union. Symbolically, the victims represented not a President, a congress, or a parliament, but an age; their killing ushered in what they hopeds was the beginning of the historical end of Euro-American dominance in the world, especially in the *dar al-Islam*. From their perspective, the empire of America must cede itself to a new age of resurgent religion. Yet, just as the beheading of King Louis XVI didn't automatically bring about the death of monarchy in all of Europe, it did illuminate a trajectory of history that could not be stopped. ISIS hopes for the same. In this sense, ISIS is making clear that they are the new agent of history in the world and they have the capacity to bend history towards their goals. History, they believe, is identical with their ideology and can be guided by their "revolutionary" terror, which is legitimated by the supreme goal of reestablishing a Syrian-Iraqi (Umayyad-Abbasid) Sunni caliphate and Islamic dominance over the Muslim world.[121] Although their actions may not ultimately witness their desired effect, their symbolic language is clear: imperial America's power to create the world in its own image no longer functions in the heart of the Muslim world. As such, they believe that both history and the divine are on their side. Unfortunately, James Foley, Steven Sotloff, David Haines, Alan Henning, and Peter Kassig who were all gruesomely beheaded by ISIS, were the first sacrifices (both concrete and symbolic) to this new era of jihādist barbarism. Nevertheless, at least for Hegel, the conditions that allowed for an "Islamic Empire" in which the Muslims were the dominant force in world history has passed; new conditions in history do not allow us to return to a paradigm that could only have existed in the past.[122] In the end, ISIS will find that it is the American and the Slavic world that is now in the forefront of the historical process and there is no way resurrect that which was only possible in another age.[123]

---

121   In no way do I think ISIS is revolutionary, but rather blend revolutionary-like violence with deeply flawed counter-revolutionary goals.

122   Hegel, *Philosophy of History*, 355–359.

123   Hitler made this same mistake; he believed he could resurrect a German empire in a time where European imperialism was coming to an end. Had he understood Hegel's

The Perverse Dialectic of Apology

In the context of ISIS's peculiar form of barbarism, a familiar phenomenon appears: all crimes committed by Muslim[s] are accompanied by the western world's demand for an apology by Muslim authorities, clerics, and the general population alike. Muslims are told they have to apologize for the suicide bombings, the beheadings, the insurgencies, and every attack on civilians that are done by others who happen to share the same faith, even if they express and/or practice that faith in starkly different ways. Consequently, a feeling of remorse, born out of a mistaken sense of collective guilt tacitly compels many Muslims to not only *condemn* act of terror – which is appropriate – but also to apologize for their fellow religious believers, as if the *ummah* bears the burden of collective *tauba* (repentance) or *metanoia* (μετάνοια – "change of mind") for the acts of all members of its community.[124] The question becomes, are these public acts of apology (1) appropriate, (2) helpful, and (3) defendable? Do they express sincere but ultimately misguided *remorse* for the violent act or would it be more appropriate if the global Muslim ummah expressed a sincere form of *sympathy* – "the act of suffering with" – instead? The question must be asked, *wouldn't Muslims have to first agree with ISIS and other forms of terrorism perpetrated by fellow Muslims and thus bear some of the responsibility for the barbarism in order to have a "change of mind," i.e. metanoia?* Or, like Horkheimer and Adorno suggested, are they partially responsible simply because they share space within the same "organized" religion?[125]

There is a piece of "common sense" (perverse ideology) in the United States that is played out within mainstream media nearly every night: when a crime is perpetrated by an African American, their *race* is to blame; when a crime was done by a Caucasian American, their *mental stability* is to blame; when a crime was done by a Muslim, their *religion* is to blame. This apothegm secretly

---

philosophy of history, he would have known that the historical conditions that allowed Europe to engage in empire making was already waning.

124 For a condemnation of ISIS and its activities that actually has both intellectual weight and authenticity, see the *Open Letter* sent to Abu Bakr al-Baghdadi by 126 Muslim scholars in the appendix. Furthermore, see Chapter 7 for a discussion of this Open Letter.

125 Speaking of religions and political philosophies in the *Dialectic of Enlightenment,* Horkheimer and Adorno write 'in this way, Christianity, idealism, and materialism, which in themselves contain truth, also bear guilt for the villainies committed in their name. In proclaiming power – even a benign power – they became themselves highly organized historical powers, and as such played their bloody role in the real history of the human species: as instruments of organization.' Horkheimer and Adorno, *The Dialectic of Enlightenment,* 186.

expresses the ideological core of America's attitude towards violence and its perpetrators: race, mental stability, and religion are all sources of irrationality and unacceptable behavior in light of the "accepted norms" of American civil society. Most concretely, it demonstrates our inability or unwillingness to abandon the *ready-at-hand* identifiable characteristics of "otherness" that American society still maintains precisely because those characteristics provide a convenient explanation for the apparently unexplainable – how could anyone transverse the "rational" norms of American democratic and capitalist culture? From an ideological perspective, when a nation is closely identified with the will of God, it becomes sacrilegious and politically heretical to oppose its "national destiny." Yet, many do oppose the prevailing ideology of the most powerful nation in the world. Why? And why specifically through the lenses of religion?

Although violence done in the name of religion (or against religion) has abated in the modern period, it is not uncommon within countries that are wrestling with cultural, political, and economic crises, including areas of the Middle East, the Indian sub-continent, Africa, *and* Europe. However, when certain actors from particular religions engage in religiously inspired violence, very rarely are their religious compatriots asked to burden themselves with the perpetrator's guilt and expand it to the whole. It is understood that individuals bear the responsibility for their own actions; that no one can alleviate the guilt of the actor by donning their "sins"; that the individual must assume full responsibility for their transgressions even if they were inspired by a religion or had felt that they acted in service to their religion. Religions are not put on trial, individuals are – religions lacks a body to incarcerate and have no soul to damn, even if they are sometimes sources of motivation for violence and terror. However, in the international public sphere, the grand inquisitor not only demands justice for the wronged by the perpetrator, but also demands the members of the religious community *apologize* for the transgressions of the one. Today, Islam may be the only religion that stands condemned within in the international public sphere for the actions of some of its members.

However, distancing average Muslims from the heinous acts of murder, barbarity, and destruction may temporarily put worried non-Muslims at ease, and therefore diminish the possibility of an Islamophobic backlash. Muslims often feel compelled to demonstrate that not all believers express their faith through violence, not all believe *jihād* is an act of *totalen krieg* (total war) against non-Muslims and minority sects, and that not all Muslims sanctify the bloody acts of the few. Indeed, from the perspective of humanistic solidarity, public condemnations of barbarity, whether perpetrated by Muslims or others, should be done; a united front of Muslims and non-Muslims against civilization's devolution into a new *Golgotha* should be expressed most force-fully. Indeed, an *inverse apologia* is an attitude more congruent with revolutionary Islam as well as the Critical Theory of Religion as expressed by the Frankfurt School; one should not simply *condemn* the act of terror, but *live in* sympathy, empathy and solidarity with the victims of religious terror regardless of sectarian considerations and regardless if the act of terror emanated from within one's own religious, national, or ethnic community. Yet, do certain Muslims' compulsive need to apologize for the violence of other Muslims somehow not perversely express to others – especially miso-Islamists who already suspect all Muslims to be terrorists – that all of the *ummah* are tacitly guilty for the crimes? Does not the apology somehow unjustly disperse some of the guilt upon the innocent? Does not the act of seeking forgiveness – the goal of apology – betray not only a misplaced blame but also a misplaced guilt?

In 1947, the German philosopher Karl Jaspers published his book *Die Schuldfrage* (The Question of Debt), exploring the issue of guilt and debt of the Germans as a whole for what was done to Europe in general and the Jews in particular during WWII. Jaspers rejected the idea of collective guilt, understanding that the individual who committed the crime cannot dilute their crime by passing guilt onto others, nor can others willfully appropriate the guilt of the criminal. He states,

> It is nonsensical, however, to charge a whole people with a crime. The criminal is always only an individual... It is nonsensical, too, to lay moral guilt to a people as a whole. There is no such thing as a national character extending to every single member of a nation... Morally one can judge the individual only, never a group... One cannot make an individual out of a people. A people cannot perish heroically, cannot be a criminal, cannot act morally or immorally; only its individuals can do so. A people as a whole can be neither guilty nor innocent, neither in the criminal nor in the political... nor in the moral.[126]

For Jaspers, to collectivize the guilt of the individual was to engage in what Adorno deemed "identity thought"; to collapse the multiplicity, the various, the particularity of each and every individual into a conceptual singularity. In the case of Islam, all 1.6 billion Muslims become the singular "the Muslim," and in this artificial singularity it bears the responsibility of all crimes that its members perpetrate, as if the sin of the individual infects the whole. With the

---

126 Karl Jaspers, *The Question of German Guilt,* trans. E.B. Ashton (New York: Fordham University Press, 2000), 34–35.

destruction of the European Jews in mind, Jaspers writes, 'for centuries this mentality has fostered hatred among nations and communities... it has been most viciously applied and drilled into the heads... It was as though there no longer were human beings, just those collective groups.'[127] For Jaspers, as well as many other critical voices who've been stigmatized by the transgression of others, this form of collective guilt – or guilt by association – has no merit, and misguided collective apologies mend no wounds, but only creates more victims. However, the most dangerous aspect of this collective guilt is that it creates the conditions for collective violence. Just as the individual perpetrator's guilt warrants punishment by a legitimate system of justice, so too does the collective if the guilt is dispersed. It is too easy, as Jaspers reminds us, to replace the individual with the guilty collective, which has only led to mass murder and genocide in the past. Yet for Jaspers, the absolution of collective guilt is not the end of the story; there is the matter of collective *liability* to consider. Again, in light of the catastrophe of the Third Reich, he writes,

> Every German is made to share the blame for the crimes committed in the name of the Reich. *We are collectively liable.* The question is in what sense each of us must feel co-responsible. Certainly in the political sense of the joint liability of all citizens for acts committed by their state – but for that reason not necessarily also in the moral sense of actual or intellectual participation in crimes. Are we Germans to be held liable for outrages which Germans inflicted on us, or from which we were saved as by a miracle? Yes – inasmuch as we let such a régime rise among us. No – insofar as many of us in our deepest hearts opposed all this evil and have no morally guilty acts or inner motivations to admit. To hold liable does not mean to hold morally guilty.[128]

For Jaspers, the collective liability for the rise of the Third Reich lies in Germany's inability and/or unwillingness to prevent, arrest, and/or destroy fascism in its infancy, to allow it to fester, and ultimately to allow it to gain control over the society. For Jaspers, too many good Germans retreated into their own private space in order to survive the fascist takeover of the state. They refused to publicly oppose fascism and because of their inaction, millions, including Germans, were killed. In the face of the Nazi's early crimes, only the Communists – and some Christians – actively opposed them; nearly

---

127   Jaspers, *German Guilt,* 35.
128   Ibid.

all other peoples of good will remained silent or acquiesced.[129] Yet, is the same true for the Muslims? Is there a form of fascism that has grown within the *dar al-Islam* that the Muslims are afraid of opposing? Do they bear collective liability if not collective guilt for the crimes of ISIS and other terrorists groups? It is clear that ISIS was not a product of a state – like the Taliban, which was created by ISI (Pakistani Intelligence Service) – but rather the absence of an Islamic alternative to the secular-dictatorial and monarchial states in the Middle East. Additionally, ISIS brutally imposed its rule upon its subjects without their democratic deliberation. In other words, it was established against the will of the populace (for the most part) and was not a product of a democratic religio-political will-formation. In the case of other terrorist organizations such as al-Qae'da, who do not swear any allegiance to any particular state, nor have they attempted to create one, the guilt of their heinous crimes cannot be made the guilt of those who have absolutely no input upon their activities. For Jaspers, the Germans may bear a certain amount of liability for fascism precisely because they allowed it to occur within their state – through parliamentary maneuvers, by giving fascism freedom to operate within the Weimar republic, which was the pre-condition for fascism's growth in the political realm. In light of this, he believes that a certain degree of liability rests with the *demos*. However, this is certainly not the same dynamic one finds amidst the Muslim world; Muslims have rarely had any democratic input in what regimes rule them for centuries, including ISIS.

Hypocritical Apologetics and the Recovery of the Prophetic

2011 saw one of the worst massacres in Europe since WWII; Anders Behring Breivik, a 32 years old right-wing Norwegian-Christian extremist, murdered 77 individuals in a bombing in Oslo and a shooting rampage on Utøya Island. Although the "mental stability" defense was attempted, claiming that he was a paranoid schizophrenic, it was clear from Breivik's manifesto *2083: A European Declaration of Independence* that he simply chose sides in what he believed was Christian Europe's need to defend itself and its values against the onslaught of the Muslims and "cultural Marxists." Although he wasn't shy

---

129 Certainly there are many exceptions, most important among them are the Protestant *Bekennende Kirche* (Confessing Church), *die Weiße Rose* (The White Rose, a group of students and professors who opposed Hitler – the most famous being Sophie and Hans Scholl), and many conservative Catholic groups, among them Father Rudolphi. See Rudolf J. Siebert, *Georg W. Rudolphi's Prophetische Politische Theologie*. Frankfurt a/m: Haag + Herchen.

about expressing his supposed devotion to Christianity, no voices of protest demanded that the rest of the Christian world (whatever that is today) apologize for his vicious attack. Although he claimed to be motivated by the defense of *Christendom* (Christ's domain), "Christendom" felt no need to apologize for what their religion "supposedly" created in Breivik; it was tacitly understood that his actions, although congruent with similar acts of terror against innocents perpetrated by the Church throughout its history, were not a reflection of the Gospels, the life of Jesus of Nazareth, nor the Church as it stands today. The sheer absence of apology in the face of mass murder demonstrates two very important insights. First, that a defense of Christendom today seems anachronistic in light of our secular society. Christianity need not be apologized for because Christianity as a social power is nearly non-existent. "Christendom" is a concept of the past, a relic of a time-gone-by, a figment of Breivek's imagination, as it has no real existence today in the minds of those supposedly within Christendom. As such it lacks agency and those who would fight for its cause appear to be anachronistic at best. In Europe, Christianity is no longer understood to be a substantive pre-political social or identity adhesive in the modern post-secular society, but rather a semblance of collectivity that remain recalcitrant despite it being obsolete (so the secularists say). Second, the West has become so individualized that it would never occur to most to think that they share in the blame of the crimes of another, even when those crimes were born out of the society that was created by its collective culture. The concept of the individual is so absolute, we no longer think in terms of our own collective guilt or even, as Jaspers would point out, our own collective liability. The radical individualism of modern capitalism, which began with Martin Luther's form of spiritual individualism, and was introduced into politics through the Bourgeois revolution, now grants no legitimacy to substantive social collectivity. It negates any possibility of thinking in terms of collective guilt or liability.

As is often pointed out through many critical voices, the Israeli state is responsible for some of the worst human right abuses in the modern era. Under state guidance (or willful neglect), Jewish settlers frequently – almost daily – attacks Palestinians, the state confiscates the Palestinian lands, robs them of their possessions, randomly fires their weapons at Palestinian protesters (who are often children), restricts access to water and natural resources, bulldozes their homes, and engages in other abhorrent practices that have been banned by international law. In light of the ongoing crimes, there is too often a deafening silence from the international public sphere. Ironically, never is the western Jewish community asked to apologize for the sins of their brethren in Israel in any meaningful way. Is this not precisely because they are not seen to be responsible for those crimes?[130] Not even when Rachel Corrie, a young American peace activist, was intentionally run over by an Israeli bulldozer in 2003, and was killed without mercy, was the Jewish community collectively asked for an apology for murdering an American civilian who posed no threat – unless one can think of "peace" as being threatening. Even though many Israelis expressed their outrage over her murder, an apology from the whole of the Jewish community was never called for, and rightly so. However, perversity arose: the Palestinians and Rachel Corrie were overwhelmingly blamed for their own victimization both in the western and Israeli press.[131] Nevertheless, when misguided Muslims in the West attack Jews and synagogues to express their outrage against Israel's aggression against Palestinians, these acts are taken as example of how Islam itself is inherently anti-Semitic, as opposed to seeing it for what it is: a criminal act of individuals of a certain faith community.

When Hindu nationalist parties, who see no future for Muslims in India, attack Muslims, their mosques and their families, does the world cry out for apologies from all Hindus? When secular right-wing anti-immigrant parties in Europe attack Muslims on the streets, does the public sphere cry for apologies from other secular communities? Clearly it does not. Yet, when a Muslims commits a heinous act of aggression, the Muslim community, from the United States to Europe, from the Middle East to Indonesia, is expected to apologize for a crime they did not commit, (and often were the victim of). However, a fatigue has set in within the Muslim community; many voices are exclaiming that they can no longer apologize for those who speak in their name but violate the most basic tenets of their faith. Although often associated with Wahhabi Islam, a *takfīri* (excommunication) impulse is beginning to emerge among Muslims who cannot identify with the brutality of some of their co-religionists.

The inner-contradiction that reveals the perverse dialect within the apology is thus: each apology further ingrains the notion that Muslims are all equally to blame for any given crime by a Muslim. With each expression of public remorse, the Muslim community inappropriately acquires and legitimates collective guilt, even if the victim of the terror is Muslim. For many, including critic of Islam such as Geert Wilders of the Netherlands, the unifying factor in all

---

130   The notable exception to this can be found in the anti-Semitic attacks on Jews in Europe and the U.S. However, this is usually the act of those who adhere to anti-Semitic sentiments regardless of the actions of particular Jews and or Israel. In other words, they are usually neo-Nazis who are pathologically against the Jews regardless of what happens in Palestine/Israel.

131   See Rachel Corrie, *Let Me Stand Alone: The Journals of Rachel Corrie.* New York: W.W. Norton & Co., 2008.

crimes made by Muslims is Islam itself. By sharing a faith – that he believes is constitutionally barbaric – all Muslims bear the guilt of their criminal minority. It is believed that when a Muslim proves to be a criminal, it is because they are faithful to the Qur'an and the example of the Prophet. When they are ecumenical, peace loving, law abiding and open for modernity, they are on the boarders of apostasy. What Wilders and others would prefer is that the Muslim community reconciles itself to its *evil* religion so that the truth about Islam would cease to be clouded by the claim that Islam is a "religion of peace," which, in their view, is a pernicious lie. This type of thinking strikes the scholar of Islam, Daniel A. Madigan, as being quite peculiar as it denies the Muslims the right to interpret their sacred texts and traditions in a more ecumenical and peaceful way. Additionally, the outsiders' interpretation of the sacred text, which privileges the "medieval voices" from the Islamic past, is an attempt to 'deny any possibility to change [the meaning] and [to engage in] dialogue.'[132] Do critics like Wilders really prefer that the Muslim world interpret their sacred texts more violently as opposed to strengthening the claims of those Muslims who see peacefulness as a supreme value emanating from within those same texts? If so, why? Who benefits from such a violent hermeneutics? Does the Muslim who sees solidarity with non-Muslims behind every verse in the Qur'an have to apologize for the crimes of those who interpret the text through a binary "us vs. them," especially if the latter is the preferred interpretation for anti-Islamic voices? We have to ask what motivates those non-Muslim critics who diminish the ecumenical voices of Islam over the violent and barbaric. What is their agenda and why are they invested not in reconciliation between peoples but increased antagonisms?

By Islamic standards of justice, unjustified killing, i.e. murder, and especially mass murder, is a grievous enough crime as to consign someone to *jahannam* (hell) for eternity. Yet many Muslims inadvertently take on the guilt of the mass murderer when they engage in collective apologies for crimes they did not do. The more the ummah apologizes for the crimes they are not guilty of, the more it draws itself into the guilt of the damned. In other words, the more the Muslim ummah apologizes for the terroristic actions of the few, the more it bears the burden of guilt for those actions, and thus the more liable it becomes. Where it was innocent, it becomes guilty; it stands condemned even though it is free of blame.

Believing that religious authorities have some influence over their adherents, many in the West demand Islamic institutions apologize and condemn

---

132   Daniel A. Madigan, "Muslim-Christian Dialogue in Difficult Times" in *Catholicism and Interreligious Dialogue,* ed. James L. Heft (New York: Oxford University Press, 2012), 63.

all terrorist acts. These demands from the various "authorities" in the Islamic world are also a misguided proposition. In this matter, it does the critical
analyst well to remember an important distinction developed by Hegel: the
distinction between "objective" and "subjective" religion. In his Tübingen Essay, written in the mid 1790's, Hegel claims there are two forms of religion, the
first being the "objective." This form, which he associates with theology, i.e.
the systematic construction of religious thoughts, institutions, and authorities, remains in the realm of the abstract for the believer. It is often outside
the world of the believer and they retain a certain level of reservation when
investing themselves within the objective. As it is "doctrine and dogma," it is
outside the purview of the average believer.[133] This form of religion is codified
and institutionalized; it is priestly and represents an outside bureaucratic authority. The average believer's religiosity often remains un-affected by official
doctrine, which proves to be incapable of penetrating the core of the believer's
religious being. In this way, the believer remains secure within his "subjective"
form of religion, which Hegel called *Volksreligion* (religion of the people).[134]
Their religiosity is not a matter of official form but of live experiences, feelings,
and sentiments. Subjective thoughts take on a religious legitimacy – they become their true religious authority despite the fact that their views may be
heterodox from the standpoint of the official tradition. Hegel states that 'everything depends on subjective religion; this is what has inherent and true worth.
Let the theologian squabble all they like over what belongs to objective religion, over its dogmas and their precise determination.'[135] With this insight in
mind, the demand for apologies from the "objective," i.e. Islamic institutions,
for the crimes of the "subjective," i.e. the individual believer, reveals itself as being impotent. The objective authorities can no more harness control over the
individual believer's subjective religiosity as can the state. The religious subjectivity of the individual is the authoritative core that motivates, legitimates,
and justifies his actions, including those actions that to many seem to be terroristic. Although the objective form of religion may condemn such actions
via official dogmas, it is the wrong standard of judgment for the believer's own
subjective religious positions and as such gains no influence on the believer.
Condemnations of the crimes may alleviate the collective suspicion of the objective religious tradition, but it will not help alleviate the tendency towards

---

133   Frederick Beiser, *Hegel* (New York: Routledge, 2005), 127–128.
134   *Volksreligion* was often times called "riff raff" religion by Islamic scholars such as Imam
      al-Ghazzali, especially in his book *Ihya al-ulum al-Din* (Revival of Religious Sciences).
135   Ibid., 128.

violence residing within the subjectively constructed religious worldview of the believer.

From the perspective of the Frankfurt School's critical theory of religion, solidarity with the suffering, remembrance of the victims, and the enactment of what Walter Benjamin described as our *weak messianic power* to bring about a more reconciled future-society is a more appropriate stance to take in the face of religiously-inspired terror.[136] Where the ummah bears collective guilt is when it collectively forgets about past suffering and fails to stop future suffering. If it collectively wants to alleviate this metaphysical guilt, it cannot do it by constantly apologizing for the actions of the guilty few, but it must rather live in solidarity with the suffering of the innocent regardless of their creed. *Solidaristic fitnah*, or a division within the ummah in the name of the suffering (and with the suffering), is the only just position to take in light of *terroristic fitnah*, which already divides the ummah among the suffering, broken, and terrorized against those who create suffering, break the body and spirit, and terrorize the populace.[137] In other words, it is only by *being-with* all victims of terror (in the name of Islam) that Muslims can affectively fight against the fitnah of terrorists. Muslims must always remain on the side of the innocent victims of history, never the cruel victors. Most dialectically, the call for fitnah amongst the Muslims is conversely a call for solidarity amongst the Muslims against oppression and terrorism, as it congeals the prophetic within Islam in the name of those who suffer at the hands of the brutal – those who have left the prophetic way-of-being in search of power, prestige, and comfort. Whenever Islam's inherent negativity, its *adversus mundi*, is perverted in such a way that it legitimates the brutality of a state, or *faux-state* as in ISIS, it has lost its essential prophetic core and is, for all intents and purposes, no longer Islamic, but just a shallow surface expression of Islam: an *ideology*, i.e. false consciousness. As long as it remains in opposition to all forms of oppression, brutality, and barbarity, including that of other Muslims, it embodies the *ruh Muhammad* (spirit of Muhammad); when that is abandoned, when it loses its *longing for the totally other than the world as it is*, it becomes more important than ever for Muslims to live with the victims of this "untrue" Islam – to witness and

---

136   It is interesting to note that Horkheimer did not believe in Benjamin's 'weak messianic power' thesis. He pessimistically believed the dead are dead and nothing the living do can redeem them of their past suffering. See John Abromeit, *Max Horkheimer and the Foundations of the Frankfurt School* (New York: Cambridge University Press, 2013), 230–231.

137   *Fitnah* is Arabic for "division," as in a division amongst a single group or collective.

confess on behalf of the prophetic and give shelter and aid to the vulnerable, abused, and hunted. The *weak* but still *messianic* power within the community is dependent on the Muslims identifying not with the victors of history, but with its victims, not the predators but the prey. It is only within such a relationship that Muslims are capable of wrestling history out of the hands of the barbaric and deliver it to a more-reconciled future state of existence.

CHAPTER 7

The Globalized Post-Secular Society and the Future of Islam

From the West to the Rest

For Habermas, the discussion concerning post-secularity is one that is squarely situated within the European and North American context, as it is the West that has been thoroughly secularized in most aspects of its society. However, with the advent of globalization, especially in the form of aggressive neo-liberalism, secularity has become increasingly normative within civil society and the state throughout the world, leading the critical observer to note that the rest of the World is now going through similar traumatic experiences that the West went through in the past couple centuries. We must now come to realize that there is a *globalized* post-secular condition, where religious societies remain within an increasing globalized secularity. These societies, especially those within the heart of the Muslim world, only a few centuries ago were predominately guided by the dictates of religion, religious institutions, and religiously rooted authorities, and could hardly have fathomed living within a society that was devoid of the guidance of the Qur'an and Sharī'ah. However, the colonial situation brought to many of these countries a new form of government, one that was tangentially – or only culturally – associated with religion but would later be steered on the basis of secular power and its way-of-being, especially instrumental rationality. These colonial powers often masked their racist-imperialism within the shroud of altruism; it was their duty to "civilize" those darker skinned people who have yet to discover the benefits of western society. The Enlightenment, as an "accomplishment solely of the West," produced an infectious arrogance that alienated many Muslims who resented their conquerors' claims of superiority. To their humiliation, the colonies not only learned secular sciences, philosophy, autonomous art, etc., but also a lesson in power and violence, as the *will-towards-freedom* of the victims of colonialism was suppressed under the rather un-Enlightened colonial boot of systematic oppression. However, as colonialism retreated into the dustbin of history throughout the 20th century at the hands of liberation struggles from Africa, the Middle East, and Asia, the secular and capitalist structures of political-economy often remained intact and served as the basis by which many newly liberated peoples constructed their own independence.[1] This can be clearly seen in places like India and Pakistan, where the remnants of British colonial rule can still be witnessed in the functioning of their administration of justice, parliament, and economic system. From traditional economics to capitalism; from religious laws to secular democratic governance; from Sharī'ah law to English Common Law, the ghosts of colonialism remains deeply imbedded within the framework of the post-colonial society. Additionally, the universal laws that have been established by the United Nations and other bodies of international governance have been introduced into the constitutions and legal systems of former colonial countries, because of which they have had to modify their own legal systems, often based in religion or religious sentiments, to accommodate for international norms (which are clearly articulated in western Enlightenment language).

In addition to this reality, former colonial states, some of who have been able to create a fairly vibrant synthesis of colonial era laws and customs with their own indigenous culture and legal norms – while many other have not had the opportunity to do so due to western interference – have had to absorb the onslaught of secular modernity while still on the shaky political-economic grounds left by colonialism. Neo-colonialism, via globalized neo-liberalism, has arrived even before the ghosts of colonialism have been exorcised. Not having fully recovered from their European occupation and exploitation, these traditional societies have become saturated with the latest version of European and American imperialism: aggressive globalized secular capitalism – this time under the camouflage of "free-trade." Once again the southern hemisphere, the "third world," and the darker segments of the global population, have found themselves ensnared in the trap of a system not of their own design or making, nor does it have their economic interests at heart. Nevertheless, they are forced to participate within the this system or accept a pariah state of international existence, as for example, socialist Cuba, who has paid a high price for their recalcitrance in the face of American aggression and for their refusal to be integrated into the neo-liberal economic system. With only a few

---

1   Evidence for this claim can be witnessed in how many former colonies attempted to overcome their colonial-capitalist past by attempting to bring about a socialist state. This is true for many of the colonies in Africa, Latin America and South East Asia. Capitalism was associated with colonialism and therefore it was thought that it must be removed in order for a more just and equal society to blossom within the post-colonial situation. Unfortunately, most of these experiments in socialism failed or dried up after the fall of their sponsor, the Soviet Union.

exceptions, participation in the capitalist system is either a voluntary surren-der or a forced integration.[2]

As stated above, this produces the condition where nations and cultures – while in the process of rethinking and retooling their own religious and cultur-al resources so that they could provide a basis for a stabilized and functioning state within the modern world – were *recolonized* by a power that is even more insidious than direct colonialism, as it masquerades as a force for good, for lib-eration, and emancipation, as opposed to historic colonialism, whose brutality was often on full display. In this sense, the world, being the stage for globalized neo-liberalism, is increasingly becoming more secularized as the culture of big business, technology, commercialization, commodification, i.e. international corporate capitalism, becomes increasingly normative. Traditional religious life withers and is replaced by the new religion of commodities, exchange and the idolatry of money. As Marx already understood, wherever the system of bourgeois capitalism goes, it destroys the native culture, it undermines the tra-ditional view of the world, it infects the family with the values of civil society, and it transforms 'all that is holy [into] profane.'[3] Because of this, traditional societies, especially in the *dar-al-Islam,* increasingly find themselves in a world that no longer speaks to the values associated with religious adherence, the spiritual life, and the guidance found within sacred traditions, personalities, and texts. In other words, religion itself has become alienated within a secular-ized global lifeworld; it no longer sees itself in the world it once molded; it no longer sees itself in itself, as religion itself has been reshaped and deformed by a secular world and its commodification of the lifeworld; it no longer sees itself in nature, as the natural world has been disenchanted and sacredness has evaporated from the environment; and it no longer sees itself within its "believers," for even they have become thoroughly secularized despite their surface adherence or their commitment to identity politics. Just as in the West, where religion is forcibly removed from being the dominant force within polity, economics, and culture, and turned into a private affair that few take seriously, the Muslim world has watched – especially since the beginning of the 20th century – as this same *weltlichen geist* (secular spirit) quickly re-placed religion in the daily life of the Muslim. In some areas this process has moved fairly slowly, such as in many of the Persian Gulf States, where others it was a enforced act of government, such as Mustafa Kamal Pasha (Attatürk)'s brutal secularization and westernization of Turkey – often called "Attatürk's

---

2   John Perkins, *Confessions of an Economic Hitman.* New York: Plume, 2004.
3   Karl Marx, "Manifesto of the Communist Party" in the *Marx-Engels Reader,* 476.

Reforms" or *Attatürk Devrimleri* – after the collapse of the Ottoman caliphate post-WWI.

However, against the classical secularization theorists, religion has not totally disappeared even as these nations have increasingly secularized, industrialized, and capitalized.[4] On the contrary, the opposite phenomenon is true; the *dialectic of secularization* has also appeared in the Muslim world; as secularization of the lifeworld has continued to expand, in equal proportion, so too has the existential crisis-conditions it creates. These "soulless" and "heartless" conditions beckon for a return to religion as a way of overcoming the reduction of the world to material acquisition as a comprehensive doctrine or way-of-being-in-the-world.[5] As secular capitalism exports its spiritual vacuousness into the Muslim world, creating a society of "having" as opposed to a society of "being" rooted within a religious worldview, Muslims have increasingly turned towards religion as a way of fixing that which capitalism broke: the human spirit and the spirit of *'asabiyya* (solidarity). In other words, the more secularization penetrates into the *dar-al-Islam*, the more many Muslims retreat into their religion as a way of opposing this new form of colonization.

There is another factor that must be understood: because of the nature of Islam, which has often attempted to reconcile its theology and metaphysics with the natural sciences, Aristotle with Muhammad, reason with revelation, the metaphysical basis of the Islamic worldview was never undermined thoroughly by western positivism and empirical sciences. Consequently, the secularization process, being a natural outcome of the diminishment of Christianity in the West – which resulted from its metaphysical deterioration in light of natural sciences, positivism, etc. – encounters a religious society that is still deeply rooted within its own faith. In other words, the necessary cracks within religion and metaphysics, by which modern doubt penetrates, are not present within the Muslim community at the level that they were in Christendom at the beginning of the Enlightenment. The Christian Church fought rearguard struggles against science for centuries in Europe, which produces significant fractures in the faith of its adherents. Whereas in the Muslim world, science was integrated within religion from the beginning and the natural sciences in particular where seen as religious disciplines themselves. Science was a religious endeavor in the Muslim world, as it corresponded to the idea of God's holistic creation – to research nature was to research the divine and its creation; to contemplate the natural world was to fulfill Allah's divine command

---

4 Habermas, *Europe: The Faltering Project*, 60.
5 Karl Marx, "Contribution to the Critique of Hegel's Philosophy of Right: Introduction," in the *Marx-Engels Reader*, 54.

to "ponder" his creation.[6] Therefore, "secular science" – science strictly outside the bounds of religion and metaphysics – is not a phenomenon that ever truly exists in the Muslim world.[7] What this demonstrates is that even though the colonial powers saturated the Muslim world with their secular (and later bourgeois) worldviews, the neo-colonial expansion of capitalism into the Muslim world is not finding a world sufficiently fractured in its religion, even if it is fractured in its polity. Religion, because it is one of the few social phenomena that are still relatively intact throughout the Muslim world, despite secularization and capitalist atomization, has become the main motivation and vehicle for the opposition to the secular neo-liberalization of the Muslim world. Notice, it is not the state that resists neo-liberalism in the Muslim world, it is not the economics systems, it is not the majority of western-oriented intellectual elites, it is the religious communities – both those in authority and laity – that voice their opposition to the globalization of secular capitalism. Yet, lest we descend into some form of religiously inspired triumphalism, we have to be very cognizant of not only the great determination of neo-liberalism to gain a strong foothold in the traditional Muslim world, but its very ability to do so, and the fact that it has *already* done so to a large degree. Traditional Islam and religiously rooted thought – post-Islamo-Marxism ala ʿAli Sharīʿati – is the only major countervailing force against neo-colonial capitalism in the Muslim world.

Because of the continual integrity of religious belief, today, many Muslims in the traditional Muslim-majority countries find themselves in a situation that appears to be similar to the Muslims of Europe and North America; they are an anachronistic religious presence within an increasingly materialistic and religionless world. Because of this, just as Muslim in Europe have to find a way to articulate their ultimate concerns, their religious norms, their protests, and their ethical and moral sensibilities in a language that is "publicly accessible" to all members of the society, Muslims now within the *dar-al-Islam*

---

6   In Sūrat al-Baqarah, 2:164, Allah says, "behold! In the creation of the heavens and the earth; in the changing of the night and day; in the ships that sail through the ocean for mankind's benefit; in the rain sent down by Allah from the skies and the life that he gives to the dead earth; in the various animals that he spreads throughout the world; in the changing winds, and the clouds that follow like slaves the sky and earth; here indeed are signs for those who are wise." (My translation). Indeed, the command to reflect, ponder, and study the creation of Allah is replete throughout the Qur'an.

7   Most Muslims certainly deny the validity of "scientism," an alternative ideological worldview that attempts to supplant religion and metaphysics with the findings of science. For Muslims, the divine is always behind that which science takes as its subject, but the scientific method is seen as ultimately deficient as it cannot account for that which is outside of the physical.

have also to find a way of (1) remaining true to their Islamic identity, while (2) fully integrating within the global community that is increasingly secular, lest they become a pariah state. The post-secular conditions of Europe and North America are increasingly becoming the post-secular condition of the world. Yet, the common language system that allows members of different societies to speak to each other via mutual-recognition and mutual-respect has not been adequately developed. Indeed, the opposite is more true; the most vocal and present response to the globalized post-secular condition has been the reactionary rejection of it, i.e. Muslim fundamentalism, extremism, and terrorism, on the one hand, and on the other hand the international struggle for supremacy by western powers that undermine the idea of the "world community," which is fostered in corporative international institutions like the United Nations. It is not the case that all Muslim have responded through violence against the pervasive secularity that penetrates the lifeworld via the expansion of neo-liberalism, but those voices who have attempted to engage in a robust dialogue, discourse and debate concerning the nature of Islam in the modern period, such as the Muslim intellectual Tariq Ramadan, have had a minimal impact within the Muslim ummah worldwide.[8] Where Tariq Ramadan and others serve as a sturdy bridge between the secular West and religious Muslims – as they are adept both in western culture, history, and philosophy as well as in the traditional Islamic sciences (theology, philosophy, law) – they are perpetually overshadowed by the reactionary violence of bin Laden, al-Qae'da, and ISIS. Likewise in the West, those anti-Islamic voices that condemn all Muslims as terrorists or potential terrorists have the loudest and most powerful platform by which they can mold public opinion. It is not the case that bridges cannot be built, but that those who attempt to build the bridge watch them burn down before they reach to the other side.

The post-secular societies, where religion and secularity are becoming increasingly antagonistic, destructive, and blind to the concerns of the other, must find within themselves representatives that can translate the thoughts, beliefs, and utmost concerns of the "other" into a common language that can serve as the basis for trans-civilizational discourse with the practical intent of increasing reconciliation, peace, and friendly living together. However, such a friendly living together could only happen if the antagonistic and oppressive

---

8 See Tariq Ramadan, *Islam, the West and the Challenge of Modernity*, trans. Saïd Amghar. Leicester, UK: The Islamic Foundation, 2001; *To Be a European Muslim*. Leicester, UK: The Islamic Foundation, 2002; *Radical Reform: Islamic Ethics and Liberation*. New York: Oxford University Press, 2009.

conditions of neo-liberalism are replace, as exploitation of one segment of humanity over another cannot serve as the basis for reconciliation. In other words, the demand for inter-civilizational reconciliation is the demand to give up the conditions that prevent reconciliation, i.e. neo-liberalism. However, the opposite as occurred; the drift between the West and the rest has continued to fuel religious fundamentalism as well as nativist racism, xenophobia, Islamophobia, and miso-Islamism.

Theocracy as a Response to the Globalized Post-Secular Society

For Habermas, the expansion of modern secular capitalism into parts of the world that are still governed, either on the political or personal level, by traditional religious worldviews, has provoked a variety or responses. They include (1) missionary expansion, (2) fundamentalist radicalization, or (3) the instrumentalization of the inherent potential for violence.[9] In some cases, more than one applies to a given group. In the case of the global Muslims world, all three have been witnessed as responses to the increased secularization and capitalization of the lifeworld.[10] For example, 'Abd al-Al'a Mawdudi (d. 1979) called for a fundamentalist-oriented evangelism as well as the necessity to defend Islam via violence (if necessary); the archetypical Egyptian activist/author Seyyid Qutb (d. 1966) and his book *Ma'alim fi l-Tarīq* (Milestones) called for the continual *jihād* (struggle/effort) within the world to spread Islam until all of humanity submits to the will of Allah, which is in stark contrast to the mere submission to the *nafs* (instincts/desires) that is more normative in the West.[11] These scholars, and many others, have synthesized Islam with anti-western, anti-colonial, and anti-modern philosophy, the result of which has brought to the foreground the hostility that many Muslims experience towards western-oriented secular modernity.

---

9   Habermas, *Europe: The Faltering Project.* 61.

10   To Habermas' first point, Islam continues to be the fastest growing religion in the world, both by birth rate as well as through *da'wa* (invitation to Islam). Indeed, with the advent of the globalized cyberspace age, Muslims have been able to propagate their message across the world through popular social media, which has led many – especially in the West – to embrace Islam as their religion and way of life. I have dubbed this use of social media for the purposes of propagating religion "cyber-da'wah" or "e-daw'ah."

11   Abu al-A'la Mawdudi, *Jihad in Islam* (Damascus: The Holy Qur'an Publishing House, 1977), 5; Seyyid Qutb, *Ma'alim fi l-tariq* (Beirut: 1982), 62–91.

Although most of the ummah experiences modernity in the same way, their responses to it have created deep divisions within the Muslim world.[12] The Muslim community has become split within itself depending on how they relate to secularity, capitalism, democracy, cultural modernity, etc. Can Islam co-exist with democracy? Is capitalism compatible with Islamic law? Is secularity a good thing if it provides political freedom for Muslims to practice their religion? To what extent should Muslim participate in contemporary culture, especially when it's morally questionable, or even unavoidable? In other words, to what degree should Muslims accommodate themselves, their societies, and their religious praxis to the secular *zeitgeist*? Should the Muslim community try to accommodate itself to technological advances and leave behind cultural liberalization? Should it reject secularity as a whole and encourage a wholesale adoption of *Shari'ah* law? Should it attempt to create its own form of Islamic modernity that determinately negates both western concepts of the secular state as well as traditional Islamic law? These and similar questions have been grappled with by Christian, Jews, and other faiths, as some have fully rejected the modern world and have become anachronistic within the world around them, while others have made enormous accommodations to modernity which threatens their very identity as believers. Although it is too broad of a topic to discuss all forms of response to the globalized post-secular age, for this study we want to focus on two of the most dynamic: the fundamentalist, who is himself the product of modernity but nevertheless rejects many aspects of it, and the guardians of traditional Islam, who view modernity with suspicion but understand that Islam cannot survive if it does not confront modernity on its own terms, and therefore seek a balanced approach to Islam in the modern secular world. These traditionalists believe that Islam has the resources within itself to not only survive modernity but to thrive within the post-secular modern world while at the same time maintain deep connections with their tradition. It is this traditionalist – but not necessarily conservative – school of thought in Islam that is most vocal against the distortion of Islam by Muslim fundamentalists and extremists; this distortion being their attempt to answer the question of Islam in modernity.

As detailed above, groups such as ISIS, The Taliban, Boko Haram, al-Shabaab and al-Qae'da reject the cultural modernization of the Muslim world, i.e. the

---

12   One should not confuse the divisions in the Muslims world regarding the appropriate method and or stance to be adopted in light of the secularity and capitalism with division within Islam itself. Muslims disagree on what would be the best way to relate to secularity, but this is not a disagreement intra-Islam, i.e. it does not affect the fundamentals of Islam itself, but rather conditions the way in which Muslims can practice their faith.

autonomy of the individual as expressed through individual rights, openness towards alternative sexualities, freedom to blaspheme, equal rights of citizens to adhere to the religion of their choosing, and "western" notions of women's rights, etc.[13] In the mindset of these believers, nothing good has come from the West; it is a cesspool of sin, over-indulgence, heedlessness, forgetfulness of the divine, irreverence for sacredness, vulgar materialism, pornography, atheism, and *shirk* (polytheism) via the gods of the market – power, status and wealth. These reactionary fundamentalists are deeply wounded by the corrosive effects of western modernization, and in reaction to that corrosion, they defensively construct an identity that is radically anti-West and anti-modern (despite being a product of modernity itself). Often unbeknownst to them, the perversity of constructing an identity on the basis of being the *other* of that which is rejected, is that the identity of the other is given the power to influence the reactionary identity thus created. In other words, in becoming the opposite of the other, the other remains an integral part of the newly developed identity; its negativity serves as the foundation of the new identity, albeit in its rejection. In this way the rejected other still has power, or is granted power, over the identity of those who reject. On the other hand, those who remain deeply suspicious of the modern world, especially as it is articulated by the post-Christian secular West, but nevertheless refuse to build an identity based upon being the opposite of the West, are able to create an identity for themselves that is dynamic, open, and on its own terms; the other is known but not given power. In other words, it doesn't allow the other to define who it is (either positively or negatively) but rather safeguards its own prerogative to do so. Because it recognizes the other for what it is, both good and bad, it doesn't create its identity *against* that of the other, but on an equal footing as the other, and thus can stand defiantly against the other while at the same time appreciating what the other has accomplished in history; it is *secure-in-itself* and therefore not threatened by the existence of the other. This tension between Muslims whose identity is rooted in the hatred for the secular West and those who have adhered to the traditional Islamic identity while honestly engaging the western world, is on full display amidst the battle between ISIS with its leader Abu Bakr al-Baghdadi and the traditional *fuquha, mutakalimun* and *'Ulamā'* (jurists, theologians and scholars) that have bravely spoken out against them.

In light of ISIS's advances within the heart of the Muslim world, many traditional scholars of Islam feared that ISIS would be witnessed as being identical with Islam; in other words, to the world, ISIS would appear to be

---

13   This is not to say that all "fundamentalist" groups share monolithic answers to their issues. This is but a general observation of their general orientation.

the perfect manifestation of all the negative accusations leveled at Islam and Muslims since the 7th century.[14] In order to counter such a threat, in September of 2014, 126 internationally-renown scholars, Shaykhs, Imams, jurists, and theologians from throughout the Sunni Muslim world, signed an *open letter* in English and Arabic to Dr. Ibrahim Awwad al-Badri, a.k.a. Abu Bakr al-Baghdadi, the leader of ISIS, as well as to 'the fighters and followers of the self-declared "Islamic State." The letter thoroughly argued 24 ways in which ISIS had distorted Islam according to an 'overwhelming majority of Sunni scholars over the course of Islamic history,' and how those distortions discredit and/or prove that the "Islamic State" fails to reflect the true values of Islam via the qualification set forth by Islam and the Qur'an.[15] Refuting many Wahhabi-Salafist interpretations of Islam, the letter was directed squarely at Abu Bakr al-Baghdadi. They declare in their letter that ISIS has,

> provided ample ammunition for all those who want to call Islam barbaric with your broadcasting of barbaric acts which you pretend are for the sake of Islam. You have given the world a stick with which to beat Islam whereas in reality Islam is completely innocent of these acts and prohibits them.[16]

The fact that ISIS appears to be the embodiment of every Islamophobe's and miso-Islamist's accusation against Islam was enough to elicit a definitive response from the highest levels of Islamic authority, with the hopes of defending Islam from those who distort its meaning and praxis from within and also to safeguard its reputation and image from those outside of Islam who would use the barbarity of ISIS as a tool for spreading their anti-Islamic message.

In light of this open letter, we must ask what exactly are these scholars safeguarding? Surely it's not the case that Muslims are innocent of all crimes throughout their 1,400 year history, or that there aren't some inherent violent tendencies within its core doctrines. All major religions have a criminal

---

14   This very phenomenon led the World Council of Churches (WCC), as well as many other non-affiliated Christian denominations to denounce U.S. President George W. Bush's 2003 war on Iraq. In an attempt to separate Christianity from Bush's "crusade" (his words), the WCC stated "war against Iraq would be immoral, unwise and in breach of the principles of the United Nations Charter... the fact that the most powerful nations of this world again regard war as an acceptable instrument of foreign policy" had to be condemned. See *Religious Groups Issue Statements on War with Iraq.* March 19, 2003. www.pewforum .org/2003/03/19/publicationpage-aspxid616/ (Accessed 10/15/2014).

15   126 Muslim Scholars, *Open Letter to al-Baghdadi,* http://www.lettertobaghdadi.com/.

16   Ibid., §18.

history and all religions have a modicum of violence or violent tendencies inherent within them, which can either take the form of direct violence, structural violence, symbolic violence, or even the threat of metaphysical-eschatological violence. To say the least, the Muslim world is not a society of angels and Islamic doctrine does, under strict circumstances, legitimate all four forms of aforementioned violence. For Muslims to think of themselves or their history as being free from criminality is an unrealistic self-image, and one that diminishes the possibility for an honest discourse with the other (and with the self), as it imbues a false aura of innocence on one civilization while demonizing the other. As Daniel A. Madigan writes, 'each partner has a strong tendency to compare his own *ideals* with the *reality* of the other. The result is that each assumes the moral high ground, and with a sense of superiority speaks down to the other.'[17] Only within the gap between the distorted self-image and the lies of anti-Islamic propaganda can one find the reality about Muslims and their history and in doing so lay down the necessary conditions for an inter-civilizational discourse.[18]

Despite these issues, the 126 scholars want to make a clear distinction between *Islam* as a religious tradition that can either be adhered to or rejected, and *Muslims*, who have the agency to adhere or reject. These two entities, Islam and Muslims, are neither synonymous nor are they identical, but often times find themselves conflicting on a multitude of matters. Muslims fail to live up to the high standards set forth by the Qur'an and the Sunnah of the Prophet, and Islam often seems to fail to supply sufficient motivation for Muslims to adhere to those strictures. Nevertheless, these scholars believe Islam represents a force for absolute good within the world, as it represents the will of the world's creator. It is this force for good that they seek to safeguard against the distortions made by ISIS and others. As such, the Wahhabi-Salafi inspired orientation within ISIS had to be publicly resisted, if only to demonstrate that the whole of the Muslim world does not identify with their violent barbarism. It was a necessary condition that this be done in the form of an *inner-critique* – a critique from within the Islamic tradition using only shared Islamic sources, i.e. al-Qur'an, Ṣaḥīḥ ḥadīth, and in some cases the *ijma' al-'aimmah* (consensus of the scholars) and the *ijma' al-ummah* (consensus of the community). For the 126 scholars, this is the shared worldview and language by which a discourse with ISIS can be made as they have become impenetrable to critiques from outside of Islam.

---

17   Daniel A. Madigan, "Muslim-Christian Dialogue in Difficult Times," 67. My emphasis.
18   Ibid., 67.

However, the 126 scholars may have been too optimistic; critiques from outside of ISIS's Wahhabi-Salafi orientation, no matter how Islamicly valid, may also fall on deaf ears as they often reject the legitimacy of arguments that do not correspond with their authoritarian interpretation, thus making their thinking an extremely closed system of self-enforcing arguments that inherently resists democratic deliberation or scholarly debate and interpretation. It may be the case that the necessary discourse partner with ISIS can only be a recognized authority within the Wahhabi-Salafi orientation of Islam, as authorities outside of that orientation lack ISIS's recognition.[19] However, such voices are often either mute or in tacit support of ISIS's war on the Shi'a and other non-Sunni forces.[20]

As Hegel demonstrated in his philosophy of history, empires that develop out of the dialectical process often prove to be civilizing forces, moving humanity closer to its realization of true freedom, breaking the chains of the previous society's irrationalism and replacing it with better and more sophisticated thought and praxis. They tear down the old society's ossified structures; they destroy its unreasonable restraints; they answer the existential questions that the old empires and civilizations fail to answer; they replace the old gods with gods that are more appropriate for that epoch's intellectual development; their historic vitality incorporates the good from the old and builds anew while it discards that which was a hindrances to humanity in the old. When we look at Islamic history, we see that the breakout of Arabia by the early Muslims of the 7th and 8th century would likewise prove to be a great leap forward in the progressive dialectic that structures the historical process. Islam brought with it a radical sense of equality, women's rights, protections of minorities (both ethnic and religious), and a new desire for learning (both religious and "secular" sciences); Islam's radicalism and spirit of progressivity broke down the decaying and often times oppressive structures of the Byzantine and Sassanian Empires, opening up the Middle East, North Africa, Central Asia, and the Indus Valley for a new civilization that was predicated on justice, the development of the intellect, spiritual inquisitiveness, moral excellence, and multi-religious

---

19   Although intra-religious exclusion is not rare in the history of religions, it is rare in Islamic history. Throughout Muslim history, differing "schools of thought" (madahib), such as the Shafi'i, Maliki, Hanbali, Hannafi, and even the Shi'i Jafar'i have been accepted as equally valid. However, the Wahhabi-Salafi orientaiton of Islam is radically exclusionary and thus overwhelmingly rejects the cacophony of authoritative Islamic voices.

20   Alastair Crooke, "You Can't Understand ISIS if You Don't Know the History of Wahhabism in Saudi Arabia," August 27, 2014. http://www.huffingtonpost.com/alastair-crooke/isis-wahhabism-saudi-arabia_b_5717157.html (Accessed 10/15/2014).

and multi-ethnic tolerance.[21] Indeed, later on in history, "Orthodox" Christians of the Balkans frequently said, "better the turban of the Arab than the miter of the Pope," as to live under the conditions of Muslim rule was much more beneficial and peaceful for "heretical" Christians ("heretical" in the Roman view) than to live under the tyranny of the Roman Popes.[22] As this quote demonstrates, even centuries after Islam's exodus from Arabia it was considered a more progressive force than those who came before – both Christian and pagan. Islam, in this view, was a force for civilizational advancement, especially when it challenged the dominance of a quickly decaying Christendom around the Mediterranean. The evidence for this advancement can be seen in the political, economic, and cultural state of the Muslim world while Europe was in its dark ages; where European civilization crashed post-Rome, which St. Augustine believed was the work of divine providence, the Muslims appropriated the knowledge of the ancient Greeks, Romans, and the Hindus, etc., to build a society that was vibrant, educated, and culturally sophisticated.[23] It developed a system of theology with the use of Greek logic; it improved on the Greek philosophical tradition and reconciled it to Qur'anic revelation; it incorporated Hindu mathematics, astronomy, and natural sciences and studied the architecture of ancient Rome. Although not at the standards of the modern period, with its secular *Universal Declaration of Human Rights*, it even cultivated a progressive form of tolerance for Jews, Christians, and other religious denominations that were the envy of those minorities living n Christendom. It founded major universities that studied all subjects, some of which are still in existence today. It invented the modern hospital, by which patients would be segregated based on their illnesses, and even pioneered forms of surgery that were considered sacrilegious in Europe. Although this would come as a shock for many in the West, especially in light of the brutality of isis, the Muslims developed a system of rights and responsibilities for prisoners of war and their captors. This system prefigured many of the stipulations with the Geneva Conventions. All in all, the Muslim world was a much more hospitable and advanced place to live during Europe's civilizational collapse into darkness.

However, the modern period, especially from the colonial period onward, has not been kind to the Muslims, who have fallen behind the West in its

---

21   Dustin J. Byrd, "On the State of Islam: Thoughts on Revolution, Revolt, and Reform" in *Global Future of Religion: Probing into Issues of Religion and Religiosity in the Postmodern World*, 289–311.

22   Eamon Duffy, *Saints and Sinners: A History of the Popes*. New Haven; Yale University Press, 2006.

23   St. Augustine, *City of God*, 2014.

technology, scientific advancements, levels of education, and tolerance, i.e. its social progressivism.[24] Now, some parts of the Muslim world have nearly forsaken the spirit of social progress that once animated the Muslims to achieve great civilizational heights. ISIS is but the latest manifestation of the descent back into pre-Islamic times; a new age of *jāhilīyah* (ignorance), where the advances made by Islam for centuries have been all but cancelled; such openness and willingness to experiment with thought is often seen as a door through which the West can enter into the Muslim world and forcibly open it up to its corrupting influence. Therefore many Muslims adopt a reactionary stance towards modernity that has had a devastating effect of their religion. They advocate a closing of Islam and the Muslim world – a retreat into a fundamentalist mindset that bunkers itself behind a preconceived orthodoxy and intellectual/ religious simplicity. Unfortunately, this regression into reactionary-ignorance is now happening in the name of the same religion that once spawned the most progressive civilization. Understanding the power differential between the Muslim world and the West, especially in terms of economics and military might, the defensive Muslims often believe that there is no other option than to fortify Islam via conservatism: it is a survival tactic, or a coping-mechanism design to respond to the trauma brought on by neo-liberal secular modernity and western aggression. However, this retreat disfigures the message of the Prophet Muhammad and the first generations of Muslims who believed in, stood up for, and built a progressive society wherein the aims were the establishment of justice, a society of learning, and a culture of equality.

This claim may strike some as biased, being that it comes from a western academic, but it is essentially the claim made by the 126 Muslim scholars who wrote the open letter to Abu Bakr al-Baghdadi. In this letter they claim that he and his group have engaged in 'warmongering and criminality,' perpetrated 'heinous war crimes,' to have committed act of violence that are 'absolutely forbidden under Islamic law,' and have destroyed centuries of work of Muslim scholars. To the last point, like much of the world, the scholars of Islam have attempted to eradicate slavery from the Muslim majority countries. However, ISIS has triumphantly resurrected various forms of slavery within the heart of the Muslim world. To this historical mistake, the scholars write,

---

24   This is most certainly a relative term, as many minorities, especially religious minorities have fared better in the Muslim world, even after it decline, than they did in the West. There is nothing comparable to the Holocaust/Shoah in the Muslim world, even if the Turkish attack (or genocide) on the Armenians in 1919–1920 is often offered up as a parallel. Nevertheless, from the perspective of the critical theory, both societies have much more work to do when it comes to tolerance and/or acceptance of minorities.

after a century of Muslim consensus on the prohibition of slavery, you
have violated this; you have taken women as concubines, and thus revived strife and sedition (*fitnah*), and corruption and lewdness on the
earth. You have resuscitated something that the *Sharī'ah* [Islamic Law]
has worked tirelessly to undo and has been considered forbidden by consensus for over a century. Indeed all the Muslim countries in the world
are signatories of anti-slavery conventions... you bear responsibility for
this great crime and all the reactions which this may lead to against all
Muslims.[25]

The scholars continue their critique of ISIS by condemning their clear viola-
tions of the Qur'an, especially its clear injunction against forcing individuals into Islam or forcing them to accept their version of Islam. *La ikraha fii
din* (there is no compulsion in religion), they remind ISIS. Invoking *Sūrat al-
Baqarah* 2:256, they state,

It is known that the verse: "There is no compulsion in religion" was revealed after the conquest of Mecca, hence, no one can claim that it was
abrogated. You have coerced people to convert to Islam just as you have
coerced Muslims to accept your views. You also coerce everyone living
under your control in every matter, great or small, even in matters which
are between the individual and God. In Al-Raqqa, Deir el-Zor and other
areas under your control, armed groups who call themselves "al-hisbah"
make their rounds, taking people to task as thought they were assigned
by God to execute His commandments. Yet, not a single one of the Companions did this. This is not enjoining the right and honourable and for-
bidding the wrong; rather it is coercion, assault, and constant, random
intimidation.[26]

What the scholars have pointed out in this particular critique of ISIS is their
transgression against the autonomous subjectivity of the individual to either
conform to Islamic norms – which the individual may or may not think to be
valid or pragmatic – or reject them. From the scholars'' perspective, the individual can only be truly religious if they take upon themselves the dictates of
the religion as their own, which must be done out of their own free will as a
free subject. In other words, they have to be convinced of their truth and freely accept them. In doing so, they "self-institute" (αυτο-νομούνται), or regulate

---

25   126 Muslim Scholars, *Open Letter,* §12.
26   Ibid., §13.

themselves out of their own conviction that the religion is true and represents the way of righteousness that they want to embody in their own subjectivity. Anything less, as the scholars have alluded to, is *heteronomy*: the forced imposition of power upon an individual, which robs them of their freedom to accept the religion or not (at least in the public sphere).[27] In legal theory, *actus me invito factus non est meus actus* can be invoked as a defense in order to plead innocence against an heteronomically imposed act, precisely because only through a free subjective appropriation of a belief can *agere sequitur credere* (actions follow beliefs).[28] In the heteronomic situation, actions come *before* belief and as such are fraudulent, or at best questionable, because they do not reflect the free conscience of the actor. In order for a true Muslim society to be achieved, it cannot be predicated upon the *heteronomic compliance*, but rather on the free identification of the self with the religious tradition and its moral claims.[29]

What ISIS has done to the people living under their control has negated their ability to autonomously choose, and therefore the ability to be truly religious. ISIS and others make a logical jump; they believe since the religious tradition itself has moral authority because it is from the divine, that they have the moral authority to enforce its ethical tenets. However, the tradition itself gives no one the moral authority to impose divine strictures on others. In doing this, they have created the *illusion* of a religious society. Yet since they have failed to convince the people via discursive means, it remains nothing but a self-satisfying illusion. Had they truly convinced the people of the rightness of their cause, they would not have to enforce their interpretation of Islam by *violence*; the *power* of the argument itself would have compelled the masses to embody their values, and thus they would auto-regulate.[30]

Ironically, under religious rule – under theocratic tyranny – the ability to produce a population that accepts religion as their own is greatly reduced; that can only be achieved in a state of freedom where the population chooses for itself to be united with and guided by religion. In this sense, *freedom to choose is the necessary pre-condition for a truly religious population*. What a state that enforces religion can produce is outward/public conformity, while the individual in his/her private life remains in defiance towards the state as a way of safeguarding their subjectivity in the face of a heteronomic power

---

27   See Immanuel Kant, *Critique of Practical Reason*. New York: Cambridge University Press, 1997.

28   "the act done by me against my will is not my act."

29   See Chapter 6.

30   Hannah Arendt, *On Violence* (New York: A Harvest Book, 1970), 35–56.

that attempts to impose upon them values that they do not claim as their own. Indeed, a heteronomic state nearly always guarantees that the religion that is being imposed will also be the religion that opposes the state, as individuals re-appropriate their own personal autonomous religiosity in defiance of the "official" (coopted) version of religion. In this case, a subjectively autonomous interpretation of Islam struggles against the objective heteronomic Islam.

Recall Iran's 2009 Green Movement, in which the discontented youth, who represented the first generation educated post-Islamic revolution, as well as many of the first supporters of Iran's 1979 revolution, expressed their discontent with the regime of Mahmoud Ahmadinejad by protesting his reelection which they believed to be fraudulent.[31] The absence of a coherent alternative philosophy was striking; what many of the protesters were calling for cannot be reduced down to a simple *political* demand – the ouster of President Ahmadinejad as a political fraud – but rather must be seen in the light of Khomeini's peculiar form of Islamism: his blending of revolutionary Shi'a Islam and the Hussein model of anti-oppression action.[32] These youth, even with their pro-western sensibilities, demanded a closer adherence to a more enlightened form of Islam – one that would be morally and ethically loosened from heteronomic state power; one that would increase personal freedom, diminish corruption, would open the doors for dialogue with the West on an equal footing, and would not deny the "civil rights' of its citizens by denying their vote (which was symbolic of their collective will). Islam, in their view, could not be identified with the clerical ruling elites, but was rather the guarantor of the civil rights that where eclipsed under the rule of the Supreme Leader 'Ali Khamenei. Their interpretation of Islam set them against those who spoke for the heteronomic "official Islam": Islam that blesses the rule of the few. Most dialectically, the more Shi'a Islam was pressed into the service of the ruling elites, the more Islam liberated itself from their rule and engrained itself among the masses. Islam, and the standards it upholds, became their weapon against those same elites. To read these protests simply as a rejection of Khomeini and the Islamic Republic in favor of a western consumer society, as many western analysts did, is entirely wrong, as it fails to see the religiously polyphonic nature of the Shi'a community in Iran as well as the commitment to the vision of a just Islamic society that was first articulated by Ayatollah Khomeini during the revolution against the Shah. The Green Movement was a *reform* movement, one that wanted to change the particularities of the state and society, but not the overall

---

31   Hamid Dabashi, *Iran, The Green Movement, and the USA: The Fox and the Paradox*. New
      York: Zed Books, 2010.

32   Byrd, *Ayatollah Khoemini*, 41–45.

structure, ideals, or philosophy of the Islamic Republic. In other words, it was not a revolution, but one interpretation of Khomeini's *Hukumat-i Islami* (Islamic governance) in conflict with other interpretations.

From the perspective of the Qur'an, in order to avoid these forms of division within the Muslim community, all forms of religious coercion, as the Qur'an states, are illegitimate and in violation of Allah's commands. Having been revealed when Muhammad regained control of Mecca, *la ikraha fii din* is normative on all levels of society; the political, economic, and socio-cultural included, and those who functionalize Islam for their own purposes, especially political purposes, inadvertently contribute to the recovery of Islam's revolutionary core: Islam as a means by which religious subjectivity liberates itself from religious heteronomy.[33] By legitimating oppressive force via Islamic language, one dialectically articulates what Islam is not; the struggle against heteronomy makes this clear to the victims of the elites.

Yet, many Muslims feel that the ummah is required to have a central authority, such as a caliphate, as the Muslims had always had such a political-religious structure of authority since the death of the Prophet, beginning with the *Khulafā'u ar-Rāshidūn* (Four Rightly Guided Caliphs) for the Sunnis, or the Twelve Imams for the Shi'a. Indeed, the 126 Sunni scholars themselves testify that, 'there is agreement (*ittifaq*) among scholars that a caliphate is an obligation upon the *ummah*.'[34] However, from the perspective of our modern secular society, and the increasingly secularization of the world, and now post-secular conditions that are appearing in various nations, can a religious authority that seizes real temporal power truly exist in a meaningful and beneficial manner? Would not a transnational religious authority be anachronistic in the modern pluralistic and multi-cultural world of the 21st century? Would the extraction of religious authority out of civil society and restoring it back to the state not be a devastating blow for the modern world, not to mention for religion itself? Furthermore, isn't there something much more perverse at the core of *theocracy* – God's rule on earth via authority invested in *homo religious*, especially when it fuses the will of man with the will of the divine?

Even if ISIS refuses to proclaim itself to be a theocracy, in that they refuse to claim that they are taking the prerogatives of the divine as their own

---

33   One shouldn't deny that there are indeed certain exceptions. Parents have a right to "impose" a religion on their children. However, when they are of the age of political emancipation, they would gain the right to choose to be religious or engage in religious activities or not. Additionally, they also have the right to demand justification for religious beliefs, i.e. to have a faith predicated on "post-conventional" morality.

34   126 Scholars, *Open Letter,* 15.

or ruling in his name, their actions, as condemned by the 126 scholars, show that they engage in theft of the divine sovereignty, especially when ISIS's members intervene in activities that are strictly between the individual and God. Furthermore, if we can define theocracy as a form of government in which the law of God, in this case *Sharīʿah*, is the governing law, and such law is rooted in or legitimized by a sacred text or tradition, and/or the leader of the religious state is said to be – or claims to be – acting as the divine's enforcer of law, thus synthesizing their will with the supposed will of the divine, then it is by all measures a "theocracy," even if it would be more accurate to describe it as a "cleritocracy" (rule of the clerics). Theocracy is an amalgamation of religion and state power; the state becomes identical with the norms and ordinances of the religious tradition, with the ultimate consequence being the legitimization of the ruler's actions by divine sanction; a human agent becomes the divine's grand inquisitor, judge, and executioner. God and temporal power become one, as the human agent serves as a conduit for the divine's will on earth, and as such his temporal powers take on the power of the absolute. To oppose the temporal authority is to oppose the will of the divine. *Aut Caesar aut nihil.*[35]

The danger of theocracy takes on a Feuerbachian meaning when one thinks in terms of how ISIS and their cohorts "project" onto the divine their own biases, animosities, and hatred, which they then legitimate via a distorted reading of the Qur'an and prophetic traditions (*ḥadīth*). In a most penetrating passage that lends itself to ISIS, Anne Lamott, a progressive novelist, wrote in her book *Bird by Bird,* 'you can safely assume you've created God in your own image when it turns out that God hates all the same people you do.'[36] The identification of earthly rule with divine sanction by way of ISIS resulted in the oppression of women, raping of girls, subjugation of religious minorities, brutal executions of Syrians and the Iraqi Shi'a and Sunni Muslims, the mutilation of corpses, the torture and burning of soldiers and dissidents, the traumatization of children, the destructions of shrines and mosques, the slander or *takfīr* (accusation of apostasy) of pious believers, and the comprehensive distortion of Islam, which Muslims believe is a *mercy* to mankind from the creator, but appears to much of the world to be more of a *curse*. It is no mistake that ISIS finds these groups to be distasteful, and thus targets them with the supposed sanction of the divine. From the perspective of the 126 scholars as well as the critical theory of religion, such a return to barbarity as a response to the barbarity unleashed by colonialism, neo-colonialism and neo-liberalism – that which continues

---

35   "Either Caesar or nothing": a phrase that embodies the absolutism of the authority.
36   Ann LaMott, *Bird by Bird: Some Instructions on Writing and Life* (New York: First Anchor Books, 1995), 22.

to divide Muslims via nationhood, tribe, and class, cause conflict within the heart of the ummah, and facilitate unending wars – cannot be legitimated via prophetic religion, Islam, nor revolutionary theory, nor can such barbarity be functionalized as being a bad means to good ends.[37] From the view of many Muslims, the only way to resist the constant destruction of the ummah via *fit-nah* and neo-liberalism's expansion is a return to a theocratic caliphate. But is that really a viable solution in today's increasingly secular world?

From the perspective of his philosophy of religion and state, the critical theorist Walter Benjamin sees a more troubling eschatological aspect of theocracy; one that makes it a misplaced phenomenon within the history of mankind. He states,

> Only the Messiah himself consummates all history, in the sense that he alone redeems, completes, creates its relation to the Messianic. For this reason *nothing* historical can relate itself on its own account to anything Messianic. Therefore the Kingdom of God is not the telos of the historical dynamic; *it cannot be set as a goal.* From the standpoint of history it is not the goal, but the end. Therefore the order of the profane cannot be built up on the idea of the Divine Kingdom, and therefore theocracy has no political, but only a religious meaning.[38]

For Benjamin, the claims of the theocratic regimes, that their rule is based within the will of Allah, that they somehow have a special status that grants them the authority to rule in the place of God (or in the place of the hidden Imam for the Shi'a), or that their regimes represents the *telos* of history, are misguided as it denies the finality that only the Messiah (or *Mahdī*) can bring to history; he, and only he, *consummates* history.[39] Therefore, that which is mediated by history, i.e. any form of political-economy, charismatic individual, clerical leadership, etc., cannot be the messianic that ends history – history does not have within itself the eschatological qualities needed in order to bring

---

37   The argument that "the ends justify the means" has been soundly rejected in Islamic thought. Forbidden (*haram*) means, even if they result in good ends, cannot be justified, as it would mean to violate the law of Allah.

38   Walter Benjamin, "Theologico-Political Fragment" in *Reflections: Essays, Aphorisms, Autobiographical Writing,* ed. Peter Demetz (New York: Harcourt Brace Jovanovich Inc., 1978), 312. My emphasis.

39   One should be aware that the *valayat-i faqīh* (the rule of the jurist), in Khomeini's thought, is only the temporary placeholder for the messianic figure, but does not appropriate the prerogatives of the Mahdi himself. Ayatollah Khomeini, *Islam and Revolution: Writing and Declaration of Imam Khomeini,* trans. Hamid Algar (Berkeley: Mizan Press, 1981), 27–166.

about its own consummation; that which has the capacity to congeal history into the perpetual *jetztzeit* (now time), to establish the messianic utopia, to realize the longing for the totally other, comes from outside of history and as such nothing burdened by the historical process can claim such prerogatives. In his philosophy, Benjamin preserves the messianic and prophetic by denying any earthly regime the right to claim itself as the embodiment of God's will. The object of the state, according to Benjamin, is to construct the coordinates of society by which man can achieve abiding and substantive felicity. Ironically, the actualization of felicity can only be done within the same coordinates of freedom that allow the believers to subjectivity realize religion. In other words, freedom is both the precondition for individual felicity and true religiosity. By imposing the "will of God" upon those who do not accept it as the will of God, nor as their own, the state destroys the possibility for both felicity and religiosity, and thus, for Benjamin, it must stay out of the messianic-utopia business.

The utopian negativity of the 2nd commandment, the *bilderverbot*, which can also be found within Islam's negativity towards the world-as-it-is and its prohibition on making *idols* of the divine, i.e. ossifying that which is created into that which creates, rejects such combination of the divine with earthly rule, as it pulls the ineffable down into the broken, the distorted and the corrupt; it makes that which is unarticulatable into that which is deficiently articulated; and falsely sanctions that which is odious by the standards of prophetic and revealed religion. No, as Walter Benjamin stated and the 126 scholars alluded to, religion cannot be legitimately co-opted by any given ruler, nor can theocracy be seen as the goal of history. In the history of Islam, never has a caliph been the *Kalām Allah* (speech of God), rather only an "*Abdallah* (servant of God), and an "*abd* (servant) knows his place.

The "political meaning" of theocracy that Benjamin invokes, can be identified only with the Messianic age, when the rule of the divine – through his Messiah – is the reality of the world, its summation and endpoint. But only the Messiah can achieve this, not Abu Bakr al-Baghdadi nor anything else that's subject to the historical process. Until the Messiah (or *Mahdī*) breaks into human history, the longing for the totally other – which is both expressed in Christianity and Islam – cannot be articulated within a deficient and temporal power, as to do so brings the authority of the *totally other* into concert with the earthly familiar, thus creating an idol. Rather, for Benjamin, being rooted in the bilderverbot, the "otherness" of the *totally other* must remain unarticulated, as it serves as the unexpressed utopian vision (rooted in negativity) of what the world ought to be, and as such it retains its revolutionary potential to critique that which is the case: the world and all its brokenness, all its brutality, and all it barbarism.

Post-Secular Solidarity: A Proposal for an Intra-religious Constitutionalism

In our struggle to find a way to abate contemporary barbarity, devolution of a world-being-towards-violence – a global civil war – we have to begin to think beyond the bounds of the traditional notions of nations and states. We have to think in terms of a global solidarity that transcends the traditional geography of national politics, religious communities, and ethnic barriers. In order to do this, I want to return briefly to a theory advanced by the political theorist Dolf Sternberger but most associated with Jürgen Habermas – "constitutional patriotism" (*Verfassungspatriotismus*) – and see if we can modify it in such a way that it can be expanded outside of national borders. In attempting this, we are in pursuit of a post-secular and post-nationalist form of solidarity; one that can serve as the basis for a more reconciled future society that transcends the bounds of civilizational particularism.

For Jürgen Habermas, the post-secular and post-metaphysical conditions of the West make it necessary for societies to create ways in which they can govern themselves democratically without appealing to pre-political foundations, i.e. race, ethnicity, common language, religious worldview, and cultural heritage, etc. Because of the plurality of its citizens, the modern cosmopolitan state is no longer capable of sustaining a close connection between "demos" and "ethnos," as it once had; the reality of multiculturalism demands a different way of formulating a national identity.[40] In other words, "demos" has to be divorced from "ethnos." Habermas observes that in secular modernity, 'each nation is now supposed to be granted the right to political self-determination. The intentional democratic community (*Willensgemeinschaft*) takes the place of the ethnic complex.'[41] Against any forms of nationalism, modern democracies and democratic cultures are comprised of a symphony of ethnicities, languages, customs, and religious beliefs, making a functioning democracy rooted in a particular *ethos* no longer viable, as it denies entrance into the citizenry to those who do not share the historical ethnos (or any given pre-political characteristic). For Habermas, something else must replace the shared ethnos that once served as the national adhesive. In searching for this, he turns his attention to the aftermath of the French Revolution, which philosophically and politically augmented the possibility of citizenship to those outside of the predominant ethnos. For the French revolutionaries, the bonds of ethnos were broken first by those who cared little for their own ethnicities, but rather

---

40   Habermas, *Between Facts and Norms*, 495.
41   Ibid., 494.

ruled solely in the interest of their class: the aristocracy. In other words, the ruling class showed scant solidarity with those in classes beneath them regardless of their shared ethnicity. This fracture in the edifice of ethnos contributed to the revolutionary Bourgeois' formulation of the universal philosophical categories: freedom, justice, and liberty, as these values transcended those pre-political foundations and are applicable to all those who assent to their validity as universals. To be a nation was to be a 'nation of citizens,' that 'finds its identity,' Habermas writes, 'not in ethnic and cultural commonalities but in the practice of citizens who actively exercise their rights to participation and communication.'[42] At this point Habermas believes that the republican form of governance completes its separation with all pre-political foundations – they simply cannot provide an adequate basis for a nation that finds its adhesive in shared ideals and shared polity. In Bourgeois society, the "demos" from this point on is not a racial group, a religious group, or a group sharing the same language; the modern demos is united as a democratic community of the will, and this will collectively adheres to certain "universal" values and together attempts to manifest those values in their polity, economics, culture, etc. In this way, the "demos" is not only a political entity within a given state, but takes on the characteristics of a way-of-being that transcends formal politics.

Yet the conditions within the contemporary democratic societies of Europe and North America have become much more complex than the Bourgeois revolutionaries could ever have imagined. The bonds created by the powerful civil religion of the United States, which has brought different ethnic and religious groups together through the past two centuries of shared civic rituals, holidays, and practices, has begun to disintegrate, transforming into mindless and xenophobic nationalism or political-economic apathy – driven by the national discourses concerning healthcare, immigration, gun control, police brutality, and the role of the state in civil society.[43] In Europe, where the philosophical values of the Bourgeois revolution have progressed beyond their original intent and freedom and has been extended beyond what was ever imagined during the Enlightenment period, strong voices of dissent among both religious and non-religious groups have questioned the legitimacy and universality of such Enlightenment values. It is often argued that those values have gone too far in their accommodation of non-European – meaning "non-liberal" and "non-democratic" – culture. Some "communities" residing in "cultural ghettos" within the demos simply cannot abandon their pre-political foundations because those foundations are essential to their cultural identity as something

---

42   Ibid., 495.
43   Habermas, *The Inclusion of the Other,* 118.

other than liberal Europeans. As such, they have difficulties integrating and assimilating into a demo that has left behind the concreteness of pre-political foundations and found their identity within particular abstract philosophical values, ideals, and notions. Additionally, other critics, such as the fundamentalist Muslims and Christians, believe the West's liberal culture is too open and free and therefore without the confines of concrete moral bearings. In the philosophical abstractness of freedom, liberty, and pursuit of happiness – which leads to radical atomization – anything is permissible to the individual and therefore there is no real community, no real demos. From that perspective, the abstractness of ideals fails to congeal the aggregate of individuals into a unity. Consequently, what in theory should unite the people – democratic and enlightened ideals – are no longer universally accepted, but are highly debated within the disjointed communities that comprise multi-cultural societies.

As not to descend into the moral and political chaos that would accompany a return behind the Bourgeois Enlightenment and re-establishing a state predicated on pre-political foundations (as many on the right demand), and to avoid cultural suicide by capitulating to the voices of Muslim radicals who condemn all things western, or nativists who demonizes all things "Islamic," Habermas attempts to find a way in which the modern cosmopolitan state can create a basis for cross-cultural national unity, discursive citizenship, and democratic stability that still preserves the polyphonic nature of modern democracy.[44]

In this pursuit, Habermas turn to Sternberger's conception of "constitutional patriotism," which can be understood as a post-nationalist adhesive within a given society in which the citizens subjectively and freely attach themselves to the values, principles, ideals and democratic procedures that have been crystalized within a democratic constitution. Symbiotically, the constitution reflects the core values of the people and the people willfully bind themselves to that document. In this sense, allegiance to the constitution is an affirmation of the values by which the individual lives; thus the citizen can recognize

---

44   Roland Boer makes an interesting observation when discussing those in Europe who are now resurrecting the 'old alliance between God and state, between Europe and Christianity.' He believes that this insistence on Europe's Christian heritage is emphasized only by those who 'only know what a church-building looks like from the outside.' This touches on an interesting point; it is not a "return to religion" that these critics advocate, but rather a sense of a pre-political foundation that includes an aspect of religion. Christianity, as part of European heritage, is juxtaposed to Islam, which is not. Religion therefore plays an important role in their emphasis on *shared history* as foundation for the society, but they do not seek a resurrection of the church in the lifeworld of the average person. See Roland Boer, *Criticisms of Theology: On Marxism and Theology III*, 38.

themself in the ideals articulated with the constitution. As such, patriotism, which does not abandon critical reflection on the way the constitution is enacted or interpreted, is cultivated outside of the bounds of the "nation" (the community of the pre-political foundations), but rather is cultivated via discourses surrounding constitutional matters. Allegiance is owed to the values of the constitution as well as to all those who adhere to those values regardless of their ethnic, religious, linguistic, etc., backgrounds. In this sense, the values expressed by the constitution have no ethnicity, no religious allegiances, and no prejudices towards a certain group; the constitution is intentionally devoid of pre-political considerations.

However, knowing the power of nationalism – man's mythical connection to his *blut und boden* (blood and soil) – many, Habermas admits, doubt that such an abstract and content-less notion can bind a diverse group of people together within one political entity; for them it is 'too weak.'[45] With that critique in mind, Habermas insists that for constitutional patriotism to work, the,

> citizens must be able to experience the fair value of their rights also in the form of social security and the reciprocal recognition of different cultural forms of life. Democratic citizenship can only realize its integrative potential – that is, it can only found solidarity between strangers – if it proves itself as a mechanism that actually realizes the material conditions of preferred forms of life.[46]

In other words, constitutional patriotism must deliver on its promises; it must not share the fate of Bourgeois society by promising greatness – such as equality, fraternity, and liberty – while systematically failing to deliver on those promises. It must demonstrate that the shared citizenship of all, that their common allegiances to the constitution, and that their abatement of radical self-interest in the search for the common good, has benefits for all who assent to this *post*-pre-political foundational collective. As such, if a country is to bind itself to the values expressed within its constitution, Habermas believes that

> each individual [must] come to recognize and appreciate citizenship status as that which links her with the other members of the political community and makes her at the same time dependent upon and co-responsible for them. It [becomes] clear to all that private and public

---

45   Ibid., 118.
46   Ibid., 118–119.

autonomy presuppose one another in the circuit of reproduction and improvement of the conditions of preferred ways of life.[47]

In many ways the constitution that Habermas is proposing is a codification of the "overlapping consensus" between various comprehensive worldviews. It is, in effect, the product of discourse between different peoples within the multicultural and cosmopolitan nation; their agreed upon values take form within legislative and democratic structures under which they agree to be governed. In this sense, the constitution preserves both the universal values as the guiding spirit of the document while understands that the document is a *living* document that is subject to perpetual contestation. If disagreements arise within the community of citizens, the constitutional values will have to judge between the interpretations as to what interpretation is most congruent with the original intent of the constitutional value in question as well as what interpretation is most adequate for the given contemporary situation.[48] The democratic process must always be regarded as legitimate, even if the outcome of discourse fails to garnish universal consensus. Peaceful and legitimate discourse is therefore an inherent component within constitutional patriotism. The allegiance to the ideals expressed within the constitution is not abandoned although they may be strained by discursive activities.

If Habermas believes that this model can be achieved within a given state, can we legitimately use it as a framework for global religious communities? Can various religions enter into a "constitutional convention" through which they attempt to create a governing and ecumenical document that expresses their "overlapping consensus" on shared concerns? Or will the secular origins of the modern notion of a constitution prove to be unworkable within a religious context?

Ecumenism and Inter-Religious Constitution Building: Modern Slavery

Soon after Pope Francis returned from his historic 2014 trip to the secular Republic of Turkey, a country that is overwhelmingly Muslim, he gathered together leaders from various world religions at the Vatican in Rome. Together

---

47   Ibid., 120.
48   We should also admit that the "original intent" thesis of a constitution is also a matter of contestation. If the original intent is no longer adequate to the times, it is a democratic prerogative to rethink the society's conception of that particular ideal.

these leaders, representing the Anglican Tradition, Orthodox Christianity, Hinduism, Buddhism, Judaism, Islam (both Sunni and Shi'a), and Catholicism, discussed, debated, and contemplated what the Pope called the 'atrocious plague' of modern globalized slavery.[49] Despite the many differences these religious leaders have in theology, eschatology, liturgy, religious philosophy, and ethical systems, they were able to each retrieve a moral commonality from within their own traditions that allowed them to come to a binding agreement with other religions concerning a pressing moral dilemma. Regardless of the presence of slavery within many of these religions' histories, slavery was universally condemned as being 'a crime against humanity' in the resulting document. In declaring it as such, these religious leaders engaged in a twofold practice; first, they were explicitly critical of their own communities that often practiced slavery (sometimes sanctioned by religious authorities), and two, they were determined to abate, arrest, and eradicate the practice within their own communities in the near future. These religious leaders were able to transcend their religious exclusivism – their particularity – in order to come to a universal consensus; together they created an inter-religious constitutional opinion that is deeply rooted within each of their religious traditions, especially their humanistic elements. By putting forward an articulation of a moral claim from within their traditions, entering into an inter-religious discourse, coming to an agreement about the nature of slavery – in this case its evilness – and then working towards a document that translates all their particular articulations into a universal declaration, they have produced a constitutional document by which they can judge themselves, their communities, and each other. This constitutional document can now serve as the starting point for a more fruitful and peaceful cooperation between religious communities on various other

---

49   Reuters, "Pope, World Religious Leaders, Pledge to Fight Modern Slavery," December 2, 2014.
        http://www.reuters.com/article/2014/12/02/us-pope-slavery-idUSKCNoJG1KM20141202
        (Accessed 12/3/2014). Below is a list of religious leaders present at the conference and
        the religions they represented: Hinduism: Her Holiness Mata Amritanandamayi (Amma);
        Buddhism: Venerable Bhikkhuni Thich Nu Chan Khong, representing Zen Master Thich
        Nhat Hanh, Thailand; Venerable Datuk K. Sri Dhammaratana, Chief High Priest of
        Malaysia; Judaism: Rabbi Abraham Skorka and Rabbi David Rosen KSG, CBE; Orthodox:
        His Eminence Emmanuel, Metropolitan of France, representing the Ecumenical Patri-
        arch Bartholomaios I; Islam: Abbas Abdalla Abbas Soliman, undersecretary of State of
        Al Azhar Alsharif, representing Mohamed Ahmed El-Tayeb, Grand Imam of Al Azhar; the
        Grand Ayatollah Mohammad Taqi al-Modarresi; Sheikh Naziyah Razzaq Jaafar, special
        advisor, representing Grand Ayatollah Sheikh Basheer Hussain al Najafi; Sheikh Omar
        Abboud; Anglicanism: His Grace Most Reverend and Right Honourable Justin Welby,
        archbishop of Canterbury.

issues that plague the modern world. If they can come to an agreement on the barbarity of slavery and its need for eradication, then it is also possible that they can come to an agreement on issues of war, abortion, economic exploitation, poverty, and many other moral conserns.

The language of the *Joint Declaration of Religious Leaders for the Eradication of Slavery* states,

> We, the undersigned, are gathered here today for a historic initiative to inspire spiritual and practical action by all global faiths and people of good will everywhere to eradicate modern slavery across the world by 2020 and for all time.
>
> In the eyes of God, each human being is a free person, whether girl, boy, woman or man, and is destined to exist for the good of all in equality and fraternity.[50] Modern slavery, in terms of human trafficking, forced labour and prostitution, organ trafficking, and any relationship that fails to respect the fundamental conviction that all people are equal and have the same freedom and dignity, is a crime against humanity.
>
> We pledge ourselves here today to do all in our power, within our faith communities and beyond, to work together for the freedom of all those who are enslaved and trafficked so that their future may be restored. Today we have the opportunity, awareness, wisdom, innovation and technology to achieve this human and moral imperative.[51]

From the perspective of the Pope, world religious communities have a potential for revolutionary and moral change even within our post-secular societies, where practices such as slavery have failed to be eradicated by secular modernity. This potential for good is augmented when there is cooperation between religious authorities, especially when they bring their moral strength to bear on their own communities.

It is also important to note that the joint declaration does not excommunicate secular voices from their attempts to alleviate the suffering of modern slavery; they intentionally included the phrase 'people of good will' as an invitation to those who can no longer believe in religion but can recognize the

---

50   The Grand Imam of al-Azhar preferred the word "religion" as opposed to "God" in this sentence. The inclusion of his concern demonstrates the recognition of the group towards certain theological sensitivities.

51   Vatican City, "Declaration of Religious Leaders for the Eradication of Modern Slavery," December 2, 2014. http://www.news.va/en/news/declaration-of-religious-leaders-for-the -eradicati (Accessed 12/4/2014).

validity of their condemnation of modern slavery. With this door wide open, religious and non-religious people can now come to an agreement about how to translate this religious document into secular language that can be fully grasped and approved of by secular humanists and atheists who also shared their abhorrence towards modern slavery.

However, certain intrinsic problems do remain; does this constitutional document simply remain a statement of common morality without the force of law, or can it become a piece of legislation that can engender within itself coercive powers? Can it become both moral law and legislative law? In other words, can this document be enforced by political and/or religious authorities among the adherents of the world religions represented at this conference? Do individual states have the ability to legally enforce what is essentially a joint statement of religious morality? Needless to say, all forms of slavery are already illegal under international law, i.e. the United Nation's Universal Declaration of Human Rights (UDHR), which in Article 4 states, 'No one shall be held in slavery or servitude; slavery and the slave trade shall be prohibited in all their forms.'[52] Does the fact that this secular legal document already exists make the Pope's *Joint Declaration* redundant and therefore facile – especially if religion has been pushed into civil society and can no longer enforce itself on its members? Such international legislation already has the force of law even if it member states fail to enforce it within their territories. Being so, is this joint declaration just an affirmation of what secular authorities have already decided?

We should remember that the particular individuals at the Pope's conference were not representatives of states, but were the representatives of religions that have very little power if any in their countries beyond the moral persuasion they hold within their own communities. However, the observer must not forget that religious power is often trans-national and not subject to political boarders. Because religious communities are international forms of identity, solidarity tends to transcend the particularities of states, and with this internationalism it wields a different form of power than the authority of the state. However, because such an international authority is often free from the political constraints of any particular state, it can be both dangerous regressive and/or progressive. History has demonstrated to us time and time again the destructive power of Popes, Caliphs and other transnational organizations; such power should be wielded carefully. On the other hand, if that authority, like the authority used to enter into a discourse with the Pope on the issue of modern slavery, is bent towards progressive means, i.e. the augmentation

---

52   United Nations. "The Universal Declaration of Human Rights," http://www.un.org/en/documents/udhr/ (Accessed 12/4/2014).

of peace, justice, and freedom, than it may very well be the form of authority most needed in a global public sphere that is often stunted by intra-state
parochialism.

What the power of these international religious authorities makes imperative is that their religious language be translated into secular language through
which their beliefs can be introduced into the public sphere including political
and legislative bodies within their own home countries. Although these religious authorities are interested in benefiting all of humanity, the *universal*, and
not just their own *particular* communities, the state must remain the agent of
the common good in society, as the state is the entity that labors on behalf of
the common good. The temptation for parochial advancement at the expense
of other sub-communities remains too strong within religions to ensure such
a task to any particular religious tradition. Because of this, the constitutional
declarations devised by religious authorities must be translated into secular
political-philosophy and debated, approved and enacted by proper state authorities. However, what then would be the purpose other than to say that this
new inter-religious declaration supports that which is already international
law, i.e. the Universal Declaration of Human Rights? What are these religious
leaders adding to this discourse? The signatory nations to the UDHR already
have the obligation to enforce its strictures within their national boarders –
would this declaration aid in their enforcement? The question for the religious
authorities is whether or not they can help enforce such tenets upon a population; not through the use of force or coercision, but through persuasive via the
language of morality?

It seems to me that this declaration could serve as the beginning of a parallel authority; one that is not rooted in a system of justice that is rather rooted
in a moral worldview that depends not on law for its enforcement but upon
the universal acceptance of the moral argument that is represented and advanced within the *Joint Declaration* (or any other inter-religious constitutional
document). Returning behind the Enlightenment and granting religious institutions the power to enforce their moral claims among their populations
cannot be the answer to modern slavery and other vices that plague the
world. What the religious leaders can do is *convince* their communities of
the legitimacy of their agreed upon constitutional moral claims, aid in their
self-regulation, and seek to transform their societies without illegitimately, i.e.
heteronomically, limiting the autonomy of the individual, but rather by augmenting their knowledge of the ecumenical nature and validity of their moral claims. Ultimately what such an inter-religious constitutional convention
can produce is a *united nations of morality* – rooted in a process of consensus
building via democratic discourse between representatives of various religions.

Additionally, as the Pope and his convention have demonstrated, this discourse must remain open to all who have a concern for the suffering of the finite individual, the plight and predicament of the broken, and the misery of those who have been damaged by world history, society, and mankind's imposition of unnecessary suffering.[53]

The procedures of constructing a constitutional document between religions that could be advanced into governing bodies are important to acknowledge. Taking a cue from the Pope's discourse on global slavery, we can see a functioning procedure develop: a twofold translation process. First, the legitimate authorities of the religious communities enter into a robust discourse concerning the constitutional values that they can all agree upon; secondly, these agreed upon values are recorded in such an ecumenical way that all the discourse partners can also agree upon the universalistic – yet still religious – language of the constitutional document, and lastly, this document is then *together* translated into secular – and most likely – philosophical language that is suitable for submission into the secular political realm. This process is slightly different than Habermas' proposal, as he would have all religious groups work independently of all others; each community is responsible for translating their own particular religious claims into secular language as well as advancing those claims through the political process. In my proposal, religious voices, especially those that have the most invested within a given society, are asked to first enter into a learning process with each other before they attempt to offer their claims to the democratic process. The benefit of this procedure is that religions first come to diminish their own antagonisms with each other to avoid becoming simply another solitary voice amongst the aggregate of voices in the democratic process. The downside, of course, is the possibility that the religious authorities will fail to agree upon certain constitutional values, their universal religious language, or the language used in their translation. However, if they fail on one or more of these accounts, there is always Habermas' individualistic approach to translating religion into secular discourse. Yet I argue that if religions can first transcend their own faith-based isolation, find common ground with other religious believers, the potential for meaningful reconciliation with secular society will be intensely augmented. The Catholic theologian Hans Küng reminds us that there must first be peace among the world religions before there will be peace among the nations. In light of that sentiment, it may be discovered that this procedure is not only a chance for religious communities to participate fully in their nation's political discourse, but also a peace process among the religious communities. How

---

53   Pope Francis, *Evangelii Gaudium*, 26–55.

powerful of an example would be set if the world religions, with all their dis-
functionality, their criminal history, and their antagonistic relationships with
each other, transcended their provinciality and came to a common agreement
rooted in common concerns, especially if those common concerns, interpretations, and remedies could be made available to the secular society? Once
again they could be a potential source of good in history. That being the case,
the post-secular society – the society devoid of God but full of prophetic and
Socratic religion – could lay the foundations for the future society of reconciliation and peace.

Conclusion

An inter-religious constitutional convention within the conditions of the post-
secular society is a start towards a more-reconciled future society that has
been the dream of many prophets, mystics, sages, philosophers, theologians,
workers, the impoverished and revolutionaries for thousands of years. Challenges and resistance will be a constant companion, especially by those who
find it impossible to shed the veil of particularity in a search for the universal,
those who believe ecumenisms is a dilution of their "pure" faith, those who
stagnate their dynamic religion through their dogmatic and legalistic understanding of "perfection," and those who fundamentally find all religions to be
the sickness of mankind instead of an agent of mercy, compassion, kindness
and a potential source for coming together. However, in the face of the growing
antagonism between the secular and the religious, the growth of fundamentalistic belief attitudes among certain religions as well as the religionless, and the
barbaric violence perpetrated upon those who have not the means to defend
themselves, what other alternative do religious communities have if they wish
to be a part of the world healing process? If religion is to maintain itself in the
face of the increasingly secular world, should it not direct its attention to the
healing of mankind and not its destruction? What can believers do if they are
in the company of men like St. Francis of Assisi and Sultan Malik al-Kamil, who
risked their lives to further peaceful reconciliation between religious communities? Can the religious communities of the modern world simply leave their
faith in the hands of the extremists and the ecumenically mute who wish to
use their religions as a tribal defense against the demonized other; can the
secular communities that wish to know their religious neighbors not so that
they can hate them more efficiently, but come to know them as friends – can
they leave their secular Enlightenment beliefs in the hands of those who would
distort them into a battering ram of western hegemony against their fellow

citizens of Islamic faith? What choice do we have today concerning the ongoing conflict between religion and secularity other than to talk with each other,
be with each other, and reason together in a respectful dialogue that takes in
account the cacophony of voices and sensitivities? If we cannot find a common language that allows us to communicate in an inter-subjective fashion,
we will only have war – either within one society or between nations. Must we
learn to witness and confess our beliefs, whether they be secular or religious, in
a way that reaches towards a vision of society of reconciliation, not reproduces
the horrors and terrors of the past. The post-secular condition is a unique opportunity for dialogue and friendly discourse, as it opens up the geography in
which members of differing religious communities and secular citizens can
engage each other in a manner that alleviates misunderstandings, hatred, and
despair. *Hoc natura est insitum, ut quem timueris, hunc semper oderis.*[54] Is it
not time for fear and hate to be replaced by recognition, reconciliation, inter-
subjectivity and unconditional solidarity? In my estimation, the world cannot
wait any longer.

---

54   "It's an innate thing to always hate the one we have learnt to fear."

Bibliography

Abrahamian, Ervand. *Khomeinism: Essays on the Islamic Republic.* Berkeley: University of California Press, 1993.

Abromeit, John. *Max Horkheimer and the Foundations of the Frankfurt School.* New York: Cambridge University Press, 2013.

Adorno, Theodor. *Negative Dialectics.* Translated by E.B. Ashton. New York: Continuum, 1999.

———. *Metaphysics: Concept and Problems.* Edited Rolf Tiedemann. Translated by Edmund Jephcott. Stanford: Stanford University Press, 2001.

———. *Can One Live After Auschwitz.* Edited by Rolf Tiedemann. Stanford: Stanford University Press, 2003.

———. *Critical Models: Interventions and Catchwords.* New York: Columbia University Press, 2005.

Adorno, Theodor et al. *The Authoritarian Personality.* New York: Harper & Brothers, 1950.

Afsaruddin, Asma. "Martyrdom in Islamic Thought and Praxis" in *Martyrdom and Terrorism: Pre-Modern to Contemporary Perspectives,* edited by Dominic Janes and Alex Houen. New York: Oxford University Press, 2014.

Ahmad, Jalal Al-i. *Occidentosis: A Plague from the West.* Edited by Hamid Algar. Translated by R. Campbell. Berkeley: Mizan Press Berkeley, 1984.

Algar, Hamid. *Roots of the Islamic Revolution in Iran.* Oneonta, NY: Islamic Publications International, 2001.

———. *Wahhabism: A Critical Essay.* Oneonta, NY: Islamic Publications International, 2002.

Ali, Ayaan Hirsi. *Infidel.* New York: Free Press, 2007.

Allen Jr., John L. "Mad at Everyone Else, Muslim Immigrants in Rome Trust the Pope." December 27, 2013. http://ncronline.org/blogs/ncr-today/mad-everyone-else-muslim-immigrants-rome-trust-pope.

Almond, Ian. *The New Orientalists: Postmodern Representations of Islam from Foucault to Baudrillard.* New York: I.B. Taurus, 2007.

Arendt, Hannah. *Eichmann in Jerusalem: A Report on the Banality of Evil.* New York: Viking, 1969.

———. *On Violence.* New York: A Harvest Book, 1970.

Armstrong, Karen. *Muhammad: Biography of the Prophet.* New York: HarperSanFrancisco, 1992.

Asad, Talal, et al. *Is Critique Secular? Blasphemy, Injury and Free Speech.* New York: Fordham University Press, 2013.

Azad, Hasan. "Why are there no Muslim Philosophers?" June 12, 2014. http://www
.aljazeera.com/indepth/opinion/2014/06/muslim-philosophers-2014
610135114713259.html.

BBC News Europe, "Paris Attack: Pope Francis Say Freedom of Speech has Limits."
January 15, 2015. http://www.bbc.com/news/world-europe-30835625.

Baker, Rob and Gray Henry, eds. *Merton and Sufism: The Untold Story – A Complete
Compendium.* Louisville, KY: Fons Vitae, 2005.

Barrett, Richard. *Foreign Fighters in Syria.* Soufan Group Report: June, 2014.

Bawer, Bruce. *While Europe Slept: How Radical Islam is Destroying the West from Within.*
New York: Broadway Books, 2006.

Beiser, Frederick. *Hegel.* New York: Routledge, 2005.

Benjamin, Walter. *Reflections: Essays, Aphorisms, Autobiographical Writing.* Edited by
Peter Demetz. New York: Harcourt Brace Jovanovich Inc., 1978.

———. *The Correspondence of Walter Benjamin: 1910–1940.* Edited by Gershom Scholem and Theodor W. Adorno. Translated by Manfred R. Jacobson and Evelyn M.
Jacobson. Chicago: University of Chicago Press, 1994.

———. *Arcades Project.* Edited by Rolf Tiedemann. Translated by Howard Eiland and
Kevin McLaughlin. Cambridge, MA: The Belknap Press of Harvard University Press,
1999.

———. *Walter Benjamin: Selected Writings Vol. 1: 1913–1926.* Edited by Marcus Bullock
and Michael W. Jennings. Cambridge, MA: The Belknap Press of Harvard University
Press, 2004.

———. *Illuminations: Essays and Reflections.* Edited by Hannah Arendt. New York:
Schocken Books, 2007.

Bin Laden, Osama. *Message to the World: The Statements of Osama Bin Laden.* Edited by
Bruce Lawrence. New York: Verso, 2005.

Binelli, Mark, "Pope Francis: The Times They Are a-Changing." *Rolling Stone,* 13 February 2014, 36–43, 66.

Blumenthal, David R. *Facing the Abusing God: A Theology of Protest.* Louisville, KY:
Westminster/John Knox Press, 1993.

Bociurkiw, Bohdan R. *Lenin: The Man, The Theorist, The Leader: A Reappraisal.* Edited
by Leonard Schapiro and Peter Reddaway. New York: Frederick A. Praeger, Publishers, 1967.

Boer, Roland. *Marxist Criticism of the Bible.* New York: Continuum, 2003.

———. *Criticisms of Theology: On Marxism and Theology III.* Chicago: Haymarket
Books, 2012.

———. *Lenin, Religion, and Theology.* New York: Palgrave MacMillan, 2013.

Borchegrevink, Aage. *A Norwegian Tragedy: Anders Behring Breivik and the Massacre
on Utøya.* Translated by Guy Puzey. Malden, MA: Polity Press, 2013.

Borradori, Giovanna. *Philosophy in a Time of Terror: Dialogues with Jürgen Habermas and Jacques Derrida.* Chicago: University of Chicago Press, 2003.

Bowen, John R. *Why the French Don't Like Headscarves: Islam, the State, and Public Space.* Princeton, NJ: Princeton University Press, 2007.

———. *Can Islam Be French?* Princeton: Princeton University Press, 2010.

———. *Blaming Islam.* Cambridge, MA: The MIT Press, 2012.

Browning, Christopher R. *The Origins of the Final Solution: The Evolution of Nazi Jewish Policy, September 1939–March 1942.* Lincoln, NE: University of Nebraska Press, 2004.

Buck-Morss, Susan. *The Dialectics of Seeing: Walter Benjamin and the Arcades Project.* Cambridge, Mass: The MIT Press, 1991.

Buruma, Ian. *Murder in Amsterdam: Liberal Europe, Islam, and the Limits of Tolerance.* New York: Penguin Books, 2006.

Byrd, Dustin J. *Ayatollah Khomeini and the Anatomy of the Islamic Revolution in Iran: Toward a Theory of Prophetic Charisma,* (Lanham, MD: University Press of America), 2011.

———. "On the State of Islam: Thoughts on Revolution, Revolt, and Reform" in *Global Future of Religion: Probing into Issues of Religion and Religiosity in the Postmodern World,* edited by Seyed Javad Miri, 289–311. London: International Peace Studies Centre Press, 2012.

———. "Fromm's Notion of Prophets and Priests: Ancient Antagonism, Modern Manifestations" in *Reclaiming the Sane Society: Essays in Erich Fromm's Thought,* edited by Miri, Lake and Kress, 147–160. Rotterdam: Sense Publishers, 2014.

———. *A Critique of Ayn Rand's Philosophy of Religion: The Gospel According to John Galt.* Lanham, MD: Lexington Books, 2015.

Carter, Chelsea J. "Video Shows ISIS Beheading U.S. Journalist James Foley." Aug. 20, 2014. http://www.cnn.com/2014/08/19/world/meast/isis-james-foley/index.html.

Casey, Michael. *Che's Afterlife: The Legacy of an Image.* New York: Vintage Books, 2009.

Castro, Fidel and Frei Betto. *Fidel and Religion: Conversations with Frei Betto on Marxism & Liberation Theology.* New York: Ocean Press, 2014.

Catholic Herald. "Pope Francis Offers Prayers for the Victims of Lampedusa Boat Sinking." October 3, 2013. http://www.catholicherald.co.uk/news/2013/10/03/pope-francis-offers-prayers-for-victims-of-lampedusa-boat-sinking/.

Chomsky, Noam. *Fateful Triangle: The United States, Israel & the Palestinians.* Cambridge, MA: South End Press, 1999.

Chua-Eoan, Howard and Elizabeth Dias. "The People's Pope." *TIME,* 23 December 2013, 54.

Connor, Tracy. "Francis Effect? Popular Pope has Catholics Praying More, Polls Find." March 6, 2014. http://www.nbcnews.com/news/religion/francis-effect-popular-pope-has-catholics-praying-more-poll-finds-n43451.

Corrie, Rachel. *Let Me Stand Alone: The Journals of Rachel Corrie*. New York: W.W. Norton & Co., 2008.

Crooke, Alastair. "You Can't Understand ISIS if You Don't Know the History of Wahhabism in Saudi Arabia." August 27, 2014. www.huffingtonpost.com/alastair-crooke/isis-wahhabism-saudi-arabia_b_5717157.html.

Dabashi, Hamid. *Iran, The Green Movement, and the USA: The Fox and the Paradox*. New York: Zed Books, 2010.

Dabiq, No. 4, 1435 Dhul-Hijjah.

Daley, Beth and Martin Finucane. "Marathon Bombing Suspect's Disrupted Cambridge Mosque on Martin Luther King Day." April 21, 2013. http://www.boston.com/metrodesk/2013/04/21/marathon-bombing-suspect-outbursts-had-disturbed-cambridge-mosque-goers/HUM4K1dm5IKWqRRKktFM9L/story.html.

Davidson, Amy. "The Mystery of Abdul-Rahman, or Peter Kassig." Nov. 17, 2014. http://www.newyorker.com/news/amy-davidson/mystery-abdul-rahman-peter-kassig.

DeLong-Bas, Natana J. *Wahhabi Islam: From Revival and Reform to Global Jihad*. New York: Oxford University Press, 2004.

Diversity Chronicle. "Pope Francis Invites the Homeless, Undocumented Immigrants and Prostitutes to Exclusive Catered Vatican Banquet." April 11, 2014. http://diversitychronicle.wordpress.com/2014/04/11/pope-francis-invites-the-homeless-undocumented-immigrants-and-prostitutes-to-exclusive-catered-vatican-banquet/.

Dorrien, Gary. *Imperial Designs: Neoconservativism and the New Pax Americana*. New York: Routledge, 2004.

Duffy, Eamon. *Saints and Sinners: A History of the Popes*. New Haven; Yale University Press, 2006.

Eagleton, Terry. *Culture and the Death of God*. New Haven: Yale University Press, 2014.

Emerick, Yahya. *Muhammad*. Indianapolis: Alpha, 2002.

Engels, Frederick. *Socialism: Utopian and Scientific*. New York: International Publishers, 1989.

Esposito, Richard et al. "Anti-Islam Film Producer Wrote Script in Prison: Authorities." Sept. 13, 2012. http://abcnews.go.com/Blotter/anti-islam-film-producer-wrote-script-prison-authorities/story?id=17230609#.UFLmFK4dWVk.

Fisher, Max. "This Map Shows Every Attack on French Muslims since *Charlie Hebdo*." January 10, 2015. http://www.vox.com/2015/1/10/7524731/french-muslims-attacks-charlie-hebdo.

Fisk, Robert. *The Great War for Civilization: The Conquest of the Middle East*. New York: Vintage, 2007.

Fitzpatrick, David and Drew Griffin. "Canadians have Joined ISIS to Fight – and Die – in Syria." Sept. 10, 2014. http://www.cnn.com/2014/09/10/world/canada-isis-jihādists/.

Follain, John. *Jackal*. New York: Arcade Publishing, 1998.

Ford, Bev and Rich Schapiro. "Pope Francis calls Parents of Slain Journalist James Foley to Give Condolences." Aug. 22, 2014. http://www.nydailynews.com/news/national/pope-francis-calls-parents-james-foley-article-1.1912382.

Frazer, Jenni. "Wiesel: Yes, We Really did put God on Trial." Sept. 19, 2008. http://www.thejc.com/news/uk-news/wiesel-yes-we-really-did-put-god-trial.

Freud, Sigmund. *Civilization and its Discontents,* Edited and translated by James Strachey. New York: W.W. Norton & Co., Inc., 1962.

———. *New Introductory Lectures on Psychoanalysis,* Edited and translated by James Strachey. New York: W.W. Norton & Co., 1966.

———. *An Outline of Psycho-Analysis.* Translated by James Strachey. New York: W.W. Norton & Co., 1989.

Fromm, Erich. *The Anatomy of Human Destructiveness.* New York: Holt, Rinehart and Winston, 1973.

———. *Marx's Concept of Man.* New York: Frederick Ungar Publishing Co., 1981.

———. *On Disobedience and Other Essays.* New York: The Seabury Press, 1981.

———. *Escape from Freedom.* New York: Henry Holt & Co., Inc., 1994.

———. *To Have or To Be.* New York: Continuum, 2000.

Fukuyama, Francis. *The End of History and the Last Man.* New York: Avon Books, 1992.

Gehring, John. *The Francis Effect: A Radical Pope's Challenge to the American Catholic Church.* Landham, MD: Rowman & Littlefield, 2015.

Giglio, Mike and Munzer al-Awad. "Smuggler: I Sent ISIS Fighters to Europe." November 11, 2014. http://www.buzzfeed.com/mikegiglio/smuggler-i-sent-isis-fighters-to-europe?utm_term=4ldqpia.

Gladstone, Rick. "Amnesty International Find Executions Rose in 2013." March 26, 2014. http://www.nytimes.com/2014/03/27/world/amnesty-international-2013-death-penalty-report.html?_r=0.

GlobalPost, "Full Text of the Last Email the Islamic State sent to the Foley Family." August 21, 2014. http://www.globalpost.com/dispatch/news/regions/middle-east/syria/140821/text-last-email-islamic-state-sent-foley-family.

Grieg, Alex. "Almost a Dozen Men from Minnesota are Fighting for ISIS in Syria, Say Officials." August 29, 2014. http://www.dailymail.co.uk/news/article-2737982/Almost-dozen-men-Minnesota-fighting-ISIS-Syria-say-officials.html.

Habermas, Jürgen. *The Theory of Communication Action: Reason and the Rationalization of Society, Vol. 1.* Translated by Thomas McCarthy. Boston: Beacon Press, 1984.

———. *Between Facts and Norms.* Cambridge, MA: The MIT Press, 1996.

———. *The Inclusion of the Other: Studies in Political Theory.* Cambridge, MA: The MIT Press, 1998.

———. *Europe: The Faltering Project.* Malden, MA: Polity Press, 2009.

———. *An Awareness of What's Missing: Faith and Reason in a Post-Secular Age.* Malden, MA: Polity Press, 2011.

Habermas, Jürgen and Joseph Ratzinger. *The Dialectics of Secularization: On Reason and Religion*. San Francisco: Ignatius Press, 2005.

Hackett, Conrad. "No Clear "Pope Francis Effect" Among U.S. Catholics." November 25, 2013. http://www.pewresearch.org/fact-tank/2013/11/25/no-clear-pope-francis-effect-among-u-s-catholics/.

Halm, Heinz. *Shi'a Islam: From Religion to Revolution*. Princeton, NJ: Markus Wiener Publishers, 1999.

Harris, Elise. "Pope Denounces "Racist, Xenophobic" Attitudes towards Immigrants." July 15, 2014. http://www.catholicnewsagency.com/news/pope-denounces-racist-xenophobic-attitudes-toward-migrants-84304/.

Heft, James L, ed. *Catholicism and Interreligious Dialogue*. New York: Oxford University Press, 2012.

Hegel, G.W.F. *Phenomenology of Spirit*. Translated by A.V. Miller. New York: Oxford University Press, 1977.

———. *Lectures on the Philosophy of Religion: The Lectures of 1827*. Edited by Peter C. Hodgson. New York: Oxford University Press, 2006.

———. *Lectures on the Philosophy of Religion: Determinate Religion*. Vol. 2 (Ed. Peter C. Hodgson) New York: Clarendon Press, 2007.

———. *Elements of the Philosophy of Right*. New York: Cambridge University Press, 2010.

Heidegger, Martin. *The Question Concerning Technology*. Translated by William Lovitt. New York: Harper Perennial, 1977.

Him, Johannes. "Will Box for Passport: An Olympic Drive to Become a United States Citizen." *The Comment*, 2010.

Hitler, Adolf. *Mein Kampf*. Translated by Ralph Manheim. New York: Houghton Mifflin Company, 1999.

———. *Hitler's Table Talk: 1941–1944*. Translated by Norman Cameron and R.H. Stevens. New York: Enigma Books, 2000.

Hobbes, Thomas. *Leviathan: Parts I and II*. Edited by Herbert W. Schneider. New York: The Bobbs-Merrill Company, Inc., 1958.

Hoess, Rudolf. *Commandant of Auschwitz*. Translated by Constantine FitzGibbon. London, Phoenix Press, 2000.

Holy Bible: Revised Standard Version. New York: Thomas Nelson Inc., 1972.

Hodgson, Marshall G.S. *The Venture of Islam: Conscience and History in a World Civilization. The Classical Age of Islam*. Chicago: The University of Chicago Press, 1977.

Honneth, Axel. *The Struggle for Recognition: The Moral Grammar of Social Conflicts*. Cambridge, MA: The MIT Press, 1995.

———. *Disrespect: The Normative Foundations of Critical Theory*. Malden, MA: Polity Press, 2007.

Horkheimer, Max. *Critique of Instrumental Reason*. New York: The Seabury Press, 1974.

———. *Dawn and Decline: Notes 1926–1931 & 1950–1969*. Translated by Michael Shaw. New York: The Seabury Press, 1978.

———. *Critical Theory: Selected Essays*. New York: Continuum, 2002.

———. *Eclipse of Reason*. New York: Continuum, 2004.

Horkheimer, Max and Theodor Adorno, *Dialectic of Enlightenment: Philosophical Fragments*. Edited by Gunzelin Schmid Noerr. Translated by Edmund Jephcott. Stanford: Stanford University Press, 2002.

Human Rights Watch. "'Bad Dreams': Exploitation and Abuse of Migrant Workers in Saudi Arabia." July 14, 2004. www.refworld.org/cgibin/texis/vtx/rwmainpage=searc h&docid=412ef32a4&skip=0&query=saudiarabiamigrantworkers.

IBTimes UK. "EU Elections: Anti-Immigrant Wave Sweeps Europe." May 26, 2014. http:// www.ibtimes.com/eu-elections-anti-immigrant-wave-sweeps-europe-1590035.

Instituut voor Multiculturele Vraagstukken. *Forum*. http://www.forum.nl/Portals/Res/ res-pdf/Moslims-in-Nederland-2010.pdf.

Ivereigh, Austen. *The Great Reformer: Francis and the Making of a Radical Pope*. New York: Henry Holt & Co., 2014.

Jackson, Roy. *What is Islamic Philosophy?* New York: Routledge, 2014.

Jacobson, Eric. *Metaphysics of the Propane: The Political Theology of Walter Benjamin and Gershom Scholem*. New York: Columbia University Press, 2003.

Jaspers, Karl. *The Question of German Guilt*. Translated by E.B. Ashton. New York: Fordham University Press, 2000.

Jay, Martin. *The Dialectical Imagination: A History of the Frankfurt School and the Institute of Social Research, 1923–1950*. Berkeley: University of California Press, 1996.

Kant, Immanuel. *Groundwork for the Metaphysics of Morals*. Translated by H.J. Paton. New York: Harper Torchbooks, 1964.

———. *Critique of Practice Reason*. New York: Cambridge University Press, 1997.

———. *Religion within the Boundaries of Mere Reason*. Edited by Allen Wood and George di Giovanni. Cambridge, MA: Cambridge University Press, 1998.

Kaufmann, Walter ed. *Religion from Tolstoy to Camus*. New York: Harper & Row, Publishers, 1964.

———. *Nietzsche: Philosopher, Psychologist, Antichrist*. Princeton, NJ: Princeton University Press, 1974.

Kerry, John. *Twitter* – 8/20/2014.

Khaldun, Ibn. *The Muqaddimah: An Introduction to History*. Translated by Franz Rosenthal. Edited by N.J. Dawood. Princeton, N.J.: Princeton University Press, 1989.

Khomeini, Ayatollah. *Islam and Revolution*. Translated by Hamid Algar. Berkely: Mizan Press, 1981.

King III, Martin Luther. Interview by Rev. Al Sharpton. *PoliticsNation*, MSNBC, 20 January 2014.

Klausen, Jytte. *The Cartoons that Shook the World*. New Haven: Yale University Press, 2009.

Kogon, Eugen. *Der SS-Staat: Das System der deutschen Konzentrationslager*. München: Wilhelm Heyne Verlag, 2006.

Kuenssberg, Laura. "State Multiculturalism has Failed, Says David Cameron." Feb. 5, 2011. http://www.bbc.com/news/uk-politics-12371994.

Kukis, Mark. *My Heart Became Attached: The Strange Odyssey of John Walker Lindh*. Washington D.C.: Brassey's Inc., 2003.

Küng, Hans. *The Catholic Church: A Short History*. Translated by John Bowden. New York: The Modern Library, 2003.

———. *Islam: Past, Present & Future*. New York: Oxford University Press, 2007.

LaMott, Ann. *Bird by Bird: Some Instructions on Writing and Life*. New York: First Anchor Books, 1995.

Lana, Sara Miller. 'French Muslims to Islamic State: We are also "Dirty French."' September 26, 2014. http://www.csmonitor.com/World/Europe/2014/0926/French-Muslims-to-Islamic-State-We-are-also-dirty-French.

Leiken, Robert S. *Europe's Angry Muslims: The Revolt of the Second Generation*. New York: Oxford University Press, 2012.

Löwy, Michael. *The Marxism of Che Guevara*. Lanham, MD: Rowman & Littlefield Publishers Inc., 2007.

Lydall, Ross. "Woolwich Killing: A Plea for Calm as Mosques are Targeted and English Defense Leagues Clash with Police." May 23, 2013. http://www.standard.co.uk/news/crime/woolwich-killing-plea-for-calm-as-mosques-are-targeted-and-english-defence-league-clash-with-police-8628387.html.

Madigan, Daniel A. "Muslim-Christian Dialogue in Difficult Times" In *Catholicism and Interreligious Dialogue*, edited by James L. Heft. New York: Oxford University Press, 2012.

Makdisi, George. *The Rise of Colleges: Institutions of Learning in Islam and the West*. Edinburgh: Edinburgh University Press, 1981.

Mamdani, Mahmood. *Good Muslim, Bad Muslim: America, The Cold War, and the Roots of Terror*. New York: Pantheon Books, 2004.

Marcuse, Herbert. *A study on Authority*. New York: Verso, 2008.

Marx, Karl and Friederich Engels. *The Marx-Engels Reader*. Edited by Robert C. Tucker. New York: W.W. Norton & Co., 1978.

———. *Economic and Philosophic Manuscripts of 1844 and the Communist Manifesto*. Translated by Martin Milligan. Amherst, NY: Prometheus Books, 1988.

Marx-Aveling, Eleanor. "Karl Marx," in *Marx's Concept of Man* by Erich Fromm. New York: Image Books, 1961.

Mawdudi, Abu al-A'la. *Jihad in Islam*. Damascus: The Holy Qur'an Publishing House, 1977.

McGrath, Alister E. *Christianity's Dangerous Idea: The Protestant Revolution – A History from the Sixteenth Century to the Twenty First*. New York: Harper One, 2007.

Miller, Jake. "Chuck Hagel: ISIS 'beyond anything we've seen.'" August 22, 2014. http://www.cbsnews.com/news/chuck-hagel-defends-failed-james-foley-rescue-attempt/.

Miri, Seyed Javad, ed. *Global Future of Religion: Probing into Issues of Religion and Religiosity in the Postmodern World*. London: International Peace Studies Centre Press, 2012.

Moin, Baqer. *Khomeini: Life of the Ayatollah*. New York: St. Martin's Press, 1999.

Moses, Paul. *The Saint and the Sultan: The Crusades, Islam, and Francis of Assisi's Mission of Peace*. New York: Doubleday, 2009.

Moss, Candida R. *The Other Christs: Imitating Jesus in Ancient Christian Ideologies of Martyrdom*. New York: Oxford University Press, 2010.

Muslim Public Affairs Council. "What you Need to Know." http://www.mpac.org/programs/hate-crime-prevention/statistics.php#.UzixcChDx94.

NBC News. "Pope Washes Feet of Detainees in Holy Thursday Ritual." March 28, 2013. http://worldnews.nbcnews.com/_news/2013/03/28/17502522-pope-washes-feet-of-young-detainees-in-holy-thursday-ritual?lite.

Nietzsche, Friederich. *The Anti-Christ: A Criticism of Christianity*. Translated by Anthony M. Ludovici. New York: Barnes & Noble, 2006.

———. *On the Genealogy of Morals*. Translated by Horace B. Samuel. New York: Barnes & Noble, 2006.

———. *The Will to Power*. Translated by Anthony M. Ludovici. New York: Barnes & Noble, 2006.

———. *The Gay Science*. Translated by Thomas Common. New York: Barnes & Nobel, 2008.

Obama, Barack. "President Obama's Remarks on the Execution of Journalist James Foley by Islamic State." August 20, 2014. http://www.washingtonpost.com/politics/transcript-president-obamas-remarks-on-the-execution-of-journalist-james-foley-by-islamic-state/2014/08/20/f5a63802-2884-11e4-8593da634b334390_story.html.

Open Letter to al-Baghdadi (126 *Muslim Scholars*). http://www.lettertobaghdadi.com/.

Ott, Michael R. *Max Horkheimer's Critical Theory of Religion: The Meaning of Religion in the Struggle for Human Emancipation*. Lanham, MD: University Press of America, 2001.

Pahlavi, Mohammad Reza. *The White Revolution of Iran*. Tehran: Kayhan Press, 1967.

Paxton, Robert O. *The Anatomy of Fascism*. New York: Alfred A. Knopf, 2004.

Pearson, Michael and Dana Ford. "Peter Kassig's Parents: "Good will Prevail"" November 17, 2014. http://www.cnn.com/2014/11/17/world/meast/isis-peter-kassig-remembered/.

Perkins, John. *Confessions of an Economic Hitman*. New York: Plume, 2004.

PewForum. "Religious Groups Issue Statements on War with Iraq." March 19, 2003. www.pewforum.org/2003/03/19/publicationpage-aspxid616/.

Pinker, Steven. *The Better Angels of our Nature: Why Violence Has Declined.* New York: Viking, 2011.

Pope Paul VI. "Nostra Aetate: Declaration on the Relation of the Church to Non-Christian Religions." October 28, 1965. http://www.vatican.va/archive/hist_councils/ii_vatican_council/documents/vat-ii_decl_19651028_nostra-aetate_en.html.

Pope Francis, *Evangelii Gaudium: The Joy of the Gospel.* Washington D.C.: USCCB Communications, 2013.

———. "Message from Pope Francis to Muslims Throughout the World for the End of Ramadan ('Id al-Fitr)." July 10, 2013. http://www.vatican.va/holy_father/francesco/messages/pont-messages/2013/documents/papa-francesco_20130710_musulmani-ramadan_en.html.

———. *A Big Heart Open to God: A Conversation with Pope Francis.* New York: HarperOne, 2013.

———. (Jorge Mario Bergoglio) and Abraham Skorka. *On Heaven and Earth: Pope Francis on Faith, Family, and the Church in the Twenty-First Century.* New York: Image, 2013.

Public Safety Canada. "2014 Public Report on the Terrorist Threat to Canada: Responding to Violent Extremism and Travel Abroad for Terrorist Related Purposes." Her Majesty the Queen in Right of Canada, 2014.

Qutb, Seyyid. *Ma'alim fi l-tariq.* Beirut: 1982.

RT. "British-born, rich & isolated Muslims more likely to be radicalized – study." September 25, 2014. http://rt.com/uk/190588-british-depressed-muslims-radicalized/.

Rabasa, Angel and Cheryl Benard. *Eurojihad: Patterns of Radicalization and Terrorism in Europe.* Cambridge: Cambridge University Press, 2014.

Rabinbach, Anson. "Benjamin, Bloch and Modern German Jewish Messianism" *New German Critique* Winter, no. 34 (1985): 78–124.

Ramadan, Tariq. *Islam, the West and the Challenge of Modernity.* Translated by Saïd Amghar. Leicester, UK: The Islamic Foundation, 2001.

———. *To Be a European Muslim.* Leicester, UK: The Islamic Foundation, 2002.

———. *Radical Reform: Islamic Ethics and Liberation.* New York: Oxford University Press, 2009.

Ramadan, Tariq and Amina Chaudary. "Tariq Ramadan: My Absence Would Certainly Be the Most Powerful Speech I have Ever Give at ISNA." August 14, 2014. http://www.theislamicmonthly.com/tariq-ramadan-my-absence-would-certainly-be-the-most-powerful-speech-i-have-ever-given-at-isna/.

Rand, Ayn. *The Ayn Rand Column.* Irvine, CA: Ayn Rand Institute Press, 1998.

Reeves, Minou. *Muhammad in Europe: A Thousand Years of Western Myth-Making.* New York: New York University Press, 2000.

Reimer, A James. "Constantine: From Religious Pluralism to Christian Hegemony" in *The Future of Religion: Toward a Reconciled Society.* Edited by Michael R. Ott. Leiden: Brill Publishers, 2007.

Reuters. "Christians and Muslims Join Forces to Combat Modern Slavery." March 17, 2014. http://www.reuters.com/article/2014/03/17/us-religion-slavery-idUSBREA2G19N20140317.

———. "Pope, World Religious Leaders, Pledge to Fight Modern Slavery." December 2, 2014. http://www.reuters.com/article/2014/12/02/us-pope-slavery-idUSKCN0JG1KM20141202.

———. "Saudi Grand Mufti Denounces ISIS." http://www.dailystar.com.lb/News/Middle-East/2014/Aug-19/267697-saudi-top-preacher-blasts-isis-as-enemy-no1.ashx#axzz3AqneMQkc Aug. 19, 2014.

Richardson, John. *Nietzsche's New Darwinism*. New York: Oxford University Press, 2004.

Rodinson, Maxime. *Islam and Capitalism*. New York: Pantheon Books, 1973.

Rubenstein, Richard L. *After Auschwitz: History, Theology, and Contemporary Judaism*. Baltimore: Johns Hopkins University Press, 1992.

Safranski, Rüdiger. *Nietzsche: A Philosophical Biography*. Translated by Shelly Frisch. New York: W.W. Norton & Co., 2002.

Said, Edward W. *Orientalism*. New York: Vintage Books, 1994.

Sánchez, Ilich Ramírez. *L'islam Revolutionaire*. Éditions du Rocher, 2003.

Sands, Philippe. *Lawless World: America and the Making and Breaking of Global Rules from FDR's Atlantic Charter to George W. Bush's Illegal War*. New York: Viking, 2005.

Schmitt, Carl. *Political Theology: Four Chapters on the Concept of Sovereignty*. Chicago: University of Chicago Press, 2005.

Scholem, Gershom. *The Messianic Idea in Judaism and other essays on Jewish Spirituality*. New York: Schocken Books, 1995.

Schweizer, Bernard. *Hating God: The Untold Story of Misotheism*. New York: Oxford University Press, 2011.

Scurr, Ruth. *Fatal Purity: Robespierre and the French Revolution*. New York: Metropolitan Books, 2006.

Segal, Ronald. *Islam's Black Slaves: The Other Black Diaspora*. New York: Farrar, Straus & Giroux, 2001.

Sharī'ati, 'Ali. *On the Sociology of Islam*. Translated by Hamid Algar. Berkeley: Mizan Press, 1979.

Siebert, Rudolf J. *Hegel's Concept of Marriage and Family: The Origin of Subjective Freedom*. Lewiston, NY: The Edwin Mellen Press, 1979.

———. *From Critical Theory to Critical Political Theology: Personal Autonomy and Universal Solidarity*. New York: Peter Lang, 1994.

———. *Manifesto of the Critical Theory of Society and Religion: The Wholly Other, Liberation, Happiness and the Rescue of the Hopeless. Vol II*. Leiden: Brill, 2010.

———. *The Development of Moral Consciousness towards a Global Ethos*. New Dehli: Sanbun Publishers, 2012.

———. *Georg W. Rudolphi's Prophetische Politische Theologie*. Frankfurt a/m: Haag + Herchen, 1993.

Simon, Jeffrey D. *Lone Wolf Terrorism: Understanding the Growing Threat*. Amherst, NY: Prometheus Books, 2013.

Slahi, Mohamedou Ould. *Guantánamo Diary*. Edited by Larry Siems. New York: Little, Brown and Company, 2015.

Smietana, Bob. "Religious Conflict isn't New to Murfreesboro: Catholic Immigrants Plan Fueled Protests in Murfreesboro in 1929." October 24, 2010. www.tennessean .com/article/20101024/NEWS01/10240382.

Smith, David Livingstone. *Less than Human: Why we Demean, Enslave, and Exterminate Others*. New York: St. Martin's Press, 2011.

Speer, Albert. *Inside the Third Reich: Memoirs*. Translated by Richard & Clara Winston. New York: The MacMillan Company, 1970.

Spellberg, Denise. *Thomas Jefferson's Qur'an: Islam and the Founders*. New York: Alfred A. Knopf, 2013.

Spoto, Donald. *Reluctant Saint: The Life of Francis of Assisi*. New York: Viking Press, 2002.

Squires, Nick. "Silvio Berlusconi says immigrants not welcome but 'beautiful girls' can stay." February 13, 2010. http://www.telegraph.co.uk/news/worldnews/europe/ italy/7223365/Silvio-Berlusconi-says-immigrants-not-welcome-but-beautiful-girls -can-stay.html.

St. Augustine. *The City of God*. Translated by Marcus Dods. Peabody, MA: Hendrickson Publishers Marketing, LLC, 2014.

St. Francis and St. Claire, Francis and Claire: *The Complete Works*. Translated by Regis J. Armstrong and Ignatius C. Brady. New York: Paulist Press, 1982.

Thompson, Augustine. *Francis of Assisi: A New Biography*. Ithaca: Cornell University Press, 2012.

Tiedemann, Rolf. "Historical Materialism or Political Messianism? An Interpretation of the Theses 'On the Concept of History'" in *Benjamin: Philosophy, Aesthetics, History*. Edited by Gary Smith Chicago: University of Chicago Press, 1989.

Todd, Emmanuel. *Who is Charlie? Xenophobia and the New Middle Class* Translated by Andrew Brown. Malden, MA: Polity Press, 2015.

Tolba, Ahmed and Michael Georgy. "Sisi Warns of Response after Islamic State Kills 21 Egyptians in Libya." February 15, 2015. htttp://www.reuters.com/article/2015/02/15/ us-mideast-crisis-libya-egypt-idUSKBN0LJ10D20150215.

Tomlinson, Simon. "#noapology: Muslims stage angry protests over *Charlie Hebdo*'s Mo-hammed cartoon as Boko Haram terror leader hails Paris massacre." January 14, 2015. http://www.dailymail.co.uk/news/article-2910126/Muslims-stage-angry-protests -Charlie-Hebdo-s-Mohammed-cartoon-Boko-Haram-terror-leader-hails-Paris -massacre.html#ixzz3OpojSdsC.

Tornielli, Andrea and Giacomo Galeazzi, *This Economy Kills: Pope Francis on Capital-ism and Social Justice*. Collegeville, MN: Liturgical Press, 2015.

Traynor, Ian. "'I Don't Hate Muslims, I Hate Islam' says Holland's Rising Political Star." February 16, 2008. http://www.theguardian.com/world/2008/feb/17/netherlands .islam.

Turner, Colin and Hasan Horkuc, *Said Nursi.* New York: I.B. Tauris, 2009.

United Nations. "The Universal Declaration of Human Rights." http://www.un.org/en/ documents/udhr/.

Vatican City. "Apostolic Journey of His Holiness Pope Francis to Tirana (Albania): Meeting with the Civil Authorities." September 21, 2014. http://w2.vatican.va/ content/francesco/en/speeches/2014/september/documents/papa-francesco _20140921_albania-autorita.html.

———. "Declaration of Religious Leaders for the Eradication of Modern Slavery." December 2, 2014. http://www.news.va/en/news/declaration-of-religious-leaders -for-the-eradicati.

Vatican Radio. "Pope Francis to Muslims: We Must Confront Common Challenges." May 26, 2014. http://www.news.va/en/news/pope-francis-to-muslims-we-must-confront -common-ch.

Wagner, Meg. "American Suicide Bomber Feared the FBI was Hunting him when he Fled from Florida to Syria." Aug. 28, 2014. http://www.nydailynews.com/news/ world/american-suicide-bomber-feared-fbi-hunting-article-1.1919902.

Wallace, R. Jay. "Ressentiment, Value, and Self-Vindication: Making Sense of Nietzsche's Slave Revolt" in *Nietzsche and Morality.* Edited by Brian Leiter and Neil Sinhababu. New York: Oxford University Press, 2009.

Warrick, Joby. *Black Flags: The Rise of ISIS.* New York: Doubleday, 2015.

Weaver, Matthew. "Angela Merkel: German Multiculturalism has 'Utterly Failed.'" Oct. 17, 2010. http://www.theguardian.com/world/2010/oct/17/angela-merkel-german -multiculturalism-failed.

Weber, Max. *From Max Weber: Essays in Sociology.* Edited and translated by H.H. Gerth & C. Wright Mills. New York: Oxford University Press, 1976.

———. *The Protestant Ethic and the Spirit of Capitalism.* Translated by Stephen Kalberg. Los Angeles, CA: Roxbury Publishing Co., 2002.

Weiss, Michael and Hassan Hassan. *ISIS: Inside the Army of Terror.* New York: Regan Arts, 2015.

Wiesel, Elie. *The Trial of God (as it was held on February 25, 1649 in Shamgorod).* Translated by Marion Wiesel New York: Random House, 1979.

Wiggershaus, Rolf. *The Frankfurt School: It's History, Theories, and Political Significance.* Translated by Michael Robertson. Cambridge: The MIT Press, 1994.

Wilders, Geert. "Mr Wilder's Contribution to the Debate on Islamic Activism." September 6, 2007. http://web.archive.org/web/20080614074737/http://www.groepwilders .com/website/details.aspx?ID=44.

———. *Marked For Death: Islam's War Against the West and Me.* Washington D.C.: Regnery Publishing, Inc., 2012.

Wolin, Richard. *Walter Benjamin: An Aesthetic of Redemption*. New York: Columbia University Press, 1982.

Yaqoubi, Shaykh Muhammad. *Refuting ISIS: A Rebuttal of its Religious and Ideological Foundations*. United States: Sacred Knowledge, 2015.

YouTube. "Inside the Mind of a Terrorist: Moner Mohammad AbuSalha (Abu Huayrah al-Amriki)" https://www.youtube.com/watch?v=HSdtCcWTaSI.

———. "Interview with Moner Mohammad Abu Salaha aka Abu Hurayra al-Ameriki Part 1: Hijra." https://www.youtube.com/watch?v=DvCUMagTiCo.

Zawahiri, Ayman. *The Al Qaeda Reader*. Edited and translated by Raymond Ibrahim. New York: Broadway Books, 2007.

Žižek, Slavoj. *In Defense of Lost Causes*. New York: Verso, 2008.

———. *Robespierre: Virtue and Terror*. New York: Verso, 2007.

———. *The Year of Dreaming Dangerously*. New York; Verso, 2012.

———. "ISIS is a Disgrace to Fundamentalism," *New York Times*. September 3, 2014.

Index